RELEASED

BUREAUCRATS IN COLLISION:
CASE STUDIES IN AREA TRANSPORTATION PLANNING

The MIT Press

Cambridge, Massachusetts, and London, England

HE
308
L4

Melvin R. Levin   Norman A. Abend

126124

BUREAUCRATS IN COLLISION:
CASE STUDIES IN AREA TRANSPORTATION PLANNING

To
George D. Blackwood
1919–1968

The need for an objective view of intergovernmental relations as they relate to large regional planning became evident to the authors during their experiences in a variety of roles in three of the comprehensive area transportation planning studies that were conducted during the 1960s. With interagency coordination required by the word and intent of the federal legislation, these studies resulted in head-on confrontations between the ideology and staff of the highway agencies and an emerging phalanx of planners whose influence and strength have been growing steadily.

While this book concentrates on area transportation studies and its conclusions are directly applicable to this exotic form of administrative organization, other multiagency efforts ranging from model cities to antipoverty programs have faced quite similar problems. The authors can predict, without a shred of qualification, that comprehensive programs aimed at upgrading the quality of the environment will replay much of the same drama in which personalities, power, budgets, and ideology meet in a series of complicated wrangles.

Both authors were closely involved in the conception and early stages of the Boston project, and one continued to play a technical role in the project over a two-year period. The other author directed the Portland, Maine, study, working as a consultant with the state highway department as the principal client. He also was codirector of the Manchester, New Hampshire, study, playing a supervisory and administrative role, this time with the state planning agency as his client. In addition, both authors have written and consulted extensively in the fields of planning, transportation, and administration of planning and transportation studies.

The research for this volume provided the authors with the opportunity to test some of the conclusions and theories they had developed during their long association with the area transportation studies. Our conclusions, as harsh or unpopular as some may appear, have received no real challenge. In fact, we have been encouraged to publish the study as a guide to government officials who are or who will be intimately involved in intergovernmental programs. The work, although reviewed in the federal establishment, has remained there and has received little or no outside scrutiny. We are grateful to the Department of Housing and Urban Development for having funded most of the basic research and to the M.I.T. Press, which has seen fit to publish the results.

Melvin R. Levin   Boston, Massachusetts
Norman A. Abend   March 1970

1 BACKGROUND   1

INTRODUCTION   3
Overview   3
Applicability of Findings   6

1 THE RESEARCH DESIGN   11
Introduction   11
Initial Observations   12
Project Design   12
Project Administration   15
Selection of Projects for Study   22
Methodology   23

2 DEVELOPMENT OF FEDERAL POLICY TOWARD
URBAN TRANSPORTATION   27
Introduction   27
The Federal-Aid Road Act of 1916   31
Federal Legislation in the Depression Years   32
The Federal-Aid Highway Act of 1944   34
Federal Government Recognition of Urban Transportation Needs   36
City Pressure for Federal Transportation Legislation   40
The Housing Act of 1961: Federal Assistance for Mass
Transportation   42
The Highway Act of 1962: Prelude to the Interagency Studies   45

2 THE AREA STUDIES   47

3 THE BOSTON REGIONAL PLANNING PROJECT: INTRODUCTION   49
Study Area Profile   49
Project Overview   55

4 BOSTON: THE FEDERAL GRANT AND ORGANIZATIONAL PROBLEMS   65
Transportation Politics   65
Overture to Disaster   74
Cold War   82

5 BOSTON: TRANSITION TO OBSCURITY   88
Honeymoon at 150 Causeway   88
The Courtiers   92
The Governor Decides   99
Last Will and Testament   105
The Last Act   115

6 THE PENN-JERSEY TRANSPORTATION STUDY   119
Study Area Profile   119
Project Chronology   125
Project Administration   134
Problems with the Model   137
The Computer, Again   141
Effect of HHFA Nonparticipation   143
Conclusions   144

7 THE NIAGARA FRONTIER TRANSPORTATION STUDY   147
Study Area Profile   147
Project Chronology   149
HHFA's Influence and Involvement in the NFTS   156
Reliability of Data: The Population Implosion   158
Relations with Local Planning Agencies   160
The Rapid Transit Controversy   164
The State Transportation Agency as a Service Organization   167
Relationship Between Area Size and Local Opposition   169
The Need for Transportation Goals and Objectives   170

8 THE MANCHESTER METROPOLITAN PLANNING STUDY   172
Study Area Profile   172
Project Chronology   174
The Role of the State Planning Agency   180
The Relationship Between Regional and Local Planning   183
HUD Objectives   187
Regional Planning versus Downtown Renewal   188
Financial Difficulties   190
Lack of Local Transportation Planning Expertise   193
The Future Land-Use Plan   196
The Myth of Regional Land-Use Alternatives   197
Project End—Advisory Committee Transition   198
Problems of a Joint Venture   199

9 THE PORTLAND AREA COMPREHENSIVE TRANSPORTATION STUDY   201
Study Area Profile   201
Project Chronology   203
Level of Detail of Highway Location   208
Intercity Travel Considerations   210
Citizen Participation   213
Coordination with Urban Renewal Projects   216
The Highway Location Emergency   220
The Transportation Consultant   222
The Role of the Regional Planning Commission   225

3 LEARNING FROM EXPERIENCE   229

10 CONCLUSIONS   231
Introduction   231
The Absence of Goals and Priorities   232
Weaknesses in the State of the Art:
The Planner Lacks Authority and Skill   236
Talent Shortage   242

11 PROBLEMS IN INTERGOVERNMENTAL AND
INTERAGENCY COORDINATION   248
Introduction   248
Federal, State, and Local Relations   253
State-Metropolitan Relations   258
The Need for Reorganization and Centralization   263
A Role for Metropolitan Agencies   268
The Role and Importance of Program Evaluation   271
Program Evaluation and Agency Reform   274

Bibliography   277
Index   283

Figure

3.1　Study Area: Boston Regional Planning Project　　　　56

3.2　Study Organization: Boston Regional Planning Project　　　57

3.3　Study Reorganization: Eastern Massachusetts Regional Planning Project　　　58

3.4　Initial Funding of the Boston Regional Planning Project　　　59

6.1　Study Area: Penn-Jersey Transportation Study　　　126

6.2　Study Organization: Penn-Jersey Transportation Study　　　127

6.3　Study Reorganization: Delaware Valley Regional Planning Commission　　　128

6.4　Initial Funding of the Penn-Jersey Transportation Study　　　129

7.1　Study Area: Niagara Frontier Transportation Study　　　150

7.2　Study Organization: Niagara Frontier Transportation Study　　　151

8.1　Study Area: Manchester Metropolitan Planning Study　　　175

8.2　Study Organization: Manchester Metropolitan Planning Study　　　176

8.3　Funding of the Manchester Metropolitan Planning Study　　　177

9.1　Study Area: Portland Area Comprehensive Transportation Study　　　204

9.2　Study Organization: Portland Area Comprehensive Transportation Study　　　205

9.3　Funding of the Portland Area Comprehensive Transportation Study　　　206

BUREAUCRATS IN COLLISION:
CASE STUDIES IN AREA TRANSPORTATION PLANNING

BACKGROUND 1

Overview

This analysis of five area transportation studies points to certain fundamental lessons for the future of metropolitan planning policy and identifies a number of specific difficulties directly associated with the organization of interagency planning projects.

Many planners, including key officials in the U.S. Housing and Home Finance Agency (HHFA; later to become the Department of Housing and Urban Development, HUD),[1] anticipated that the studies would result in an improved quality of highway decisions because they would help to inject planning expertise into route location decisions. In most cases, however, these decisions were not included in the scope of the studies since they were viewed either as local matters unsuitable for regional consideration or as faits accomplis not subject to further review. Despite, or perhaps partly because of, this self-imposed limitation, the problem of highway route locations in urban areas continues to be a major battleground between planners and highway engineers.

The federal and state planning agencies hoped that the cause of interagency harmony would be furthered by convincing the highway agencies of the benefits of coordinating highway and land-use plans. They were also firmly committed to the concept of genuine citizen participation, compared with the perfunctory statute-satisfying public hearings conducted by the highway agencies. Finally, the planning agencies were hopeful that a new brand of action-oriented research would emerge from the studies and that it would include information of great value to decision-makers.

Officials in planning agencies at all levels of government apparently expected that existing planning techniques and staff organization would be adequate in the early stages of the studies, while the needs for new comprehensive planning skills would be clarified during the course of the studies. These agency planning officials, not all of them card-carrying members of the American Institute of Planners, were also sincerely convinced that their conceptual approach, skills, and participation were desperately needed by the highway agencies and would be enthusiastically embraced by the traffic engi-

---

[1] On September 9, 1965, President Johnson signed P.L. 89–174, which created th Department of Housing and Urban Development. The legislation basically upgraded the existing HHFA to cabinet-level status. The secretary was given all the powers, functions, and duties of the Housing and Home Finance Agency and its components. The Community Facilities Administration and the Urban Renewal Administration, both of which were administratively created within the HHFA without specific legal authorization, were transferred with modifications to the new agency; however, overall responsibilities continued. The Community Facilities Administration (HHFA) was responsible for the so-called 701 program under which the transportation planning funds were granted.

neers. By and large, these expectations were not realized.

The cooperating federal and state highway agencies entertained more limited but clearer expectations about the use of the area transportation studies. They were interested in one aspect of basic research, namely, the development of a low-cost transportation model that would permit future studies to be conducted with considerably less data collection—in particular, fewer expensive road and home interviews. On the whole, however, the traffic engineers were perfectly satisfied with their existing capabilities to conduct area transportation studies. They were less interested in exploring new forms of comprehensive planning than in securing sanction and validation for existing highway goals and plans. However, the attempt of the Bureau of Public Roads (BPR) and the directors of some of the larger projects to use the area studies as proving grounds for computer-oriented transportation planning caused major difficulties in the Penn-Jersey and Niagara Frontier studies and lesser problems in the Boston area study. Contrary to early hopes of a breakthrough in comprehensive planning, the studies concentrated on preparing what were basically master highway plans rather than broad transportation policy. Land-use considerations, aesthetics, economic base, public transportation, and other parameters were not directly related to highway proposals.

One major problem arose because too little attention had been paid to staffing. Competent planners skilled in regional planning rather than in traditional local planning were much scarcer than had been thought in the euphoric, design phases of the studies. Events were to prove that city planning experience was not directly applicable to the demands of regional planning. Even such a relatively simple task as making a land-use inventory proved troublesome when the scale of operations and expenditures was greatly magnified.

Another type of staffing problem emerged in HUD's monitoring and supervision from its regional offices. Too few qualified people were available, and most of those assigned to the area studies had been accustomed to the different demands of small-town planning operations and city urban renewal projects.

One reason for the highway orientation of the area studies grew out of HUD's inability to supply the kind of continuing close supervision and monitoring that the Bureau of Public Roads was able to provide with its long-established and well-staffed state and regional offices. When the studies began, the planning profession was poorly versed in transportation procedures, objectives, and personnel. Many planners involved in the studies were apparently unable to master unfamiliar techniques and complex administrative problems quickly enough to give the highwaymen a run for the money. A vacuum in leadership, skills, and doctrine emerged, which was filled by the highway agencies. It is not surprising that the Bureau of Public Roads and the state highway agencies are relatively pleased with the outcome of the area transportation studies since they regard them as successful in terms of achieving agency objectives.

The experience of the area transportation studies suggests that it may be too early to expect a significant contribution to development decisions from regional planning organizations. There is neither an adequate underpinning of useful research on regional plans, consequences, and alternatives nor a recognized, coherent set of conclusions and goals to guide such decisions. The regional planning organizations are controlled essentially by technicians with varying political expertise, operating under the loose control of laymen. They are not suitable administrative structures for arriving at consensual regional goals—if such there be—nor are they capable of imposing community and agency adherence to such goals. To the extent that regional planning agencies attempt to exercise a serious impact on the flow of decisions, they become one contender among many in a complicated game involving an intricate mix of local, state, and federal participants.

This book suggests, however, that, despite the imperfections just noted, both HUD and the BPR can be reasonably satisfied with the outcome of the studies in the smaller areas such as Manchester, New Hampshire, and Portland, Maine. Small metropolitan areas are simpler organisms. They lack a significant public transportation component, and they do not suffer from the shortage of open space, the traffic congestion, and the massive housing, minority group, and poverty problems besetting the larger areas. In consequence, the Manchester and Portland studies proceeded fairly smoothly and produced what seem to be regarded by the BPR, the state highway agencies, and the affected local communities as satisfactory highway plans.

The situation in the three large metropolitan areas reviewed (Boston, Philadelphia, and Buffalo) was far different. There were substantial difficulties in developing a satisfactory administrative and research approach to undertake large-scale studies.

Because they could not restructure themselves to play a substantive role in meeting emerging urban crises and because they could not produce a timely, acceptable product, the studies in the larger areas have had only a peripheral influence upon major development decisions on land use, transportation, and other issues. The presence or absence of HHFA-HUD in the large studies was apparently of little consequence. As the text of Part 2 indicates, the Penn-Jersey and Niagara Frontier studies, in which HHFA-HUD did not participate, ran into problems comparable with those encountered by the Eastern Massachusetts project, for which HUD contributed half the total funding.

Applicability of Findings

In view of the fact that the five area transportation studies chosen for review are in the northeast portion of the country, the cover of the book might have included the phrase "prices slightly lower west of the Mississippi" (or south of the Mason-Dixon line) on the ground that the conclusions derived from the analysis have only a limited applicability to other parts of the country. The authors do not believe this is the case. Because this work represents the first, if not the only, intensive analysis of intergovernmental relations in the area of transportation studies (as well as criticism and evaluation of other aspects of these studies, including their techniques and usefulness), it has been difficult to find direct evidence to corroborate the findings from other parts of the nation. Nevertheless, from time to time occasional rumblings have been heard that can be interpreted as partial validation of the authors' conclusions. For example, a brief look at the articles in *Traffic Quarterly* in 1968 and 1969, one of the more prestigious periodicals dealing with urban transportation, reveals isolated articles dealing with some of the shortcomings of area transportation planning projects in terms of their technical and administrative aspects.[2]

The decision to adopt a qualitative approach to the research limited the effort to relatively few areas, while budgetary constraints effectively confined the selection of the projects to be evaluated to the northeast. Final selection of the five areas was made after consultation with federal officials. Although few in number, the areas included a cross section of the study area types in terms of population size, method of funding, and administrative organization. They ranged from Manchester's 113,000 population to the Penn-Jersey area with over 4,500,000 people. (The Portland area contained 140,000; Buffalo, over 1,000,000; and the Boston area, over 3,500,000.) In terms of funding, the studies ran the gamut from the 100 percent BPR funding of the Buffalo study to the 50 percent HHFA-BPR funding of the Manchester and Boston studies. (In all the studies, federal support required some state funds.) The Penn-Jersey study began mostly with highway funds but, since its transformation

[2] See, for example, Norman Ashford, "The Developing Role of State and Government in Transportation," *Traffic Quarterly*, vol. 22 (October 1968), p. 455; Donald F. Wood, "State Level Transportation Planning Considerations," ibid. (April 1968), p. 191; Martin Wachs and Joseph Schofer, "Abstract Values and Concrete Highways," ibid., vol. 23 (January 1969), p. 133, which deals with the need for establishing goals and objectives prior to highway planning; and Thomas B. Schocken, "Splitting Headaches," ibid., vol. 22 (July 1968), p. 389, which deals with the shortcomings of modal split formulas.

into a regional planning agency, has received increasing support by HUD grants. The administrative organization of the studies also represented a variety of approaches. In the two small studies, technical work was conducted by consultants. In the larger areas, one was conducted by the state highway agency (New York), one predominantly with staff (Penn-Jersey), and one with a combination of consultant and staff (Boston).

Although the lack of common denominators such as size, source of funding, and administrative organization made it impossible to make certain types of direct comparisons between the various studies, the findings in each of the area studies evidenced considerable consistency between the three large areas and between the two smaller ones. The authors believe that this pattern is broadly applicable. The serious problems identified in the larger study areas were similar to those found in other major study areas, while the relative lack of difficulty in the organization and conduct of small metropolitan area studies is also fairly typical. In addition to comments in the literature, discussions with federal officials, press reports on transportation problems elsewhere in the nation, and personal contact with state and local officials and members of the academic community lend support to these conclusions. In short, although no comparable research is available, the evidence suggests that experience in the area transportation studies elsewhere has been quite similar. Perhaps the most significant symptom of the transportation study shortcomings in the large metropolitan areas has been the continuing eruption of freeway revolts. The controversy has centered around opposition to major urban expressways in most of the nation's large cities. The *Christian Science Monitor,* in a series of ten articles appearing between June 4, 1968, and July 9, 1968, highlighted some of the more notable problems.[3] Stories in the *New York Times*[4] and other publications lead to the conclusion that the area transportation studies apparently played little or no role either in resolving this critical issue before the open confrontation or in providing acceptable guideposts after battle had been joined. An examination of issues of professional publications, including the *Journal of the American Institute of Planners, Urban Affairs Quarterly,* and *Land Economics* as well as *Traffic Quarterly,* reveals an interesting silence. The findings and recommendations of the comprehensive transporta-

[3]This series of articles, entitled "The Highway Revolt," was written by Lyn Shepard, a staff correspondent of the *Christian Science Monitor,* who had visited twelve cities where proposed highways were being disputed. He discussed the freeway revolt in the metropolitan areas of Philadelphia and Boston, which are included in this analysis, as well as some other cities—San Francisco, Nashville, New Orleans, New York, Cleveland, and Los Angeles, among others. See also Lyn Shepard, "Backup on the Pork Barrel Highway," ibid., October 8, 1968.

[4]"Mayor Abandons Plans for Expressways," *New York Times,* July 17, 1969, p. 1, and Ada L. Huxtable, "Politics of Expressways," ibid., p. 51.

tion studies seem to have received the scantiest of attention in subsequent discussions of the transportation issues besetting many urban areas. For whatever reasons, metropolitan planning, urban renewal, and public transportation agencies (as well as scholars) appear reluctant to cite the area transportation studies as firm guideposts and benchmarks. Certainly, the relatively minor concern with developing a major role for public transportation evidenced in the selected study areas held true in other areas. In the Boston and Penn-Jersey areas, public transportation research for the most part was carried on independently of the area transportation studies, and the same pattern holds in other parts of the nation.

Serious technical problems arose in each of the three larger area studies in attempts to construct computer models for land-use and transportation planning. This difficulty, too, was encountered in studies elsewhere in the nation. A 1968 conference on urban development models produced ample evidence that modeling has been beset by unsolved problems.[5] This sober evaluation is in contrast to the rather cocksure statements of the practitioners involved in the area transportation studies of the early 1960s.

Moreover, this analysis points out that concentrated research efforts on model development (which cost dearly in terms of time and money), especially in the Penn-Jersey study, had little relevance to the final study recommendations, which in any event had little impact upon major transportation decisions in the regions. As Britton Harris notes:

The existing practice of BPR and HUD of attaching major research efforts to operational projects in the form of major urban transportation studies, community renewal program studies, and 701 studies has the advantage of bringing research into contact with realistic decision-making problems, but it has the disadvantage of funding research at inadequate scales and of failing to provide continuity. Not only continued research, but also the actual functioning of agencies has suffered from the consequent lack of capacity to capitalize on previous research progress.[6]

Harris, who was a principal adviser on model building for the Penn-Jersey study, underscores one finding of this volume: a major emphasis on pure research and a simultaneous requirement for routine studies with production deadlines are not compatible. In two of the three larger studies, research on new models proved costly and unproductive, and in the Penn-Jersey study, the heavy emphasis on pioneering research had effects approaching the point of disaster.

Some persons closely associated with the area transportation studies would doubtless dispute the authors' contention that (particularly in the larger

[5] Highway Research Board, *Urban Development Models*, Special Report no. 97 (Washington, D.C., 1968), p. 22.
[6] Ibid., p. 13.

areas) the studies failed to come to grips with live issues. In 1968 the director of the Chicago Area Transportation Study (CATS), the grandfather of the area transportation studies of the 1960s, maintained that "two separate agencies can, with particular skills and specialties, successfully work together in preparing and evaluating land-use and transportation plans."[7] He also indicated that the CATS research provided a large body of statistics in support of the CATS expressway proposals. Yet at the same time that the director's statements were published, it was apparent that substantial segments of the community found the CATS material unconvincing. A new type of study has been initiated to resolve Chicago's transportation issues:

The Chicago Department of Public Works has switched to the design-team concept in a last-ditch effort to develop acceptable, comprehensive plans for its $500 million, 22-mile long cross-town expressway (I-494). A team of engineers, architects, city planners, sociologists and other professionals is now working on the route location. A report on the first two and one-half mile stretch is due this summer.[8]

The story in the *Engineering News-Record* is indicative of the manner in which area transportation studies have been ignored. In Baltimore and Boston as well as Washington and Chicago, a new generation of transportation studies is under way. In effect, they represent a tacit admission that in the larger areas the comprehensive transportation studies failed to achieve even their limited highway agency objective of providing solid, persuasive arguments for highway plans.

The five area studies encapsulate what seems to have been a typical chronology of the entire program. There was the brave beginning, when the studies were acclaimed as heralds of a new era in transportation and land-use planning. This was apparently followed in most areas by internecine struggles over control of the study organization. After this flurry of activity, the studies seemingly faded from public view as they attempted to adhere to a timetable embracing a rigid scope of services that not only bypassed emerging urban issues but failed even to confront simmering transportation problems.

Insofar as the authors can judge, the planning profession and the planning agencies everywhere were inadequately equipped with a sound body of concepts, doctrine, and knowledge to counterbalance the narrow certainties of the highway engineers. For their part, the highway agencies seem to have won a victory by dominating virtually all of the studies, even those in which HHFA-HUD contributed half the financing. But their triumph was hollow in the larger areas, which are still riven by controversy over expressway routes

[7] Highway Research Board, *Transportation System Evaluation,* Highway Research Record no. 238 (Washington, D.C., 1968), p. 116.
[8] "Cutbacks Hit Interstate Progress Last Year: Urban Binds Persist," *Engineering News-Record,* May 1969, p. 32.

because the studies did not create a suit of planning armor to ward off the growing public clamor against the highway bulldozer.

We seem to be entering into a new generation of studies aimed at reexamining the individual pieces of the highway system that have met with opposition, particularly those deeply involved with housing, slum, and poverty problems. In brief, for all the early talk of careful consideration of alternatives and the overt attempts to secure citizen participation and to link the studies to the decision-making process, the basic job remains: in many large urban areas new kinds of joint studies emphasizing human and design dimensions are under way. Furthermore, the transit agencies are continuing to finance their own research, while significant studies of urban issues like housing, poverty, and race are being conducted with barely a reference to the costly study Leviathans that have vanished into limbo.

In short, available evidence at practically all levels supports the principal finding: most of the painfully achieved reports produced by the quarter of a billion dollars invested in the area transportation studies seem to have been largely abandoned by their sponsors and by their participants.

Introduction

Urban and regional planning and programming efforts have been moving away from single-agency projects to new and broader concepts that demand participation from a number of agencies. These agencies may be federal, state, or metropolitan, and their interests may range from direct involvement to watchful observation. Up to the present, such intergovernmental and interagency convergence cannot be judged an unqualified success. This volume presents a number of suggestions aimed at improving interagency and intergovernmental operations, particularly in the metropolitan areas, which pose some of the nation's most critical urban development problems.

The metropolitan areas contain most of the nation's population and economic power and are likely to continue to capture the lion's share of national growth. They are also characterized by a high degree of political fragmentation. As a result, in past years heavily funded state and metropolitan agencies, especially highway agencies, have been able to pursue their objectives with only token opposition. The introduction of broader regional planning considerations, as reflected in the Department of Housing and Urban Development (HUD) programs of the 1960s, represents a new departure from past policies. Although the day of unchallenged supremacy for functional planning is over, far too little is known about what should replace it. Many of the strains and problems identified in this study are of the kind that are always found in transitional eras when disenchantment with the old has not yet led to the evolution of satisfactory new systems.

While the requirements for interagency coordination have greatly increased since the mid-1960s, with the passage of such legislation as the Model Cities Program, most agencies have had little useful experience in mounting these complicated operations. Moreover, agencies that have already been involved in cooperative programs have rarely had the opportunity to evaluate their past experiences and apply the lessons to present needs.

Scholars have begun to amass a history of intergovernmental operations in metropolitan areas. The research for this book, through an evaluation of the experiences of the area transportation studies, was primarily intended to assist the Department of Housing and Urban Development—and perhaps other agencies—in designing, supervising, and evaluating future interagency programs.

For all departments, whether federal or local, a key problem is how best to plan, organize, and implement extremely multijurisdictional programs involving the participation of agencies at all levels of government and also a variety of interest groups. On the basis of the experience of the interagency transportation projects, substantial problems can be anticipated at every stage: in defining goals, in designing the project, in measuring performance, and in ensuring that a major public investment will yield a reasonable harvest. The area transportation studies, begun in the late 1950s but now mandatory for urban areas of over 50,000 population under the Federal-Aid Highway Act of 1962, offer useful lessons in identifying some of the problems and potential associated with large-scale interagency projects.

Initial Observations

The present research was begun on the basis of a number of preliminary observations. These were founded in the available literature, published reports, and evaluations of the area transportation studies throughout the nation and on the actual experience of the principal researchers in these studies and related activities. The following section presents a list of the observations made prior to the actual research and later subjected to examination and testing. They represented an identification of key areas for study and served as a preliminary set of working hypotheses. These observations are divided into two major categories, project design and project administration. Both categories reflect a strong emphasis on questions that are likely to be relevant to future interagency operations.

In addition to the hypotheses identified prior to initiating the research, a number of other important questions were answered during the course of the study. The selection of study areas, in fact, reflects to some extent the supplementary issues that were to be raised. For example, the role of the consultant is an important consideration for future planning efforts. The research also considered the benefits and disadvantages of centralization and decentralization and the impact of HUD participation or nonparticipation on the studies. The research was directed, for the most part, to examine and test the initial observations and to answer related questions that were raised as it progressed.

Project Design

1. Problems Increase Geometrically with Area Size. It is probable that the complications inherent in interagency projects increase immeasurably with the size of the urban area. The special difficulties found in the larger metropolitan complexes include, for example, the presence of a substantial public transportation system.

In larger areas, public transportation is sufficiently important to warrant extended study and analysis as part of the transportation planning process. The existence of large autonomous or semiautonomous public transportation organizations with multimillion-dollar resources (not to be confused with profits) increases the complexity of transportation planning. In contrast, in smaller urban areas public transportation is a relatively small factor; studies can therefore be designed and conducted with far fewer inherent frictions and problems. In both of the smaller study areas included in this study, as in many other areas of less than 100,000 people, public transportation is a comparatively minor factor.

2. Slow Studies and Fast Decisions. One of the more serious problems in the area transportation studies involved their time schedules. Although the larger studies were generally launched in a crisis atmosphere of urgent need, the actual design called for research to proceed at a measured pace, with the result that years passed without the studies producing any hard recommendations. There was a marked tendency, therefore, for the studies to be overtaken by unpostponable decisions.

As roads and transit lines were approved and built without reference to the ongoing studies, participants, as well as informed members of the press and political and civic leaders, came to the conclusion that the studies were of little relevance. In brief, because the studies and the persons responsible for their design and conduct were not geared to the realities of legislative and administrative timetables, they were unable to exert much influence on the problems they were asked to solve.

3. Strains on a Frail Administrative Structure. In most urban transportation studies, a "memorandum of agreement" between the participant agencies was the working basis for organization and administration. Such a memorandum suggested equal-partner relationships among the federal signatories. Subsequently, however, problems arose because of basic differences in philosophy and approach toward supervision. The Bureau of Public Roads (BPR) relied almost completely on its local offices for supervision of the day-to-day conduct of its urban transportation studies. Because these offices were adequately staffed, the BPR was able to participate thoroughly in every phase of the project and to give close supervision to those portions of the research that were most relevant to its own interests. On the other hand, HUD's normal relationship with the states (as well as stated policy) dictated an arrangement that resulted in limited participation. HUD's continuing supervisory responsibility was delegated to the BPR or assigned on a formal or informal basis to local or state planning agencies. In most cases, a limited number of HUD personnel were assigned to supervision of the studies. Moreover, the few HUD members who were assigned to the projects from regional offices seemed to be uncomfortable in a process totally alien to their previous experience and training.

4. Techniques versus Research. The development of an array of old and new tools, such as computers, organization charts, "PERTing,"[1] and the study of land-use alternatives, opened up a number of fashionable temptations to indulge in expensive experimentation. One result of this manipulation of unfamiliar instruments was that even simple endeavors, such as land-use data collection, ran into serious trouble.

Another set of major problems arose because technicians stressed the pioneering research aspect of project objectives. Some area transportation studies that were designed to develop specific planning recommendations degenerated instead into continuing explorations into the wonderful world of research. In part, this tendency can be attributed to the Chicago Area Transportation Study (CATS) syndrome. Although CATS experienced difficulties in developing acceptable recommendations for transportation construction, it was widely regarded as a successful research endeavor that pioneered many planning processes for subsequent studies. Following the CATS example, some technicians were not satisfied with the studies if their sole purpose was to develop a transportation plan. They sought to make a personal contribution to the solution of a variety of knotty research problems in metropolitan areas. This tendency created a certain dilemma for project administrators. It is difficult and perhaps unwise for any administrator to discourage innovation and new techniques. However, he runs the risk that the would-be pioneers will run away on costly, time-consuming exploration of untested research techniques.

Part of the blame for this can be laid at the federal door. For example, the BPR's long-range objective of developing a "model" that, with a minimum of time, cost, and effort, could predict transportation requirements in urban areas was fully reflected in the model-building propensities of most of the studies. Unfortunately, this particular activity did not necessarily lead to better planning at the local level, whatever the benefit to the Bureau of Public Roads.

5. Action Programs or Educational Devices? As suggested, the area transportation studies moved at such a slow pace that they exercised little influence over many of the major issues that impelled their creation. The question then arises: Having missed the bus for the 1960 decade, can they possibly have a powerful influence on the decisions of the 1970s and 1980s? If they cannot reasonably be regarded as action programs for the present or near future, can the studies be considered adequate educational devices to assist in decision-making over the coming two or three decades? Are they, in effect, an adult seminar to lay the foundation for informed choices involving

[1] PERT refers to the Project Evaluation and Review Technique that was originally developed to coordinate components of construction projects.

highway plans, proposals for transit and airport expansion, regional land-use control, and upgrading the urban environment after 1972, the original estimated completion date of the Interstate System (now estimated for 1975)?

It is too soon to answer these questions, but it does seem that great opportunities were missed in developing the educational aspects of the studies—in translating into relevant terms their objectives, facts, methods of analysis, and alternative recommendations. Moreover, the audiovisual methods used to display the results for the public tended to be unsatisfactory.

Extraordinary efforts to muffle controversy also hindered the educational process. It is important that people who are participating in the planning process for the first time begin to develop firsthand acquaintance with the problems of administration, organization, goal selection, and choice of priorities. However, when news of hidden struggles and problems leaks out and the participants have not been treated frankly and openly, the cynicism toward government that is already far too prevalent is exacerbated.

Project Administration

1. The Role of Planners versus Other Agencies. Interagency projects by their very nature involve a certain amount of conflict between the participants. In such conflicts, planners and planning agencies often appear to be less combative and less effective than other agencies. When other agencies come to the arena armed with solutions, the planner may often be at the stage of beginning the search for solutions.[2]

Most federal, state, and local agencies involved in transportation services are single-purpose agencies with narrowly designated functions as denoted by their titles or by their legislative mandates. Thus the Massachusetts Bay Transportation Authority and the Chicago Transportation Authority are primarily concerned with providing transportation services to the public, and doing so principally by conventional methods such as rapid transit and bus. Their interest in other transportation facilities, such as highways, or in related matters, such as land use, is not clearly and directly linked to their operating function and therefore tends to become a tertiary or, at best, a secondary consideration.

Perhaps the most powerful of the single-minded agencies are the state highway agencies, the functions of which—until quite recently—were solely to design, build, and maintain highways. The initial efforts of the highway agencies in most states revolved around the conversion of dirt and mud roads to hard-surface, year-round, all-weather facilities. Long- or short-range planning involving all transportation systems or nonhighway factors was not

[2] See Alan A. Altshuler, *The City Planning Process* (Ithaca, N.Y.: Cornell University Press, 1965), chap. 1, "The Intercity Freeway," pp. 17–83.

considered relevant. With the completion of the primary task of road building before World War II, the state highway agencies shifted their attention to the construction of higher-quality facilities, for example, expressways and elaborate interchanges. Despite some prodding from the Federal Bureau of Public Roads and others, the state highway agencies are still principally concerned with road construction and maintenance to the exclusion of other interests. Their participation in interagency efforts represents in some cases a genuine effort to upgrade the scope and quality of highway planning, but in others it appears to be both a reluctant and a defensive measure designed to safeguard the agency from the threat of encroachment.

In contrast to the transportation agencies (and quite possibly renewal, education, and other agencies), the regional planners are by their nature not firmly committed to specific strategies to solve specific problems. Thus, when approaching an urban transportation problem, they are not strongly wedded to a single solution. This lack of prior commitment usually means that they are weak and unarmed. Planning agencies attempt to represent a rather diffuse, undefined public interest, and they lack the underpinning of a vocal constituency that is supported by enormous financial resources. The planning agencies seek solutions that appear to meet a broad spectrum of public needs, but they are constrained by the practical necessity of satisfying their more dogmatic colleagues in cooperating agencies. Far from being convinced that planning or any other profession has all the answers, planners tend to regard their function as one of exploration and questioning, of developing tentative hypotheses and alternative solutions. However, because this open-minded approach to the solution of urban problems is frequently not shared by representatives of the operating agencies, the planning agencies have often been forced into validating substantive proposals advanced by the operating agencies. The planning agencies may be assigned to more congenial, ephemeral, and broad-brush aspects of the study, such as preparing work programs and alternative land-use maps, while the key development decisions are made elsewhere.

2. Politicians versus Planning Technicians. For a number of reasons, some politicians tend to discount the ability, sincerity, and wisdom of the planning technicians who are involved in the urban transportation planning process. The planner remains an intruder; politicians, who are used to dealing with the regular transportation agencies, are prone to protect these relationships and to continue to rely on these agencies for advice. As a result, the planner and his planning agency are frequently mistrusted as researchers who are practiced in esoteric arts—including tapping the federal treasury—but who are out of touch with the real world.

The mistrust is often mutual. The planners employed in such studies are sometimes repelled by the behind-the-scenes arrangements and closed minds of political leaders and their transportation agency alliances. Moreover, beyond the practical, immediate causes for hostility, there are traditional rationalizations for such attitudes. Politicians have sometimes suggested that an expert's advice on controversial issues must be discounted since the technician has never been elected to public office and therefore does not have a grass-root grasp of what the people want and need. On the other hand, planners are occasionally tempted to write off as hopeless the possibility of educating and persuading elected officials to their side in view of the latter's alleged mental and moral deficiencies. It may be that the area transportation studies, like other intergency operations touching on delicate issues, tend to draw to the surface the latent feelings of mutual distaste between planners and politicians.

3. Crisis and Response. Many of the crises that inevitably develop in the course of interagency studies are impossible to predict in advance. Some of the crises are clearly of incendiary origin, perpetrated by individuals and agencies seeking to obtain a particular advantage or concession. Others are attributable to unexpected delays in funding or to prolonged, fruitless commitment to unproductive research, the inability of assigned staff or consulting firms to meet their time schedules, sudden resignations, or changes in the political leadership. The area transportation studies were for the most part overplanned, with elaborate time schedules and work charts that left insufficient room for handling prolonged internal crises or other mishaps. They also tended to be muscle-bound—unresponsive to new problems, poor at improvisation, and, in general, unable to respond quickly to the unexpected. As a result, many studies in the larger metropolitan areas fell well behind their original schedules and also lost many of their skilled staff, who had not been prepared to face frustrations and delays.

4. Resolving Interagency Conflicts. For the most part, metropolitan-level agencies are weak in comparison with long-established state agencies. The area transportation organizations are even weaker. Since they are outside the normal jurisdictions of executive power, disputes between agency participants cannot easily be resolved through the regular machinery. Such dilemmas must therefore be shifted to a controlling level, either the governor's office or the federal funding-sponsoring agencies. Since the decisions are made by nonparticipants, frequently without all the facts at their disposal, the referees' choice may lead to further problems. Moreover, this practice leads participants to be tempted into playing a "courtier" role, forsaking reasoned argument and enlisting higher authority to resolve conflicts in their favor. The result may be a form of three-dimensional infighting harmful to the calm pursuit of objective and factually based recommendations.

In this connection, it is well to review the role of consultants. Not infrequently, a specific consulting firm will be retained to perform a technical task because of its reputation, know-how, and presumed readiness to proceed immediately. It is also thought that a consultant, by virtue of his private status, will retain an independent role both in the conduct of a study and in his ultimate responsibility for making recommendations. Experience has shown that consultants may be useful in organizing a study, in collecting data, and in preparing it for analysis. Beyond this point, however, the consultant tends to become a participant and/or a pawn of participant interests. Few consultants are able to proceed in their work without becoming closely involved with and directly affected by the interagency conflicts that may arise.

5. Talent Shortage. The urban transportation studies were large-scale pioneering efforts that flowered at a time when qualified planners were already in short supply. The imposition of this new pressure for staff resulted in further strains on the limited reserves of trained personnel. For a number of reasons, Washington has generally been able to attract sufficient talent. Despite the high salaries offered, many of the study organizations experienced considerable trouble in attracting and retaining qualified staff. The same observation was, and is, true of the lower echelons of the federal and state governments. Unfortunately, staffing shortages in the transportation studies were exacerbated by the unusual talents required for pioneering studies; a modest competence was not enough. Furthermore, the supply of available talent was not always wisely used; resignations were frequent, partly because technicians were assigned to administrative and policy-level posts beyond their depth. Reliance on consulting firms did not always help matters. The consultants, too, were short of qualified technicians.

The chronic shortage of planners and the variety of posts open in the studies led in some instances to appointing persons with marginal technical qualifications to key positions. In some studies, a substantial proportion of the funds was allocated to the salaries of chairwarmers rathers than competent professionals. Large-scale interagency efforts involving a number of ill-defined administrative tasks always offer temptations for appointments of the unqualified. Furthermore, disillusionment with the pace of results can lead to desperate, often poorly conceived, moves to replace technicians with hard-driving administrators who have legal or business backgrounds—on the theory that personalities specializing in tough-minded action rather than thoughtful, time-consuming research are needed.

6. Untoward Results of Political Change. Interagency projects tend to be fragile, easily derailed structures that can function only in an atmosphere of political tranquillity. An election, a major appointment, or other significant alteration in the power structure at the state or metropolitan level is likely to show that the studies were victims, not beneficiaries, of a changing of the guard. The staff that had time to build a rapport with one set of officials faced difficulties as it tried to build new bridges during an interregnum. This difficulty led to a decline in the overall efficiency and conduct of the study.

Constructing a comfortable relationship may not be an easy task. The newly elected official is often mistrustful of experts who have been closely associated with his predecessor, particularly if activities undertaken by the experts have become election issues. This raises long-standing problems of program continuity and implementation of recommendations.

The head of the agency responsible for the conduct of the studies can be expected to be replaced as part of a political changeover. On the other hand, the technician normally expects to remain. There are instances, however, when technicians find it expedient to resign. For example, the technician who believes that close involvement with political leaders is essential if his efforts are to bear fruit may risk replacement if his political allies are defeated. Whatever the reasons for turnover at the top, the consequences are likely to be confusion and delay. Urban transportation studies, because of their size and complexity, are frequently cumbersome to administer and, once deflected from their basic objective and having lost momentum, are difficult to reinvigorate.

7. Communication and Dialogue with Citizens. Problems of area transportation, unlike the federally assisted poverty program, are usually matters of secondary interest and priority to the citizenry. There is often a genuine interest in transportation proposals, but it tends to be highly localized. Strong reactions are generated only by a new access road or by a change in public transportation schedules. However, certain regional problems do arouse varying degrees of interest. These include such matters as rush-hour congestion, declining revenues of small, publicly owned bus firms, higher fares, and highway route location problems. As a rule, area transportation studies have not been able to stimulate continuing interest and response. It is frequently difficult, but probably not impossible, to translate results of a broad-brush transportation study into terms that local participants can comprehend. Indeed, some of the studies have not made a serious effort to create a meaningful dialogue. Presentations and reports have dwelt on the technical aspects of the studies, apparently addressed primarily to audiences of fellow technicians. In many cases, contact with the public has taken the form of bland, reassuring placebos, avoiding rather than meeting urgent local problems.

The transportation issues that did arouse local interest, such as local interchanges or routes through parks and slums, were frequently dismissed as too parochial to be worthy of consideration in regional planning. Moreover, partly because of the inflexible manner in which the studies were organized and administered, they were often unprepared to deal with regional matters until the time for decision had long since passed.

For these reasons, the area studies received rather little attention from the local press, the general public, or local civic groups. Occasionally, prominent local citizens were appointed to advisory committees and were thereby concerned with their progress. However, even in these instances, interest slackened as the studies dragged on and the prospects for exciting results grew dim. Broad-brush programs do not engender continuing interest and participation except among agencies and individuals directly involved in their conduct. Study publications mirrored the consistent lack of participation in meaningful regional and local issues.

This lack of bite in published study materials can be attributed in part to the desire to avoid controversy; participant agencies exercise a veto power over material that might be considered detrimental to their interests. Unfortunately, it is precisely this kind of disputatious information that may be of paramount interest. In more instances, however, the expert has simply not learned to communicate successfully. Frequently, the terminology and tabular material contained in a report dealing with land use, modal splits, trip generation, and trip distribution are understandable only to an experienced technician. This observation also applies to "informational" meetings that dwell heavily on the technical aspects of a study but have little relevance for policy or action on the local level.

8. How Much Real Commitment? The fundamental assumption of an interagency effort is a genuine commitment by all the participants. Unfortunately, a gap between words and deeds can develop if there are differing interpretations of documents and of verbal commitments. Trouble may also be generated by the sort of difference in outlook that separates top-level echelons from regional and lower-echelon staff. An agency chief is likely to have a broader outlook, to be more alert to current needs, and may be more at home in high-level interagency maneuvering than is a lowly staff member. In fact, the real commitment of the lower-level staff, who have the responsibility for day-to-day participation in an unfamiliar endeavor, may be highly unsatisfactory.

Firm policies and directives from agency headquarters can be useful correctives for ensuring at least reasonable cooperation. The fact that such direction has not always been forthcoming raises serious questions. In some cases, it seems that the studies were conducted to meet minimal requirements for further funding rather than to achieve solid objectives.

9. Results Not Commensurate with Expenditures and Promise. The area transportation studies were extremely expensive in comparison with their predecessors, the regional planning studies. Persons who deal with expenditures and their consequences—auditors, elected officials, and the press—have not always been convinced that the results were worth the effort and the money expended.

Many people contend that comprehensive planning has been ignored and that the public transit sector has been shortchanged, that is, that the highway agencies dominated the studies. In many cases, the studies were financed on a fifty-fifty basis by the two federal agencies—HUD and the BPR—but most local planning officials maintain that the HUD money was really used to augment the highway planning funds of the Bureau of Public Roads. The studies, they feel, served to underwrite proposals that would, in any case, have been advanced by the highway agencies, and they have had little impact in producing coordinated land-use and transportation plans. This disillusionment has been most pronounced in areas where there has been an active local planning organization. Negative reactions seem to have been strongest where the most glowing promises were made to local planners at the time the studies were initiated. There was, in short, a credibility gap, which sometimes served to obscure the modest but real contributions made.

The beginning phase of many of the transportation planning studies involved extensive promises about local participation, exaggerated claims about the results that were to be obtained, and, in general, a loud trumpeting of official speeches and public relations handouts. The loud braying that is often associated with the launching of new and difficult endeavors cannot fail to lead to disillusionment as time passes. The relative lack of excitement in the day-to-day routine of these studies was often cause for disappointment.

The raising of false hopes and excessive expectations often led to allegations of underperformance. Thus a study that presented local, state, and federal officials with a modest product was denigrated because of the false hopes that had been created among local officials. Furthermore, some politicians apparently believed that the studies would take the worry out of close decisions because they would present incontrovertible proof that a single alternative was the only correct solution. They were unhappy when they discovered that such projects cannot help them evade critical, controversial decisions. Moreover, local officials who welcomed the idea of participation in transportation planning were dismayed to learn that the final reports apparently grew out of a technical, barely comprehensible process in which their affirmation rather than their participation was solicited.

However, there are other reasons for disillusionment besides escalated rhetoric. In some instances, for example, local officials felt they had been issued an ill-fitting garment; the studies were not flexible enough to be tailored to local needs. Standardized procedures and uniform criteria for measuring results are, of course, needed to achieve national transportation planning objectives, but the cookbook approach may have neglected some local appetites. It also proved difficult to rearrange brand-name prescriptions. In particular, their resentment has centered on the broad-brush treatment that tended to ignore troublesome local issues on the ground that they were insufficiently regional in scope or that it would be premature to make substantive recommendations before the study was completed. This experience suggests that interagency efforts must be reasonably responsive to local requests if they wish to retain local support, even if these requests do not, strictly speaking, fall within the original scope or timetable of operations.

Selection of Projects for Study

Since the research design was predicated on a detailed review of comparatively few studies, it was decided to limit the analysis to five projects. This was considered to be the minimum number that would allow for a sufficient variety of comparisons among the various projects. The authors believed that extensive familiarity with the subject matter was essential to produce a meaningful study. For this reason, three of the five areas selected for study were ones of which the authors had substantial prior knowledge. The following area studies were chosen with the approval of HUD:

1. The Boston Regional Planning Project (BRPP), which later became the Eastern Massachusetts Regional Planning Project (EMRPP), covering the Boston, Massachusetts, area.

2. The Portland Area Comprehensive Transportation Study (PACTS), covering the Portland, Maine, area.

3. The Manchester Metropolitan Planning Study (MMPS), covering the Manchester, New Hampshire, area.

4. The Niagara Frontier Transportation Study (NFTS), covering the Buffalo–Niagara Falls, New York, area.

5. The Penn-Jersey Transportation Study, which involved the Philadelphia, Pennsylvania, and Camden and Trenton, New Jersey, area.

The projects were chosen to provide a variety of situations and types of project organization. Each was located in a different state. However, the five studies came under the jurisdiction of only two regional offices of the Bureau of Public Roads and two regional offices of HUD.

The Boston project, covering an area with a population of 3,300,000 people, was the largest project in which HUD and BPR participated on a fifty-fifty basis through a joint revolving fund. It was one of the later area transportation studies to be undertaken, and at that time it represented the most expensive joint planning effort of any type by two federal agencies.

The Portland and Manchester studies are typical of the numerous smaller urban area transportation studies. Although their sizes were comparable (involving populations of 100,000–200,000), the administrative procedures were significantly different. In the Portland study, which preceded the Manchester one by three years, HHFA and the BPR independently financed specific portions of the study. There was no joint revolving account, and the work program was rather simplistic in the light of subsequent efforts in other areas. The Manchester study was a fifty-fifty HUD-BPR effort with a joint revolving fund similar to that for the Boston project. Its work program was more comprehensive, and regional planning and transportation were more closely interwoven than in the Portland study.

The Niagara Frontier Transportation Study was totally funded and administered by the Bureau of Public Roads, and it provides a control by which to measure the administrative procedures of the joint studies. Furthermore, the NFTS study area population of about 1,000,000 persons provided data on the effect of this key population size on transportation systems. As noted elsewhere, it is at this population point that public transportation becomes a significant factor. The Buffalo study also represented the first major effort to conduct a series of transportation studies using one centralized transportation staff.

Penn-Jersey, perhaps the granddaddy of the "production" studies, in which plans rather than research were the principal objectives, was chosen for a number of reasons. The region, which contained 5,400,000 people, mounted one of the most costly studies undertaken in the nation. It was perhaps the longest running in terms of time spent from initiation of the study to preparation of plans, and it was also the only one of the five to include parts of two states. Finally, Penn-Jersey also represents the only study that had nearly 100 percent local staff.

Each of the five studies presented a unique situation, yet it is feasible to make comparisons among the study areas and to measure the impact of differences in project organization and administration.

Methodology

This research examined some of the salient problems and the key accomplishments of five area transportation studies, and it suggested possible ways to maximize the achievements and reduce the problems of future interagency programs. The research was qualitative, concentrating on a limited number of cases and agencies, since this was the only way in which a reasonably intensive study could be conducted. The research did not present extensive statistics on the area studies, nor did it attempt to develop mathematical relationships between causes and effects. The objective was to probe a range of projects in areas that varied greatly in size and experience.

The basic research tool was a series of interviews with persons involved in the studies chosen for evaluation. Based generally on the observations and hypotheses outlined earlier, the interviews were conducted by the two authors, both of whom had considerable prior familiarity with the technical aspects of area transportation planning and with the administrative conduct of such studies. As a result, the interview process produced revealing opinions and insights as well as suggestions for potential solutions.

In all, the authors interviewed about sixty persons in the course of their research while observing dozens more in action in the Boston, Manchester, and Portland areas. The research design recognized the need of obtaining information from comparable actors in each of the study areas. The authors had had direct association in one form or another with the Portland, Manchester, and Boston studies and were able to draw upon their own experiences and memories along with additional interviews on a formal and informal basis to round out the picture. In the two areas where the authors had no direct association—Buffalo and Philadelphia—they were required to reconstruct long-past events.

Interviews with participants who not only enjoyed an excellent vantage point in the study organizations but also possessed good memories made it possible to develop a reasonably complete picture. Bureau of Public Roads personnel associated with each of the studies were interviewed at the state level. In all cases, the state's BPR planning and programming engineer, the executive closest to these studies, was either interviewed or observed in action. In the Penn-Jersey and Buffalo studies, current and former project directors and state highway officials responsible for state highway planning were asked to comment on their experiences. Moreover, Bureau of Public Roads and HUD officials in Washington were interviewed at the outset of the study, and HUD executives were contacted at the division level in Region I in New York and Region II in Philadelphia.

In all areas, interviews were conducted with staff members of regional planning agencies. In Buffalo, an interview was held with the technical chief of the urban renewal agency that had battled the study organization over certain transportation proposals. Renewal agencies in Philadelphia and Boston were not included because they had not been embroiled in similar conflicts over intown highways. On the other hand, renewal agency staffs in Manchester and Portland, who had become involved in controversies over downtown highway proposals, were observed during the conduct of the studies.

One inconsistency related to interviews with members of lay committees. In the Portland, Manchester, and Boston studies, citizen advisory committees were observed in operation; but in the Buffalo and Penn-Jersey areas, because of the large number of persons involved and the problems of attempting to locate these persons and to elicit useful comments and observations, it was not considered worthwhile to allocate the necessary time and effort.

To gain perspective, most of the interviewing was conducted by a pair of researchers. The length of the interviews varied from a minimum of an hour to a half day. Tape recorders were not used for obvious reasons: persons reviewing past events are more candid in their impressions and observations when they know that their words are not being indelibly recorded.

Much of the basic data of this research consists of notes taken at the interviews. These notes and observations were supplemented by information obtained from published documents and by interviews with comparably placed persons in other studies. The same techniques that were used with relevant press and citizen representatives were used in conducting interviews with federal and local officials. In this manner it was hoped that the project processes could be meaningfully analyzed and compared. As was expected, common patterns were identified for closer study, and follow-up interviews were made in some cases. Members of the research team worked independently but coordinated their activities during the interview phase of the research. Occasionally, joint interviews were conducted, particularly in communities remote from Boston. This approach was used in the Niagara Frontier and Penn-Jersey studies with which the research team had had no previous direct contact.

The interviews were guided by a general outline that was based on the observations and propositions outlined earlier. The absence of a definitive interview form was intentional. It was expected that many interviews would cover a broad range of subjects which might or might not be relevant to the problem at hand but which would provide useful background information. Moreover, in the absence of a tightly organized questionnaire, it was hoped to obtain different opinions and insights in describing each of the various studies and events. All interviews and information have been held in the strictest confidence.

It should be made clear that the intent of this research was not to discredit individuals or agencies. The objective was to identify and analyze problems, experiences, patterns, and achievements for a spectrum of interagency studies and thereby to help improve the planning and conduct of future interagency endeavors. A clear understanding of individual and agency decisions, and the reasoning leading to these decisions, may well point to improved procedures and techniques for future programs.

Introduction

The nation's rather late start in attempting to solve some of its urban transportation problems stems in good part from a lack of federal concern. Not until fairly recently have the nation's urban transportation problems been seriously considered by the rurally dominated federal and state legislatures. The problem is compounded because most urban transportation problems cannot be solved on an individual municipal basis but must involve hundreds of municipalities and often more than one state. (About 10 percent of the nation's metropolitan areas straddle state boundaries.) Urban highways, which now serve a majority of the country's transportation requirements, were for many years excluded from federal support and still continue to receive only limited funds from Congress despite the fact that the nation has rapidly become urbanized.

There is a further complication. Mass transit, which in many urban areas is a viable alternative to elaborate and expensive highway construction, originated within the private sector of the economy. Only in recent years have most of the nation's mass transportation companies converted to public ownership. To a great extent, governmental acceptance of responsibility for public transportation has come about through recognition that it provides the only form of transportation for significant segments of the population.

Because the federal government has been taking a more active role in urban transportation planning, programming, and financing, it is significant to review what has taken place in the past so that current actions can be put in their proper context. Accordingly, this chapter attempts to follow the sequence of events leading to the 1962 Highway Act. It is intended primarily for those readers unfamiliar with the field, who may wish to obtain a broader background before reading further.

Urban transportation, a conglomerate of public and private enterprise, has not had the benefit of coordinated attention or regulation by the federal government. Until the present, federal policy has consisted of occasional, usually unrelated actions and attempts to solve parts of what are identified from time to time as problems. Policy has not changed materially in recent years despite a growing national awareness of urban needs, major interagency efforts, and sporadically applied congressional pressure. Perhaps because of its newness, the recently created U.S. Department of Transportation (DOT) has so far done little to improve the situation; it has not yet produced a consistent federal policy and has had little success in resolving existing conflicts.[1]

[1] DOT did not assume major responsibility for the administration of mass transportation, including the authorization to make grants and loans for the acquisition, construction, and improvement of facilities and equipment, until July 1, 1968. The

These comments should not be construed as a singling out of the transportation agencies. The lack of any consistent federal policy has been noted in many, if not most, areas of domestic and international affairs. In the past few years, for example, much attention has been devoted to the problems created by overlapping and conflicting programs in the fields of housing and community development, manpower training, poverty, education, and communications, as well as transportation. Perhaps the important fact is that the deficiencies are finally beginning to receive more serious attention.

Until the twentieth century, the nation's urban problems were relatively small scale. The United States was not yet an urban society; not until 1910 did more than half the population live in urban areas. Active federal participation, as a policy maker and investor, in urban transportation did not begin to emerge until about a decade later, in the 1920s. The federal government had played an active role in railroad, canal, and harbor development throughout the nineteenth century but was much slower to become involved in urban transportation. City streets were considered a local responsibility, and most long-distance roads were poorly articulated arrangements of locally financed routes and streets.

Federal hesitancy in moving into the cities was based on several factors. For the most part, the various forms of intercity transportation had long been under private control. Coastal packets, steamships, and ferries, the numerous toll roads, railroads, and interurban transit systems were all privately operated, although they were often the beneficaries of major public subsidies for construction and maintenance. Public transportation was provided by corporately owned vehicles on corporately owned rights-of-way or on publicly owned rights-of-way. By the twentieth century, the transportation system that had evolved consisted almost entirely of individually owned vehicles operating on publicly owned rights-of-way.

This capsule description necessarily emphasizes highways. It may be noted that the need for federal intervention to strengthen urban transportation was not recognized until the early 1960s. Highways rather than public mass transit still receive virtually all of the available transportation funds and exercise the principal influence on urban transportation planning. Witness the authorization of another 1,500 miles of interstate highways by Congress in 1968.[2] It is significant that even as late as 1968 some important congressional

Department of Housing and Urban Development retained authority over transportation planning as it relates to urban development. DOT and HUD are jointly responsible for establishing criteria applicable to local planning agencies in developing coordinated transportation systems as a part of comprehensive urban development programs.

[2] S. 3418, the Federal-Aid Highway Act of 1968, authorized 1,500 additional miles to the previously authorized 41,000-mile Interstate System.

leaders were still heavily committed to highways. The 1968 bill authorized the construction of four major Washington, D.C., highway projects, although these projects were being opposed by proponents of local rapid transit, who believed that rail rapid transit should be constructed first. After criticizing the strict highway requirements for Washington, President Johnson reluctantly signed the bill, despite the unusual provisions for specific highway projects. After the president signed the bill the chairman of the House Subcommittee on Roads of the Public Works Committee, Representative John C. Klucz-ywski of Illinois, told the *Washington Post,* "the District won't get a dime for a subway until it does what we want it to do to highways."[3]

It may be useful to review briefly at this point the conditions that led to the current transportation crisis and provided the launching pad for the transportation studies of the late 1950s and early 1960s.

From 1900 to 1930 the number of automobile registrations in the country increased from 8,000 to over 26,000,000.[4] Over the next fifteen years, 1930–1945, the economic pressures of the Great Depression and World War II resulted in a further increase of only 5,000,000 vehicles. Automobile sales, which had shown sharp gains during the twenties, slowed, and registrations by 1945 had climbed to only 30,600,000 vehicles. Following the war, there was again a massive outpouring of demand for new cars. Between 1945 and 1955, registrations doubled, rising to 62,000,000. The rate of increase declined considerably in the next decade, but the national registration figures climbed by an additional 32,000,000 vehicles. By 1970, vehicle registrations had reached the 100,000,000 level.

Widespread ownership of automobiles had a strong impact on public transportation. In 1935 the nation's urban transit lines carried 9.8 billion passengers. Ten years later, because of wartime restrictions, these same transit lines carried 19 billion passengers, an increase of nearly 100 percent in the ten-year period. However, with the removal of wartime restrictions on automobile manufacturing and the end of gasoline and tire rationing, the trend changed radically. By 1955, transit line patronage was cut in half, revenue passengers having declined to 9.2 billion, a level below that of twenty years earlier. One significant factor in this rapid decline was that the nation's public transportation equipment, under great strain during the war years, had long ago begun to show the effects of age. Many of the systems begun during the early 1900s and 1920s were utilizing equipment purchased when they were first established, and companies equipped with old transit vehicles were not in a

---

[3] *Congressional Quarterly Weekly Report,* vol. 26, no. 35 (August 30, 1968), p. 2320.
[4] Data in this section are derived from Automobile Manufacturers Association, *Automobile Facts and Figures* (Detroit, 1967).

position to compete with the attractions of new private automobiles.

The 1920s produced the first wave of automobile congestion, as evidenced by photographs of the snarled conditions of Boston, New York, and Chicago streets during this period; the nation was hard pressed to produce the necessary miles of improved city streets. It was not until the 1930s that major highway construction projects were begun; yet these projects were more concerned with providing jobs than a sound highway system. With the advent of World War II the country turned to problems abroad, and highways were set aside except for a few emergency and defense projects.

In the decade following the war, the nation's manufacturing industry that had geared up to produce military vehicles, including tanks and airplanes, met the accumulated demands of a more affluent public by converting its large military production capabilities to the construction of private vehicles. Again highway construction did not keep pace with automobile production. Faced with the backlog of problems after a five-year moratorium, highway construction bogged down in the postwar period. During this decade a number of states, acting under virtual emergency conditions, established turnpike authorities as a means of bypassing the cumbersome and comparatively poorly financed highway agencies. These turnpikes satisfied only minimally the requirements posed by the massive increase in vehicle ownership and use. As a result the nation's urban areas began experiencing traffic congestion far surpassing the traffic jams of the 1920s. To help close the gap between growing numbers of cars and limited roadway capacity, the federal government in 1956 authorized the so-called Interstate System.[5] Although not new in concept, the interstate network represented a major step forward in the federal government's commitment to highway construction.

The nation's expenditures for highway construction and maintenance doubled from $1.3 billion in 1921 to $2.6 billion in 1930. After a temporary decline in the early 1930s, the national investment in highways continued at about $2.6 billion per year, although automobile registrations did not increase during this same period. By 1945, however, because of wartime restrictions, yearly highway expenditures had declined to $1.7 billion, most of it allocated for maintenance work and interest payments on outstanding debts. Between 1945 and 1960, national highway expenditures rose by about

[5] The National System of Interstate and Defense Highways was actually authorized in 1944; however, the 1956 Federal-Aid Highway Act is generally recognized as the beginning date of the system since it provided for 90 percent federal support for construction of the system, thus assuring its timely completion. As an added measure of insurance for construction of the Interstate System, the 1956 act also created the Highway Trust Fund, fed by federal gasoline taxes, which provide an untouchable source of federal funds for the system.

$3 billion per year during each five-year period to nearly $11 billion by 1960. By 1965 the annual figure had risen an additional $2 billion. Figures for the fiscal year 1970[6] indicate an expenditure of about $6 billion from federal funds alone for highway construction.

On the other hand, the amount of new investment in public transportation facilities was insignificant. In fact, the industry was undergoing a vast depletion of its resources as it vainly sought to replace its obsolescent equipment in the face of steady reductions in ridership. Between 1945 and 1960 the total miles of electric railway track declined from 17,700 miles to 3,150 miles. Motor bus mileage, however, did increase slightly in the same period, from 90,000 to 109,000.[7]

Thus the nation as a whole, after being repressed for fifteen years by depression and war, radically transformed the nation's transportation balance. The congestion of the late 1940s continued to worsen during the 1950s. As a result the period from 1955 to 1960 might be classified as the transportation crisis phase for the nation's urban areas. Today, the high-priority crises of poverty and law and order have moved transportation from center stage to a comparatively minor role in the urban landscape. But before this shift in emphasis occurred, the nation's vast transportation planning activities had been undertaken.

The Federal-Aid Road Act of 1916

Transportation planning for cities had its roots in the 1916 Road Act, which was concerned primarily with stimulating intercity highway construction. The major forces for federal action were a combination of agrarian, automobile, and, surprisingly, railroad interests. The agrarian interest in intercity roads was understandable, since farmers needed access to city markets. Previous federal involvement with roads had had an exclusively rural emphasis, as indicated by the location of the U.S. Bureau of Public Roads (BPR) in the Department of Agriculture. Allied with the farmers was the burgeoning automobile industry, which foresaw that intercity highways would promote more automobile usage and ownership. Finally, the railroads saw the advantages of having roads linked to rail terminals because they would promote farm shipments by rail freight.

Absent in this early coalition of interest groups were spokesmen for the cities. Although this may have been understandable during the early 1900s, when urban congestion was not a problem, it is surprising that the cities were

[6] "Federal Road Aid Extended Despite D.C. Project Dispute," *Congressional Quarterly Weekly Report,* vol. 26, no. 35 (August 30, 1968), p. 2321.
[7] American Transit Association, *Transit Facts and Figures: Annual Report, 1968* (Washington, D.C., 1968).

not pressing for direct federal aid to urban transportation by the late 1920s. City planners, especially those who belonged to the city-beautiful movement, were interested primarily in architectural aesthetics, and their concern with city design did not extend to the operational requirements of mass transit systems. For example, they did not worry that transportation systems might encroach on open space. There were a few early rumblings: in Boston, a Park Department report[8] in 1926 expressed concern over the use of parkways for "general traffic" and the use of park lands for new highways. However, characteristically, the park officials accepted the need for new highways while urging that they should be built outside of park areas. This illustration was a harbinger of things to come. Over the years, planners have been either resigned to or enthusiastic for new highways, although they have been more sensitive than most to the attendant problems. On the whole, it is probably fair to conclude that city planners, like other people, failed to anticipate the true impact of the automobile either on traffic congestion or on land use.

The 1916 Road Act resulted in a federal-state partnership under which most transportation planning and highway construction was determined by state highway agencies. The program was administered by the Federal Bureau of Public Roads in conjunction with the states, and the BPR set uniform standards of organization and procedure. A provision prohibiting municipalities with populations of 2,500 or more from receiving highway aid stressed the construction of rural highway connections between cities. There was one exception: municipalities could receive aid for those portions of streets on which the houses were on the average more than two hundred feet apart, presumably rural territory. This discrimination against built-up urban areas, while considerably altered, still exists in principle in most states. City streets have long been a no-man's-land, as well as a no-money-land, for state highway agencies. This situation is gradually changing. As state legislatures increasingly reflect apportionment changes, urban needs are receiving greater recognition.

Federal Legislation in the Depression Years

Federal aid for highways, including assistance for roads that might be built in urban areas, increased during the 1930s, but this aid was not accompanied by efforts to promote comprehensive planning. In the midst of the Great Depression, the primary goal was to provide jobs and relief from unemployment through road construction projects. Through the Emergency Relief and Construction Act of 1932, the federal government provided funds for a broad program of state-administered public works. Under this legislation the states

[8] Boston, Park Department, *Future Parks and Playgrounds,* report prepared by Shurcliff and Merrill (Boston, October 1926).

were not required to match federal funds, and they were permitted to use funds to improve roads within the urban areas that had already been designated for federal assistance. In 1933 came the National Industrial Recovery Act (NIRA), which contained much broader provisions for spending federal funds in urban areas. The act stated that funds would be available

for expenditure in emergency construction of the federal aid highway system, an extension thereof into and through municipalities, including costs of surveys and plans, grade crossing eliminations, bridges and construction of routes to avoid congested areas.[9]

The Hayden-Cartwright Act of 1934, which provided additional funds for highway construction, represented a continuation of the NIRA and added an important new feature—the authorization of planning funds. Under this provision, up to 1.5 percent of combined federal and state highway construction moneys could be allocated by the states for use in surveys, planning, and engineering investigations. At the same time, the legislation also called for the appointment within each state highway agency of a planning and programming engineer.

While urban area transportation planning may possibly have been a consideration in the establishment of the 1.5 percent provision and the creation of a new planning post, these changes were mostly intended to improve and accelerate the programming of federal and state funds for highways. Much of the emphasis in the investigations financed with the 1.5 percent funds was on materials research (for example, asphalt versus concrete surfaces) and highway location (cut and fill balancing), both of which flowered during the 1930s and 1940s and diminished in importance during the 1950s as answers were found to these problems. Furthermore, the act did not require that these planning funds actually be spent for planning or engineering investigations. In fact, there was a construction bonus if the 1.5 percent funds were not used for research purposes; in that event, the funds could be used for road building. As a result, state highway agencies succumbed to the temptation to spend the available research funds for construction purposes. Finally, even in the states that used these funds for research, they were administered by state highway agencies, which traditionally, and specifically, ignored city transportation needs.

In summary, federally aided highway construction during the 1930s represented a continuation of the pattern established in the 1916 Road Act. The public works program was new, but the basic means for dealing with urban transportation requirements were determined by the Federal Bureau of Public Roads working in close cooperation with the state highway agencies.

[9] George M. Smerk, *Urban Transportation: The Federal Role* (Bloomington: Indiana University Press, 1965), p. 124.

Despite the traffic congestion of the roaring 1920s no efforts were made toward comprehensive regional planning. Perhaps one reason was the antagonism displayed by highway engineers toward city planners; this antagonism was evident as early as the 1930s at the state and federal levels and was to burst into full bloom in the 1960s. The cities were not prepared, either technically or financially, to combat this attitude, particularly during a time of national economic crisis.

The federal government established no guidelines to promote urban area planning in the 1930s, although there were numerous federally sponsored or federally aided activities in national, regional, and state planning. Thus throughout the 1930s, transportation programs in which the federal government was involved continued to have a highway emphasis that was strongly reinforced by the state highway agencies.

At the same time, public transportation in urban areas began to show the effects of neglect and changing traffic patterns. Plagued by the depression and increasing competition from the private automobile, many of the largely unregulated, privately owned transit companies began to lose interest in retaining their properties. Many prescient companies had already unloaded their white elephants on the municipalities ten or twenty years earlier. By the late 1930s, some cities had begun to call for increased federal aid to improve urban transportation; but, for the most part, improvements were envisioned as more of the same, that is, more highways. Their pleas were met with sympathy, but the intervention of World War II brought a postponement of all federal aid for highways except in defense plant areas.

The Federal-Aid Highway Act of 1944

As World War II was coming to an end, the federal government feared a reversion to mass unemployment with the cessation of war spending, and it moved to provide funds to reduce the backlog of highway building. The Federal-Aid Highway Act of 1944 called for continued federal-state cooperation in designating a national system of interstate highways to connect the principal metropolitan areas of the country. The act paid particular attention to urban areas by specifying that a percentage of the funds be allocated to cities of over 5,000 population. The appropriations under the 1944 act were apportioned as follows: 45 percent for primary roads in the federal system, including some urban extensions; 30 percent for selected roads in the federal-aid secondary system; and 25 percent for federal-aid highways in urban areas with a population of over 5,000 persons. The 1944 act was notable for continuing the emphasis on a highways-only policy at a time when the greatest urban decentralization the nation had ever seen was about to take place. In fact, federal highway policies after 1944 further accelerated the urban sprawl.

A rash of postwar transportation studies, financed under the 1.5 percent provision of the 1934 act, developed master highway plans for a number of the nation's urban areas. For the first time, there was some recognition of public transportation systems, where these existed, but most of the reports only acknowledged their existence and the need for their continuation. The drastic reductions in mass transit ridership that took place in the late 1940s and 1950s were totally unexpected. The highway engineers were confident, however, that an expanded highway system would be capable of absorbing the former transit riders. Planning funds continued to be used exclusively for highway studies except in the very few cases where cities were able to convince their state highway agencies to consider the overall transportation picture. This trend was consistent with state-aid distribution formulas, which continued to favor rural roads at the expense of urban areas.[10]

The highways-only policy of the 1944 legislation set the pattern for subsequent federal appropriations until 1961. Several reasons account for the continuing emphasis on roads. First, the federal-aid program for highways was an accepted and traditional program. For thirty years the federal government had helped to meet urban transportation needs solely in terms of highway construction. Second, the highway program was an accepted governmental responsibility, one that clearly could not be handled by the private sector of the national economy. Third, the great change in mass transportation ownership from private to public was and continued to be a very gradual one; although municipalities were up to their ears in streetcar, bus, and subway systems by the 1940s, the federal government did not, until much later, share responsibility for what many saw as a purely local problem. Perhaps most important, rural and small-town interests in both the U.S. Congress and the state legislatures opposed federal legislation that increased aid to urban transportation at the expense of the vast road-building program in outlying areas. The powerful automotive industry, of course, supported more road building as a means of stimulating the purchase and usage of automobiles, and it saw little advantage in diverting federal transportation funds to help the subways and buses. Finally, the Bureau of Public Roads tended to discourage any programs or financing that would diminish its status and influence.

In the face of such a formidable coalition, the cities, which lacked technical and financial support and which were also underrepresented in the state and federal legislatures, saw little hope in altering the entrenched transportation program. Furthermore, many urban spokesmen sensed that they were cham-

[10] Robert S. Friedman, "State Politics and Highways," in *Politics in the American States,* ed. Herbert Jacob and Kenneth N. Vines (Boston: Little, Brown and Company, 1965), pp. 428–429.

pions of a lost cause. They had to concede that the average citizen, given his choice, favored the private automobile over public transportation. It must be noted, however, that the average citizen has had little incentive to urge widespread aid for public transportation. Transit companies and commuter railroads have constantly bemoaned their financial losses and decline in ridership and have continually reacted by cutting service and requesting higher fares. Many transit companies in the last stages of private ownership, or in the struggling period of new public ownership, have suffered from an accumulation of ailments ranging from old equipment and obsolete terminals to sullen, mutinous employees. Thus public transportation during the late 1940s and 1950s came to be viewed as an unwanted but necessary evil.

Unfortunately, the cities were not organized to lobby in Congress for a change in policy, and state governors, even in urban states, were not urging immediate action on behalf of the cities. Nor was any effort made initially by the federal government to tie community planning to the highway program, even though the multibillion-dollar Interstate System begun under the 1956 Federal-Aid Highway Act was bound to have an enormous impact on urban transportation. Wilfred Owen, a noted expert on metropolitan transportation, made this observation about the 1956 Federal-Aid Highway Act:

The new interstate highway program places special emphasis on the urban area. Construction of the system will to a considerable degree determine the character of the community. But it would be folly to design and locate the new highways without the guidance of area plans that dictate future population densities, land uses and therefore demands for transportation. Comprehensive planning for the urban area therefore is a prerequisite to sound highway planning.[11]

Despite this warning and the accelerating rate of deterioration in public transportation in the mid to late 1950s, it was not until the 1962 Federal-Aid Highway Act that any real changes were made.

Federal Government Recognition of Urban Transportation Needs

To provide the reader with a sense of perspective, it is necessary to discuss briefly the changing outlook of the federal agencies with respect to urban transportation problems. By the late 1950s, it was evident that the answer to urban transportation needs involved more than new roads. Large numbers of people commuting during peak hours could not be handled by a highway system, and many others—the old, the infirm, children, and the poor—needed good public transportation. It also seemed that the steady decline of public transportation patronage would not be reversed. Meanwhile, a conflict arose between the Bureau of Public Roads and city repre-

[11] Wilfred Owen, "What Do We Want the Highway System to Do?" in Tax Institute, Inc., *Financing Highways* (Princeton, N.J., 1957), pp. 9–10.

sentatives, particularly city planners. The BPR contended that the interstate highway program would do much to relieve automobile congestion in the cities; the representatives of the cities strongly challenged this position. In many of the nation's largest cities as much as two-thirds of the total downtown land area was already dedicated to streets and parking, and some planners gloomily predicted that much of the remainder would be converted to serve the automobile unless strenuous efforts were made to curb highway construction.

The federal government was beginning to realize that the massive highway construction program was aggravating rather than relieving urban transportation problems. Under Section 701 of the 1954 Housing Act, Congress provided $5 million in matching grants to the states for urban and mass transportation planning, which was to be administered by the Urban Renewal Administration of the Housing and Home Finance Agency (HHFA).

In 1961, two important reports were released by the federal government: an analysis by the Advisory Commission on Intergovernmental Relations (ACIR),[12] and *National Transportation Policy,* prepared for the U.S. Senate Committee on Interstate and Foreign Commerce.[13]

The ACIR report noted two general characteristics of the urban transportation problem. First, transportation facilities in most urban areas failed to meet community standards, and consequently, there was a widespread feeling that transportation was inadequate. Second, the general public was frustrated with the inability of the cities to remedy transportation inadequacies. The ACIR suggested that one of the principal reasons for both problems was the lack of federal funds for mass transportation on a scale similar to the funding available for highways. There was clearly a highway bias in local transportation planning and financing.

The *National Transportation Policy* report spelled out the particular deficiencies in federal policy toward urban transportation. It indicated that the political and administrative problems included the following:

1. Present facilities fail to form a coherent system. Since transportation facilities were built up over a long period of time, people tend to look at city transportation in segmented terms, such as bridges, streets, tunnels, parking lots, and rail lines.

2. Areawide systems require areawide plans. Such planning must relate

[12] U.S., Advisory Commission on Intergovernmental Relations, *Intergovernmental Responsibilities for Mass Transportation Facilities and Service in Metropolitan Areas* (Washington, D.C.: Government Printing Office, 1961).
[13] U.S., Congress, Senate, Special Study Group on Transportation Policies in the United States, *National Transportation Policy,* preliminary draft of a report prepared for the Committee on Interstate and Foreign Commerce, 87th Congress, 1st session, January 3, 1961.

transportation to other metropolitan investments and land use.

3. Governmental fragmentation in metropolitan areas leads to competing jurisdictions that attempt, often unsuccessfully, to handle urban transportation requirements.

4. Financing of public facilities and services has no rational basis. There is a hodgepodge of financing similar to the hodgepodge of facilities.[14]

A document prepared by the U.S. Department of Commerce in 1960 had also called attention to the need for federal support in urban transportation. It noted that metropolitan areas continued to be congested and that rush-hour jams, parking area deficiencies, and commuter and rapid transit losses had become chronic problems of the urban scene. The federal government was recognized as a major contributor to the problem through its huge highway program.

The report recommended that the federal government (1) encourage communities to make broad land-use plans including transportation as an essential part and (2) consider the total urban transport situation, so that federal participation might further the acceptance of transportation as a system rather than as a grouping of individual components.

These reports by the ACIR, the Senate Special Study Group on Transportation Policies, and the Commerce Department agreed that the federal government had failed to assist urban areas in meeting their transportation requirements. They all noted the lack of comprehensive areawide planning, but none strongly recommended federal aid for public transportation. The studies implied that neither Section 701 of the Housing Act of 1954 nor the 1.5 percent provision of the highway legislation was generating much areawide transportation planning. The 701 projects were primarily general planning studies with only a minor focus on transportation. Furthermore, most of them were conducted in small towns and medium-sized cities rather than in the nation's largest urban areas.

On the other hand, the Bureau of Public Roads did begin to modify the highway bias in its planning during the late 1950s. In a policy statement issued in December 1959, the BPR ruled that the 1.5 percent funds could be used for comprehensive transportation studies if they were made at the same time as highway studies.[15] This concession encountered numerous problems, however; for example, state constitutions barred the diversion of highway

[14] Ibid., pp. iii–iv.
[15] Ibid., p. 615. See also Lyle Fitch and Associates, *Urban Transportation and Public Policy* (San Francisco: Chandler Publishing Co., 1964), pp. 64–65, and Richard M. Zettel and Richard R. Carll, *Summary Review of Metropolitan Area Transportation Studies in the United States* (Berkeley: University of California, Institute of Traffic and Transportation Engineering, 1962).

funds for other uses. Perhaps the most important difficulty was that the new concept was not binding on the states. The state highway agencies still determined the use of the 1.5 percent planning funds—if they were to be used at all—and were much more interested in designing and constructing new roads than in engaging in metropolitan transportation planning.

Nevertheless, pressure was developing. In November 1960, the U.S. Department of Commerce (BPR) and the U.S. Housing and Home Finance Agency agreed to work jointly to provide funds for metropolitan transportation planning. The Department of Commerce directed the BPR to encourage the use of the 1.5 percent planning funds for urban transportation needs, and the HHFA expanded urban renewal planning authorizations under Section 701 to cover areawide transportation planning. This interagency coordination between the BPR and HHFA was an important step forward. It should be noted that all of this cooperation was taking place in Washington. Out in the real world, it was business as usual.

After considerable analysis and negotiation, the two agencies submitted a joint report to the president in March 1962. They pledged to continue joint planning, and they pledged interagency coordination in meeting transportation needs at both the national and regional levels.[16] The Commerce-HHFA joint agreement represented an initial step in providing federal leadership for urban transportation policy. But several problems remained in reconciling the diverse orientations toward urban transportation of the Bureau of Public Roads and HHFA. The BPR was accustomed to working with the state highway agencies, and HHFA dealt mainly with municipalities and area planning agencies on land-use problems. The BPR was interested in the interagency arrangement primarily because of its implications for new road construction, while HHFA was interested because of its alarm at the impact of highways on urban neighborhoods and public transportation. Considering these divergent concerns, it was somewhat doubtful that the ad hoc joint planning agreement first initiated in 1960 could effectively promote metropolitan transportation planning. Although both Commerce and HHFA officials felt that there was ample precedent for combining urban and highway planning, there was little guiding experience. Neither agency had been involved in large-scale comprehensive transportation planning in the past. Both agencies stressed the importance of local responsibility for areawide planning, but they did not specify the federal government's role. In effect, the Department of Commerce and HHFA were delegating responsibility for areawide planning

[16] U.S., Congress, House, Committee on Banking and Currency, *Urban Mass Transportation Act of 1962: Hearings on H.R. 11158,* 87th Congress, 2nd session, 1962, pp. 43–44.

to the urban areas at a time when the urban areas lacked the capability to pursue this approach. More effort was needed in the form of new federal legislation to provide the funds, personnel, leadership, and direction for encouraging integrated metropolitan transportation planning.

City Pressure for Federal Transportation Legislation

By the late 1950s, the nation's larger cities had begun to bring pressure on Congress for changes in urban transportation policy. Faced with increasing traffic congestion, failing commuter services, and the need to improve mass transit facilities, a procession of urban leaders trooped to Washington seeking federal participation in urban transportation.[17] This was considered by many to be the keystone to a solution of city problems.

Perhaps one of the first bits of evidence that the cities were acting in concert on transportation problems was the formation of the National Committee on Urban Transportation in 1958. With the assistance of the Bureau of Public Roads, the committee prepared a report, *Better Transportation for Your City*,[18] which noted that one of the major problems was the absence of effective intergovernmental coordination and metropolitan planning. The committee's efforts were taken over on a continuing basis by the American Municipal Association.

A more dramatic presentation of urban transportation needs, however, took place in 1959, when a group of twelve mayors and the heads of seventeen railroads met in Chicago to discuss the crisis situation of commuter railroads. It is significant that, by this time, most of the nation's large mass transportation systems had been taken over by public agencies while the commuter railroads were still privately owned and operated. More strictly regulated than the transit companies, the railroads, to a degree, were able to offset revenue losses with freight revenues. Caught in a bind between federal and state regulations and potential financial disaster, the railroads joined forces with city officials in attempting to obtain public subsidies for passenger service or, alternatively, in eliminating this service. In 1959 a Senate committee headed by Ray Dilworth of Philadelphia issued a survey report on commuter rail studies in five cities—New York, Chicago, Philadelphia, Boston, and Cleveland. This report, entitled "The Collapse of Commuter Service," recommended the following action by the federal government:

(1) That a national policy should be established by the Congress for a balanced and coordinated transportation system.

[17] These included representatives of the American Public Works Association, the American Municipal Association, the International City Managers Association, the National Association of County Officials, and the American Society of Planning Officials.

[18] National Committee on Urban Transportation, *Better Transportation for Your City* (Chicago: Public Administration Service, 1958).

(2) That the Federal, state and local governments be asked to develop rational tax policies for the railroads.

(3) That Federal loans be made available where necessary to municipalities or publicly constituted bodies for new commuter equipment and improved facilities and for the improvement of intracity mass passenger transportation facilities; these to be long term, low interest loans.

(4) That a study should be made of grants-in-aid by the Federal Government to communities or duly constituted public bodies which have a sound plan for the permanent improvement of commutation or other intracity transportation facilities, this to be modeled on the present urban renewal program.[19]

The Dilworth report presented perhaps the first concrete recommendations to the federal government relating to urban transportation problems. However, it dealt specifically with the rail commuter situation, and the recommendations for congressional action were restricted to this aspect of urban transportation. It omitted discussion of a regional approach to urban transportation and failed to press for a coordinated system that would also include highways, automobiles, buses, and rapid transit. Perhaps the greatest significance of the Dilworth report was its recognition that federal financial support for commuter facilities was a necessity.

Senator Harrison A. Williams, Jr., of New Jersey used the Dilworth report as the basis for a bill that he introduced in March 1960. The bill called for a new federal policy to encourage state and local governments to plan, coordinate, and financially assist their public transportation systems. It authorized $100 million for long-term, low-interest loans to public bodies for mass transportation improvements; priorities were to be given to applicants with urgent needs and workable plans for coordinated transportation systems. Senator Williams also proposed that Section 701 of the 1954 Housing Act be amended specifically to authorize federal aid for transportation planning. The bill passed in the Senate but came to grief in the House.

Although Congress did not pass the Williams bill in 1960, it is important to note that urban pressures were leading in the direction of new federal legislation. The cities had joined forces to dramatize their problems. The Dilworth committee recommendations and the Williams bill emphasized the need for a change in federal policy toward urban transportation. Both recognized that urban transportation systems must be coordinated and that areawide comprehensive planning was first required as the basis for an overall approach to the problem. However, the city spokesman and Senator Williams failed to consider fully the problems entailed in undertaking such a new program. There was general agreement in Washington, and there were numerous gentlemen's

[19] In U.S., Congress, Senate, Committee on Banking and Currency, *Urban Mass Transportation—1961: Hearings on S. 435,* 87th Congress, 1st session, March 20, 21, and 22, 1961, p. 122.

agreements between officials of both HHFA and the BPR, but it was difficult to see how the cities could begin to plan in view of the very powerful role still played by the Bureau of Public Roads and the state highway agencies in the federal-aid program. While both the railroad leaders and federal officials pressed for federal aid, they did not attack the existing road-building program, nor did they argue forcefully for a balanced national urban transportation policy. No one recognized that effective areawide planning would have to cope with the difficult task of taming the semiautonomous highway agencies. In the absence of any effective cooperation and coordination in the past, there was no assurance that a new joint interagency effort could be successfully developed.

The Housing Act of 1961: Federal Assistance for Mass Transportation
By 1961, with 70 percent of the nation's population living in urban areas, federal officials had become convinced that only with federal aid could the cities make a dent in their accumulation of transportation problems. More than 300 cities, towns, and villages had lost all of their public transportation since World War II because private bus, railroad, and streetcar companies had eliminated routes or gone out of business.[20] Many of the remaining transit and commuter services were in poor physical condition, and decreasing public use of mass transportation led to higher fares for increasingly poor service. At the same time, the massive road-building programs could not keep pace with the demands of the automobile.

In January 1961, Senator Williams and seventeen Republican and Democratic cosponsors reintroduced an expanded version of the unsuccessful 1960 urban transportation bill. The new legislation called for $325 million in federal assistance and a three-part program:
1. $250 million in a revolving loan fund for the purchase of new rail and bus equipment, rights-of-way and terminals. Loans would be available for state and local governments or public authorities to be used in transportation programs but not for carrier operating expenses.
2. $50 million in matching grants to state or local governments for demonstration projects to show the feasibility of new transportation methods and systems.
3. $25 million in matching grants for area or regional planning for mass transportation.[21]

This bill not only recognized the urgent need for assisting mass transportation facilities but made provisions for stimulating interagency coordination and intergovernmental cooperation through areawide planning. With the $25 million in matching grants, the federal government would provide substantial

[20] *New York Times,* April 10, 1961, p. 1.
[21] Ibid., March 20, 1961, p. 24.

aid for planning, an urban transportation component that had been badly neglected since the 1940s.

The demonstration grants and urban planning assistance provision of the 1961 legislation represented the key components of a long-range attack on urban transportation problems. However, the Williams bill did not include guidelines for developing regional planning. It was also vague on the relationship between demonstration projects and regional planning. For example, it was not clear whether such projects should precede or follow area planning or whether they should be conducted simultaneously. In point of fact, the demonstration programs were often used as simple subsidies for operating railroad and bus companies to buy time and continue rail commuter lines while permanent solutions were being arranged. Moreover, the Williams bill did not provide for a federal-state partnership in urban transportation nor for a city-federal partnership in attempting to find more permanent solutions.

The testimony before the Housing Subcommittee of the Senate Banking and Currency Committee in March 1961 produced a wide range of support for the Williams bill. With the lone exception of the U.S. Chamber of Commerce, all witnesses endorsed it. However, this broad coalition of interests, comprising the big-city mayors, urban renewal experts, city planners, and transit and commuter rail spokesmen, did not see the urban transportation problem in overall perspective. The testimony revealed that there was no broad national consensus within the ad hoc constituency for urban transportation. Everyone wanted to see his own particular problem solved by the new legislation but was not interested in coordination with other potentially competing modes. Furthermore, it was notable that urban-state governors and federal administrators were missing from the list of witnesses. Only one or two witnesses stated that the proposed bill was merely a stopgap measure to save the commuter railroads, arguing that panic solutions and huge outlays of federal money would not solve the urban transportation problem; in particular, subsidization of the commuter railroads was perhaps not the best approach. Aside from these few voices, however, the witnesses mainly viewed federal aid in terms of immediate relief for urgent crises. (The situation was comparable to early highway legislation, which was also aimed at resolving immediate problems.) In short, it was apparently the consensus that transportation planning was necessary, but very little was said about the machinery that would be necessary for an areawide approach.

Agreement was unanimous that HHFA rather than the Commerce Department would be the appropriate federal agency to administer any mass transportation program. Witnesses argued that HHFA's long experience with urban renewal had established that agency's expertise in dealing directly with cities and with urban problems. In contrast, the Bureau of Public Roads in the Department of Commerce was accustomed to working only with the state highway agencies. Witnesses were critical of the BPR for neglecting city transportation requirements while providing millions for new highway construction. Furthermore, because many witnesses represented cities, there was an emphasis upon developing close city-federal relationships through HHFA, which would bypass the state highway agencies and the rurally controlled state legislatures. This technique had proved effective in the urban renewal program, for which a working city-federal relationship had been established that made only the barest reference to the role of the states. It was hoped that the same pattern could be carried over into the mass transportation program, since there was a distinct antagonism between city and state interests. However, this was a weak position for the cities because the state highway agencies controlled an integral part of the city's transportation systems. Yet, despite the necessity for close participation with the state highway agencies, the Senate testimony did not include any spokesmen for the latter.

The urban mass transportation provisions of the 1961 Housing Act were passed by Congress on June 28, 1961. Proponents in the Senate were largely responsible for congressional approval of the legislation, since the House of Representatives did not include any assistance for urban transportation in its version of the housing bill. Even so, the mass transportation provisions were almost defeated in the Senate when attempts were made to delete the loan and grant provisions. President Kennedy was active in urging the House to add the urban transportation section to its version, and Senate and House conferees subsequently agreed to include urban transportation in the omnibus housing bill.

Opposition to the transportation provision of the Housing Act focused primarily on the degree of federal financial support. As finally enacted, the 1961 legislation represented a drastic reduction from the $325 million in federal aid originally proposed by Senator Williams. The revolving loan fund of $250 million for transit facilities and equipment was reduced to $50 million in the final bill. The $50 million in matching grants for demonstration projects was pared to $25 million. Only the assistance for planning was increased. The Section 701 authorization for mass transit planning purposes was raised to $75 million. However, the entire 701 program was reduced even further; the $150 million authorization was cut back to $42.5 million in actual appropriations.

Thus the legislation represented a rather inauspicious beginning in federal assistance for urban mass transportation. The most hopeful sign was the recognition of planning as an important aspect of urban transportation needs. Nothing was done, however, to alleviate the interagency administrative problems that had already become evident. Furthermore, no recognition was given to the need for the federal government to have a transportation policy covering all modes of transportation. An urban transportation administrator was not appointed by HHFA, and the new act contained no provisions for improved interagency coordination between HHFA and the Bureau of Public Roads, the state highway agencies, and the cities. The act bore no relationship to the massive highway programs, and no provision was made for subsequent reevaluation as areawide planning and demonstration projects proceeded. In effect, Congress was providing a short-term crash program of financial assistance to begin a limited attack on selected urban transportation problems.

The Highway Act of 1962: Prelude to the Interagency Studies

The 1962 Federal-Aid Highway Act specified that future federal highways in urban areas must conform to a plan for comprehensive development for the entire region. It further specified that the deadline for this requirement was July 1965, a short three years after passage of the act. The act did not specify that comprehensive development plans had to be conducted in cooperation with other state, federal, or city agencies, but it did state that they should be initiated and undertaken by the state highway agencies. As a result, the Bureau of Public Roads emerged as the federal agency most instrumental in expanding regional planning in the nation's metropolitan areas.

Perhaps of greatest significance, the potential existed for an annual expenditure of $75 million for planning out of the annual national expenditure of approximately $5 billion on federal-state highways. This calculation is based on the 1.5 percent formula. The 1962 Highway Act finally specified that these funds had to be spent for studies and could not be used for construction.

HHFA offered to participate as an equal partner with the BPR in urban transportation planning. The offer was due to a combination of previous cooperative efforts, a willingness to participate, and, perhaps most important, a desire to influence the course of urban transportation planning. Initially this cooperation was on an ad hoc basis, whereby HHFA would finance those portions of a study in which it was interested; however, the program soon developed into a joint affair with both agencies contributing equally to the effort. Thus began the great urban transportation planning program of the 1960s.

From the outset, despite numerous signs of cooperation at high levels, a difference in supervisory and administrative techniques between the two agencies was a forewarning of future interagency difficulties. The Bureau of Public Roads retained its traditional pattern of dealing only with the state highway agencies. While upper-echelon Washington officials of the Bureau of Public Roads appeared to be sincerely interested in joint area transportation planning, the administrative procedures and staff attitudes at the lower levels did not reflect this ecumenical spirit. The BPR was accustomed to conducting large-scale transportation studies in which the state highway agencies worked closely with personnel of the Bureau of Public Roads who were stationed in the states. HHFA, on the other hand, did not have the administrative experience, nor in most cases did it have a staff at the state level. Consequently, much of its contact with the urban transportation studies was made directly by Washington officials. They were frequently confused by the apparent sympathy and goodwill of BPR officials in Washington and subsequently dismayed by the hostile and rather parochial views of state and BPR regional highway engineers.

The decision to participate in joint efforts in the area transportation studies was based upon earlier memoranda of agreement dating back to 1959, but the new wave of post-1962 joint studies did not result in any better solutions to the problems of interagency coordination than had been offered in earlier years. The same problems that confronted the earlier joint proposals confronted the joint studies. The question is whether federal agencies, particularly those involved with urban transportation, will continue to attempt large interagency planning efforts without prior investigation of the attendant pitfalls and problems. Since the 1962 Highway Act has provided a large pool of study funds, it is clear that failures in urban transportation planning can no longer be attributed to a shortage of money to support large-scale efforts. It has become apparent that solutions to urban transportation problems, like other urban problems, cannot simply be purchased with money alone, even if available in large quantities.

THE AREA STUDIES 2

Study Area Profile

The area selected for the Boston Regional Planning Project (BRPP), later the Eastern Massachusetts Regional Planning Project (EMRPP), is bounded on the north by the New Hampshire border, on the west by a line roughly following one tier of communities outside Interstate Route 495 (the so-called Outer Belt that runs around Boston at a radius of twenty-five to thirty-five miles from the center of the city), on the south by the Rhode Island state line and the boundary of the Southeastern Massachusetts Regional Planning District, and on the east by the waters of Massachusetts Bay.

The planning region included 152 cities and towns. In 1965 the population of the region was over 3,500,000, accounting for two-thirds of the population of Massachusetts and almost one-third of the population of New England. The area contains virtually all of four Standard Metropolitan Statistical Areas (SMSAs) and small parts of two others. The Boston SMSA, the nation's seventh largest, comprises 77 percent of the population of the region.

Census data reveal that between 1950 and 1960 the population in the planning region increased at a rate slightly more than half the national growth rate. From 1960 to 1965 the region's population increase was less than half the national rate, only 3.1 percent compared with the nation's 8.1 percent, indicating a further decline in the growth rate. Since the regional natural increase rate (births minus deaths) was not significantly lower than the natural increase rates in other major urban areas, it is apparent that some of the region's population has been drained away through migration.

The regional population growth pattern, however, has been far from uniform; while 1950–1960 population losses were as high as 13 percent in the city of Boston, some suburban areas doubled in numbers. The population in the fourteen inner communities increased by 100,000 during this period, while the total population in the remainder of the region climbed by 400,000. Although more recent, fully comparable figures are not available, the 1965

Authors' note: The story of the Boston project is best told in consecutive stages. It has a prelude, a dissonant overture, a cold war, and an unexploited victory, followed by a prolonged paralysis punctuated by minor disasters and continuing reorganization, ending in apathy. The first period, the prelude, covers the nine months prior to legislative approval in July 1962. The final phase continued through 1968, when most of this research was done. The Boston study was finally laid to rest in 1969, when a final report was published.

The reader will note that almost a quarter of this study is devoted to the Boston project, about three times as much space as any of the other four projects. The reason for this disproportionate allocation is simple. The authors were familiar with the Boston project and had participated in its formative stages and in its early travails. This personal experience provided the seedbed for the hypotheses that guided the study as a whole and that, for the most part, have been validated by the research in other areas.

state census indicates a continuation of this suburban growth pattern, while Boston has continued its rapid decline.

If the region's population continues to increase at the rate of 10 percent per decade over the next forty years, it will approach 5,000,000 by the year 2000. Virtually all of this growth can be expected to occur in suburban territory, which would increase by more than 75 percent over 1960 levels. While the core area might, at best, maintain its present population level of about 1,400,000, the suburban population increase in the 1960–2000 period is likely to be larger than the total present population of Boston and the thirteen other core communities.

In spite of three hundred years of urban development, two-thirds of the total land area of the region—over 1,000,000 acres—is still available for development. Only about 6,000 acres (less than 3 percent of the total) are still undeveloped in the core city, but over 100,000 acres are available for development in the fast-growing inner suburbs, and over 900,000 acres of vacant land are located in the thinly populated outer suburbs. On the basis of recent land-use and population trends, the open space is sufficient to satisfy the region's development needs for a minimum of forty years, despite the growing trend to large-lot zoning in many communities. However, unless there is a shift toward multifamily zoning, the supply of open, readily developed land in the core and inner suburbs may be exhausted by the early 1980s. In consequence, development will increasingly shift to the outer suburbs.

The region's zoning reveals a pattern that is similar, in some respects, to the actual regional land-use pattern. Roughly the same percentage of zoned open land is allocated for future single-family residential and industrial use as is currently being used for these purposes. However, the zoning pattern for multifamily housing is far different from the current land-use pattern; most suburban communities have allocated little or no land for apartment, town house, or duplex construction. In fact, only 1.4 percent of all open land in the region is zoned for multifamily use, compared with 11.4 percent of the developed land currently used for that purpose.

In the course of its long history, the planning region has weathered severe stresses, financial panics, recessions, and dark years of depression. Its present economy represents a distinct break with the relatively stagnant patterns of the past century, when the economy was largely based on low-wage industries. The region now has a diversified economic base underwritten by great financial strength and stimulated by national preeminence in the research and development sector's growth industries. As the economy has increasingly shifted to a reliance on intellectual capital, some of the region's traditional assets have become less significant. It no longer contains an enormous unskilled labor pool of the type that was one of its strengths in the nineteenth century and that still persists in other major cities. Instead, the economy of the region runs mainly on the products of its major universities and on the skills and intelligence of a high-quality core of financial, professional, and technical personnel.

Serious problems remain, however. Unemployment in certain parts of the region is relatively high, and average factory wages are somewhat below the national average. The region is fortunate in that most of its military equipment and communications production activities have been subject to rapid advances in technology; but, with the exception of three big industries—ordnance, electrical machinery, and rubber—it has not participated to any great extent in the upsurge of employment in the nation's growth industries.

Although per capita income in Massachusetts has been consistently and substantially higher than that of the nation as a whole, this pattern is changing. For some years the state ranked 30 percent or more above the national average, but it fell to only 11 percent above the U.S. average in 1950. Total personal income in Massachusetts is expected to increase by 43 percent between 1957 and 1970, which is substantially smaller than the 54 percent increase projected for the nation as a whole. In 1975 the national per capita personal income is expected to be about $3,000; in Massachusetts it is expected to be almost $3,300.

The region is one of the nation's leading retail centers; about $5 billion was spent in its retail establishments in 1963, an increase of about 16 percent since 1958. The Boston SMSA accounts for about 80 percent of the region's total receipts in retail trade. In addition, retailing is a major source of regional employment. Over 22 percent of the region's nonagricultural jobs were included in this category in 1960. Despite the rapid suburbanization that has taken place in the Boston area, the region's central cities were still capturing a substantial, although a declining, proportion of the total retail spending of suburban residents. The central business district in Boston accounted for roughly 8 percent of the region's retail sales in 1963, compared with 10 percent in 1958. However, this was a substantial decline, from almost 15 percent of regional sales in 1948.

Recent trends suggest that the core will continue to be the region's major employment center. It is expected that in 1975 it will still retain well over one-third of the region's total employment; jobs in the city of Boston will account for one-fifth to one-fourth of all jobs in the region. Boston and the inner core will remain a job-surplus, in-commuting area, since their respective shares of the regional population are expected to be much smaller than their proportion of regional jobs.

Historically, the region has been a leading innovator in each new technical phase of public transportation. Early mass transit vehicles, such as the omnibus and the horsecar, were introduced in the Boston area between 1825 and 1850. Boston's large urban street railway became the first to electrify in 1900, thereby leading the way for the acceptance of electric railways in other parts of the country. However, the pace of these early advances was not maintained. As with most other types of regional development, the transit system did not continue to grow out of a comprehensive rational plan based on prudent cost-benefit evaluation.

Each phase of mass transportation innovation and extension has left enduring effects on the region. The horsecar and omnibus provided the basis for the first commuting suburbs for the wealthy, and the low-fare electric railway permitted people with lower incomes to live at some distance from their place of employment. Rapid transit generated high-density commercial and industrial mass transportation to relatively low-density suburban areas.

The current transit service district of the Massachusetts Bay Transportation Authority (MBTA), formerly the Metropolitan Transit Authority (MTA), covers an area of 1,022 square miles and services an average population density of only 2,550 persons per square mile. The former MTA district covered an area of only 123 square miles but had a population density of 11,700 persons per square mile. (By way of comparison, the Chicago Transit Authority serves a population density of 17,600 persons per square mile; the public transit system in Philadelphia serves a density of only 6,300 persons per square mile.) Density in the present district ranges from 24,000 persons per square mile in the city of Somerville to only 100 persons per square mile in outlying communities. Only eight of the seventy communities in the district have an average density of over 10,000 persons per square mile.

The number of transit passengers has shown a significant decline similar to the trends elsewhere in the country, and this has been consistent with the national pattern. In 1959 the MTA system carried about 800,000 passengers per day on about 800 miles of routes. By 1968 the daily passenger load was estimated at 550,000 persons, about half of whom were carried on the 64 route miles of rapid transit lines.[1] The Boston MBTA system has the highest percentage of rapid transit passengers (including streetcar subway lines) of any of the four major eastern cities with transit systems. Mass transportation carries the bulk of total peak-hour trips entering the downtown commercial district of Boston.

[1] Gunther M. Gottfeld, *Rapid Transit Systems in Six Metropolitan Areas,* staff report prepared for U.S., Congress, Joint Committee on Washington Metropolitan Problems, 86th Congress, 1st session, November 1959.

The MBTA uses four types of vehicles: rapid transit cars, streetcars, trackless trolleys, and motor buses. Over half of the vehicles are buses. There has been a significant decline over the past twenty years in the number of trackless trolleys in service on the MBTA system. The number of buses has increased by about 50 percent during the last few years, after remaining at a level of 600 to 900 since 1947.

It is generally accepted that the rapid transit system is essential to the economic life of the Boston region. While opposition to the MBTA is substantial, eventual extension of rapid transit to suburban areas appears probable because of widespread recognition that the region's transit coverage is inadequate. Major decisions face the region in locating, designing, and servicing suburban extensions to obtain the greatest benefit from the large capital investments required for this purpose.

By the mid-1970s these suburban MBTA extensions will make commuter railroad service unnecessary. Meanwhile, there are many problems in keeping the railroads operating until they can be replaced. Perhaps the most significant characteristic of the railroad system in the region is that, while most lines and branches radiate from downtown Boston, none of the lines effectively connect with each other. All trains to and from the north use North Station, while trains to and from the west and south use South Station. There is no rail passenger connection between the two stations, and MBTA service between the two lines is inconvenient; although both stations are served by rapid transit lines, buses provide the only direct connection between the major terminals. Part of the problem arises because three separate railroad companies have served the region—the Boston and Maine (B&M), the New York Central (which absorbed the Boston and Albany), and the New York, New Haven and Hartford. Only since the Penn-Central merger have any lines been eliminated. Yet the merger merely combined the two smallest commuter operations, and even unifying all the railroads would not overcome the system's inherent physical problems.

The downward trend of railroad commuter volume in the Boston region has been consistent over the past two decades. In 1959, transportation patterns in the entire South Shore, including the heavily populated Quincy area, were drastically disrupted by the abandonment of the Old Colony line of the New Haven Railroad. This discontinuance occurred concurrently with the opening of the six-lane Southeast Expressway and was the major reason for the congestion that has plagued the expressway since its opening day.

Only five major cities in the United States—Boston, New York, Chicago, Philadelphia, and San Francisco—are served by commuter railroads. As might be expected, Boston ranks near the bottom, in fourth position, well behind the other regions in the number of commuter passengers. However, Boston's railroads rank second to New York City in the total route mileage of track in suburban service.[2] Numerous main-line and branch routes are a legacy from the nineteenth century, when the economic prospects of the region stimulated railroad overexpansion. Boston has almost one-third more miles of railroad line than Philadelphia but less than half as many rail commuters, and, instead of being concentrated along a few major axes, railroad passengers in the Boston area spread out in a diffuse pattern along numerous travel corridors.

The decline in Boston's rail commutation has been somewhat more severe than in other railroad commuting centers. It fell by over 75 percent from 1948 to 1961. By 1961, only 23,000 weekday passengers were carried by the commuter railroads leading into Boston, and by 1966 the volume had dropped to 17,000 passengers. The peak hours accounted for 50 percent of the total weekday numbers. By 1959, only 7 percent of all person trips to downtown Boston were made by rail, compared to 11 percent in 1950. The railroad commuter service in the region is in a precarious position. The trend has been continuously and irrevocably downward, and there are no indications of a significant reversal in the future.

As with the rail service, responsibility for highways is fragmented. Within the region, five public agencies build or operate highway facilities: the State Department of Public Works (DPW), the Massachusetts Turnpike Authority, the Metropolitan District Commission (MDC), the Massachusetts Port Authority, and individual cities and towns. Between 1964 and 1975, the State Department of Public Works will be spending about $150 million annually on highway construction, of which about 50 percent will be allocated to the Boston region.

Concentration of traffic on relatively few arterial streets, coupled with neglect of feeder streets, has resulted in severe congestion in the Boston region, particularly in the core communities. The highest traffic volume in the region—110,000 vehicles per day—has been recorded on the John F. Fitzgerald Expressway (Central Artery). Only a few years earlier, traffic volumes of this magnitude were unknown in the Boston area. Furthermore, the construction of high-capacity, limited access roads has placed an unprecedented traffic load on other major routes. Within a period of fifteen years, maximum volumes on the order of 40,000–50,000 vehicles per day in 1951 doubled. In the core cities, traffic volumes of 30,000–40,000 vehicles per day had been

[2] American Municipal Association, *The Collapse of Commuter Service: A Survey of Mass Transportation in Five Selected Cities* (Washington, D.C., 1959).

recorded since the 1930s, reflecting existing street capacity rather than potential demand.

Inside Route 128 (the major circumferential highway located on a ten- to twelve-mile radius from Boston), the region's major radial arterials carry volumes generally ranging between 20,000 and 40,000 vehicles per day. Beyond Route 128, volumes decline to 10,000–20,000, leveling off as these roads become rural highways connecting major cities throughout the state. On routes in the areas between major radials, lower traffic volumes prevail—in most cases running below 10,000 vehicles per day.

The future, of course, promises further increases in traffic, resulting from increased vehicle ownership as more suburban familes acquire a second or even a third automobile, as well as increased population. It is quite likely that travel in second and third cars will be confined to the suburban and rural portions of the region and will occur during off-peak travel periods. Thus the increases in vehicle ownership and mileage may raise daily traffic levels on rural roads, but not necessarily the critical peak-hour flows.

Despite its relatively lower rate of population expansion, per capita travel appears to be growing more rapidly in the region than in the nation as a whole. Vehicle travel per person in the region increased at twice the national average during the 1950–1960 decade. One probable cause of this large increase is the great amount of highway capacity that became available in the region during this period, permitting a massive shift in travel habits.

As the limited supply of land in the core areas is depleted, land for expressway construction is becoming extremely difficult and expensive to obtain. Objections to virtually every proposed expressway are being raised by neighborhood groups fearful of the impact of six- and eight-lane highways on their homes. Family displacement by the Inner Belt alone is expected to be in the thousands. The large number of families being relocated by highway construction has become a serious regional problem, particularly since it is accompanied by growing relocation as a result of increased urban renewal activities. Any future highway plans must consider the requirements and effects of family relocation.

Project Overview

Boston's $5 million area transportation study illustrates three points. First, such costly efforts may have little influence on important events. Reform of the regional transit agency, breaking the logjam on transit extensions to the suburbs, reorganization of the Massachusetts Public Works Department, and creation of a permanent metropolitan planning agency all occurred during a period when the project was spending over $1 million a year in planning and

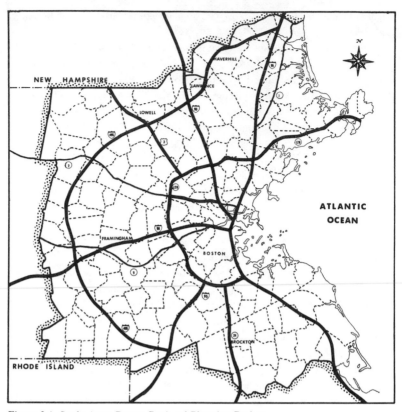

Figure 3.1. Study Area: Boston Regional Planning Project

transportation studies, yet there was no perceptible cause-and-effect relationship between the transportation planning project and the events that occurred in state government in 1964. Quite conceivably, all of these things could have happened if the project had never been undertaken, although it is also conceivable that useful outputs from the project could have improved the quality of some of the decisions.

Second, the conflict that racked the project for over a year involved issues of project control rather than a dispute between pro-highway or anti-highway factions. The two factions tacitly agreed on the necessity of accelerating existing plans for both the highway and the transit agencies.

Much of the initial support for the project came from the highway agencies, and in makeup and orientation it reflected a vested interest in the major source of funds. The persistent weakness of the federal planning agency offi-

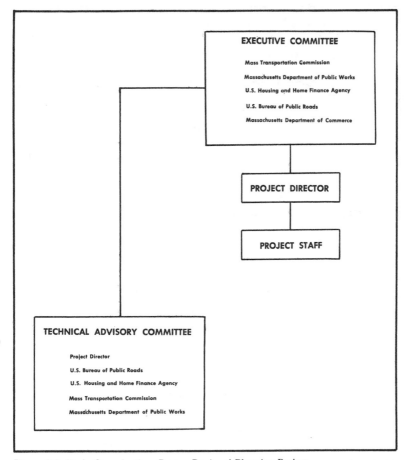

EXECUTIVE COMMITTEE

Mass Transportation Commission

Massachusetts Department of Public Works

U.S. Housing and Home Finance Agency

U.S. Bureau of Public Roads

Massachusetts Department of Commerce

PROJECT DIRECTOR

PROJECT STAFF

TECHNICAL ADVISORY COMMITTEE

Project Director

U.S. Bureau of Public Roads

U.S. Housing and Home Finance Agency

Mass Transportation Commission

Massachusetts Department of Public Works

Figure 3.2. Study Organization: Boston Regional Planning Project

cials who supervised the project, in the face of the U.S. Bureau of Public Roads (BPR) and the state road agencies that were represented on the state's Mass Transportation Commission (MTC—Massachusetts' multiagency transportation agency during the 1959–1964 period), guaranteed a strong voice if not a sweeping victory for the highway viewpoint, and would have done so even if a struggle over the directorship had turned out differently. The very independent position of the MTC's director presented a source of danger so far as the highway officials were concerned.

Third, the great stumbling block to the Boston project and to other substantial programs is the shortage of talent in local and state agencies. Then, and

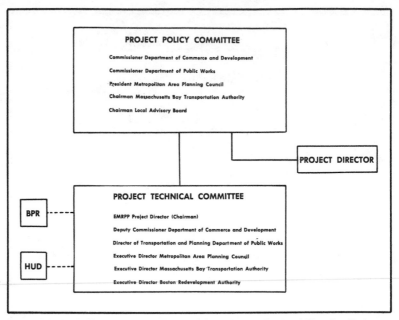

PROJECT POLICY COMMITTEE

Commissioner Department of Commerce and Development

Commissioner Department of Public Works

President Metropolitan Area Planning Council

Chairman Massachusetts Bay Transportation Authority

Chairman Local Advisory Board

PROJECT DIRECTOR

BPR

HUD

PROJECT TECHNICAL COMMITTEE

EMRPP Project Director (Chairman)

Deputy Commissioner Department of Commerce and Development

Director of Transportation and Planning Department of Public Works

Executive Director Metropolitan Area Planning Council

Executive Director Massachusetts Bay Transportation Authority

Executive Director Boston Redevelopment Authority

Figure 3.3. Study Reorganization: Eastern Massachusetts Regional Planning Project

still more now, many local and state agencies were unfit to handle routine operations, let alone new program responsibilities. The imminent retirement of many qualified higher executives who were recruited in the Great Depression, when alternative jobs were scarce, is all the more serious because of their failure to recruit young talent. The federal agencies are better off, but they, too, are stretched thin. The staffing problem is rendered acute by the tremendous demands on talent created by the complex new programs in planning, transportation, poverty, and other fields. The project's history suggests that goals of federal programs will continue to be alarmingly elusive, particularly if there are strong prejudices against using effective people who do not conform to conventional standards. There seems to be a gap of only a year or so after the initiation of imaginative new programs, bold in concept and convincing in rhetoric, before disenchantment sets in, due in large measure to faulty execution (on the state and local levels).

In the fall of 1961 the Mass Transportation Commission gave hardly any indication of the broad scope of its powers to study public transportation, land use, and practically anything else on a statewide basis. At that time the MTC professional staff was miniscule. In addition to the executive director,

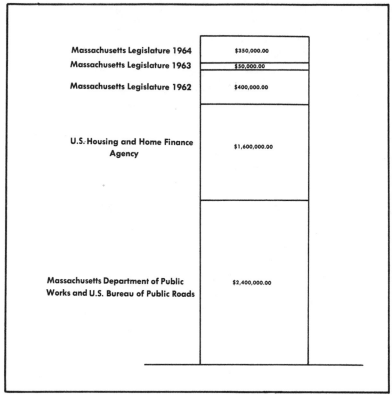

Massachusetts Legislature 1964	$350,000.00
Massachusetts Legislature 1963	$50,000.00
Massachusetts Legislature 1962	$400,000.00
U.S. Housing and Home Finance Agency	$1,600,000.00
Massachusetts Department of Public Works and U.S. Bureau of Public Roads	$2,400,000.00

Figure 3.4. Initial Funding of the Boston Regional Planning Project

there were only a secretary and a part-time attorney. The director, formerly an assistant professor of political science in New York City, had been working as an administrative and political man-of-business for Governor Furcolo.

Following Governor Furcolo's disastrous defeat in the Democratic senatorial primary of 1960, the former professor chose to accept the position with the MTC. To an ambitious, imaginative administrator, the statutory powers of the MTC offered a wide scope. A statute enacted in 1959 empowered the commission to investigate mass transportation problems and to plan coordinated mass transportation facilities and land-use policies in the state and in metropolitan Boston.[3] The commission was also empowered to investigate and study the relationship of mass transportation facilities, land use, urban

[3] Massachusetts, "Act Creating the Massachusetts Mass Transportation Commission," *Massachusetts Acts and Resolves, 1959.*

renewal, and development to the economy, related social problems, and the state highway program.

The new governor, John A. Volpe (Republican), found the director a useful source of advice on public transportation issues. He even gave his support to the director's prosposal for an integrated transportation program, which required squeezing a sizable state matching contribution out of a thin state budget.

This $10 million program, devised in 1961, resembled a large Christmas tree with gifts for everyone. It consisted of a $4.8 million planning project and a $5.4 million demonstration project. It promised rational planning for the intellectuals and reformers, transit extensions for the deficit-ridden transit system, and improved highway planning and continued highway construction for the highway agencies. The U.S. Bureau of Public Roads was eager both to participate in a pioneering effort and to expose the backward Massachusetts highway agency to advanced practices; federal highway officials had long deplored the level of staff competence in the Department of Public Works. The program also offered exciting experimental possibilities to the BPR and to the U.S. Housing and Home Finance Agency (HHFA, reconstituted as the Department of Housing and Urban Development in 1965) for launching a major cooperative planning project in conjunction with large-scale public transit demonstrations. The least enthusiastic participant, the State Department of Public Works, went along with it as a means of satisfying the BPR and of ensuring future federal highway allocations to the state.

The Boston area planning project was to proceed in the following sequence: (1) an inventory of population, land use, and economic base, (2) a study of transportation facilities, traffic patterns, transportation requirements, population size and distribution, and land-use patterns, (3) preparation of alternative projections based on predicted economic growth, land-use patterns, and transportation needs, (4) refinement and testing of plans, cost estimating, recommendation of priorities and methods of financing, (5) discussion of alternative choices with decision-makers and the public to achieve broad agreement upon a general plan of land-use and transportation development, and (6) formulation of methods to continue collection and analysis of data as part of a continuing planning process.[4]

The companion demonstration project involved fare decreases and improved services on the commuter railroads, MBTA lines, and private bus company facilities. This project, which began early in December 1962, was designed and initiated in an atmosphere of crisis. Between 1949 and 1962 the number

[4] Massachusetts, Mass Transportation Commission, "Approved Work Program," May 1962.

of weekday railroad passengers to Boston's North and South stations declined by 75 percent, falling from 80,000 to less than 20,000 passengers per day. For some time the Boston and Maine Railroad, carrying 7,000,000 passengers annually into downtown Boston, had been preparing to abandon all its commuter lines. Receivers of the bankrupt New Haven and of the New York Central's Boston and Albany commuter railroads, carrying about half the volume of the B&M, were also planning for early abandonment.

Other major public transportation systems had suffered from a comparable decline in ridership. The average number of daily passengers on the MTA dropped by over 50 percent between the peak year of 1946 and 1960.

The demonstration experiments were to include an analysis of the railroad company books to determine how much money they were actually losing on commuter business. This information was then to be used as the basis for establishing the subsidies needed to keep the commuter lines in operation until the mass transit extensions could be constructed.

The Mass Transportation Commission was to conduct the planning project on behalf of the State Department of Public Works and the two cooperating federal agencies (the BPR and HHFA); it was to secure federal and highway agency concurrence on all contracts, but otherwise could run the project with a fairly free hand. This kind of arrangement had been explicit in the May 1962 contract between the Mass Transportation Commission and the Housing and Home Finance Agency and in the agreements between the MTC and the two highway agencies—the Federal Bureau of Public Roads and the State Department of Public Works. Once the MTC director had secured firm legal agreement from the State Department of Public Works, he was confident of fast federal approval; he could thereupon proceed to hire staff and let consultant contracts.

However, this course of action was not followed. Although it is not possible to identify with any precision the reasons for the distinct cooling in the relations between the federal agencies and the director, he apparently aroused suspicions among federal officials: his flamboyance, his acknowledged ability to get along with suspect state legislators, and his frank discussions of government corruption were unfamiliar characteristics to federal officials, who expressed a preference for a traditional planner to run the study. In addition, the two federal agencies were not initially enthusiastic over the director's assurances that the Massachusetts Department of Public Works could assume responsibility for selecting consultants to perform effective, honest work on the planning project.

Yet by September this lack of confidence in the DPW had been dispelled. More important, by then HHFA and the BPR did not regard as binding the administrative structure specified in the original May contract, which had provided that the MTC would direct the planning program. The federal highway agency was also apparently reexamining its original approval of the MTC application. One member agency of the MTC, the Department of Public Works, had been the subject of numerous investigations by federal agencies and by a congressional committee, while another, the Metropolitan District Commission, had been purged as a result of a state investigation of improper and illegal contracting practices.

The distrust of the MTC director led to the immediate formation of a broad coalition of the two federal agencies, the DPW, and the planner who had been hired by the MTC director to undertake the technical direction of the planning study. In effect the federal agencies decided to rewrite the original contract to strip the director of most of his power. The director's appeals for a reversal of judgment proved fruitless, and his pleas to the governor's office were equally unavailing. Before the project actually got under way in October, the simple one-agency operation approved in May was converted into a consensual, cumbersome, four-agency administrative structure.

An unintended by-product of the organizational arrangement ultimately approved was the four-agency veto, shared by the participating federal agencies. Normally, veto power over a local project is avoided by federal agencies. Yet the interagency organization in Boston gave each participant final approval on mass transit, highway, and other recommendations directly affecting the future prestige, size, and appropriations of its sister agencies. The project immediately bogged down in prolonged disputes over the organization, content, and schedule of the research.

Between October 1962 and May 1963 the project had succeeded in hiring some staff and in letting only two consultant contracts. The first was for a $1,000,000 traffic inventory; the second was a $330,000 contract to prepare a land-use inventory for the study area. By the summer of 1963 the traffic inventory had collected sufficient data to begin a trip distribution analysis. Under normal conditions the travel and land-use inventories should have been completed simultaneously. But the land-use contract, as discussed later, became yet another unfortunate episode in the Boston project.

By this time, the project seemed to be sinking into an administrative morass. Federal officials had long been wary of the prospects in Massachusetts, but they had believed that the chief danger was corruption. Instead, they were constantly confronted by administrative tangles, which were referred to them for action month after month, and they grew increasingly disturbed. They had acted, they believed, briskly and efficiently to remove the chief obstruction: the project had been removed from the control of the MTC director and given to the professionals. Yet there was still little progress on the substance of the study. During the summer of 1963, both the federal agencies and the MTC director appealed to the governor to resolve the dispute.

The governor responded vigorously. Beginning in early 1963, his personal representative from the Executive Commission for Administration and Finance attended in a nonvoting capacity virtually all project Executive Committee meetings. The project, however, was only one of a number of crises that besieged the governor. Thus, after his initial decision in February to exercise personal leadership, he appeared to be at a loss to know what form his intervention should take. By actual count, a dozen advisers in or around the governor's office were called in from time to time to suggest how to reorganize the area planning project.

Meanwhile, the federal agencies had grown increasingly disillusioned as they were constantly drawn into long-winded, pointless discussions over the hiring of minor personnel, press releases, community relations, unpaid telephone bills, cramped office space, and nonexistent stationery and pencils. This was hardly the great experiment in joint cooperation on a major project and far from the portentous shaping of high-level policy that the interagency agreement had promised.

While the struggle for control of the planning project continued, the demonstration project had been operated and completed on schedule between December 1962 and March 1964. During this period the MTC secured a consistently favorable reaction from its Boston and Maine and New Haven railroad experiments and mixed reactions from private bus and MBTA demonstrations. The MTC program suggested that an overhaul in MBTA management was long overdue, particularly since the MBTA commissioners had to be coaxed and subsidized into conducting experiments (like reducing parking fees) that could easily have been undertaken without outside financial aid.

The governor decided to assume major control over the planning project in late 1963. By early 1964 the chairman of the MTC had been replaced by the governor's appointee, and the search was on for a new superplanner who could pull the faltering project together and move it toward a conclusion. The federal agencies, by this time, had reverted to a well-insulated "concurring" role that they had been seeking for over a year.

In a further move to reorganize and reform state government, the governor decided in August 1964 to create a new Department of Commerce and Development (DCD). The MTC was abolished as a separate entity and absorbed by the DCD, which inherited the MTC's role in the planning project. At this time the MTC director submitted his resignation and completed the final report on the demonstration program. Not long afterward the project's planning director also resigned to take a higher paying, but less exposed, position in the newly organized Massachusetts Bay Transportation Authority that replaced the MTA.

The DCD had difficulty in developing a suitable organizational framework. Conditions might have improved at this point if the governor had remained in office, but unfortunately, in September 1964, he failed to secure renomination. This event perhaps destroyed the last chance for a speedy conclusion of the project. The new head of the DCD's Division of Planning discovered that he had inherited many of the enemies and obstacles to progress that had been plaguing the project from its inception. Nevertheless, in 1966 and 1967 the remaining consultant contracts were mostly completed, over the strenuous opposition of some of the participating agencies.

During this period, the project administration, located in the DCD's Division of Planning, was under continual fire from two major fronts. It was regarded as a rival by the Metropolitan Area Planning Council (MAPC), the permanent regional planning agency created by the previous governor, and the commissioner of the Executive Commission for Administration and Finance, who feared that the DCD's Division of Planning, which proposed a broad program of state planning, would emerge as a rival superpower in state government. The commissioner bitterly opposed two planning project studies involving surveys of state agency operations as they related to the project study area. Partly as a result of this dispute, the head of the DCD Division of Planning transferred to a new position.

Finally, in late 1968 all of the project consultant studies had been completed, and by early 1969 they had been finally approved. The final report was released in mid-1969. Thus the project, originally scheduled for completion in December 1964, was roughly four years behind schedule.

Transportation Politics

Some of the problems facing the director of the Mass Transportation Commission (MTC) stemmed from Massachusetts politics. The spotlight was focused on the more sordid side of Massachusetts well before the MTC applied for large amounts of federal funds. "Baystatology" has been one of the more popular forms of academic expression in recent years, partly because Massachusetts is well endowed with publishers and university scholars who have discovered the availability of useful research material right under their noses. States with equally dubious politics, but which contain fewer academicians, have escaped the benefits of such searching scrutiny.

Richard Abrams[1] suggests that the state was honestly and efficiently run until the first decade of the twentieth century; it enjoyed the benefits of much progressive legislation and a well-deserved reputation for cleanliness, which confounded Lincoln Steffens, the muckraker, in his grand tour of municipal corruption at the turn of the century.

Whatever the date of Massachusetts' take-over, politics in the state tends to be tribal and oriented around personalities.[2] It still reflects the standards and objectives of poor immigrants who see little harm and much benefit in early and prolonged attachment to the public payroll. For example, a candidate's relative voting strength in Democratic primaries is reported to depend on the allegiances of political jobholders and jobseekers to their sponsors.

The federal agencies negotiating the project might not have been quite so concerned perhaps about Massachusetts political patterns if a series of disclosures and investigations had not been in full swing during the contract negotiations and if the director himself had not drawn much of his support from some of the state's most investigated agencies: the Department of Public Works, the Metropolitan District Commission, and the Turnpike Authority. They may also have felt that the bad habits were not surface blemishes but deeply ingrained features of the state's basic structure, reaching back at least two generations.

In late 1961 the *Atlantic,* a Boston-published periodical, carried an article naming three of the six constituent agencies of the MTC as key elements in a debased system of politics.

The year's disclosures began with an investigation of Greater Boston's Metropolitan District Commission. . . . The M.D.C. investigation was followed closely by another legislative probe, this time of the Massachusetts Depart-

[1] Richard M. Abrams, *Conservativism in a Progressive Era: Massachusetts Politics, 1900–1912* (Cambridge, Mass.: Harvard University Press, 1964).

[2] Whalen sees the Kennedys as the heirs and beneficiaries of this chieftain tradition rather than as a distinct break with the past, despite their Harvard and "social" background. See Richard J. Whalen, *The Founding Father* (New York: New American Library, 1964), p. 44.

ment of Public Works. . . . Still under way is a federal grand jury inquiry into conspiracies to defraud the United States in connection with the D.P.W.'s administration of the federal-aid highway program in Massachusetts. . . . Not all Massachusetts politicians are venal. . . . Nonetheless the political processes of Massachusetts are deeply infected . . . jobs, contracts and miscellaneous favors became the life-blood of Massachusetts politics. They still are. . . . For William F. Callahan, now Chairman of the Massachusetts Turnpike Authority, and past master of the art of Massachusetts politics, it would seem that this nightmarish world of vendetta and intrigue is the only one that really exists.[3]

The director had remarkable success in his ability to communicate with some of the state's less savory agencies and political leaders, and also in keeping abreast of the new federal programs. He displayed a remarkable willingness to enter into the bureaucrats' semantic framework. He was ready to echo it on paper, while at the same time reserving for himself a wide area of freedom in the form of carefully worded hedges. While much admired, this glibness provided grounds for suspicion. Furthermore, in Washington as in Massachusetts, he was viewed by some as a power-hungry political operator.

An important feature of the director's early successes was careful timing. Although the chief executive was a Republican, Governor John A. Volpe, both houses of the legislature were controlled by the Democrats in 1962. Successful strategy called for the necessary legislation to be introduced by the Democratic legislative leadership and subsequently to be endorsed by the governor along with many of the Commonwealth's civic, business, and labor leaders. It was also necessary to secure commitments from the U.S. Housing and Home Finance Agency (HHFA) and the Bureau of Public Roads (BPR) so that he could convince the local political leadership to vote the necessary matching funds. Although the federal agencies could not legally allocate money until the state share was on hand, the director was able to generate a network of expectations and understandings and to eliminate any doubts that a state appropriation would be followed immediately by a two-to-one federal outlay. He tended to minimize the state share of highway funds involved in the project (actually about 22 percent) so that the enterprise resembled a sure-thing jackpot.

A critical element in the director's success was the unswerving support he received from the Republican governor. As the nation's first federal highway administrator under President Eisenhower and the former state DPW commissioner, Governor John A. Volpe was thoroughly conversant with highway problems, although he was less familiar with those of public transportation.

Governor Volpe's 1960 platform revolved around the standard efficiency,

[3] Elliot L. Richardson, "Poisoned Politics: The Real Tragedy of Massachusetts," *Atlantic,* October 1961, pp. 77–79.

honesty, and economy featured in Republican candidacies. Unlike Governor Endicott Peabody, whose brief tenure (1962–1964) his terms of office bracketed, Governor Volpe tended to concentrate much of his attention on moderate fiscal reforms and a few key programs rather than attempting to engage in a stem-to-stern overhaul of state government. However, their administrations were lamentably similar in their effects on the regional planning project; neither governor succeeded in stimulating the project to produce a timely, useful product.

Relations between the director and his operating environment were excellent throughout 1961, and the project received the support of the press and of the articulate letter-writing and speech-making public. It was accorded the approbation of the minority of intellectual "gown" representatives in and out of the legislature, who tend to be oriented toward reform issues, and the tentative approval of the stronger "town" elements and special-interest groups, whose orientation is more strongly directed to bread-and-butter problems. Among the latter goups was the collection of corporate specializations that comprised the MTC itself: the transportation agencies, the transit union, the commuter railroads and railroad brotherhoods, and their political allies.

To the state legislator, the program offered an inexpensive method of qualifying for more highway funds and securing federal money for transit extensions. Some legislators were involved in saving or expanding mass transportation in one form or another, while many were interested in the patronage possibilities.

The demonstration half of the project offered special charms of its own, including temporary financial aid and good public relations for the railroad and bus carriers and jobs for the unions. However, the other half, the planning project, was sold primarily as a means of qualifying for future federal grants by satisfying requirements for a comprehensive regional plan. There was some skepticism over the prerequisite calling for comprehensive area plans before further federal funds would be granted for highways. The skeptics doubted that the post-1965 federal criteria would really be strictly imposed, and they maintained that federal officials would be easily satisfied by pro forma action combining interim memoranda and paper promises to produce comprehensive plans. Nevertheless, the argument for the project carried considerable weight among both the relatively few legislators who believed in the inherent merits of planning and the others in the legislature who viewed the formal prerequisites for comprehensive planning as the key to more federal highway money.

However, negotiations for state and federal approval between November 1961 and July 1962 were far from smooth; they were more like navigating a battleship through a minefield. Several notable clashes occurred that barely averted an early demise of the project. One of these encounters was with the Metropolitan Transit Authority, whose engineers were disdainful and fearful of the MTC, which seemed to be encroaching on their own senior and privileged position in the transportation field. Partly to forestall the MTC, the MTA twice attempted to develop demonstration projects of its own, but it failed to secure federal approval.

Another, more serious clash occurred with the commuter railroads, all three of which reacted unfavorably at first to the demonstration program. Eventually the two larger railroads were convinced that they would not lose either money or time by participating. Moreover, they finally agreed that the demonstration program was likely to provide ammunition to hit two targets: a faster discontinuance of commuter passenger service and a special subsidy while they awaited construction of transit extensions to replace their railroad lines. The Boston and Albany division of the New York Central declined to join, however, apparently on the grounds that any form of participation might delay the company's speedy exit from the commuter business.

Another major crisis arose over the initial opposition of the development administrator of the Boston Redevelopment Authority (BRA). The administrator, a dynamic and combative figure, thought that participation of the Boston and Maine's Reading line in the experiments would delay BRA plans to remove the MTA elevated structure running through an urban renewal project in the Charlestown area of Boston. This removal was part of a plan to replace the old elevated line with a new rapid transit line running to, or part way toward, Reading, a suburb north of Boston. Without this removal, he believed that the renewal project was not viable. After two or three decreasingly acrimonious discussions with the MTC director, the BRA administrator agreed that the timing of the MTC Boston and Maine demonstration experiment did not threaten the timing of his Charlestown plans, which, in any case, had not yet fully matured. He then withdrew his threatened opposition to the MTC program both locally and in Washington.

In developing the broad coalition of interests needed to get a two-thirds vote through the legislature, the MTC had one powerful weapon—patronage. There were jobs for railroad union members and MTA employees in the experiments themselves, jobs on the MTC staff, jobs on the project staff, and hundreds of temporary "census taker" level jobs with the traffic and land-use consultants. Patronage is, of course, meat and drink to the political process. In close elections, a dozen well-placed jobs can be decisive. Awarded to grateful recipients from large families or funneled through responsive fraternal organizations, even a modest amount of timely patronage, scheduled for issuance prior to the 1962 fall election, might be extraordinarily helpful to the legislators.

It has been suggested that, so far as patronage is concerned, Massachusetts is something of a special case, perhaps because of its immigrant-based political heritage. For a person at the bottom of the social and economic ladder, political jobs are often the breath of life, and strict employment criteria represent a heartless barrier between his family's needs and the obvious means of satisfying them.

Patronage, like nepotism and other aspects of power, has ancient roots in private as well as public life. In many areas, including Massachusetts, contractors doing business with government are called on for party contributions and special favors, including providing jobs in their companies for politicians and their designees. This is normal practice, as is the technique of allocating brief interludes of public employment (on highway department rolls, for example) as frequent incentives for lower-echelon party workers.[4]

The largest source of part-time patronage jobs in Massachusetts, as in most states, is the highway department. As a rule, highway jobs are known quantities spoken for well in advance. For this reason, the possibility of opening up a virgin employment area with an entirely new program was an enticing prospect. Unfortunately, as the MTC director was to learn, the loyalties of patronage appointees are only secondarily to the appointing authorities; they are primarily to the sponsors who located the jobs.

The potential patronage pool was enormously increased in May 1962 when, at the insistence of the Bureau of Public Roads, the planning program was enlarged to update the Boston area's 1948 highway plan and to educate the Commonwealth's backward Department of Public Works. This increase in the planning project from $1.5 to $4.8 million also offered an opportunity to the HHFA and the BPR to put into effect, on a large scale, the cooperative planning effort that the agencies had discussed for some years but had never put into practice.

As it later transpired, most of the seeds of future troubles were planted in this honeymoon period. One was the promise of early delivery of patronage to the legislators. Another was the director's penchant for courting publicity, a practice that aroused envy and suspicion. During this period also, he appointed to the staff a project planner with whom he was soon to be locked in combat. But most of all, the roots of disaster lay in his agreement to operate the project on an integrated basis, thereby linking the future of the project

---

[4] Harvey C. Mansfield, "Political Parties, Patronage and the Federal Service," in The American Assembly, *The Federal Government Service,* ed. Wallace S. Sayre (Englewood Cliffs, N.J.: Prentice-Hall, 1965), pp. 117–120.

to the State Department of Public Works and its federal counterpart, the Bureau of Public Roads.

But this was the end of July, and for the moment the director had triumphed. Starting from a tiny office furnished with a ragbag collection of cast-off furniture, he had put together a remarkable coalition of diverse interests in the first part of 1961, had mastered many minor and even major crises, had secured the required two-thirds majority in a faction-ridden legislature, and had received $1.7 million from a tight state budget for a program that few legislators understood. It was a great victory, not to be repeated.

While the Boston project had unique elements designed by the director and his staff, it was similar to other major transportation studies in the nation. It was to include a study of public transportation as well as the traditional regional planning analyses of population, land use, and economic base. Data were to be collected and processed for hundreds of traffic zones, and federal, state, and local agencies were to be represented on advisory and supervisory committees.

The key study product, the plan, was expected to nudge public and private decisions and actions in the proper direction. The project organization was designed to attract high-salaried temporary staff, to insulate them from outside pressure (including patronage appointments to technical positions and consultant contracts), and to preserve staff time and energy for long-range planning.

A policy committee was established to review and evaluate the study design, oversee the conduct of operations—including staff and consultant contracts—and, most important, appraise the transportation land-use alternatives developed by the study staff. In practice, however, the technical staff (in Boston as elsewhere) was in a strong position to influence the committee because it largely controlled the presentation of information.[5]

The original planning proposal, developed in the fall of 1961, contained the rationale of the three key studies for which the MTC was to do battle so long and with so little success. The first priority topic was an analysis of the deficit-troubled Metropolitan Transit Authority.

Although a member of the MTC, the MTA was the sole direct target of the MTC's administrative reorganization studies. Its remarkable vulnerability in this situation can be explained by the fact that the MTA chairman, who was

[5] These choices were to be presented in the form of alternative "models," for example, a compact radial regional pattern of development oriented toward heavy reliance on mass transit reaching into the suburbs, or a dispersed, highway-oriented development pattern. For a useful discussion of the possibilities and limitations of model building, see *Urban Development Models: New Tools for Planning,* special issue, *Journal of the American Institute of Planners,* vol. 31, no. 4 (May 1965).

the agency's representative on the MTC, was unsympathetic to much of his staff and to the MTA's long castigation by the press and public for its continued deficits and alleged mismanagement. In short, the MTA was a popular subject for overhaul with legislators, the public, and others, including its own chairman.

The planning proposal published by the MTC in December 1961 explained that the elements of the integrated project covered ground familiar to many of the Commonwealth's opinion leaders who had been seriously concerned with the unsatisfactory conditions of mass transportation in the Greater Boston region.

With remarkable optimism considering the events to follow, this proposal for a broad study cutting across traditional jurisdictions explained that bickering was most unlikely because "all of the key agencies were either represented on the MTC or had enthusiastically agreed to cooperate with the agency."[6] The MTA was to be dissected by an independent consulting firm from outside the area. The DPW was not to be renovated but had to permit a nationally reputable, out-of-state traffic consultant to conduct the critical planning operations, which included transportation inventories, interviews, and preparation of a new plan to supersede and update the 1948 highway plan. As might be expected, neither the MTA nor the DPW was comfortable with the arrangement, but for the moment they both seemed acquiescent.

As a first priority, $300,000 was allocated to planning studies designed to analyze the feasibility of rapid transit extensions. A second allocation of $200,000 was made for the analysis of the organization, financing, and management of the transit authority. It was assumed that no agency can clean its own house. (The hatchet men were to be out-of-town consultants with no local ties or early expectation of working in the transit industry.) The proposal suggested that transit extensions were contingent on a genuine effort at reorganizing the MTA, which had been the subject of controversy in recent years and whose extension to suburban areas had met with bitter opposition.

Yet another study was designed partly to bury the ghost of monorail, strongly advocated by some local political figures, and partly to ensure that transit extensions would not become rapidly obsolete.

Further, $200,000 was allocated for a technological impact study to examine changes in transportation and communications technology. Since transit capital equipment has a lifetime measured in decades, it was considered necessary to evaluate technological trends that might have drastic effects on its

---

[6] Massachusetts, Mass Transportation Commission, "A Proposal for an Integrated Mass Demonstration and Planning Program," submitted to the U.S. Housing and Home Finance Agency, December 1961.

future utility. The study was also to consider changes in communications techniques, housing technology, and shifts in employment patterns caused by automation for their potential impact on transportation.[7]

The most distinctive feature of the MTC proposal, and one that fell victim to the later dispute over the management and organization of the project, was a cost-benefit analysis. This study would have analyzed various mixes of transportation systems and services and would have included an evaluation of indirect as well as direct costs. Despite the fact that no wholly satisfactory method has been developed to measure the full range of costs and benefits accruing from any particular project, it was believed that this type of analysis held particular advantages for the evaluation of alternative transportation systems.

One reason for the stress on a cost-benefit analysis was its use as a propaganda device in public education. The extent of public acceptance of transit extensions to the suburbs was unknown when the project was in its planning stages. It was assumed that the unfavorable community attitude toward mass transit was due to the wide publicizing of deficits, while tangible and intangible benefits had been unquantified and too frequently overlooked. It was therefore reasoned that an objective analysis of the costs and benefits of alternative transportation "mixes," including abandonment of mass transit, might do much to alter this widespread attitude.[8] Later, as the project changed hands, the proposed cost-benefit study was gradually submerged by an economic base study proposed by the planning project staff but totally rejected by the MTC.

For the rest, the planning project was designed to resemble standard transportation and regional studies, containing elements familiar to the Bureau of Public Roads and to the Housing and Home Finance Agency. It included the usual population, land-use, and economic base studies and a costly highway inventory and planning study that was to absorb half of the $4.8 million in project funds.

Aside from the discarded cost-benefit analysis and the study aimed at replacing the MTA top management, the Boston project was primarily focused on achieving an objective that had eluded the region for a generation, the construction of transit extensions to the suburbs. Its secondary objective was to qualify the region for more federal highway funds by producing a new highway plan and a regional plan. The director, in short, was not proposing a rebellion but an instrument to help achieve a previously unobtainable goal—modernization of the public transportation system, including transit

[7] Ibid., p. 8.
[8] Ibid., p. 10.

extensions a dozen miles into the suburbs. There was little danger that he would make a direct attack on the highway agency; but, as a semiautonomous power center, the MTC under his direction clearly embodied a potential threat to the highway interests. The Boston area could meet the planning prerequisites for more highways, many believed, without financing an independent, uncontrollable dukedom of uncertain intentions.

Despite the MTA's predominant role in public transportation, the MTC allocated three-fifths of the $5.4 million in demonstration funds to rail experiments involving fare reductions and service increases with the Boston and Maine and the New Haven railroads. Roughly 20 percent was allocated to the Metropolitan Transit Authority for bus and parking experiments, 12 percent was budgeted for the private bus company experiments, and the remainder was for analysis, supervision, and administration. This limited allocation of funds to the MTA, compared with the lavish rail experiments, caused bitter criticism on the part of local transit proponents.

There were several reasons for the MTA's small share of the total experiment money. Bad as conditions were on the MTA, there was no prospect of abandonment, as was the case on all three of Boston's commuter railroads. As a rule, deficits do not have quite the same disastrous effects on public agencies as on private corporations. In addition, MTA management had proved unimaginative in designing experiments, and the MTA was reluctant to yield primacy in the transportation field to the MTC. Moreover, the commuter rail experiments had been designed to prepare the way for future MTA construction and were visualized as a stopgap measure. The rail lines were to be helped to continue service until suburban transit extensions could be developed. The MTA might have been expected to support this MTC plan since, for over two decades, it had been an article of faith with the management that suburban transit extension was the cure for the chronic deficit problem. If the MTA could only follow its customers to the suburbs, it was argued, the decline in passenger volume could be reversed. The data, however, seemed to indicate that it was the old core-area customers who had vanished: population in the MTA district had decreased by only 10 percent in the decade but MTA passenger volume had declined by almost 60 percent. Nevertheless, as late as 1966 the move to reach out into the suburbs was still thought to be the solution to declining passenger volume. Only actual field tests of one or more extensions in the 1970s may provide a definitive answer to this question.

The demonstration program was considerably shorter than the planning project, eighteen months compared with the original planning project schedule of thirty months. This reflected the director's belief (accurate as it was proved) that the region's key transportation decisions would be reached well before the planning project was due to expire at the end of 1964.

The process of designing and securing legislative, corporate, and federal approval for the experiments was a process even more complex and hazardous than the development of the planning project. Hard cash, rail profits, jobs, franchises, and wages were at stake; and carriers, unions, and experts could never be fully satisfied, no matter how funds were juggled. The latent ill will, particularly of key carriers, was to have a serious impact as the program proceeded.

Overture to Disaster

An action that was destined to have major effects on the course of the planning project occurred in July 1962, when the director appointed a project planner. The man appointed was well thought of in the planning profession. Moreover, as planning administrator of the Boston City Planning Board (later incorporated into the Boston Redevelopment Authority), he had made few enemies and had earned a reputation for integrity. The project planner's agreement to handle the technical aspects of the project was thought to be a master stroke on the director's part. Highly regarded by most professionals, the planner also provided reassurance to the local communities and civic leaders who did not know quite what to make of the director's flamboyance and working agreements with widely mistrusted agencies and personalities. The planner's air of quiet competence and integrity also cheered the HHFA planning officials, who admired the director's political acumen but wished to ensure that a qualified planner would supervise the technical aspects of a continuing program. The director was apparently regarded as valuable in getting the project started, but the planner was seen as the professional who could help to establish a solid, permanent, and respected institution.

Initially, the planner was less welcome to the Department of Public Works and the Bureau of Public Roads, both of which had hoped that a traffic engineer rather than a planner would be placed in charge of the study. It was not without strenuous argument that the director managed to secure approval of his appointment in September 1962.

The director resorted to an ingenious administrative practice in establishing the job description for the project planner's position and for the remainder of the project planning staff. He prepared a job description that approximated a biographical sketch. The remaining positions were described in similar technical fashion as a means of fending off potential patronage raids. An ostensibly confidential but widely circulated "staff document" asserted that the MTC job descriptions were formulated "after extensive and intensive discussion with the appropriate federal officials, and are the basis for federal approval of the MTC applications."[9] The memorandum claimed that the federal agencies explicitly reserved their right to prior approval of individual appointments to each of these positions and that federal Civil Service qualifications and standards would be applied "where possible."

"In addition, the Project Planner will represent the project in speaking engagements and in high level staff conferences." For the project planner's job, the description resembled biographical notes based on the applicant's past experience: "public speaking ability, advanced degree in planning from accredited institution, full membership in the American Institute of Planners, eight years of experience in directing major planning." And, to add a final authentic note of alleged federal rigor, "must be qualified for appointment as GS–17, federal urban planning appointment, or equivalent."[10] The planner's ability to serve as the living model for the job description suggests that the director had apparently made an excellent choice.

With the help of fictionalized federal pressure, the director was able to insulate the project's key appointments from politics. Hinting at close federal scrutiny of all applicants, he earnestly solicited the support of local politicians in locating planners with a master's degree in city planning and five years' experience, and traffic engineers capable of directing the operations of a transportation bureau. Depending on the extent of their shrewdness, some elected officials dismissed this offer of high-paying jobs out of hand while others trotted out candidates with a year or two of junior college, only to be solemnly and regretfully informed that the "feds" would not hear of it. However, a number of clerical positions and a few vaguely worded community and public relations jobs were deliberately kept open for trading purposes. As anticipated, most of the political figures with job seekers in tow settled for either secretarial positions or the $70-a-week traffic-counting jobs with the traffic consultant. With the exception of jobs for attorneys and positions in shadowy areas like public and community relations, few of the politicians had qualified advanced-degree candidates to offer. As one prominent political figure phrased it, the people who came to see him "need a political job because they couldn't get one someplace else." He could not, he said, provide professionals if even a modest amount of technical background was required.

The MTC was to conduct the planning project on behalf of the DPW, BPR, HHFA, and other participating agencies. The MTC director, therefore, was hopeful that contracts with consultants could be let quickly. The boom,

[9] Massachusetts, Mass Transportation Commission, "Proposed Project Staff," memorandum, May 1, 1962.
[10] Ibid.

however, was about to fall. After months of unbroken success, the director was to fail completely in this last objective. Although he was apparently considered trustworthy enough by HHFA to run the even larger companion demonstration project, and although he was respected for his success in maneuvering a complex program through a balky legislature, the director had made enemies at the DPW and, more important, had aroused serious doubts among federal officials. They questioned his ability to operate an honest and technically competent planning program; equally important, they were not ready to fund a transportation empire.

It should be stressed that the director's personal financial honesty was never really called into question. Dark hints were passed around; nonetheless, there has never been any evidence of pilferage or even of attempted peculation in either the multimillion-dollar demonstration program or the planning project. Contractor payoffs, charged or proved in other transportation contracts in Massachusetts and elsewhere in the nation, were never an issue.

Over and above the question of personal fitness, some federal officials were unimpressed by the director's technical abilities. This was a critical element in his losing battle with the project planner, who was regarded as a model of technical competence. The director's political, nontechnical image was established in part by his manner, which tended to conceal his genuine talents and suggested, erroneously, that his standard of tolerance for misbehavior might be somewhat elastic. He added strength to the opposition by his habit of referring to himself as a "political broker." Categorizing himself as a quasi-politician who was completely untutored in technical planning skills, he repeatedly stated that he was only too willing to leave complex subjects like planning to persons better qualified in these areas.

Whatever the underlying reason, in the summer of 1962 many federal officials believed that the director was not qualified to run a $5 million planning program. By default, the palm of victory went to the project planner, and it was not the federal agencies but the State Department of Public Works that led the decisive attack.

Over the course of negotiations in the winter and spring of 1962, the director had carefully encouraged federal distrust of the Department of Public Works by transporting, on each of his many trips to Washington, copies of newspapers detailing the Blatnik Committee's revelations of the latest landtaking scandal in Massachusetts. During the spring, the director seemed to have succeeded and to have convinced the federal officials that he, therefore, and the MTC must be relied on to conduct an honest program.

The director had good reasons to be confident. Despite his activities in Washington, his relations with the Department of Public Works appeared to be cordial. Not only had the top-echelon officials in the DPW provided all the written and verbal assurances of cooperation with the MTC requested by the federal agencies, but they had freely made available a large proportion of the department's 1.5 percent highway research funds (1.5 percent of federal-aid highway construction expenditures are earmarked for research purposes). It was thus something of a shock to find that the last and relatively simple step of drafting a legal interagency agreement was alarmingly elusive.

The legislature voted the required state appropriation at the end of July. Then, during the first two weeks of August, the director found it somehow impossible to contact DPW officials. Their secretaries always reported that they were out or engaged in important conferences. Finally, in late August, the DPW produced a draft agreement that was totally unacceptable to the MTC. Belatedly aroused to the dangers of a transportation project operated by a potential rival, the DPW now wanted to be a full codirector. In other words, it deliberately reneged on its earlier agreement. This new move was in total contradiction to the director's organization proposal under which the DPW, along with the federal agencies, was to play a "concurring" role: the MTC was to run the project, and prior federal and DPW approval was to be secured only on major policy matters and on the hiring of key personnel.

The DPW's proposal established for itself and the federal agencies a far more important role, reducing MTC power to a fraction of what had been agreed on in May. It was clear that a major rift had developed between the MTC and the DPW. Not recognizing the risk, the director tried to settle the problem by calling in his federal friends for a face-to-face meeting to chasten the DPW and force it to accept the MTC version of the interagency agreement. In early September 1962 a special project meeting was arranged; it was to include Washington and regional representatives of the two participating federal agencies. The director, who had counted on federal assistance, was to be totally disappointed.

The minutes of the meeting do not give evidence of the depth of the bitternesses that were to be revealed in coming months. In the session itself, there were only two clear notes. The first was the initial hostility of the highway agencies toward the director's choice of the planner as project director and their reluctant agreement to approve his appointment. Second, to the director's surprise, the DPW's proposal that the project should be administered jointly by the four agencies was greeted with serious interest by the federal agencies. The director objected that the type of collective leadership implicit in the DPW proposal would create a cumbersome, unworkable arrangement that would raise serious legal as well as administrative problems. He was sure that his logic and eloquence had convinced the federal officials to dismiss the disconcerting DPW proposal, but he could not have been wider off the mark. The real danger sign for the director was the unexpected harmony between the two federal agencies and the DPW. Early agreements calling for the MTC to direct the project were now considered not binding, and the DPW's proposal seemed to be in favor. The director, accordingly, redoubled his efforts to secure DPW and federal approval of an interagency agreement in line with the MTC grant contract of May 1962. All was to no avail. A prolific memorandum writer, the director dispatched five revised interagency agreements to the DPW. Finally, in desperation, he drew up still another version, which split the program down the middle: $2.4 million in highway studies was to be administered by the DPW, $2.4 million in planning studies was to be conducted by the MTC. By then, October and most of November had passed, and the climate had significantly changed. A new governor had been elected, and the director's position within and without the MTC had become increasingly untenable.

In constructing the local base of support for the program, the director had earlier promised that a substantial amount of patronage would soon be available. The failure to meet the great demand for summer jobs could be laid at the door of the legislature, which had failed to appropriate the funds until late July, but the delay in August, September, and October was ruinous. The elections were near, and, on the strength of the director's promises, legislators had made commitments of their own. They showed little interest in the baffling complexities of interagency agreements and grant contracts. They had been promised jobs, and they wanted delivery. The director's position within the MTC also began to deteriorate as the project slowed, then halted. Because federal approval for the demonstration project was made contingent on interagency agreement on the planning project, no progress at all could be made until that question was resolved. The second, even more catastrophic event for the director was the election of a new governor, because the director, though a Democrat, had established a close relationship as a useful trouble-shooter for the Republican governor.

It would be impossible to reconstruct the tangled skein of intrigue and counterintrigue—lunches, memoranda, letters, telephone calls, cajolings, persuasions, and assurances—that occurred in the fall of 1962. It is known that agency participants communicated with each other frequently, often leaving behind them erroneous impressions. The planner had also been involved in a number of discussions in this period, which led him to an altered formulation of his role in the project. He grew more and more convinced that he needed a free hand to administer and direct the study, subject only to a fuzzily defined policy area in which the four agencies would have major responsibility. This assumption led to the conviction that his contract with the MTC, requiring him to work under the director, must be modified or replaced. He came to regard the MTC work program that had been approved in the May 1962 application as a working draft rather than a firm commitment. He also decided that the consultant proposals to undertake the various planning phases of the program, which had been submitted and theoretically approved with the application, were subject to substantial change. The planner's willingness to assume direction assured members of the Washington and local planning offices, as well as the federal agencies, that the project would be operated independently of the MTC as a clean, technically competent program.

As October turned to November, no solution to the deadlock was yet in sight. Finally, the federal officials made a move: the director was invited to the HHFA regional office in New York City to settle the matter on the spot. All of the participating agencies were to be present. The unsuspecting director brought with him his eloquence, his MTC chairman, and copies of his latest draft proposal for an interagency agreement.

The meeting of November 19, 1962, the director's Waterloo, came as a complete surprise to him. Prepared for verbal combat and lengthy argument, in which his persuasive abilities would bring victory or, at a minimum, an acceptable compromise, he did not expect a stunning defeat. He certainly had no premonition that he and the MTC rather than the Department of Public Works would be regarded as the obstacles to progress. To his consternation the MTC delegation was handed an ultimatum that posed two alternatives: immediate acceptance of the DPW work program that he had previously rejected, or probable HHFA withdrawal from the project. The HHFA officials also made it clear that canceling the project implied termination of the $5.4 million demonstration project that was scheduled to get under way only a week later, early in December 1962. The HHFA counsel indicated that, in his opinion, the proposal did not represent, as the director contended, a conflict with the May contract between the MTC and HHFA. The attack had been unanimous. Spearheaded by the Bureau of Public Roads, it was seconded by HHFA officials and by the DPW.

Faced with this kind of pressure, the MTC had few alternatives. They could tell the assemblage to go to blazes and threaten to issue their own statement at a press conference. This course of action presumed that the middle-management officials were bluffing and that neither federal agency really wished to share the onus of cancellation. Alternatively, the director, the chairman, or both could resign or threaten to resign—with appropriate publicity—as a method of bringing pressure. Or they could advise the MTC to accept the federal challenge and refuse to participate in what they sincerely believed was an unworkable arrangement. Or finally, they could yield to the federal ultimatum and surrender three-quarters of their influence over the planning project.

Months later an observer at the November capitulation meeting maintained that the federal regional officials were gambling on a quick collapse, that a firm negative response, or even a demand for adjournment, would have broken their nerve. The director and the chairman were unwilling to risk a fight. In their view, surrender gave the MTC half a loaf. It provided assurance that the demonstration part of the project would be approved and would be directed under sole control of the MTC.

The agreement reached at the November meeting embodied twelve points, of which the following were the most significant:

1. This program shall be conducted by the four agencies involved through an Executive Committee which shall be responsible for the over-all direction of the study.

2. The Study Director is to report directly to the Executive Committee and is responsible for direction of the administrative and technical operations of the Study.

3. The entire Study is to be a coordinated, integrated, single package and is not to be broken up or administered by, through or with any individual Agency represented on the Executive Committee.

4. Separate quarters for the Study staff will be set up and financial support therefore, can be approved by BPR: The Study Director will proceed with this matter in the immediate future.

5. It is noted for guidance that the approval by HHFA of the P-34 contract was broad in scope and contemplated that the Study thus authorized would probably involve clarification and possible revision as studies proceed.

6. In order to enable the overall Study to proceed without further delay, the Inter-agency Agreement—which has been found acceptable in principle by BPR and HHFA—should be executed immediately.[11]

Two weeks after HHFA, together with the BPR and the Massachusetts highway agency, had dictated these surrender terms to the MTC, Robert Weaver of HHFA (later appointed to head the Department of Housing and Urban Development) delivered a statement in which he reaffirmed the traditional federal stand on the sanctity of the grass roots. Mr. Weaver asserted, "This country is too vast and its conditions too diverse to be able right here in Washington to coordinate programs and projects affecting specific metropolitan areas even if this were otherwise desirable." Proceeding from this assumption, Weaver concluded that "we certainly do not deem it appropriate for us to specify to any metropolitan area what type of governmental forms it

[11] Massachusetts, Boston Regional Planning Project, "Minutes of Meeting of HHFA, BPR, DPW, and MTC," November 28, 1962.

should have for the performance of planning and other local functions."[12] On another occasion an HHFA administrator disputed proposed legislation that would require the HHFA administration to pass on new federal capital improvements in metropolitan areas with the statement that "this bill would, in effect, place with the administrator a veto power over the actions of other federal agencies. This is a veto power that the administrator certainly does not care to exercise."[13] Yet this is just what happened with the Boston project. If civil war between the federal agencies was averted, it was because HHFA tended to fade into obscurity with time.

The director, and a group of MTC commissioners, spent the next year vainly trying to win back the ground lost on that November afternoon. One question that puzzled observers then, and later, was why the director did not use any of the fabled political influence that had helped him to win state and federal approval of the integrated program. There is no clear answer to this question, although it is possible that the director actually possessed little of the influence ascribed to him by himself and others. The pressure he was able to mobilize to secure the state appropriation either was in the form of harmless pro forma endorsements or was based on a promise of favors to come. Both types of support were ebbing fast as the project's momentum was lost and the expected patronage was not forthcoming. Moreover, the knowledge that the director could be beaten without danger of political reprisals was important news to disgruntled officials who had credited him with enormous power.

There was, however, one man who might have resolved the issue in favor of the MTC. Republican Governor Volpe could have intervened on its behalf. So far as is known, his aid was never requested. One explanation may be that the governor, ending his two-year term, was busy running for reelection. It is more likely, however, that the director failed then, or later, to recognize either the number of his opponents or the depth of their unrelenting hostility.

Over the long term, he was enormously confident of his powers of persuasion, if not in Massachusetts certainly among the relatively cerebral federal agencies. While he had written off his adversaries at the DPW, he simply could not conceive that the upper echelons of HHFA and the BPR did not want him to run the planning project. Given the opportunity, he was sure

[12] Robert C. Weaver, statement in U.S., Congress, Senate, Committee on Government Operations, Subcommittee on Intergovernmental Relations, *The Role of the Federal Government in Metropolitan Areas,* 87th Congress, 2nd session, 1962.
[13] Victor Fischer, statement in U.S., Congress, Senate, Committee on Government Operations, Subcommittee on Intergovernmental Relations, *Metropolitan Planning: Hearings,* 88th Congress, 1st session, 1963.

that, in time, superior logic would convince any fair-minded listener. Yet a further possible explanation for his failure to make a move is that he was subject (along with his supporters) to the very human trait of letting events slide in the hope that an unpleasant situation would somehow go away.

Cold War

The agreement of November 19, 1962 deprived the MTC of the primary responsibility for running the planning project. As a consolation prize, the director was named chairman of the project's Executive Committee.

Since the agreement required unanimity of all four agencies on all matters, it left wide scope for disagreements on such vital matters as the new work schedule. The director was determined to fight to retain the substance of the project as approved in May 1962, particularly the three high-priority studies—transit extensions to the suburbs, analysis of MTA management, and examination of new transit technology. On the other hand, the project planner was equally determined to rethink, reshape, and redesign the project within the budgetary constraints, and he looked to the federal officials for advice. But the MTC director was unable to win back the power he had lost. The MTC retained legal responsibility but little control; its priorities were flouted, and its approved consultants forgotten.

By December, it had become apparent that the multilateral veto mechanism was unworkable unless the MTC was willing to become a rubber stamp. Since the majority of the commissioners remained firm behind the director and were resentful of the federal *démarche,* the only way in which the deadlock could be broken was through a federal appeal to the governor to force the MTC's hand. The interagency veto courted a paralysis that could be ended in two ways: cancellation of the program or intervention from a higher authority to chastise the offending member agency.

Ordinarily, the planner would have run into immediate roadblocks from the director in making any substantive changes in the work program, but the preparation of drafts was classified as a technical task from which the director, as a self-acknowledged policy maker, was naturally excluded. The planner was thereby able to secure prior federal and DPW technical approval, which was automatically translated into support at the policy level.

During December the planner held a number of conferences with a score of federal officials. The major changes recommended by the federal agencies were a stronger commitment to work closely with the communities in the Boston region and an explicit agreement to develop a continuing planning process that would carry on when the planning project terminated. The federal agencies were willing to accept the proposals to stretch out the project by an additional fourteen months and to increase the planning staff from eighteen to fifty. The stronger emphasis on staff was in line with federal policy and involved a transfer of $600,000 from consultant to staff services. However, in view of the size of the project, this was all minor rather than major surgery. Three-fourths of the original work program had been unchanged. Yet it was discovered that the three key studies—transit extension, technology, and a management analysis of the MTA—had been relegated to a secondary, temporal position.

The director and the MTC commissioners regarded the three studies as vital to the success of the demonstration program: they had to be completed rapidly if the results were to be available before the end of the eighteen-month demonstration project. Considerable distress was caused by the comment of a Department of Public Works representative, who appeared to question the status of the three studies:

The question now before the Executive Committee is whether the studies as originally recommended by the Legislative Committee should now be carried out, how rapidly, and by whom. This was followed by the BPR representative who said that any such studies proposed should be conducted in accordance with a master work program for the entire project. He said that he thought an agreement on such a work program is the most important next step, and that the selection of consultants for elements of the study should follow that. [14]

In short, only if the MTC agreed to the planner's work program was there any hope that the priority studies would be approved; but even if they were, there was no guarantee that the consultants whose proposals had been submitted and approved in May would in fact be selected. The director was also distressed about the planned shift to staff from consultants. He had become doubtful of the possibility of assembling first-rate personnel quickly enough to meet the project's tight schedule. At this stage, however, there was no formal way for the director to express dissent.

Meanwhile, the demonstration project took up much of the MTC's attention. The first small bus experiment began in the first week in December 1962, and the large ($2,200,000) Boston and Maine experiment was due to begin in the first week of January 1963. It was imperative, therefore, that the preexperiment passenger market be measured to provide a yardstick for the impact of the impending fare and service changes anticipated in the experiments. The MTC was anxious to secure approval by the Executive Committee and the four agencies of a small ($120,000) traffic consultant contract to conduct this passenger survey. The planner was almost as interested in getting fast approval on this particular consultant contract because it included preliminary traffic studies that would lay the groundwork for the highway

[14] Massachusetts, Boston Regional Planning Project, "Minutes of the Executive Committee," special meeting of December 2, 1962.

phase of the planning project's work program. Unless the highway consultant contract could be approved quickly, the entire project was in danger of stalling. Despite their growing coolness, the director and the planner formed the first of a series of temporary alliances. As a result the four agencies acted in faster time than was ever to be achieved again; by mid-December, the traffic consultant was able to start work on his contract.

This temporary concord was shattered when the revised work program reached the policy level in early January. This draft program represented months of hard labor, and the federal agencies were committed to it if only because of their long list of objections to the first and second drafts. The MTC director fired off detailed criticisms covering virtually every aspect of the work program, but the federal officials still approved the draft. In their eyes, the director appeared to be asserting that he was a better planner, a more qualified transportation expert, and a more competent administrator than most of the federal bureaucracy.

In a memorandum to the other agencies in mid-January, the director once again suggested that the MTC had a special responsibility for the project. The MTC had assured the legislature, he maintained, that the entire project would be conducted in accord with the procedures, budgets, staffing, and time schedules incorporated in the original application. He raised four questions that he considered to be the heart of the dispute:

1. Why cannot the approved application be implemented? 2. Why cannot the Project be completed within 30 months? 3. Has, for example, the traffic consultant indicated any change from his June 1962 proposal to finish his work within the specified time-table? 4. Have the other consultants whose proposals were incorporated in the approved application indicated that they cannot complete their work schedules within the approved time-table?[15]

The planner responded that the previous work program and, in fact, the original MTC contract with HHFA were only tentative documents subject to substantial, subsequent reshaping. One of the first duties of the project planner, he held, was to present to the Executive Committee for its review and approval a work program to indicate how he proposed to conduct the project.

As the Project proceeds, periodic adjustments and modifications in the work program will be required. On occasion, such modifications may require budget amendments and/or amendments to the Urban Planning Grant Contract and/or the Inter-agency Agreement. In any event, such proposed modifications shall be submitted by the Planning Project Director to the Executive Committee for its consideration.[16]

[15]Massachusetts, Boston Regional Planning Project, "Memorandum from MTC Staff," January 12, 1963.
[16]Massachusetts, Boston Regional Planning Project, "Reply to Four Questions Raised by MTC Staff, January 21, 1963," memorandum no. 7 to members of the Executive Committee.

He received immediate firm backing from his agency allies on this and other points. By mid-January 1963, however, the director had made progress in one direction because the BPR now agreed that the three priority studies should proceed.

In late January the director distributed an MTC memorandum demanding written proof that the planner, his own choice, was in truth qualified by experience and successful achievement to direct a $5 million planning project. Whatever doubts federal officials conceivably may have had were dismissed in mounting irritation against this seemingly endless paper warfare. In the first week in February, top-level HHFA and BPR officials visited the governor and requested his intervention to bring the director to heel. They flatly labeled the director's continued resistance to the new work program as arrant obstructionism that placed the entire project in jeopardy. Under instructions relayed from the governor, the director in the first week of February 1963 recommended to the Mass Transportation Commission that it approve the new work program. After six months of struggle, the cold war had ended in a second disaster for the director and the MTC.

However, the federal officials were not sure that they had seen the end of the rebellion. On February 4, 1963, the director was asked point-blank if he really meant to cooperate or, conversely, whether the federal agencies should cancel the project? Of course he promised to cooperate. But since this verbal evidence of what he termed "a new spirit of cooperation" was followed immediately by his further criticism of the organization and administration of the project, the federal officials were by no means completely sanguine about their victory. Perhaps they sensed the trouble that was yet to come.

In February 1963 as in November 1962, the MTC director and commissioners had the option of resigning or threatening to resign. However, this possibility was never seriously considered, particularly because the demonstration program apparently displayed so much promise. (The experiments, begun in December, were providing a modest amount of patronage and considerable newspaper coverage for the governor and other political officials, although no gratitude was expressed toward the MTC.) Moreover, the MTC believed that subsequent events would alter the situation in its favor. These hopes were based on a growing conviction that the planner was going to run into trouble. The federal agencies and the DPW had created an administrative tangle, and it was quite possible that he would fall afoul of the cumbersome four-agency organization. In contrast, the director believed that the MTC, in the absence of the four-power inertia, would march on from triumph to triumph.

The director rejected one possible method of dramatizing this contrast and the possibility of securing control. The MTC could give the planner a sixty-to ninety-day deadline to initiate the three key studies. The idea was attractive. If the planner met the deadline, he would help to assure the success of the demonstration program, and the MTC would be able to claim credit for designing and implementing the only elements of the planning program that were comprehensive and attractive to both legislators and MTC commissioners. If he failed to do so, he would provide prima facie justification for immediate dismissal. However, the director once more decided to avoid a battle. Instead, he inserted a vaguely worded sentence in his February 1963 surrender document, warning that the "MTC might be obligated to take appropriate action if the time schedule in the revised work program approved on February 4, 1963, was not fulfilled."[17]

If the Planning Project is not substantially and expeditiously implemented after this Executive Committee meeting, I will be compelled to advise the members of the MTC that they review and reconsider the basis of their participation in the multi-agency project.

This will be the second occasion in which, against my better judgment, I will have recommended that the MTC yield to the insistent pressures and threats of the other agencies in revising the basic methods incorporated in the approved application. If the Boston Regional Planning Project does not expeditiously contract for the basic studies to be performed in the Extension, Administrative Analyses and Technological portions, then I shall recommend to the MTC that it seriously reconsider the practicality of its continued participation in the Boston Regional Planning Project as constituted.[18]

These two concluding paragraphs of the director's memorandum provoked a pointed and bitter reaction from the planner's allies. A letter from the division engineer of the Bureau of Public Roads, dated February 8, 1963, expressed strong support for the planner, and another scathing letter from the HHFA New York office was addressed directly to the MTC director. It was apparent that officials of the federal planning agency were prepared to write and send letters of the kind that are sometimes written to relieve animosities but are usually consigned to the wastebasket after prudent second thoughts.

As finally approved, the work program schedule called for the three key studies to be given priority status. Moreover, the MTC expected that the victory would be complete in that the planner would recommend an immediate approval of the consultant draft contracts included in the approved 1962 application, since there was clearly insufficient time to effect substantial revisions or to seek out, interview, and develop new proposals from new consultants.

Meanwhile, in the midst of the organizational turmoil and the heated

[17] Massachusetts, Boston Regional Planning Project, "Fourth Draft of Work Program," memorandum to members of the Executive Committee, February 4, 1963.
[18] Ibid.

argument over the work program, the planner gave a good deal of attention to the question of choosing a suitable name for the Boston Regional Planning Project. Most of the nation's metropolitan transportation studies were referred to by their initials, in the tradition of the WACS and WAVES. The Chicago Area Transportation Study became known as CATS, the Pittsburgh study became PATS. Buffalo, in an attempt to avoid the inevitable BATS, was named the Niagara Frontier. To avoid the same unflattering designations of BATS, the planner initially accepted the term Boston Regional Planning Project.

The simplest and shortest of the generally accepted titles has been used until a final decision could be made. In view of the foregoing, it would appear that no markedly superior name will emerge. Therefore, it is my somewhat reluctant recommendation that the temporary title be adopted for the duration and that the Project be officially known as the BOSTON REGIONAL PLANNING PROJECT.[19]

Unfortunately, no one foresaw "BRPP" (pronounced BURP), which quickly became the accepted nickname. Almost two years later the project was redesignated as the Eastern Massachusetts Regional Planning Project, possibly in an effort to escape the taint of failure, which by that time was synonymous with "BURP."

While the planner was concerned about nomenclature, the project continued to drift, lacking strong leadership from either a willing director or a reluctant governor. The arbiter of conflict was the governor. It was to him rather than to the big-city mayor that the federal agencies turned, and it was the governor who settled the Boston area's major transportation issues, including reorganization of the region's metropolitan transit agency and the State Department of Public Works. This record suggests that Richard Meier's, Richard Duke's, and Michael Danielson's characterization of the central-city mayor as the natural spokesman for the metropolis[20] may have considerable validity; but in the final analysis much more power seems to lie with the governor.

[19]Massachusetts, Boston Regional Planning Project, "Planning Project Name," memorandum no. 8 to members of the Executive Committee, January 23, 1963.
[20]Richard L. Meier and Richard D. Duke, "Gaming Simulation for Urban Planning," *Journal of the American Institute of Planners,* vol. 32, no. 1 (January 1966), pp. 3–16. See also Michael N. Danielson, *Federal-Metropolitan Politics and the Commuter Crisis* (New York: Columbia University Press, 1965).

Honeymoon at 150 Causeway

The preceding chapter dealt with the genesis of the Boston Regional Planning Project (BRPP) and the turmoil surrounding its organization in the final months of 1962 and January 1963. This chapter takes up the narrative from the brief, peaceful interlude that followed and carries it on through further bitter struggles to the final, anticlimactic phase.

From February through April 1963 the planner was given a free hand in running the planning project. The federal agencies were firm in their support. Their role was essentially passive and neutralizing; they were there to ensure that the Mass Transportation Commission (MTC) would not interfere with the planner. The only question remaining was, how effectively could he move? As it turned out, the planner was to be given the same kind of brief, frustrating honeymoon that the MTC had enjoyed in August and September 1962.

There were three basic tasks: hiring staff, setting up a permanent office, and securing approval of major consultant contracts from the four agencies. Of these, the least troublesome proved to be staffing. The planner quickly succeeded in compiling a backlog of a dozen or so project applicants, with the assistance of the Boston Redevelopment Authority (BRA). Offering the enticement of salary increases ranging from $1,000 to $3,000, it was comparatively easy to fill the open boxes in the organization chart. However, the other two elements in the early timetable were to prove more difficult.

In the fall the Bureau of Public Roads (BPR) and the Massachusetts Department of Public Works (DPW) had offered to supply an estimated $200,000 in overhead costs, since the original budget with the Housing and Home Finance Agency (HHFA) made no provision for the substantial overhead expenses involved in setting up a large, independent office. This increased the total amount to be expended on the project from $4,800,000 to $5,000,000. It also made the project's office arrangements dependent on the DPW and a sometimes suspicious state auditor's office.

This simple step—renting adequate office space (and securing equipment and supplies)—proved to be one of the project's major hurdles. For most of its existence the project operations exhibited all the permanence of a roving encampment of impoverished gypsies. There were not enough stamps, and mailings were late or delayed. There were no drafting tables or equipment, so this work was performed at the home of one of the project draftsmen. Jammed into one room at 150 Causeway Street, near the DPW headquarters, it was a frustrating experience for the project staff, who had hoped for far more lavish space allocations than the meager quarters supplied by the MTC.

It has been hypothesized that the move away from the MTC offices may have been effected by the highway agencies in the hope of combatting MTC influence and because they believed that physical proximity to the DPW would help to ensure protection of the highway interests. Whatever the motivation, the project staff soon encountered problems in attempting to secure overhead support from the Department of Public Works. For example, not until April 1964 was the project able to move to "permanent" quarters in a building scheduled for demolition in 1966 as part of Boston's Government Center renewal project.

Trouble also came from an unexpected quarter. The Department of Public Works, it seemed, was almost as wary of giving the project staff free rein as it was of allowing freedom to the MTC. The DPW assigned two inspectors to oversee the management of the project, and these men were assigned space in the one-room office at 150 Causeway Street. The introduction of project inspectors was not a happy innovation for most of the project staff. The inspectors helped to prepare the large highway consultant contract and helped with other technical matters. Some of the staff complained, however, that they were full of dismal predictions of impending disaster; and even more irritating, they were stool pigeons for the DPW and were expected to check on staff activities. The BPR also assigned a staff representative to the project, but he apparently limited himself to technical matters. Neither HHFA nor the MTC assigned full-time personnel to the project.

The DPW inspectors, in addition to their other tasks, were supposed to expedite the acquisition of project supplies, space, and equipment. As the months passed, many of these efforts seemed to founder in a sea of misplaced or misworded applications and clumsy procedures. Partly as a consequence, the close ties that had existed between the project staff and the DPW appeared to loosen. Desperate for such working essentials as stationery and stamps, the project staff protested (mostly in vain) the DPW's failure to provide its promised overhead support. At a series of Executive Committee meetings beginning in the spring of 1963, the DPW became the target of complaints. The overseer-expediters attempted to blame the project staff, particularly a recently resigned project office manager, but the criticism rankled. One consequence of this new breach between the project and the DPW was that the highway agency lessened its conflict with the MTC and by May had switched to a more neutral position.

Since the Executive Committee had by this time given the project staff only ninety days to push through the key consultant contracts, it was likely that anything reasonable in the way of working arrangements was certain to meet with federal and DPW approval. More important, personnel and consultant contracts were likely to pass through the MTC barrier without difficulty.

The planner's immediate problem was to help prepare the large ($1,400,000) traffic consultant contract and to shepherd it through the designated hurdles. This process proved far more time-consuming than anyone had anticipated. First, not unexpectedly, the investigation-shaken DPW was slow to act; second, some MTC commissioners were fearful that any consultant contract would be an invitation to inquisitive federal investigations. Two commissioners managed to create a delay even though the director of the MTC and most of the commissioners actively supported this particular contract. The enormous effort involved in preparing the large traffic consultant contract helped to remove any serious possibility that the planner could ready the three transit-oriented studies for fast interagency approval.

The planner was faced with a clear time-power relationship in February, March, and April 1963. The project staff's decision to rewrite substantially, or ignore, all of the consultant contracts included in the May 1962 application ensured months of rethinking and renegotiating. By the time the new versions were ready, the MTC had recovered its power to the point where it could block action on contracts of which it disapproved.

Perhaps of all the decisions made by the planner and his staff this was the most crucial. If he had approved the priority studies as requested by the MTC he could have prevented much of the strife that followed, and would have achieved at least a year's immunity from controversy. Moreover, it was dangerous to delay the features of the project that were of special interest to the MTC and the legislators, and to arouse the director's wrath, because the power of the MTC waxed appreciably and its morale strengthened as the demonstration program progressed. Whatever the reasons, the spring of opportunity passed the project by. After late June, nothing proposed by the project received MTC approval except employee contracts. By August 1963, even these were resisted.

The political heat that had troubled the MTC since September 1962 was now turning in the direction of the planning project. The director referred the steady stream of legislators with job applicants directly to the project. A number of old MTC promises thus came to roost in the project's yard, and it was soon discovered that the distribution of a limited supply of jobs among a number of voracious legislators was an unpleasant, thankless task.

By the summer of 1963, federal officials were becoming concerned over the lack of progress, which was obvious, despite their effort to solve the problem by transferring project control from the MTC to the DPW. They requested an audience with the governor, indicating that the project was in trouble and that dynamic gubernatorial leadership was needed to break the MTC-DPW impasse. Thus, again, high federal authority appealed to the governor for action to break the logjam. This time, however, the MTC came in for less direct criticism. The DPW, their former ally, was accorded a share of the blame by implication, and a direct hint was made that more drastic intervention might be needed to bring both local agencies into line.

In early 1963 the federal agencies had begun to absolve themselves from any responsibility for the ills of the planning project by suggesting in private comments and memoranda that the project's difficulties were purely local in origin. In a letter to the governor, the Urban Renewal Administration commissioner and the federal highway administrator of the BPR wrote that they had agreed that

the success of the Boston Planning Project is dependent upon continuing surveillance and supervision by your office. We are pleased that, as a result of your intercession, the project work program was approved by the Executive Committee at its February 4th meeting. . . . You will agree that we must be assured that the project will not continue to be jeopardized by the lack of effective cooperation between the two State agencies involved.

We enthusiastically support your idea for the appointment of a representative of your office to the Executive Committee of the planning project. This, in our opinion, would be the most effective means of bringing your influence to bear upon the conduct of the study.[1]

The letter included a brief reference to the lack of local participation in the deliberations of the project.

The Executive Committee has thus far not fully determined the extent and form of local governmental participation in the project. Effective local participation is required under the policies of both agencies and is, in our opinion, essential to the acceptance of planning recommendations by the local governments of the region. We would suggest your early attention to this problem with specific consideration of the desirability of providing local representation on the Executive Committee.[2]

This was to become a recurring theme later on.

In response to the initial federal request, the governor had assigned an observer to the project as his personal representative. This observer became a nonvoting member of the Executive Committee in March 1963. He more or less inadvertently elicited a discussion that had considerable consequences for the project. He questioned the participants at an Executive Committee meeting about the progress of the project. The director indicated that things were difficult but improving. The DPW seconded, explaining that certain minor problems like stamps and stationery, once troublesome, were fast being overcome. But, when queried, the federal representatives strongly demurred. On the contrary, things were not going well, the BPR representative stated, and

[1] Letter to Governor Endicott M. Peabody from the Urban Renewal Commissioner, Housing and Home Finance Agency, March 11, 1963.
[2] Ibid.

something had to be done quickly. The HHFA representative concurred, indicating that there was strong dissatisfaction in his agency with the slow progress of the Massachusetts project. The planner, much to everyone's surprise, inclined strongly to the federal viewpoint. His exact words were not recorded, but participants agree that he suggested that the project was falling below his standards of tolerance and, as of that moment, could be considered a "failure." He ascribed the blame for this on the DPW, which had failed to provide the promised overhead support, and on the MTC, which was too slow in processing personnel and consultant contracts.

These comments evoked immediate reactions from the DPW and the MTC. Under hostile prodding, the planner admitted that the project's overhead problem was partly the fault of his departed office manager. Also, everything considered, he admitted that the MTC had not constituted a serious road-block, since no contract, up to that time, had been delayed by more than four or five weeks by that agency. Nevertheless, a gloomy note had been struck and it was to reverberate.

The reasons for the depressing statement concerning the "failure" of the project are not entirely clear. It may have been an unguarded remark, made in heat and brought on by temporary irritation. However, in this as in other cases, the planner's manner was unfailingly calm and dispassionate. He never appeared to speak on impulse. In consequence, this passing comment had far greater weight than he wished; in coming weeks and months, he was to attempt unsuccessfully to reinterpret it.

Before springtime ended, another event of consequence occurred. In May, on the recommendation of the project staff, the four agencies approved a $344,000 contract with a land-use mapping consultant. The contract was to be with a firm other than the one included in the original grant application, but the MTC, having no strong opinions and expert knowledge in this field, approved the contract with no more delay than was inherent in the normally slow four-agency process. Commission members did raise questions about the consultant's previous bankruptcy, but they were assured by the planner that a well-respected accounting firm had issued a clean bill of financial health for the consultant. This objection answered to their satisfaction, the MTC approved the contract as recommended. This decision turned out to be catastrophic, as is detailed later.

The Courtiers

From early May to mid-October 1963, strenuous efforts were made by the chief protagonists to win the favor of the governor. On one side, the director and a group of MTC commissioners tried to win back control of the planning project. They maintained that both the project staff management and the four-agency administrative organization had been totally inadequate and that the obvious, simple solution was to turn the planning project over to the MTC, which had proved its abilities by successfully operating the companion demonstration program.

On the defensive, the planner and the project staff were faced with the task of proving that the situation was not as bad as the MTC claimed or, at the very least, that the MTC was responsible for those problems that did exist. The federal agencies were no longer as firm in their support of the planner's stewardship as they had been months earlier, but some federal officials remained adamant on one point: the director himself, under any circumstances, was wholly inadmissible. He was viewed as completely incapable of running an honest and competent planning project; yet strangely it was admitted, somewhat grudgingly, that the MTC was effectively administering the demonstration project. On the whole the DPW tended to remain neutral; in the spring and summer of 1963, that agency retreated farther and farther from the debate because it had become involved in battling the governor's plans for its own reorganization and in meeting the mounting pressure from multiple federal investigations.

The fate of the planning project after November 1962 cannot be considered apart from the character and outlook of Governor Endicott Peabody. Governor Peabody's performance elicited mixed reactions. To his outright enemies, Republicans and hostile Democrats, "Chub" Peabody represented an accident in power, with his high-minded rhetoric concealing nothing more than a typical politician's urge for power.

To his supporters, who included many members of civic reform groups, the governor's liberalism, honesty, and unimpeachable intent far outweighed minor lapses in syntax or halting delivery. Their faith was buoyed by the contrast between the governor and his enemies. To not quite half of the Democrats voting in the September 1964 primary, the governor shone like a beacon in a fog, partly because of his remarkable record in reorganizing and cleansing state government during the second year of his term.

Suspicious of those outside the administrative family, particularly incumbent officials, and sure of its ability to use power wisely, the Peabody administration was marked by active, and successful, efforts to strengthen the governor's control over the state agencies, including the MTC.

At this time, Governor Peabody apparently shared the belief, common to many aspirants to high office, that problems of government are not as complex as they are made to appear. He and his staff were also inclined to equate the value of advice with the assigned morality rating of the adviser. In consequence, they sometimes acted on bad advice from those they trusted and sometimes ignored wise counsel from those of whom they were skeptical. They were crusaders, moreover, and as such they tended to be wary of the prudent and noncombative types within the governor's circle who sought compromise solutions.

One of the more endearing traits of the Peabody administration was its youthful enthusiasm and tenacity. If fitful and occasionally misdirected, the administration's bulldog vigor succeeded where its predecessors had failed, particularly in restructuring key areas of state government. This energy was closely linked to decisive-sounding rhetoric. The very mention of the need for further consideration of alternatives, or expressions of doubt, was suspect. To remain a member in good standing of the governor's intimate circle, it was necessary to simulate a ringing optimism. There was also a certain reliance on oversimplified solutions that would resolve intricate problems to which no one clear answer was possible.

The administration's manner toward the planning project illustrated a number of these tendencies. Flashes of revelation in the governor's circle included the decision to find a superman to take over the project, the governor's seizure of project control in October 1963, and his appointment of a "hard-nosed" lawyer in early 1964 to chastise the director and reinvigorate the project. The failure of each initiative was followed by a period of depression, a feeling of having somehow been cheated by someone or something. The psychological backlash had an adverse effect on the seers who had accurately forecast disaster. Like the ancient bearers of bad tidings who were executed for their pains, these cautious administrators came to be strongly associated with the catastrophes they had predicted. This had an unfortunate effect on later decisions and was one reason why the governor's office seemed not to profit from past errors: as time passed, the counselors of prudence were gradually excluded from policy meetings. Since they also tended to be professional administrators, their removal was partly responsible for the practice that evolved: overlong delays followed by hasty, ill-considered improvisations.

The history of most organizations suggests that the inability to anticipate crises leads their administration to degenerate into a series of last-minute salvage operations in which key personnel are shunted about like firemen in a town overrun with arsonists. When this frantic pattern comes to be accepted as the normal way of conducting government business, the effects can be disastrous. The planning project was only one casualty of this practice; the governor's defeat in the September 1964 primary is at least partly attributable to his public image as a fumbling administrator.

It became increasingly apparent during 1963 that the administration regarded the planning project and its bothersome troubles as a minor ailment unlikely either to explode into a major disaster or to produce major results. In consequence, it never really came to grips with the reorganization. Instead, the problem was handled almost in an absent-minded fashion whenever limited staff resources could be spared from more pressing matters.

For a considerable time, the MTC's attempts to elicit a clear response from the governor's office seemed totally fruitless. For example, in May or June the director wrote several long memoranda, citing planning project history and administrative practice, detailing project failures, and promising (if the project were returned to the MTC) speedy, high-quality achievement based on the proven record of success with the demonstration project. No response. In July the missives grew shorter, limited to brief expositions of project ineptitude and promises to make fast delivery on priority transit studies for such critical areas as the South Shore. Result: a mixed but mildly encouraging reaction. In August and September the director condensed his memoranda still further, coming at the very last to billboard slogans of this type: "THE PROJECT STAFF CAN'T DELIVER. WE CAN. LOOK AT THE MTC DEMONSTRATION PROJECT." Result: silence.

Failing to make any headway with the written word, the director attempted to mobilize the support of everyone who could conceivably influence the governor's final decision. MTC supporters were pressed into service to persuade politicians, administrators, newspapermen, relatives, and friends of the governor of the justice of the director's cause.

The project staff was by no means idle during this period. One of its major defensive tactics was to rekindle the latent sympathy of the federal officials. It also made efforts to reach key figures in the governor's circle. Both attempts seemingly met with some success. As at other times, the project staff was considerably aided by the favorable personal reactions that the planner always seemed to evoke. By mid-1963, attitudes toward the director had hardened, and his circle of enemies had expanded to include most of his operating universe. Few genuinely doubted his intelligence or talents; but an informal tabulation revealed that eight out of every ten people connected with the project apparently found him untrustworthy, and some felt that he was personally obnoxious. Assuming the accuracy and applicability of Richard Neustadt's well-known comment on the day-to-day market fluctuations in presidential power[3] and assuming that it is equally applicable to bureaucrats, the director's reputation for influence was selling at a discount everywhere save the MTC. On the other hand, the planner was viewed by many as a solid professional who was being martyred by a malevolent cabal. Even his

---

[3] Richard E. Neustadt, *Presidential Power* (New York: Signet Books, 1960), chap. 3, "The Power to Persuade."

detractors said that he was honest and well-meaning, floundering in deep administrative waters.

One hypothesis for this wide difference in reactions to the two contenders is that the planner did not represent a threat to established power, while the director did. The former had stepped on far fewer political, bureaucratic, and corporate toes, and it was clear that his ambitions were far more modest than those of his adversary.

During this half year the planner and his staff were busy on the work-a-day operations of the project. In June, July, and August 1963 they submitted a number of proposed consultant contracts for MTC approval. They also offered for approval a large-scale combined population-economic base study, a consultant contract for processing and storing project data, and a PERT[4] study to diagram the various work elements of the project in their proper time sequence. The director raised technical objections to each, which appeared sufficiently substantive not to be dismissed as frivolous. After considerable discussion at a dozen or so MTC meetings and private sessions with MTC subcommittees, the planner and his staff refused to revise them as the MTC desired. Eventually, by February 1964, all were withdrawn. Clearly the assignment of project staff personnel to fruitless and prolonged contract negotiations and to wrangling with the MTC interfered materially with the project work schedule; but, until the question of control was settled, progress was not in the MTC's interest.

The muteness of the governor's office during this particular six-month period cannot be fully understood but can be partially explained. From time to time, numerous advisers were consulted in an attempt to solve the project's defective organization. Various teams pondered the problem. Week after week, apparently to placate the impatient (or force itself to act), the governor's office promised that the long-awaited decision was imminent. But the late spring and summer passed, fall began, and the revelation was not forthcoming.

During most of the summer, the MTC kept a "hot line" open to the governor's office, and HHFA headquarters in Washington were alerted for a call from the governor. Time passed, deadlines for gubernatorial decisions were forgotten, and the MTC and the project staff waited.

One document of this middle period was a twenty-seven-page memorandum prepared by a staff member in the governor's budget agency, outlining eight alternative methods of reorganizing the project. Of the eight, two were unacceptable to most participants: abandoning the project or leaving its

[4] Program Evaluation and Review Technique is a method of organizing project tasks on the basis of temporal and input interrelationships.

organization unchanged. The favored alternative was a surgical operation giving the MTC's three priority studies to that agency and leaving the remainder of the project to the planner within a reorganized planning project under the general direction of the governor's office. Lower on the priority and feasibility scale was another alternative, a return of the entire project to the MTC.

There was some possibility that a compromise might have been arranged since, by this time, all parties were weary of the deadlock. One obstacle to compromise, however, was a feeling that victory for the MTC was imminent. Virtually all the commissioners seemed to be solidly in favor of regaining control over the project. Morale soared when this prospect appeared to receive a favorable reception from some of the governor's key advisers and, most important, when it looked as if the federal agencies might go along, too.

It seems obvious that HHFA, and possibly the BPR as well, had quickly regretted the regional office initiatives that had made them codirectors. The federal withdrawal began in the spring, and by June 1963 it was signalized by the continued absence of the HHFA representative from the project's Executive Committee meetings and by a less argumentative attitude on the part of BPR officials. From July 1963 to February 1964, personnel from HHFA were never at the regular meetings.

In September 1963 the planning project finally succeeded in persuading the DPW to advertise for bids on enlarged project offices. Learning that tentative quotations were coming in at $5 to $6 a square foot, the landlord renting the MTC offices quoted a price that beat the lowest alternative bid by a wide margin. Space was available one floor above the MTC offices, and the accommodations, though primitive, nevertheless represented a vast improvement over the project's bullpen at 150 Causeway Street. The project staff was confronted with an unpleasant dilemma. Refusal of the low bid could lead to accusations that the project was deliberately squandering public funds. True, the amenities provided in the low-rent space were far below the standards for which the staff had hoped, but disqualification was a risky course to take when the larger MTC demonstration project had been running smoothly out of even more substandard quarters on the floor below. On the other hand, a meek relocation close to the MTC would put the project physically near the headquarters from which it had been extricated, only after a great struggle, less than a year earlier. If the planning project was just a few steps away, the chances of its being reabsorbed might be increased immeasurably.

A possible defense against the low bidder could be found in the text of the interagency agreement; there it clearly stated that the planning project was to be sheltered in quarters removed from the MTC offices. After perusal of the document, the project staff persuaded itself that, in any event, the agreement implied more than a token separation of only thirty vertical feet. The BPR representatives apparently agreed. It was rumored that the planner would raise the issue of physical separation to the BPR representative, and the BPR would agree that a substantial distance was necessary and that the project need not accept the low bidder. However, as sometimes happens when firm verbal commitments are to be translated to paper, the BPR had second thoughts, and no strong backing emerged to assist the project's resistance to propinquity. However, the planner was far from submitting tamely. While the technical staff moved to offices above the MTC, the planner himself, along with his policy staff and community and public relations personnel, remained safely in place, a full mile away from the MTC.

The lack of BPR support on the issue of office space lent credence to the director's belief that the project staff had lost firm federal support. The MTC was convinced that the governor's office had narrowed the alternatives down to either an MTC take-over or some, as yet unidentified, candidate for project director, and it redoubled its efforts to secure control.

As time passed, two further elements were added to the campaign. The first was a three-day MTC meeting in late August at a Cape Cod resort. There, on the southern shore of the Cape, the director attempted to secure solid backing from the commissioners as the capstone of his effort to secure a solid majority vote. The Cape Cod debate and confrontation consisted of two phases. In the first—a regular MTC session—the planner was exhorted to supervise consultants more carefully, and the commissioners decided to delay action on personnel contracts. The expected telephone call from the governor's office on his reorganization plan never came because the governor had not yet reached a decision. The following afternoon the commissioners gathered to hear the planner and his lieutenants explain patiently the need for quick approval of proposed consultant contracts. On the whole, their reaction was negative. They asked searching questions, expressed serious doubts about each proposal, and ended by approving none, then or later.

The second element of the MTC offensive was an attempt in September to prove that the project was falling behind schedule. The objective was to underscore the need for progress rather than to suggest that the planner was overdue for dismissal. While project progress had undoubtedly slowed considerably since May, the planner could have retorted, with some justice, that the director was partly to blame because of his frequent use of the MTC veto. In fact, however, evidence was produced purporting to show that the project was actually on time. The MTC meeting in September turned into a battle of charts and supporting analyses. As in all such internecine technical warfare, the audience found the material boring and inconclusive. The commissioners were unable to decide which technical presentation was correct, and, in the end, the problem was left unresolved. The experience of the Massachusetts project was similar in this respect to Mowitz's and Wright's findings in Detroit:

Our cases show the prominent decision making role now played by bureaucracies. . . . As functional activities become more firmly grounded in science and technology, the lay citizen will encounter increasing difficulty in challenging policies and decisions based upon technical determinations of the bureaucracy . . . to the citizen certain internal bureaucratic struggles are subliminal.[5]

It might be pointed out, however, that many of the technical complexities that laymen find baffling are not inherent in the subject matter but are the result of miserably uncommunicative, windy presentations of material.

In defending their project administration, the project staff explained that much of the time between November 1962 and September 1963 had necessarily been devoted to supervising consultants and "detailing of the study design," a process that had

included specifications as to the specific contents for the preliminary comprehensive Regional Plan plus a more detailed description of work activities and potential techniques of analysis. This had included the expansion of the roughly 70 general tasks outlined in the approved Work Program to approximately 250 more detailed tasks.[6]

The staff claim that most disturbed the director was that

Overall, the Planning Project is currently progressing generally on schedule. However, a number of key decisions in the very near future will distinctly influence the ability of the Project to maintain its schedule. . . .

Current progress for both the Demonstration Program and the Planning Project are very nearly on schedule. There is not anticipated at the present time any difficulty in meeting the scheduling objectives designed to meet the requirements of Federal legislation; assuming future progress is comparable to past performance.[7]

The Governor Decides

A few days before a scheduled MTC meeting in October 1963, the director was informed that the governor's budget commissioner had developed a new organizational structure to operate the project. The governor had determined to make a personal visit to Washington to discuss the situation with upperechelon officials of HHFA and the BPR, and in late September a summit

[5] Robert J. Mowitz and Deil S. Wright, *Profile of a Metropolis* (Detroit: Wayne State University Press, 1962), pp. 632–633.
[6] Massachusetts, Boston Regional Planning Project, "Staff Programs Report to the Executive Committee," September 25, 1963.
[7] Ibid.

meeting was arranged for the governor and his budget commissioner.

The governor, at this point, had apparently not reached a firm decision on whether to retain the director. According to informants, he had two meetings with HHFA officials. At the first, it was merely agreed in general terms that firm gubernatorial leadership was needed to reinvigorate the project. No specific candidates for director were discussed. The second session was with an upper-echelon HHFA official who had a personal dislike of the director. He stated flatly that the incumbent director was "totally unacceptable" to HHFA, and, for that matter, to the Bureau of Public Roads. This remark was to have momentous consequences. At the minimum it would lead to continued project paralysis and the director's departure from Massachusetts. These few words would not, of course, have had such a staggering impact had it not been for the year-long campaign by HHFA and the BPR to replace the director, the persistent efforts of the director's many local traducers, and his total inability to win the governor's confidence. As it was, the statement fell on fertile soil, confirming the governor's fully aroused suspicions.

The governor and his key staff, after their return to Boston, concluded that a new organization plan should be prepared forthwith, that the director's powers over the project should be further reduced, that a strong new leader should be found to head the project, and that quick HHFA approval of the new plan of organization could be anticipated.

In early October the governor announced his reorganization plan and asked for quick approval at the MTC's regular monthly meeting, scheduled for October 11. Since the governor's proposal represented a further diminution of the MTC role, the director responded with intensive efforts to round up commissioner votes in favor of an alternate plan that would give face-saving ceremonial functions to the governor but reserve controlling power for himself and the MTC.

The situation appeared encouraging to the director. He was apparently assured of a solid block of six votes—a majority—and stood an excellent chance of picking up two more. Surprisingly, considerable verbal support was forthcoming from the governor's appointees, one of whom was the governor's spokesman on the MTC. Both of these commissioners were apparently unhappy with the governor's proposal. As a result, the day before the meeting, the director's mood was ebullient.

Meanwhile, armed with HHFA backing, the governor's office was equally active in rounding up MTC votes. Far from being solidly in favor of MTC control, three commissioners, including two of the director's long-term supporters, were enlisted in the governor's cause, while another key vote would not be cast.

The meeting of October 11 was held in a room at Boston's Parker House. It quickly became apparent that a bitter wrangle was in prospect, and the MTC hurriedly went into executive session. While the aisles and adjoining rooms were crowded by planning project and MTC staff, sounds of a loud verbal brawl penetrated through the door. Later, after hours of fruitless discussion, the official meeting was opened for the record; for the benefit of the tape recorder and the press, both sides repeated their arguments.

To digress briefly, the practice of recording everything said at MTC sessions and meetings by the planning project Executive Committee began in the MTC. Starting in the fall of 1962, one of the commissioners took to delivering rambling, impassioned speeches addressed to his necktie, inveighing against the alleged corruption of consultants and enlarging on his reasons for voting against all proposed consultant contracts. Several weeks later he cleared up the mystery when he revealed that he had been dictating all this time to a small microphone attached to his vest, which was further connected to a pocket tape recorder. This personal recording system was, he explained, necessary for self-protection in the likely eventuality that all responsible for the project would be required to justify their behavior before grand juries.

After the initial consternation had subsided, the MTC commissioners voted to tape-record all of their meetings, a practice that was followed except in executive sessions when tempers ran particularly high and abusive language was exchanged. Shortly afterward, tapes were introduced at planning project Executive Committee sessions.

Unexpectedly, the introduction of recording equipment at meetings did not inhibit discussion as some had predicted. On the contrary, as at the October meeting, it stimulated a remarkable outpouring of repetitious oratory. Occasionally, a tape was replaced for the benefit of the recording secretary to help in preparing the minutes. Less frequently, a particularly lively sequence would be replayed for the edification of bored, but unfailingly polite, captive audiences.

Returning to the October 11 meeting, the dispute boiled down to a question of faith in the governor's leadership and a corollary concern about whether the agency's status would or would not be adversely affected by the governor's proposal. Proponents of the MTC take-over asserted that acceptance of the governor's plan was illegal and would remove all reason for the agency's continued existence, but the argument fell on deaf ears. The director's long courtship of his commissioners had proved unavailing. By a five to four vote, the governor's plan was approved.

The strange part of the meeting was the subsequent vote on another piece of business. The MTC, accepting the advice of its counsel, proceeded to vote by a six to three majority to submit the plan they had just approved to the state's attorney general for an opinion on its legality.

The substance of the governor's proposal to reorganize and direct the planning project is summarized essentially in a key paragraph from the amendment approved by the MTC at that October meeting:

The Planning Project shall be conducted by the agencies through an Executive Committee consisting of three members, one of whom shall be a member of the Board of Commissioners of Public Works and one of whom shall be a member of the Mass Transportation Commission or a representative of the Commission designated by it, and one of whom shall be an individual nominated by the Governor, acceptable to the agencies, who will serve at the pleasure of the agencies, jointly and separately, as Executive Secretary of the Planning Project Advisory Board established herein. The Executive Committee shall provide overall policy guidance for the Planning Project.[8]

The sole change in the final version approved by the MTC was a requirement that Executive Committee votes be unanimous, a change that theoretically reinstated the MTC veto. The proposal was submitted to HHFA for federal approval, along with the interesting warning that the attorney general's opinion had been requested on its legality, a clear danger signal for a prudent federal official.

In the request for an opinion, the MTC asked the attorney general two questions, neither of which was destined to be answered:

1. Can the Commission authorize and empower an Executive Committee consisting of three members, of which the Commission shall have one member, functioning by majority vote, to assume obligations and enter into contracts, in the name of the Commission?
(i) to engage consultants and individuals as members of the Planning Project Staff for the purpose of undertaking, supervising, administering and completing the Planning Project; and (ii) to incur other related expenses for and on behalf of the Planning Project?
2. Can the Commission authorize an individual, to be appointed by the Governor, to serve at the pleasure of the Governor, at a salary to be designated by the Governor, and therefore not subject to control by the Commission, to act for the Commission as the executive and administrative head of the Planning Project?[9]

In the next few days, while the request to the attorney general was being prepared by the MTC counsel, a series of newspaper articles apparently giving the director's side of the controversy enlivened the local press. The first two articles raised no storm, but the third suggested that the governor's reorganization plan had been drawn up without reference to the controlling legal documents. The imputation of the article, seemingly based on

[8] "First Amendment to the BRPP Inter-Agency Agreement" (proposed by the Commissioner of Administration and Finance and accepted by the MTC), October 11, 1963.
[9] Letter to the Honorable Edward W. Brooke, Attorney General, from the Mass Transportation Commission, October 16, 1963.

inside information, was that the governor's legal staff had not done its home-work. This caused considerable distress in the governor's office. Although no immediate action was taken, partly because of a well-founded belief that such one-shot, minor attacks have little real impact, another black mark was placed against the director's name.

The optimism of the governor's staff was apparently based on verbal assur-ances proffered by the Housing and Home Finance Agency, which was expected to furnish a letter to the governor's office approving the reorganiza-tion plan. This letter would then be presented to the Commonwealth's attor-ney general, presumably as convincing evidence that the federal agencies found the plan legally sound. However, this sequence was aborted when the officials at HHFA decided not to send such a letter on the grounds that it would constitute prior federal approval over a legal matter that had not yet been resolved at the local level. A letter was subsequently furnished by HHFA, but it was entirely noncommittal, indicating only that HHFA would not act one way or the other until the Massachusetts attorney general had issued his decision. Since an unfavorable opinion could prove an embarrass-ment, the attorney general's office was reportedly instructed by the governor's staff to go slow in ruling on the governor's plan. In the absence of any ruling, the director tended to operate as if the project were now solely the governor's responsibility, and from mid-October 1963 through February 1964 there was another period of paralysis. By then, however, most of the original partici-pants had abdicated, leaving the governor's office free to find a solution.

The governor's staff was much taken up with the planning project during the late fall and winter of 1963/64. One major problem arose because an adequate substitute for the director was not easily located. The talent search revolved around finding a kind of planning superman, an individual of awe-some professional reputation who would serve as the living proof that guber-natorial leadership had put the project back on the rails. However, prospec-tive directors were either unattractive or unavailable. It is possible that the difficulties encountered were never overcome because no planning giant existed or because none applied for the job.

It is not surprising, therefore, that before long the governor's staff's talent search turned away from the super planning technician in favor of the hard-headed, no-nonsense lawyer or businessman capable of getting quick results. There was no shortage of aggressive attorneys at the governor's call, and all that seemed to be needed now was a project reorganization that would pro-vide elbow room for new vigor.

By the end of February 1964, the governor had replaced the chairman of the MTC with his own appointee and had proposed a modified administrative structure for the project. There was to be a three-man Executive Committee headed by the MTC chairman. The federal agencies would recede to the insulated, concurring status they had vainly sought for almost a year.

This reorganization plan implied that the planner would remain in technical and administrative control of the project but would be carefully supervised by the governor's MTC chairman, a prominent attorney. While the administrative maneuvering continued, the project continued to founder during the winter of 1963/64.

An event of note was the bankruptcy of the land-use inventory consultant that left this critical part of the project incomplete, with some of the work scattered from Texas to Toronto. In a detailed memorandum, the planner suggested that a mounting body of evidence had steadily led him to the conclusion that the land-use consultant was in default of his contract, which had been agreed on in May 1963:

> It has come to my attention that the Internal Revenue Service has filed a tax levy against the firm; and that there is a very real possibility that the firm will petition for bankruptcy in the very near future if it has not already done so. . . . They have stopped all work in their Boston Office on the contract as of November 6, 1963, with work remaining to be done. The landlord has advised us that they are closing the office for non-payment of rent.
> . . . The only conclusion that can be drawn is that satisfactory close working liaison with the Planning Project Staff is no longer being maintained by the contractor. . . . I, therefore, recommend that the contract be terminated.[10]

The director secured MTC approval for a technical inventory of the land-use contract to determine the probable extent of financial losses and to develop a method of preventing a recurrence of the problem. He then prepared a frightening memorandum, which suggested that serious, legally intricate problems were likely to arise, involving joint law suits, substantial losses, and other unpleasant happenings.

> An independent technical audit of a vital phase of the Boston Regional Planning Project has revealed serious administrative and technical deficiencies in the Project management. It appears that staff supervision of a third party consulting contract, a $344,500.00 land use inventory and study, was wholly inadequate.
> A number of unfortunate, complex, legal and financial consequences may arise from this situation. In particular, action is indicated to recover project materials from the bankrupt firm, which are scattered in various cities in the United States and possibly in Canada and Mexico, and to establish a fair price both for these materials and for consultant work now in possession of the Planning Project.
> The former Project Manager for the land use consultant, a resident of New York, has informed the MTC in a letter dated November 23rd, that he will

[10] Massachusetts, Boston Regional Planning Project, "Recommendation for Termination of Contract," memorandum no. 45 to members of the Executive Committee, November 14, 1963.

retain project materials in his possession until he and his assistant are paid almost $3,000.00 in back wages. The MTC has also learned that other unpaid employees of the consultant have approached Massachusetts legislative leaders toward introducing legislation for a state appropriation of their back wages.

The MTC has been notified by the Alamo National Bank of San Antonio, Texas, that the bank is seeking to assert its rights under assignment agreements with the bankrupt land use consulting firm. The bank maintains that this claim has a time priority over the liens which have been brought against the consulting firm and served to the MTC by the Internal Revenue Service.[11]

The news that the project administrators, led by the planner, had seemingly committed a clear and demonstrable error might have provided useful ammunition to the director in the spring or summer, but in the growing chill of winter he decided to distribute the consultant audit quietly to the other three agencies and the governor's office for eventual action.

There was also little reaction when the project staff submitted a new work program in February 1964. This program (destined to be scrapped within six months) called for a substantial increase in project staff to perform tasks originally allotted to consultants—including the economic base study, the population study, and the PERT study. Some months earlier the MTC might have reacted vigorously to this proposal, but now it barely made a move. Instead, by agreement, the director withdrew from his position on the project Executive Committee in favor of the new MTC chairman. By mid-February, the director had completely vanished from planning project operations.

The director's lack of interest in the project at this time was only partly a result of the governor's take-over of responsibility. He had been almost completely preoccupied since September with preparing a large-scale plan for the total reorganization of public transportation in the Boston region. This program was to be his monument and contribution to the MTC and to the Commonwealth.

Last Will and Testament

As early as September 1963, the director had informed the governor that he intended to leave the state employ after his contract expired in June 1964. He planned, he said, to remain only long enough to regenerate the planning project and complete the demonstration project. However, at that time he might well have been susceptible to a draft for a postcontract extension had the governor so desired. With the MTC solidly behind him, it was conceivable that he might have been willing to take a chance on outlasting the governor. Governor Peabody was then (erroneously) rumored due for a tough fight in the spring preliminaries and (accurately) reported to face a close

[11] Massachusetts, Mass Transportation Commission, "Memorandum on Management of the Boston Regional Planning Project," January 24, 1964.

contest in the September primary and the November election. However, since the director was a consultant, not a civil servant, and was without either a federal or a local base of support, any hope of outlasting the governor was probably out of the question. As a result his attention was concentrated on two objectives, locating a new job and ensuring that his demonstration program would be an outstanding success. The latter goal was dependent on gaining adoption of his recommendation for a new Massachusetts Public Transportation Authority, a proposal that was derived, in large part, from the demonstration experiments.

A separate and rather long study would be needed to reflect all the complexities of the demonstration program and its administration. This chapter will consider only those aspects of the demonstration program that were directly relevant to the planning project and to its principal participants.

The Boston and Maine Railroad commuter experiment had been judged successful. The B&M had succeeded in expanding off-peak passenger travel by 75 percent, while peak commuter traffic volume was increased by a more modest 40 percent.

One surprising feature of the Boston and Maine experiment was the continued gain in passenger volume after August 1, 1963, when peak-hour fares were raised by about 30 percent, a return to about the same fares that were in effect before the experiment began. Fares were increased even though the results of a survey of the commuter passengers had indicated that lower fares rather than more service had attracted them back to the B&M. As a result of continued gains throughout the fall, B&M ridership was running at the rate of almost 8,000,000 a year, and by the end of 1963 the clock had been turned back four years to the passenger levels of the late 1950s. Observers were able to report standing room only on some rush-hour trains. All in all, the prophets of gloom should have been silenced.

Results on the New Haven were considerably less spectacular, although passenger levels on the New Haven's off-peak main-line commuter service to Boston did rise by 50 percent by the end of 1963. This was a remarkable gain considering that (1) the line operated hoary, antiquated equipment (versus the Boston and Maine's air-conditioned modernized Budd cars), (b) the fare levels were about a third higher than on the Boston and Maine for comparable distances, and (c) only relatively minor tinkering with New Haven operations took place under the experiment.

Puzzled observers could not explain the sizable passenger increase except in terms of the heightened regional awareness of transportation systems. The MTC was giving considerable publicity to the experiment in the press and at public meetings in the local communities with a "use it or lose it" theme.

Strangely, some passenger increases occurred on lines where fares and service had been left untouched. Rail commuters seem to evince remarkably warm reactions to even a moderate display of kindness and attention.

Results on both of these railroads contrasted sharply with passenger trends on the New York Central's Boston and Albany division, which carried about 10 percent of the rail commuters into Boston. The Boston and Albany had refused to participate in the program on the grounds that this might impede its exit from the commuter business; for this railroad, 1963 was just another typically bad year.

The modest success in stimulating rail ridership was counterbalanced by a few fizzles, including experiments with connector buses to commuter rail stations, suburban bus service to manufacturing plants, bus service to old-age housing projects and shopping centers, and bus service through a tenement district near a decayed central business district. There were very few successes with private bus companies, for example, bus service from low-density suburbs to downtown, suburban service through a densely settled suburban area to a rapid transit station, and service to a particularly well-favored shopping center.

The experimental program suggested that public transportation is most seriously threatened in the smaller areas, with populations ranging from 50,000 to 500,000. The MTC's subsequent recommendation for a statewide public transportation authority was based on the conviction that any effort to solve transportation problems must recognize that public transportation is not solely a big-city headache.

About a dozen experiments were conducted with Boston's Metropolitan Transit Authority. Because of the MTA's relatively large passenger volume, in comparison with the commuter railroads, passenger subsidies for the MTA were not feasible within the limits of the MTC budget. The MTA was given the opportunity of developing bus and parking experiments. After much discussion, a million dollars was put into experiments, some of which failed but some of which were quite successful. Among the failures, a suburban-to-downtown bus service attracted no passengers, three parking lots at drive-in movie theaters that were linked by bus service to downtown Boston were almost totally unpatronized, and a circumferential bus service three miles from downtown Boston attracted all of its riders from other lines.

However, three other MTA experiments met with excellent responses. As in many other cities, major rail stations in Boston are distant from each other and from the downtown area. One fruitful experiment was North Station to South Station bus service, in which headways were stepped up from twenty-five minutes to five minutes. The results pointed out that a high-frequency bus operating in a downtown area can attract a sufficient number of riders to make it self-supporting.[12]

The second successful experiment was a circumferential bus service operating at a five-mile radius from downtown Boston. There was some evidence that a market exists in large urban areas for a circumferential transit line to supplement traditional radial transit service.

The third real success was an MTA experiment with reduced parking fees at outlying lots located on transit lines. When parking fees were cut from thirty-five cents to ten cents, usage doubled, with the result that a thousand cars were kept off Boston's congested streets while the MTA net revenue was increased by $200,000 a year.

It will be recalled that the director had to some extent regarded the November 29, 1962, federal ultimatum as a compromise, since it had ensured a clear field for his demonstration program. As the months went on into the late spring and summer of 1963, he rarely referred to the planning program and confined himself to eulogies of the demonstration experiments. A steady stream of favorable newspaper comments was generated during the later winter, spring, summer, and early fall of 1963. Occasionally, there were jarring notes, for example, references to a particularly barren MTA bus service, complaints from a bus carrier that it was being mortally injured by a rail experiment, but they were rare.

The director, however, received little credit for his successful operation of the demonstration program. His achievement in securing local, federal, and carrier approval for the design of the experiments and for his negotiations with carriers and unions left his enemies unmoved. Nor was he given any credit as an administrator or as a source of patronage.[13] In fact, some of his difficulties arose just because he was a source of patronage. For over two years he was forced to struggle through persistent problems created by some of his non-technical project personnel, virtually all of whom were political appointees. The director's secretarial, administrative, and legal staff was a political mosaic, each piece owing its lodgment to a direct recommendation from a prominent member of the Massachusetts House or Senate, the governor's office, or congressional sponsors. Some staff members were extremely talented, while others in many varying degrees were not.

[12] Massachusetts, Mass Transportation Commission, *Mass Transportation in Massachusetts: Final Report,* July 1964.

[13] Later, he received no credit for another unexpected by-product of the demonstration program: the recommended long-term continuance of subsidized rail commuter service until transit extensions could reach out to the far corners of the region. See Massachusetts Bay Transportation Authority, *A Comprehensive Development Program for Public Transportation in the Massachusetts Bay Area,* 1966.

Life was also complicated by a number of the professional liaison staff, who seemed to specialize in bearing news of impending disasters. Others gloomily concentrated on tale-bearing between the MTC and the Massachusetts Senate and House, while several acted as tipsters for unfriendly commissioners, hostile newspapermen, and other enemies. The absence of any real loyalty to the director was wholly understandable since this portion of his staff believed, correctly, that they owed their jobs to their political ties rather than to his favor. Following the director's October 1962 and February 1963 defeats and the abolition of the MTC as a separate agency, the less employable members of the staff worked feverishly to renew ties with sponsors and to curry favor within the new power constellation.

One of the director's techniques for ingratiating himself with the political leadership was his observance of the unwritten rule that good news is trumpeted by politicians (or highly placed political appointees) while bad news is publicly released by civil servants who do not have to stand for reelection. Accordingly, the governor, the Democratic senator (Edward M. Kennedy), and local legislative leaders were given their opportunities for newspaper coverage. For the benefit of press cameras they greeted commuters, hailed the initiation of new experiments, and pointed with pride to just received federal checks to pay for the experiments. However, the director also chose to picture himself in the press as a public benefactor. Since this role is coveted by politicians, his public relations practices gave rise to certain unassuaged anxieties and suspicions regarding his future ambitions. Professors are supposed to write unreadable articles for obscure technical journals circulated to other professors; they disturb the balance of nature when they compete for press coverage.

In the fall of 1964 the B&M and New Haven railroads petitioned to get out of the commuter business. (The New Haven asked to abandon only half of its service.) This brought into play the crisis that the director had long anticipated as the proper setting for his comprehensive solution to regional transportation problems.

After considerable discussion and analysis, he conceived of a program calling for the creation of a new Massachusetts Public Transportation Authority (MPTA), including abolition of the MTA and its absorption by the new agency. The plan included MTA purchase of private bus lines in the Boston area and a five-year lease-purchase arrangement for continued rail commuter services until suburban transit extensions could be constructed. Unfortunately, in pursuing this objective he was handicapped by his troubles with the project. He believed, for example, that he needed research results from the planning project, especially proof that (1) the top-echelon MTA management was unfit, and (2) specific suburban transit extensions were financially feasible. Because the project had not produced this detailed, objective information, he was forced to use such material as was available, a technique that left him open to charges of bias. Moreover, the project could not produce the information on the nature of the predemonstration mass transit market that was needed to gauge the impact of the experiment. This information was held up in the consultant's workroom for various administrative reasons, and the director was thereby prevented from pinpointing, as fully as he would have liked, the changes in commuter habits brought about by the rail experiments. For this reason, critics, including captious commissioners, were able to point out that only a limited numerical change had occurred in passenger volume as a result of the big Boston and Maine rail experiment and other operations; in consequence, they suggested that most of the director's demonstration program was an arrant failure.[14]

In the broader sense, the loss of the planning project was the missing horseshoe nail that lost the kingdom. Largely because of the federal disparagement resulting from the prolonged struggle for control of the project, the director was never able to gain the confidence of the governor. Opponents of his comprehensive program for a Massachusetts Public Transportation Authority were therefore highly successful in fanning further suspicions in the governor's office. Without the supporting information from the planning project, it was difficult to offer convincing proof that the comprehensive transportation plan was a sound proposition.

Meanwhile, in a desperate attempt to prove his disinterestedness and ensure a fair hearing for his proposal, the director attempted to rule himself out of the Massachusetts landscape. Opponents had charged that his MPTA was a device designed to provide him with a $40,000 a year job as the head of an independent transportation empire. Vainly he protested that he had no intention of staying on in Massachusetts government, that his ambitions were in the academic field. Finally, in early February 1964, he fulfilled his earlier pronouncements by officially announcing to the MTC that he would leave when his current contract terminated in June 1964. (Although a staff member of a permanent agency, the director was technically a consultant, and his contract was subject to yearly renewal.)

The net effect was the reverse of what he had intended. Opponents who had alleged that he was a power-mad empire builder now dismissed him from

[14] For example, a pamphlet containing a series of newspaper stories on transportation (A. S. Plotkin, "The Crisis in Greater Boston's Public Transportation," *Boston Globe*, January 12–19, 1964) stated flatly that "a number of competent observers feel that MTC missed the big chance" by allotting too much money to the railroads and too little to the MTA (p. 9).

consideration as a lame duck, attempting to foist an unworkable monstrosity on a Commonwealth that he was soon to desert. His figures were challenged, his conclusions discounted, and his claims for the proposal denied. Enemies who had begun by suggesting that the proposed bonds for the new authority were totally unsalable later declared, after their marketability had been assured, that the bonds represented a "loan shark giveaway."

Despite these criticisms, the director's proposal for a new MPTA was later adopted almost in its entirety by the governor. In essence it provided that

1. the MTA commissioners be dismissed,

2. new commissioners of substantial independent reputations be appointed,

3. the name of the agency be changed (in the director's version renamed as the Massachusetts Public Transportation Authority; in the governor's proposal, Massachusetts Bay Transit Authority),

4. the transit district be substantially enlarged,

5. the authority be authorized to float a $225 million bond issue to finance the transit extensions,

6. the commuter railroads be subsidized at a cost of $10 million to continue service until transit extensions were constructed,

7. where appropriate, the authority be authorized to aid bus companies; $15 million was set aside for this purpose.[15]

The penultimate chapter in the director's service came in late February 1964. The chairman of the MTC rewrote the interagency agreement as well as the MTC regulations to shift most of the director's remaining powers to the chairman's hands. By March the director had accepted another job, and in May, after completing the final report of the demonstration program and six weeks before his contract was due to expire, he left the Commonwealth for a new overseas position with a foundation.

There had been no serious effort on his part, however, to influence the course of the planning project since mid-October 1963. By early February 1964 he was effectively shorn of influence, not only in the affairs of the planning project but in the MTC as well, and there were hopes in some quarters that the project's troubles were over. By summer he had faded from view.

The first step in securing gubernatorial control over the project had been achieved in the October 1963 vote at the MTC meeting. The second step was the appointment of a close political associate of the governor to the MTC

---

[15] The original proposal can be found in Massachusetts, Mass Transportation Commission, "Demonstration Project Progress Report No. 5," November 1963, pp. i–viii. A summary of the governor's proposal, as adopted, is available in Mass Transportation Commission, *Mass Transportation in Massachusetts*, pp. 116–119. See also Joseph F. Courtney, "State and Municipal Government Law," chap. 19 in *Annual Survey on Massachusetts Laws* (Boston: Little, Brown and Company, 1964).

chairmanship, and the third step was the creation of the new three-man project Executive Committee on which all three votes were controlled by the governor. In April a fourth step led to immediate, explosive consequences. The governor suggested that the new MTC chairman would be appointed by the MTC to direct the planning project for a fee of $25 an hour; this fee would be paid to the chairman's law firm for a maximum of 100 hours monthly. Meanwhile, the new man was to retain the MTC chairmanship. This self-selection, presented to the MTC without prior warning, led to an immediate and very negative reaction and was leaked to the press—all of which suggested that the agency was not yet completely docile. Press comment on the proposal was extremely unfavorable. The newspapers had been quick to point out that $25 an hour for 100 hours a month represented a $30,000 a year salary for part-time work.

The furor was not abated by the new chairman's accurate insistence at press conferences that $25 an hour is considered a modest fee for a successful attorney, and his suggestion that the hourly arrangement would be only for a few months, that is, until June when the director's contract was to be terminated and the MTC would be absorbed within the new Department of Commerce and Development. However, after the proposal was withdrawn, the storm soon subsided; by the first part of April, life on the project returned to its normal equilibrium. By this time, it had been made clear to the public that the director was on his way out. A news story on March 24 announced that he had been quietly relieved of his duties.

The next difficulty with the planning project arose as a legacy of the bankruptcy of the land-use consultant. A second corporation was requested to prepare a proposal to finish the work. After inventorying the available material, the firm suggested that the entire study would have to be redone from scratch, involving an additional, unanticipated cost of about $170,000. However, a third firm proposed that the bankrupt company's work was usable and that the project component could be wound up in only five months and at little increase in budget. A proposal to finish the work in five months was submitted and accepted in July; approximately two and a half years later the study was completed.

Also in July the Massachusetts legislature was reported (falsely) to be ready to vote on a bill requiring the MTC to pay $9,000 in unpaid back wages to the former employees of the bankrupt land-use consultant. The argument in favor of the Commonwealth assuming this responsibility, to which it was not legally bound, was based on the supposition that the unpaid workers, by alerting the MTC to the impending collapse, had staved off a much larger loss, including a $90,000 undeserved payment to the consultant. The consultant's employees were overjoyed at the promise of receiving their past due wages. Some of them suggested that a public ceremony be arranged as a demonstration that Massachusetts was a Commonwealth with a heart, since it had voluntarily chosen to assume an extralegal obligation. The employees were surprised to find that this suggestion for public fanfare was quietly shelved by an appropriate authority.[16]

Later in July another attack on the MTC's handling of the land-use consultant's bankruptcy was launched by the state auditor. The MTC chairman publicly stated in response what the planner had already indicated, that the bankruptcy was an unfortunate and unforeseeable accident but one that would not add to project costs.

Another problem developed over new living quarters for the project staff. In April the Department of Public Works had announced that more than $60,000 in rentals would be saved by providing office space for the project in a decrepit building scheduled for demolition. Once again the failure to provide adequate overhead support was to have harmful effects. The choice of the condemned property failed to take into account the fact that the structure was in extremely poor condition and, most important, was lacking in modern conveniences. Specifically, washrooms were scarce and substandard. In May, under the direction of a traffic engineer, a staff investigation was proceeding on the possibility of installing chemical toilets. Later, the washrooms were repaired, but they remained on the primitive side.

The failure to provide adequate living space was only a part of the continuing troubles resulting from DPW control of overhead charges. A DPW policy of either picayune harassment or prudent control over costs (depending on the point of view) was still flourishing in the spring, summer, and fall of 1964. Stamps remained difficult to procure, requisitions were returned, and travel vouchers were rejected for slightly overstating the standard figures listed in official mileage tables.

Other events in the late spring and summer included the resignation of the planner's chief lieutenant and steadily mounting pressure from the Bureau of Public Roads. The BPR wanted more technical staff hired and fewer clerical aides and legal, liaison, and public relations personnel. The BPR also made it clear that it expected the project to develop at least a preliminary land-use, economic base, and population study by the spring of 1965, a deadline, like all the others, that was to be reached and passed without result.

In August 1964 the MTC was abolished as a separate entity and absorbed by the new Department of Commerce and Development (DCD). It was suggested that the new Executive Committee take stock of where the project

[16] The appropriation for back wages was never approved.

stood and consider the possibility of altering its course or changing its emphasis. One of the critical questions was to identify, again, the scope of the planning project's objectives. A special staff report outlined the basic concerns of four different fields of planning: transportation, land use, economic development, and social welfare.

Through a long chain of reasoning, the staff recommended that the scope of the Boston Regional Planning Project's activities focus on transportation planning and land-use planning since "technical and conceptual problems as well as budgetary and time limitations tend to preclude the Planning Project from effectively contributing to economic development and social welfare planning at this time."[17] There was the familiar complaint that the general public lacked understanding of the regional planning process, as evidenced by the often repeated statement, "the time for studies is past—it's now time for action," and the constant cry for quick and easy solutions. Because of this public lack of comprehension, the report suggested that "it is difficult for a publicly sponsored study such as the Boston Regional Planning Project to take large amounts of public funds and retire into isolation to undertake basic research."[18]

The report concluded that a practical and realistic "middle ground" must be established, involving "primarily getting specific usable results in, and secondarily advancing the state of the art and science of transportation planning and physical land use planning."[19] Thus, as is often the case in searching self-analysis, it was concluded that the project was already following the proper course of wisdom and early accomplishment.

In one respect, it must be admitted that the director's departure had made a tremendous difference in the planning project. Executive Committee meetings lost their tense, grim, and feverish quality. If they had once been accused of resembling a confrontation between the Mad Hatter and the March Hare, they later seemed to fade into the languid grip of the Dormouse. A gentle, slumbering quality was dominant. Moreover, the project's quiet glide toward some far-off destination was barely disturbed by the political earthquake of September 10, 1964.

Governor Peabody, who had been considered a certainty to win the Democratic nomination and to be the likely victor in the November election, became the second incumbent governor in a quarter century to lose the party's nomination. The atmosphere of decomposition, uncertainty, and delay

[17] Massachusetts, Boston Regional Planning Project, "Policy Objectives and the Scope of Planning for the Boston Regional Planning Project," Special Report no. 4, May 1, 1964.
[18] Ibid.
[19] Ibid.

that accompanies a political changing of the guard merely created some new difficulties for a project already well behind schedule. In October 1964 another change in the timetable was approved by all hands: the project was now to conclude in February 1967. To help provide sufficient financing for staff salaries, it was decided to reduce the amount allocated for certain consultant studies; for example, the population–economic base study, originally approved for $400,000, was subcontracted to the Metropolitan Area Planning Council for only $117,000.

It would not be accurate to characterize the entire period as one of sheer stagnation. During the fall, winter, and early spring of 1964/65, there were in fact some hopeful signs that completion of the project was at last in sight. The Department of Public Works promised and by mid-1965 had delivered new project offices in a newly created Transportation Research Center. Furthermore, an emissary from the New York regional HHFA office attended a project committee meeting. This solitary visit was in sharp contrast to the regular calls paid by the Bureau of Public Roads, but it did seem to indicate that HHFA had not entirely lost interest in the technical product of the study.

The promise of one season was once again to be blighted in another, a familiar pattern in this strangely hexed operation. One reason for the relative burst of speed had been constant prodding from the Bureau of Public Roads to produce a plan by July 1, 1965, the original deadline it had laid down in 1962. In May came a new BPR directive indicating that a plan was not necessary; just a "planning process" in operation on July 1 would suffice. This removal of the last remaining reason for urgency apparently had fatal effects on a project all too prone to relapse into a coma. It was immediately decided to expand and intensify the pace and scope of the regional plan that was to meet a fall 1965 deadline. This was later extended to the spring of 1967. Unfortunately, shortly after this decision was made, the planner departed, joining an exodus that included the project's computer expert and other key staff.

The Last Act

The interagency agreement of September 1965 represented a major turning point in the chronology of the project. The new agreement effectively terminated the previous modus operandi and dictated the rules for what was essentially a new ball game. At that point in time, nearly half of the original $4.8 million in planning funds still remained in the treasury (a little over $2 million) and, of this amount, a good proportion, roughly three quarters, was still unencumbered.

A significant difference between the old and the new project organization was that four agencies were now party to the interagency agreement. One new member was the Boston region's new Metropolitan Area Planning Council, formally authorized by the state legislature only the year before. Another was the Massachusetts Bay Transportation Authority, the Boston region's public transportation agency. This step was significant because, for the first time, an area public transportation system was formally recognized as a participant in the area transportation study. Even in the Penn-Jersey study, where public transportation accounted for a much greater percentage of trips than in Boston, the organizational structure did not include direct representation from any official of a public transportation operation. The Mass Transportation Commission was defunct by this time, and its place among the four agencies was taken by the state's new Department of Commerce and Development, which of course also had responsibilities for area-wide and statewide planning. The fourth was still the DPW.

Each of the major participating agencies received membership on the Policy Committee as well as on the Technical Committee of the new project. The MAPC was given the authority to prepare planning studies in its operating area, principally metropolitan Boston. It was also primarily responsible for preparation of the final project planning report on regional development guidelines.

As part of the new division of labor, DCD was generally confined to conducting basic studies on water and sewer problems and on open space and land use in the arc of communities on the fringes of the region. The DCD also was given responsibility for some analyses on state goals, conceptualization of information, data systems, and tourist studies, none of which was specifically oriented toward the preparation of a transportation plan for the Boston region.

The DPW retained its key prerogative, responsibility for transportation planning, including data collection and the preparation of transportation projections and plans. The highway agency continued to do most of its own transportation work with the aid of computers and models and with the assistance of transportation consultants. The MAPC did a large portion of its work with its own staff, although consultants were used to hire full-time staff, which the agency otherwise could not have obtained on its limited budget. DCD, because of the specialized nature of its delegated responsibilities, parceled out most of its work to a variety of consultants, although it, too, retained some small work project items for its own staff.

It should be noted that the MBTA was given no direct project responsibilities during the three-year period between the reorganization of the transportation study in 1965 and the presentation of the Eastern Massachusetts

Regional Planning Project report on developmental guidelines in 1968. In late 1968 the MBTA's regional planning responsibilities were mainly confined to detailed consultant engineering studies of its extensions and to refurbishing its stations. There was, however, some discussion with the DPW on a joint proposal for a transportation corridor to the south of Boston. Overall, it would be fair to say that the participation of the public transportation agency was of little consequence to the conduct of the project.

A point of interest in the new interagency agreement was a change in the name of the project from the Boston Regional Planning Project (BRPP) to the Eastern Massachusetts Regional Planning Project (EMRPP). No doubt this was aimed at distinguishing the new multiagency project from the earlier unsuccessful effort that had drawn unfavorable attention.

By late 1968 the EMRPP had not yet completed a transportation plan for the Boston region. Not only had the original project completion date of November 1964 proved overly optimistic but a first extension to May 1965 was missed, a second extension to March 1967 was overrun, and a third extension to September 1967 had also been overshot. However, most of the planning inputs had been completed. During 1968 the MAPC reported that most of its project funds had been expended, the work completed, and publications presented. The DCD had also completed most of its project work items, although some of the studies had not yet been printed. What was still lacking in late 1968 was the keystone of the arch: the transportation plan for the Boston region.

In theory the end product achieved in 1969 benefited by the repeated slowdowns in at least one respect. The EMRPP transportation plan theoretically received the support of the major planning and transportation agencies in the region since they all belonged to the project's Policy and Technical committees that approved the report. The long-drawn-out research and planning process should have resulted in a consensus among the region's transportation agencies. The question arises as to what decisions were left for the final report. The MBTA had emerged with its master plan, the DPW had already submitted its post-1972 state highway proposals to the Bureau of Public Roads, and the MAPC was about to publish a study calling for a second major airport in metropolitan Boston. This would imply that the final project transportation plan was a validating instrument rather than a plan in any real sense of the word.

In conclusion, the Boston project presents a classic case study of the problems in interagency planning. After much painful maneuvering, the project was reorganized and slowly ground its way toward completion. It took almost seven years to complete a project that was originally scheduled for two and a half years. The big question in Boston, as in most other regional transportation planning projects, is whether the project recommendations will bear any meaningful relationship to regional development decisions.

Study Area Profile

The nine-county Penn-Jersey Transportation Study area covered five counties in southeastern Pennsylvania (Chester, Delaware, Philadelphia, Montgomery, and Bucks) and four southwestern counties in New Jersey (Gloucester, Camden, Burlington, and Mercer), an area of about 3,800 square miles. However, the highly urbanized central portion of the nine counties included only about 1,200 square miles, or a little less than one-third of the total.

The planning region is located approximately midway between the New York and Baltimore-Washington metropolitan areas. Its strategic location at the confluence of the Schuylkill and Delaware rivers, at the head of the navigable Delaware estuary, provides the site for a major industrial and commercial center. It occupies a position close to the center of the East Coast megalopolis and is highly accessible by established transportation routes, including Routes U.S. 1 and I-95, the major East Coast north-south highways. In addition, the Pennsylvania Turnpike, the eastern end of which starts in the region, provides a direct route to the Middle West. Philadelphia is also a focus for rail activity in the Middle Atlantic states, partly because of its importance as a deep-water port. Access to the Penn-Jersey area by air, on the other hand, is less fully developed because of the availability of massive terminal and transfer facilities at nearby New York airports and the continued availability of good rail service to both New York and Washington. In terms of downtown-to-downtown travel time, the railroad schedules from Philadelphia to New York and Washington are competitive with airline travel times.

A dredged channel permits large ocean-going ships to travel the hundred miles from the Atlantic Ocean and dock at Philadelphia on the west or Camden on the east bank of the Delaware River. Although the total tonnage of cargo handled is roughly one-half that of the port of New York, Philadelphia is still the second largest port in the nation. However, the volume of more lucrative passenger and general cargo activities is only a fraction of that of the port of New York. This differential is reflected in the average tonnage values, which are roughly 15 percent of the New York level.[1]

The pattern of activity at the port lends support to oft-repeated claims that Philadelphia's close proximity—ninety miles—to the giant New York metropolis has tended to stunt or perhaps deform economic and cultural growth patterns. Since 1890, however, Philadelphia has kept pace with New York in population growth; the ratio has not widened over the years, remaining at about 1:2.5.

[1] U.S., Army, Corps of Engineers, *Waterborne Commerce of the United States* (Washington, D.C.: Government Printing Office, 1967).

The range of manufacturing activity in the region has been virtually unlimited because of the excellent accessibility to coal, cement, and steel. More than half of the region's manufacturing employment is located outside Philadelphia County (which is coterminous with the city) in the outlying medium-sized and smaller towns, especially in the Delaware and Schuylkill valleys. The region's dependence on industry is reflected in the fact that slightly more than one-third of the labor force is employed in manufacturing. In contrast, in metropolitan New York and Boston this figure is about one-quarter, and in the heavily industrialized Buffalo area the ratio is one-half.

Philadelphia, like most metropolitan centers, has developed a growing emphasis on finance, retail and wholesale trade, and professional and business services. An unusual development has been the establishment of a large nucleus of federal and regional headquarters. The city contains the regional offices of the Department of Housing and Urban Development (HUD) for the Middle Atlantic states; it is also the center of a district for the Federal Reserve Bank, the Census Bureau, and the Interstate Commerce Commission, among others. Medical facilities, universities, insurance, and banking industries accord the region a central position in the Middle Atlantic states.

At the outset of the Penn-Jersey study, the population of the region was 4.6 million, 2.6 percent of the United States total (1960). The region's percentage of the nation's population remained unchanged between 1940 and 1960, indicating a population growth rate for the region paralleling that of the nation as a whole. Moreover, the growth rate in metropolitan Philadelphia between 1960 and 1965 was 7.4 percent, which suggests that growth during the whole 1960 decade was not appreciably lower than in the 1950s.

It is also apparent that the primary source of population expansion has been the surplus of births over deaths rather than inmigration. In the 1940–1950 decade approximately two-thirds of the increase in the region's population growth resulted from natural increase and the remaining one-third from net inmigration. By the 1950–1960 decade, net inmigration accounted for only one-fifth of the region's total gain, a pattern that appears to have held true for the 1960s.

The population of the region as a whole grew by 18 percent between 1950 and 1960, but the central city of Philadelphia decreased by 3 percent, manifesting a trend common to many urban regions. Between 1950 and 1960 the cities of Trenton, Camden, and Philadelphia (excluding the northeast section of the city) lost 7.5 percent of their populations. Thus nearly half of the loss during the past thirty years occurred during the 1950s. The region's smallest cities grew by a little over 8 percent during the same period, while suburban areas grew by nearly 150 percent. This pattern appears to have continued in the 1960–1970 decade.

The most densely settled portion of the region, including the city of Philadelphia (which is also the oldest portion of the region), lies north of the confluence of the Schuylkill and Delaware rivers. The central city of Philadelphia, with a population of 2,000,000 in 1960, accounted for 45 percent of the region's population. As is the pattern in most urban areas, growth of the nonwhite population of the region was concentrated almost entirely in slum neighborhoods in the central city. In 1960, approximately 25 percent of the population of the city of Philadelphia was black. By 1965, this figure was 29 percent.

In the face of a long-term decline in the growth rate of manufacturing employment and in the share of manufacturing activity, the economic vitality of the central city, and indeed the future of public transportation, is closely linked to continuing strength in nonmanufacturing activities. As in other metropolitan regions, the high retail employment densities, as well as the largest concentrations of office employment, are found in the central business district. Despite population losses, the central city has retained its importance as an office and retail center, although it has suffered in relation to other parts of the region. A study conducted in 1967 shows that in a one-month period only 23 percent of the region's families shopped in the downtown area.[2]

Reflecting the effects of suburbanization, Philadelphia's share of regional employment has been steadily declining. In 1940, 69 percent of southeastern Pennsylvania's employment was in Philadelphia; by 1950 the figure had dropped to 58 percent, and by 1960 the city accounted for only 48 percent of the region's jobs.[3]

Less than 20 percent of the land in the entire study area was in urban use in 1960,[4] yet urbanization of the region had been proceeding at a rapid pace. During the fifteen-year period between 1945 and 1960, over 100,000 acres of land were developed—75,000 for residential development and 30,000 for nonresidential purposes.[5] This change reflects a redistribution of population

[2] W. R. Simmons and Associates Research, Inc., *Philadelphia Market Newspaper Profile: Sunday Newspaper,* 1967 edition (Philadelphia: Philadelphia Bulletin Co., 1967), p. 155.
[3] Charles E. Gilbert, *Governing the Suburbs* (Bloomington: Indiana University Press, 1967), p. 24.
[4] Grace Milgrim, *The City Expands* (Philadelphia: University of Pennsylvania, Institute for Environmental Studies, 1967), p. 25.
[5] Penn-Jersey Transportation Study, vol. 1, *The State of the Region* (Philadelphia, 1964), p. 7.

within the region, the provision of necessary commercial and community facilities for the growing suburban shopping centers, and some small expansion of manufacturing activity (intensive manufacturing and office employment have not, in general, displayed much tendency to decentralize).

Despite the high rate of development, there is still a considerable amount of nonurbanized land. In 1960 over 500 of the 1,200 square miles within the central portion of the region was still classified as nonurban. In the areas more distant from Philadelphia, conversion of land for urban purposes has proceeded at a much slower rate. As in most metropolitan areas, the percentage of land in urban use varies widely within the region. In 1960, 90 percent of the land within the Philadelphia city line was developed, but only 7 percent of the land in Burlington County, New Jersey, at the eastern end of the study area was in urban use at that time.

The Delaware River is both physically and politically a major dividing line of the region. Politically, it separates the states of Pennsylvania and New Jersey. Because of its great width, it is spanned by relatively few bridges. There are two bridges at the core of the region between Philadelphia and Camden; another one about eight miles to the north; the Bristol-Burlington span of the Pennsylvania Turnpike, which crosses the river south of Levittown; two bridges at Trenton; and no bridges south of downtown Philadelphia. All require a toll, a factor that no doubt reduces interstate trips in the region. Although most of the region's large cities lie on the Delaware, development within the region has not shown any significant propensity to locate along the river as, for example, in the Buffalo area. Rather, most of the development seems to have occurred radially from the central Philadelphia-Camden core. Trenton, at the northern end of the Penn-Jersey study region, is separated from Philadelphia by comparatively undeveloped land. However, south of Philadelphia, outside of the study region, development has reached its greatest intensity along the river. This exception to the overall regional development pattern can be attributed to the fact that the Delaware River is open to ocean-going vessels at this point and offers opportunities for the expansion of low-cost marine facilities.

One of the most striking land-use changes since World War II has been the development of the northeast corner of the region in the vicinity of Trenton, New Jersey, and Levittown, Pennsylvania. In 1950 the United States Steel Company located their Fairless Works, a large manufacturing component, in this area, about twenty-five miles from downtown Philadelphia. Although it is impossible within the scope of this study to speculate on the reasons for this choice, it does not appear that transportation linkages to Philadelphia were a significant determining factor. The nucleus of commercial and industrial development in this area was the strip development along Route 1 between Trenton and Philadelphia, but even in 1950 that route did not present a particularly attractive transportation facility. Moreover, the railroad connections to Philadelphia from this area are only fair. Most Levittown residents work nearby, relatively few commute to work in Philadelphia, and the same pattern is likely for the residents of other towns in the area.

On the average 1960 weekday, over 8 million person trips were made in the Penn-Jersey study area. Except for Philadelphia-Camden, only Trenton with a population of 119,000 can be classified as a major focus of travel. Most of the other cities in the region have travel patterns that are distinctly related to downtown Philadelphia. The area has the most elaborate public transportation system of any of the five study areas in this volume. However, only 16.5 percent of all trips were made on public transportation in 1962. Of this total, 10.4 percent consisted of bus and trolley passengers, 5.0 percent represented subway and other rail rapid-transit passengers, and only 1.1 percent were railroad passengers. This public transportation figure of 16.5 percent compares to about 7.5 percent for the Buffalo area, approximately 14 percent for the Boston area (exclusive of school bus trips), and less than 5 percent in the Manchester and Portland areas.

Despite the heavy reliance on public transportation and the sharp decline in ridership following World War II (Philadelphia patronage declined by 41 percent between 1946 and 1960), the Penn-Jersey study was not perceived as an emergency program aimed at saving public transit. Unlike Boston, where the Boston Regional Planning Project received its impetus from the threatened discontinuance of railroad commuter service, the Penn-Jersey study adopted a rather leisurely research approach to the broad problem of urban transportation.

As might be expected, public transportation plays its most significant role in travel to and from Philadelphia. For travel to the central part of Philadelphia (the area bounded by Vine Street, the Delaware River, South Street, and the Schuylkill River), a greater number of persons used mass transportation than automobiles in 1962.

Maintenance of high employment levels in the core of Philadelphia has resulted in a continuing major reliance on public transportation.[6] So has the large low-income black population located near public transportation routes. On an average weekday about 60 percent of all travelers to this area used

[6] Delaware Valley Regional Planning Commission, *1985 Regional Projection for the Delaware Valley,* Plan Report no. 1 (Philadelphia, 1967). The *Philadelphia Market Newspaper Profile: Sunday Newspaper,* 1962 edition (Philadelphia: Philadelphia Bulletin Co., 1962), showed that 27 percent of the region's (8 counties) workers used public transportation to get to work.

some form of public transportation. Once outside the area, however, the percentage dropped drastically, perhaps as a result of a sharp reduction in available service. Only 6 percent of all trips in the Pennsylvania counties outside Philadelphia were made on any form of public transportation, and in the New Jersey suburban counties the comparable figure was 4 percent. In the city of Camden, 17 percent of all trips to the central city were by public transportation, and in Trenton the comparable figure was 7 percent. Public transportation usage into downtown Philadelphia is high for all trip purposes, perhaps because of the availability of an extensive and at the same time low-fare public transportation system. This distinction may also be related to the fact that the highway system within the region lacks any discernible pattern and is clearly not yet integrated. Unlike the Boston area with its distinctive circumferentials and radials, or Buffalo with the clear outline of an existing and projected circumferential and radial highway network, Philadelphia's highway pattern shows no such order. Except for the Pennsylvania Turnpike and the New Jersey Turnpike, neither of which is of critical significance to the region's densely developed core, only one high-capacity road, the Schuylkill Expressway, ties together the major developed portions of the region. It extends from the southern part of Camden, across the Delaware River, along the southern and western edges of the central portion of Philadelphia, and leads generally in a northeast direction, eventually interchanging with the Pennsylvania Turnpike. This route does connect the two turnpike facilities and provides access to at least the periphery of the central city. One major highway proposal being considered faces many difficulties because it must pass through a densely developed part of the city, although it presumably would provide the central city with some east-west expressway service. Continued high usage and the availability of a rather extensive public transportation system may account for the relatively slow development of expressways in the Philadelphia region compared with other regions. Between 1946 and 1960 Boston's public transportation patronage declined by over 55 percent, but Philadelphia's declined by only 41 percent. In 1960 there were 160 miles of turnpike and expressway in operation in the Philadelphia region, compared with approximately 350 miles in the Boston region, where the population was a third smaller.

Few streets in the central city permit operating speeds of over twenty miles per hour or even continuous movement. Outside the central city, however, higher speeds are attainable on most of the region's important highways. Traffic volumes on major highways do not generally exceed 15,000–20,000 vehicles per day. Exceptions to this are the toll turnpikes, the southeast-northwest Schuylkill Expressway, and small portions of other important routes where volumes may be two or three times as great.

Despite what appears to be a low-mileage highway system in the region, the volume-capacity ratio of the principal highways in 1960 showed an interesting pattern.[7] Within the central city several small nodes of business activity, most of which were located on the north-south axis, were shown as being congested. For the most part, all of the east-west connectors were in the no-delay to minimum-delay range. On the periphery of the region, a few roads were shown as congested or very congested. In an intermediate area located about three to six miles outside the city, the radial and circumferential routes displayed noticeable trends toward congestion. This pattern existed on both the Philadelphia and the Camden sides of the Delaware River. The city of Camden, located about three miles from the center of Philadelphia, appears to be caught in this intermediate area of congestion.

Although this chapter does not permit a detailed evaluation of the technical aspects of the Penn-Jersey study, it is interesting to compare the volume-capacity ratio pattern of highways with public transportation usage in the region. Much of the public transportation usage is by core-area residents traveling within the core area. The band of highway congestion three to six miles from the city may in fact be protecting the central area from even more serious transportation problems.

One problem facing public transportation in the study area is the lack of connection between the various railroads, in particular, the Pennsylvania Railroad and the Reading Railroad, the two major commuter lines into Philadelphia. Both lines have separate central-city terminals located about a half-mile apart. Renewal plans for Philadelphia include a consolidation of these terminals, with the expectation that this will result in greater utilization of commuter service. Significant economies are also expected as the two "dead-end" stations are consolidated into one "through" station, enabling trains to be routed directly through the city on a continuous track.

Project Chronology

Perhaps the official birth of the Penn-Jersey study can be pinpointed to September 1957, when the Program Planning Committee, an informal group set up by the Pennsylvania Department of Highways, submitted to the Organizing Committee a report whose stated objective was "to establish a transportation planning process."[8] The report provided the basis for the initial prospectus, which furnished the Penn-Jersey study with an outline of the

[7] Penn-Jersey Transportation Study, *State of the Region,* map 51, p. 114.
[8] "Report of Program Planning Committee to Organizing Committee for meeting September 12, 1957," in Penn-Jersey Transportation Study, *Prospectus* (Philadelphia, December 11, 1959), p. A-7.

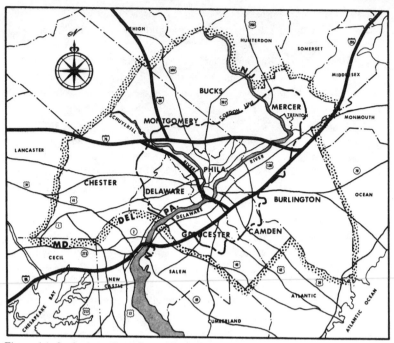

Figure 6.1. Study Area: Penn-Jersey Transportation Study

work to be undertaken and a detailed financial statement, including the anticipated sources of project funds. (The prospectus was updated in October
1962 and again in November 1963. These documents served as guides for the
project until 1964.) This report consisted primarily of a general statement of
technical methods. The study outline contained provisions for a broad land-
use analysis and socioeconomic planning, even though all members of the
Program Planning Committee were road engineers. (Six of the nine committee members were employees of the Federal Bureau of Public Roads [BPR]
or the two state highway departments.)[9]

Although not clearly enunciated, many of the policies that have now become standard in area planning and transportation planning were delineated in this initial report. The establishment of a continuing study and planning process, the representation of sponsoring agencies on committees to
determine organizational and operational policies, and the participation of
local planning professionals in the study were just beginning to emerge in
the late 1950s as firm criteria for area transportation studies.

[9] Ibid., p. A–12.

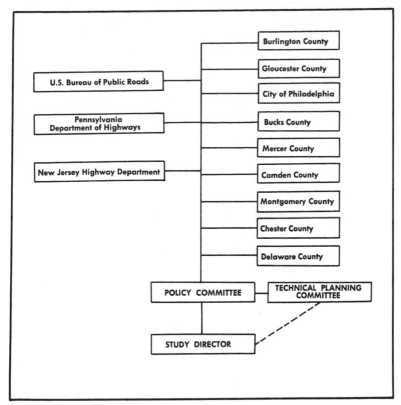

Figure 6.2. Study Organization: Penn-Jersey Transportation Study

The Penn-Jersey study was undoubtedly the most ambitious transportation study ever undertaken up to that time. It spanned the gap between the studies of the 1950s, such as the Chicago Area Transportation Study (CATS), and the area transportation studies of the early 1960s. The latter have taken advantage of recent computer advances and have been geared to producing transportation plans to comply with federal regulations rather than dramatic advances in research.

The study development represented a fortuitous convergence of local and federal interests. The traffic and transportation board of the city of Philadelphia and faculty from the University of Pennsylvania were responsible for originating the initial recommendations for the study. At the same time, the Bureau of Public Roads, encouraged by the results of earlier research-oriented transportation studies like CATS, was seeking important new in-

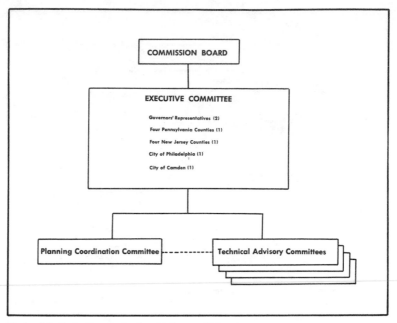

COMMISSION BOARD

EXECUTIVE COMMITTEE

Governors' Representatives (2)

Four Pennsylvania Counties (1)

Four New Jersey Counties (1)

City of Philadelphia (1)

City of Camden (1)

Planning Coordination Committee - - - - - - - - - - Technical Advisory Committees

Figure 6.3. Study Reorganization: Delaware Valley Regional Planning Commission

formation. Using Penn-Jersey as a laboratory, the BPR hoped to develop a universal formula whereby future transportation demand for urban areas could be forecast at a small fraction of the cost of normal prediction procedures. With BPR backing, the Pennsylvania Department of Highways served as the prime mover in organizing the study, providing the necessary financial assistance, and formulating the initial administrative machinery necessary to get the project started. New Jersey, partly because only about 20 percent of the study area was located within its borders, was very much the junior partner, responding to the initiatives of the Bureau of Public Roads and the Pennsylvania Department of Highways.

A formal agreement establishing the Penn-Jersey Transportation Study was signed by the BPR and the participating states and counties in January 1959. The study was to be broad and comprehensive, in transportation terms, and was designed to take advantage of the 1.5 percent federal and state highway funds available for highway planning and research. The $2.5 million study was financed principally by the Bureau of Public Roads, then in the U.S. Department of Commerce, and the Pennsylvania and New Jersey highway departments. Some local funds, which might be considered token contribu-

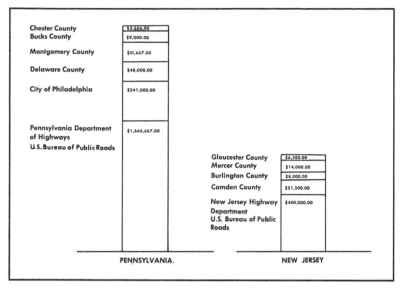

Figure 6.4. Initial Funding of the Penn-Jersey Transportation Study

tions demonstrating sincere interest, were also obtained for the first three-year period from the region's counties. A total of twelve government agencies at all levels were specified in the agreement establishing the study, and the cost was to be shared among them according to a detailed formula specified in the agreement. Local financial participation in area transportation studies, aside from reducing the federal and state shares, was recognized as a key to obtaining interested local involvement in the study process.

The purpose of the study was to

help the nine-county metropolitan region to develop a transportation system adequate for moving its people and goods. The immediate objectives of the Study are to develop a plan and program for the staged development of transportation facilities to serve the evolving area and to recommend some form of continuing agency to carry on after the initial study period has ended.[10]

However, soon after the study began, these very objective and specific goals seemed to lose their urgency as technical aspects posed more challenges to a research-minded staff. Many of the delays encountered resulted from the emphasis on techniques rather than plans, since methods already developed elsewhere could have been adopted to produce a transportation plan.

It was not until the summer of 1959 that the substantive work of the study began. By this time, sufficient staff, including several with experience in

[10] Ibid., p. 1.

CATS and the Detroit study, had been assembled, and the planning of technical operations could get under way. The first task was to prepare a prospectus incorporating a detailed design of the work and a schedule. This step was completed by the end of 1959. The stated objectives of the study appeared to be wholly pragmatic. It was to use the data collected to develop alternative regional transportation proposals and to test alternatives to produce final recommendations. There was a brief outline of the various models to be used for achieving study goals, but this was followed by the significant statement that "the regional growth model is an indispensable element of the study because its operation is essential to yield inputs for the traffic model."[11] Thus the creation of a new growth model was made the key prerequisite for substantive planning.

Although implied rather than clearly stated, the prospectus contained provisions for an elaborate research effort that had to prove successful before any recommendations or projections could be made. This attempt to create a viable regional growth model was to delay the project well over two years and was to be the element most disruptive to the technical procedures and administrative organization of the study.

Most of the data collection for the Penn-Jersey study was performed in 1960 and was completed by the end of 1961. Since two years had already expired since the initiation of the study in 1959, it was generally agreed that the initial three-year deadline could not be met but that the study would be completed by the end of 1963. By the end of 1962 the data were partially collated. Still to be designed was the model to be used to allocate regional growth and provide a basis for projecting transportation needs. A year later, when the 1963–64 prospectus supplement was issued,[12] the model had still not been completed. Another revision in the schedule was made, proposing a revised work program separating the development of the transportation plan into two stages: one for 1975 and another for 1985. The November 1963 prospectus anticipated that the transportation plan for 1975 would be completed by the end of 1963 and that a final report, prior to making the transition to a continuing agency, would be available by the middle of 1964. By this time, the Penn-Jersey study had become a five-year project, and the estimated cost had risen from $2.5 million to $5 million, from an originally estimated 60 cents to $1.20 per capita.

Each time the Penn-Jersey schedule was revised, the completion date was estimated at not more than a year away. These estimates were obviously

[11] Ibid., p. 13.
[12] Penn-Jersey Transportation Study, *Prospectus Supplement, 1963–64* (Philadelphia, November 1963), p. 2.

optimistic, since key elements of the study considered essential to its conclusion had not yet been prepared. The rather sanguine estimates may have been related to pressures from federal officials. The tendency to underestimate completion dates was nurtured by federal officials; they not only accepted such estimates but often requested reductions in schedules because they were impatient with the lack of correlation between expenditures and results.

One serious delay in the Penn-Jersey study arose because the Bureau of Public Roads insisted that the percentage of home interviews be doubled over the level originally planned for. Aside from the problems and costs of mounting a much larger home-interview survey, the increase in data began to clog the computers and to cause a variety of related data-processing problems. By 1963, computer problems were disrupting the schedule rather seriously. It often took from six weeks to six months to get Electronic Accounting Machine (EAM) material processed through the system. By today's standards the data-processing techniques of this period were fairly primitive. Moreover, they were not totally adaptable to the requirements of transportation planners. In 1964 the problem was resolved when the staff finally received permission to obtain direct access to a computer with a much greater capacity.

During 1964 a number of salary and administrative problems plagued the project. It was extremely difficult to hire staff because of the low salary levels, which were pegged to the state highway department rates. Moreover, there was a general shortage of specialized personnel, such as programmers and data analysts, because of the enormous demand in private industry. Another complication involved benefits for staff employees. Since some staffers were members of the Pennsylvania Department of Highways and others were officially members of the New Jersey Highway Department, there were variations in fringe benefits, such as per diem travel allowances and paid vacations. In an attempt to solve some of these complications, staff personnel were transferred from one bookkeeping system to another, but such problems persisted through most of the study and led to considerable irritations and a drain on the time of the staff.

Although consultants might have been available to perform the entire work program or to act as advisers on specific parts of the work, the emphasis in Penn-Jersey was on staff capabilities. Yet specialists in some of the more detailed technical procedures were not readily available as full-time staff members. Despite this the study administrators were not given permission to hire adequate numbers of specialists as consultants. The attempt to use the consultant approach was also, of course, a technique to detour around the antiquated state civil service laws. It was difficult for staff members to convince the state highway departments that consultant specialists might help put the study on a more successful track.

A series of reports, entitled the "Penn-Jersey Papers," were prepared by the staff as a means of disseminating the interim results of the study (a well-known technique used successfully by the often imitated CATS study). These reports documented the research results, and several won praise and professional recognition at Highway Research Board meetings in Washington, but they did not noticeably advance the study toward a transportation plan. Moreover, the reports were of no value to the various committee members because of their highly technical and theoretical content.[13]

By the fall of 1964 it was anticipated that another year would see the preparation of the 1985 traffic estimates. Not only was this a scheduled commitment but the executive director of the project had personally promised Governor Scranton that a late 1965 deadline would be met. The governor had been alerted by dissident Policy Committee members that the project was becoming bogged down in endless research, and he hoped that his interest in the project and a commitment from the staff would be sufficient pressure to assure a speedy completion of the project.

Meanwhile, state and federal officials, as well as local elected officials from both sides of the state line, were discussing the possibility of establishing a bistate regional organization for the Philadelphia area. By mid-1965 a possible organization and distribution of responsibilities had been formulated. It was also clear by this time that the Penn-Jersey study would probably not reach its December 1965 deadline. The organizers of the regional planning organization decided to take over the Penn-Jersey Transportation Study and to attempt to replace the executive director but retain most of the agency's staff as a nucleus for the new regional planning commission. The new commission would be given the responsibility for continuing and completing the transportation study.

On July 1, 1965, the Pennsylvania legislature passed a bill creating the Delaware Valley Regional Planning Commission (DVRPC) and authorized it to take over the Penn-Jersey Transportation Study on behalf of the state. Parallel action was taken by New Jersey, and this officially marked the end of the Penn-Jersey study, the duties, staff, and facilities of which were transferred to the DVRPC. Although the new commission's purpose was to "undertake continuous, comprehensive and coordinated planning for the growth and development of the region,"[14] its single initial responsibility was to

[13] See, for example, David R. Seidman, "Report on the Activities Allocation Model," Penn-Jersey Paper no. 22, November 17, 1964.
[14] Delaware Valley Regional Planning Commission, *Important Facts about the Delaware Valley Regional Planning Commission* (Philadelphia, 1967), p. 3.

complete the area transportation study. Consequently, its first financing came entirely from the highway agencies that had initiated and supported the earlier effort. (It should be noted that, following the initial funding for the three-year period, participating cities and counties terminated their financial contributions to the Penn-Jersey study.)

Although the structure of the project was changed when it was absorbed into the DVRPC, the technical emphasis on model research remained unaltered. The lack of change in direction brought into the open a conflict between the project director, supported by the Bureau of Public Roads (the chief sponsor), and disenchanted members of the new planning commission, who demanded a basic change in project leadership. Most of the controversy revolved around the eagerly awaited model, which was designed to predict future growth patterns in the region. During 1964 and 1965, faith in the executive director's capabilities was clearly fading. His promise to Governor Scranton to complete the study by the end of 1965 had not been kept. After a year and a half of constant trouble, during which time the director was subjected to scathing criticism by increasingly hostile opponents, he resigned. The personal attacks, the hectic meetings, the charges and countercharges that occurred bear a strong resemblance to the turmoil in the Boston study.

Since 1966 the regional planning commission has undergone major changes. Research efforts on the regional growth model were relaxed in favor of more traditional, less exotic techniques. As a result, a 1975 traffic estimate had been prepared by 1965,[15] and a 1985 estimate was completed in late 1968. In addition, the agency's financing has been revised. The study's supporters now include the Department of Housing and Urban Development: HUD's percentage of the total operating funds went from zero in 1966/67 to over 20 percent in 1968/69. This percentage is expected to increase even more in the future. The shift in sponsorship and financing has also been reflected in the broadened scope of the regional planning commission's efforts.

Certainly, one positive effect of the Penn-Jersey study was that it provided the nucleus of a permanent regional planning commission, the DVRPC. However, while this change may be good for other aspects of regional development, transportation planning in the Philadelphia area may not necessarily benefit to the same degree.

The beginning of the Penn-Jersey study coincided in time with the establishment of a regional organization known as the Regional Conference of Elected Officials (RCEO). The RCEO was comparable to the councils of local governments (COGs) that have been formed elsewhere. The RCEO found itself

[15] Penn-Jersey Transportation Study, vol. 3, *1975 Transportation Plans* (Philadelphia, May 1965).

underfinanced, in competition with other regional organizations, and with little control over regional development decisions.[16] Penn-Jersey staff members were associated with the RCEO operation from its inception, and this perhaps partially explains the good local relations enjoyed by the transportation project. Staff members, seeing an opportunity to proselytize, frequently attended meetings of the RCEO and used such opportunities to explain the project to local officials and gain their interest and support. In May 1968 the Delaware Valley Regional Planning Commission and the RCEO issued a statement aimed at defining the role of each organization and stressing the need for coordination between the two agencies.[17] The statement suggests, however, that the RCEO will continue to play a secondary role.

One potential complication was caused by the creation early in 1964 of the Southeastern Pennsylvania Transportation Authority (SEPTA), with its own capabilities for financing transportation projects. The DVRPC still retained as one of its functions the preparation of transportation plans, but it had no financial capability of its own, whereas SEPTA was able to float bonds for transportation projects but had no planning arm. (As of 1969, SEPTA's most significant action was the acquisition, for about $48 million, of the Philadelphia Transit Company, the local privately owned public transit company.) Conceivably, the solution to this separation of functions may lie in the operating procedure, which gives the regional planning commission review authority over capital improvements. There is, however, some question whether this review authority covers special bond issues. The situation in Penn-Jersey seems to be comparable to that in Buffalo: the responsibilities for transportation funding and programming and those for planning are not combined within the same agency. This will no doubt create difficulties in the planning and construction of new facilities, and it suggests the need for some type of marriage between agencies whose attributes and capabilities complement each other.

Project Administration

The Penn-Jersey project was the only one of the five studies covered in this research that was a bistate effort. The project area, as noted, comprised five counties in southeastern Pennsylvania and four New Jersey counties, including the cities of Camden and Trenton. Representation on the various committees was about equally divided between Pennsylvania and New Jersey, but most of the population, the urban development, and the transportation prob-

[16] See U. S., Advisory Commission on Intergovernmental Relations, *Metropolitan Councils of Government: An Information Report* (Washington, D.C.: Government Printing Office, August 1966).

[17] Delaware Valley Regional Planning Commission, *Delaware Valley Planning News*, vol. 2, no. 4 (June 1968).

lems were within the state of Pennsylvania.

The Policy Committee was the highest level authority in the conduct of the study. Reporting to it, and under its authority, was the Technical Planning Committee. This was an offshoot of the Policy Committee, with each member appointing a technical counterpart. The city of Philadelphia was the only municipality directly represented on the Policy Committee; other municipalities were indirectly represented through their counties. The committee was given the responsibility for general management, direction, and control of the study, selection of a general transportation plan and program, and establishment of an effective administrative basis for effectuating any recommendations that were to be forthcoming.[18] Unfortunately, the last two responsibilities, no doubt the most important in terms of transportation planning, were not carried out because the study never reached the point at which the Policy Committee could act on these matters.

The study's Executive Committee, which consisted of individuals who were also members of the Policy Committee, had responsibility for the administrative supervision of the study. Members of the Policy Committee who were concurrent members of the Executive Committee included representatives of the Bureau of Public Roads and one representative from each of the Pennsylvania and New Jersey counties. Also included was a representative from the city of Philadelphia.[19]

The Technical Planning Committee was established to advise the Policy Committee on technical problems and on the conduct of the study.[20] Presumably, this was the group that would alert the Policy Committee to deadlines that were not being met, technical problems that were being encountered, or major objectives that were not being reached. There was significant overlapping among the Policy, Technical, and Executive Committee members, which made for continuing harmony. For example, the New Jersey highway representative and the three BPR members of the Technical Committee were also members of either the Policy or the Executive Committee. Unlike the pattern of most later efforts, BPR personnel were genuine participating members of the various committees. In later studies, both the Bureau of Public Roads and the Department of Housing and Urban Development tended to regard their positions on these committees as ex officio in order to emphasize local responsibilities and participation and to calm local fears over federal control of the projects.

[18] American Association of State Highway Officials, Committee on Urban Transportation Planning, *Organizational Procedures of Seventeen Urban Transportation Studies* (Washington, D.C., 1963), p. 55.
[19] Ibid.
[20] Ibid.

Between 1959 and 1964, there was not much change in the administrative organization of the project. The BPR continued to have three members on the Policy Committee, and each of the nine counties and the two highway departments were similarly represented. In 1966, when the project was incorporated into the Delaware Valley Regional Planning Commission, a major change in the administrative organization of the study took place. The policy and technical committee concept was scrapped in favor of a more traditional regional planning commission, which usually combines the functions of technical and policy committees and often excludes federal and state officials as key members. Another significant change was the addition of representatives from each of the large cities. Thus the eighteen-member DVRPC board includes representatives from the cities of Chester, Trenton, and Camden, as well as Philadelphia.[21] Perhaps even more important was the inclusion on the new board of members from each of the state's planning agencies. The executive director of the Pennsylvania State Planning Board and the commissioner of Community Affairs of New Jersey are both on the board, reflecting the importance placed upon the new commission by the two states. The federal participants from the BPR and the Department of Housing and Urban Development (HUD) have restricted themselves to nonvoting membership in the new regional planning commission, indicating a new policy of limited intervention by the federal agencies.

Establishment of the DVRPC required legislative action in both states before the necessary agreements could be made. Most of the problems that were encountered revolved around the bistate nature of the commission's jurisdiction. Because of political, geographical, or other clear differences, bistate efforts do not always receive the support that they might get if the area were totally within one state. Often a large urban area covers a large part of one state and only a small part of another, and the minor state is not impressed with the urgency of a particular project. In some cases the regional planning agency covering the area prefers to remain aloof. In Penn-Jersey, there was only the barest pressure from the New Jersey state planning agency to participate. HUD and BPR influence no doubt helps on such occasions.

For obvious reasons the New Jersey Highway Department was decidedly less interested in the study than its Pennsylvania counterpart. Although Trenton, the state capital, was included in the study area, much of the New Jersey department's activities were centered around the New York area. New Jersey is one of the most urbanized states in the union, yet planners face the complication that most of the state's urban areas are considered part of met-

[21] Delaware Valley Regional Planning Commission, *1985 Regional Projection*, p. 3. There are also three nonvoting members on the board.

ropolitan regions of New York and Pennsylvania. The large northern New Jersey cities adjacent to New York City are part of the New York metropolitan area, while its southern cities, such as Trenton and Camden, are regarded as part of the Philadelphia area. As a result, much of New Jersey's transportation planning and construction efforts relate to its position as a primary center of transportation. Bistate agreements involve an equal partnership between the states regardless of their relative financial contributions. On more than one occasion, delays were encountered in the Penn-Jersey study because of New Jersey's reluctance to participate. At one point, it even indicated that future participation in the project was doubtful.

Another impasse developed between the two states over the issue of organization. New Jersey preferred a more monolithic state organization with little citizen participation; state officials wanted to fill key positions in the new agency from the ranks of state-level agencies. Pennsylvania was interested in encouraging local participation to a much greater extent and was willing to permit the commission to operate with leadership selected from the participating communities. These differences were obviously set aside when the DVRPC was formed.

Problems with the Model

Since the land-use model was a critical factor in the Penn-Jersey project, it may be useful to review briefly the state of the art in transportation planning. During the 1950s, fairly reliable transportation planning techniques had been developed, including sophisticated trip distribution formulas and traffic assignment techniques for projections of future traffic volumes on transportation facilities.[22] For example, modal split formulas, a refinement just beginning to appear, permitted an allocation of trips to either public transportation systems or highways in those cities where there was a choice. While the concepts were easily understood, the data tabulation required a large input of man-hours for routine mechanical calculations. The introduction of computers was a logical step. The computer was a much quicker, less expensive, and certainly more glamorous replacement for the long and tedious mathematical operations. Thus early efforts aimed at using computers in transportation planning revolved around reducing manpower requirements.

Soon after this innovation, however, the fascinating possibilities of the computer began to be recognized. The opportunities for developing mathematical models that had been uncovered in the earlier transportation studies,

[22] For a discussion of planning models, see Highway Research Board, *Urban Development Models,* Special Report no. 97 (Washington, D.C., 1968), or *Urban Development Models: New Tools for Planning,* special issue, *Journal of the American Institute of Planners,* vol. 31, no. 4 (May 1965).

coupled with the vastly increased capacity and speed of the newer computers, made model building an attractive effort.

Large industrial corporations, for example, IBM and the General Electric Company, saw potential new markets for their software and spent their own funds to develop programs for the transportation planning industries. (Software is that portion of the computer industry that does not pertain directly to the design, construction, and sale of machines, including components and attachments.) The actual performance of work on a computer, such as running programs and assistance in substituting advanced computer technology for procedures still being performed more primitively, are part of the software market that industry seeks to exploit. However, problems developed with the suppliers of computer softwares when they entered the complex world of urban planning. While these companies were successful in interesting transportation planners in the new technology, the available programs and even many of those presumably designed for the urban transportation planning process bore little resemblance to the types of programs that were eventually developed or were really needed.

In the Penn-Jersey project, the period between 1962 and 1965 turned out to be a continuing battle between the proponents of the new land-use model and their opponents, including some members of the technical staff and some Policy Committee members who doubted the efficacy of such developments.

Throughout the Penn-Jersey-DVRPC history, the land-use model (now more specifically labeled the Activities Allocation Model [AAM]) always received a prominent place in formal presentations. For example, in the regional projections for 1985, the following paragraph describes the value of the AAM:

Apart from its present use as a tool in transportation planning, the Activities Allocation Model may have general application to the broader field of regional planning. The model might be viewed as a major step toward establishing a much needed scientific means for forecasting and analysis. The AAM permits the quantification of previously qualitative factors in planning, such as the reservation of large areas of land for non-urban uses or the manipulation of densities. Within the context of a comprehensive regional planning process this more scientific approach could provide a better basis for both public and private decision making.[23]

Despite this matter-of-fact statement, the same page contains an expression of concern mixed with pride:

The second consideration concerns the AAM exclusively. In assessing its adequacy to meet the needs of the transportation planning process, the AAM should be viewed as a first generation effort. While it falls short of the conceptual goals that inspired its creation, it nevertheless does qualitatively surpass all traditional land use forecast techniques. Moreover, it has met exist-

[23] Delaware Valley Regional Planning Commission, *1985 Regional Projection,* p. 4.

ing needs and affords a meaningful basis for further innovation in the field. [24]

However, the AAM has yet to be tested or fully evaluated. The creation of a universal land-use and transportation model suitable for all conditions and all places is a major objective of the Bureau of Public Roads. In the 1950s many of the transportation study budgets contained special allocations for research aimed at accomplishing BPR research objectives. Penn-Jersey came in this category. It was not unusual for BPR-financed studies to contain provisions for the collection of certain data that were to be used subsequently in studying national transportation patterns. Later studies jointly financed by HUD and the BPR were less oriented toward long-range research and were more directed toward local problem solving. Although time-consuming delays were encountered with the model, BPR officials felt that the experiment was well worth the continuing investment. On one occasion, a representative indicated that the research for the model seemed to have made very great progress; consequently, the BPR consistently supported the project director, a strong proponent of continued model research. When the BPR accepted the final report of the outgoing Penn-Jersey project with the model still unfinished, it was considerate enough to reward the director with a letter of commendation for his work in furthering the land-use model and the use of computers in transportation planning. It must be conceded that for the Bureau of Public Roads the stakes were quite high, and it was obviously willing to experiment in Penn-Jersey. If the study had indeed developed a universal model, the ultimate savings in transportation planning studies would have been in the tens of millions of dollars.

By mid-1965, when the Penn-Jersey staff was attempting to tie down the Activities Allocation Model, a number of alternative types of models for the region were being considered. These alternatives were based on a variety of assumptions, such as residential development and separate distributions of manufacturing jobs, and were somehow to be integrated in a general land-consumption model. This model would have provided an indication of where new growth would occur in the region, together with a certain amount of detail about the type of growth to be expected. The problem that was never solved, however, was how to coordinate the different models. For example, the allocation activity forecasts for commercial, residential, and industrial uses proved difficult to synchronize. Compounding the problem of model coordination was the massive amount of data manipulation that was required.

An Activities Allocation Model was completed in 1966 by the DVRPC staff. However, despite the amount of money spent on research in the study, much

[24] Ibid.

of it directed toward the development of this model, work on the project since 1966, including estimates of trips to future transportation networks, does not utilize the AAM. Most of the additional data collection and the DVRPC work have utilized earlier techniques that are much less sophisticated than those developed in Penn-Jersey. It is possible that the AAM, which has not been tested in a large urban area, will have little use anywhere. It is probably much too complicated for smaller urban areas, although it could just conceivably be used in areas the size of Penn-Jersey. In Pittsburgh, Pennsylvania's other large metropolitan area, use is being made of a model developed by the Upstate New York Transportation Study organization. It may be noted that proponents of the Penn-Jersey model now feel that it can be made to work if less data are stored and newer computers with greater storage capacity are used.

Aside from the real problems involved in model building, there is the basic question of accuracy once the equations are derived. Technicians are quick to refer to a model as an "approximation," a "caricature," a "generalization," or some other euphemistic description. However, these guarded synonyms are, in fact, caveats often ignored by those closest to the actual work. Only when the model's accuracy and value are questioned are these descriptions used. One expert on the subject is quite candid:

I have deliberately avoided the question probably of most immediate interest to my readers: How well does each model work? I have avoided this question because I don't know the answers in each case and have little hope of finding them. The authors of the San Francisco model say bluntly, "The accuracy of the Model (s forecasts) cannot be determined with presently available data." This statement would apply with little qualification to the other six models reviewed.[25]

What happened in Penn-Jersey provides a lesson for government in general. At some point, a decision has to be made either to abandon an idea, admit defeat, and carry on with already demonstrated procedures or to continue the experimental program ad infinitum with the hope of a successful conclusion. The decision is complicated because there is usually a minority of true believers who have an emotional investment in the program and are totally unwilling to accept major changes in direction; rather than accept such changes, they are prepared to resign. The administrator, therefore, has a difficult time determining whether there is any hope for the program or whether it is propitious to eliminate it. Unfortunately, the administrator's advisers are often the program's proponents. When this happens the resolution of the dilemma must await the decision of a higher executive authority.

[25] Ira S. Lowry, "Seven Models of Urban Development: A Structural Comparison," in Highway Research Board, *Urban Development Models*, p. 145.

The Computer, Again

In most of the transportation studies, serious delays in completing the research work could be attributed to unanticipated problems with the computer. In the Niagara and Penn-Jersey studies, both of which were conducted in the early 1960s, the staffs seemed to have had more than their share of computer problems—at least a two-year delay in both studies can be attributed to this factor. In Boston the problems with other aspects of the study were so great that the computer never became an issue. In the two smaller studies, Manchester and Portland, rather simple programs and procedures were followed, so that few problems were encountered.

Computer difficulties in the Penn-Jersey study stemmed from two sources: the standard problem of computer technology in which the programmers and the individuals operating the computers make mistakes, and the simple continuous transfer of data from one type of storage to another to permit use of the latest computer models. Data that were originally put on punched cards were subsequently converted to tapes and then, in some cases, reconverted or transferred to tapes with higher capacity.

These problems were magnified in Penn-Jersey because the emphasis in the early part of the study was on Electronic Accounting Machines, which were generally slower and less sophisticated than other machines that were beginning to appear at this time. The project was also collecting enormous amounts of data and eventually began to suffer from data constipation.

In the early stages of the project, the Penn-Jersey staff requested permission to obtain direct access to a computer rather than work through the Pennsylvania Department of Highways. However, the Department of Highways, the major sponsor of this study, refused, apparently for two reasons: its general reluctance to increase the cost of its contracts (as a general rule of thumb, new computers are more expensive), and its desire to consolidate computer operations at the state capital in Harrisburg. In the interests of efficiency and economy, Penn-Jersey could utilize the computer at this central location. However, the Penn-Jersey's computer needs would have amounted to half the total capacity of the Harrisburg operation. By the end of the first three-year period, Penn-Jersey did get permission to use its own computer, which then enabled the staff to begin constructive work on the development of the model.

Perhaps the greatest effect of the modern high-speed computer on the Penn-Jersey study was the temptation it offered the staff to embark upon the development of models that, for all practical purposes, were either too complicated to manage or too unrealistic. As noted, computers were initially utilized in transportation studies to save time, money, and labor; however, as the capacity of the machines increased, the planners began to realize the possibilities of undertaking more detailed analyses that should, presumably, have increased costs only slightly. Unfortunately, use of the computer was comparable in many cases to the first drink for an alcoholic.

It is apparent that the computer problems of the Penn-Jersey study were further complicated by the massive amount of data collected for the study. For example, the increase in sample size did not make the development of a model more difficult but it did increase computer requirements. In addition, the Pennsylvania Department of Highways, in an effort to save money, had the Penn-Jersey study staff develop data on traffic volumes for the ramps of proposed interchanges as well as for the main portion of the transportation network. It was reasoned that it would be less expensive to do everything at once than to proceed sequentially. This decision made the work load enormously complicated because of the great increase in the volume of data; the staff, at that time, was still using EAM techniques and did not have the capabilities of the faster computers.

In a period when computer technology was sweeping like wildfire through other sectors of engineering, a great reliance on computers and their technology was considered essential in transportation planning. It was recognized as a research tool of the highest order, but its limitations were sometimes overlooked. The planners suffered from the basic human fault of respecting the unknown and being afraid to fall behind technologically.

As an outcome of this emphasis, individuals who had mastered the early techniques of computer applications in transportation studies were in extremely high demand and, literally, toured the country with their skills. Technicians who had had experience with the machines but were limited in their transportation experience were able to move into key positions. At the same time, others who understood the working of the participating agencies and had had experience in transportation planning but were unable, for one reason or another, to utilize or adapt themselves to the computer found themselves in secondary positions. The transportation expert who was capable both of conducting an efficient transportation study and of understanding the intricacies of computer application was indeed a rare commodity. Many of the people who were to become important transportation planners came from among the ranks of those who tended to place strong emphasis on the computer. As a result the area transportation studies served as guinea pigs: they provided the first applications on a regional basis of computers to large-scale planning.

It is safe to say that the reports of the transportation studies of the early and mid-1960s were for the most part unreadable by the average person and even by the average engineer. The terminology was new, confusing, and highly specialized. Even in conversations among transportation planning technicians, the arbitrary and often misleading definitions continually disrupted communication. Because of the peculiarities of certain types of transportation formulas, such as the gravity model, the words "trip attraction," "trip production," and "traffic generation" have meanings that are specific, not generic. For example, in certain models, the average household considered by many to be a traffic generator is instead considered partly a traffic producer and partly a traffic attraction.

Problems of communication and terminology were indicative of the deteriorating situation in the software component of the transportation study's computer input. The computer industry grew so rapidly during the early transportation studies that it was difficult for one individual to become totally familiar with any particular program. What were once characterized as simple operations became nightmares of errors, oversights, misplaced data, and a variety of small mistakes that one would normally expect to avoid in an orderly scientific endeavor. For example, tapes were erased in error and other tapes were misplaced, never to be found. The accumulation of simple mechanical errors resulted in a loss of time and money, leading to setbacks for the projects.

Recent literature in planning appears to be more conservative in its appraisal of computers and, in particular, of their use in model making. Earlier articles exhorted the reader to use computers and generally implied that the road to better planning was paved with magnetic tape. More recent evaluations, however, also warn the reader about pitfalls and suggest a cautious and prudent approach. Partly because of past computer problems and partly because of a new qualitative approach, transportation planners are placing more stock in their own judgments. As a result, computers are correctly coming to be used as planning tools rather than as decision-making machines.

Effect of HHFA Nonparticipation

HHFA was minimally involved in the Penn-Jersey study, since none of its money was invested in the project. At the same time the comprehensiveness of the Penn-Jersey study (particularly its attention to land-use and other planning elements) must surely have exceeded any of HHFA's expectations. It would appear, then, that while HHFA-HUD participation in transportation studies may have stimulated more attention to land-use and other factors, the trend toward a broader perspective for transportation planning had already been established by the Bureau of Public Roads. Since the BPR has traditionally limited its concern to highways, it is perhaps surprising that in the Penn-Jersey study the BPR encouraged relatively large expenditures on questions relating to land-use and other nonhighway factors in preparation of a definitive land-use model. For a period of time, roughly between 1960 and 1963, this study probably contributed more research materials to the files of the Highway Research Board than any other operational study. The BPR, moreover, provided all of the financial support for the legally constituted Delaware Valley Regional Planning Commission which succeeded the Penn-Jersey project and which undertook a substantial program of planning in addition to completing the transportation study. Only since 1967 have HUD funds been made available for the Penn-Jersey regional planning effort. It is apparent that the BPR did not always need HUD prodding to broaden the base of its transportation studies.

Despite the lack of HHFA-HUD participation, Penn-Jersey made some progress toward the federal agency's planning goals. It ensured local participation in the planning process, and it made greater use of socioeconomic factors in transportation planning. At the same time, many of the problems encountered in the Penn-Jersey study have not been avoided elsewhere in projects that have enjoyed HUD financial participation. One may ask, however, whether HHFA's participation might not have curtailed the long costly search for the perfect land-use model. Although HHFA-HUD has always wanted to see the provision of numerous land-use alternatives from which a lay group can presumably pick a winner, the agency has tended to seek pragmatic planning goals rather than to engage in research efforts with a comparatively long-term payoff. In studies in which HUD money has been specifically earmarked for identifiable work items, these have been rather routine tasks. Perhaps this has been due to its long experience with the Section 701 program, where conformance with tried and accepted techniques has been seen as proof of acceptable performance of basic planning tasks. In any case, HHFA-HUD did not appear to be interested in becoming involved in basic research for regional planning efforts.

Conclusions

The Penn-Jersey study can be reviewed most effectively in terms of three distinct time periods. The first, from 1959 to 1962, covered the initiation of the study, the collection of data, and the beginning of analysis. The objectives of this phase were clear, and the data collection did not involve major experimentation. The second period, from 1962 to 1965, was marked by a near disintegration of the project due to difficulties encountered in simple analyses and to strong differences of opinion over the use of mathematical models as a basis for projecting transportation needs. The most recent phase, which began in 1965 after the transportation study had been transformed into a regional planning effort, began as one of recuperation. Research efforts were curtailed, and the emphasis was placed on producing acceptable plans.

Special significance can be attached to the 1962–1965 period because it was characterized by sharp divisions among staff members, highway officials, and local technical and political participants over the basic objectives and rationale of the project. This period was dominated by the staff and advisers; with almost religious zeal they sought to produce a land-use model through the use of new and untried mathematical formulas. As time passed and no plan was forthcoming, this group came under increasing pressure to abandon much of the research and to use existing data and techniques. The net result was confusion, acrimony, and a significant loss of time and money. Because of this, the Penn-Jersey study had an extremely high turnover of technical personnel.

In retrospect the Penn-Jersey study may be viewed as a transitorial organism; it originated during an age of transportation research and was completely transformed in the subsequent period of "action planning." A major lesson learned from the project was the utility of the policy and technical committees. This concept was new in 1959 and has become a standard arrangement for transportation studies. Its usefulness, however, varies greatly and depends upon the local participants.

Although the Penn-Jersey study area involved both Region I (New England, New York, and New Jersey) and Region II (Middle Atlantic states, including Pennsylvania) of the Bureau of Public Roads, this did not cause any problems. BPR policy, particularly in regard to the area transportation studies, was set in Washington. Individual regional representatives did not face the coordination problems that the separate state highway departments had to overcome.

The general merits of local participation in area transportation planning are discussed elsewhere. In Penn-Jersey, local participation appears to have been more effective than in other instances. The original organization was never, of course, faced with the task of evaluating, supporting, or presenting final or tentative transportation plans and alternatives. Yet the organization of the project changed little during its entire lifetime from 1959 to 1965, which attests to the viability of its administrative structure.

While the scope of Penn-Jersey's work was more comprehensive than that of earlier transportation studies, it began in concept as a straightforward transportation planning effort and was not specifically oriented toward other regional planning and development problems. It is significant, however, that the top technical position in the Penn-Jersey study, that of executive director, was continuously filled by a planner rather than by a highway engineer. This may explain why the Penn-Jersey project could eventually be so readily absorbed into a regional planning agency.

Some of Penn-Jersey's many problems stemmed from its massiveness. Within a few short months after the project got under way, the staff totaled nearly 700 persons. Such rapid growth, together with the strains of a research process that had not yet been standardized, created numerous difficulties in the project's early stages.

Other problems came to the surface because the study was conducted by a staff located a hundred miles from the Pennsylvania Department of Highways headquarters. Early experience with the Penn-Jersey project showed how unsatisfactory this arrangement was to the highway department. The double standards that quickly developed between the headquarters staff and the study staff caused concern among staff officials in Harrisburg and study staff in Philadelphia. In Philadelphia, study officials were concerned over the need to attract and retain skilled persons who under normal conditions would not go to work for the Department of Highways, with its reputation for low wages and lack of mission.

The Penn-Jersey study overcame the major problem that afflicted it during its data-collection and model-building phases, and it has now officially entered the "continuing" phase. The road behind is strewn with abandoned research, unmet commitments, and a few broken spirits. Undoubtedly one of the most ambitious programs undertaken in its field, Penn-Jersey became sidetracked in its effort to produce a transportation plan for the Philadelphia region. Its chief failure was its fruitless attempt to develop a pioneering land-use model. This proved to be extremely harmful to the primary objective. Certain features of the study, however, were demonstrated to be sound. For example, the administrative structure lasted throughout the project until it was converted into a regional planning agency, and this structure was utilized in later studies. The project has also provided lessons: since the Penn-Jersey study, the BPR and HUD have shown a greater propensity to keep their eyes on the ball by attempting to separate research and plan-producing functions. As one federal official has noted, if a project does not fulfill its objectives it becomes an "educational experience." In this sense, Penn-Jersey provided the equivalent of a Ph.D.

Study Area Profile

The Niagara Frontier Transportation Study (NFTS) covers the Buffalo metropolitan area and includes Niagara and Erie counties. (The transportation survey did not actually include the total area of the two counties except for statistical purposes.) Although the Niagara Falls urban area logically covers adjacent land in Canada, the constraints of an international boundary and minimal transportation connections across the river prevented the creation of what might well have been the first bination transportation study.

In 1960 the Buffalo metropolitan area was the fourteenth largest in the United States. It consists of two urban centers, the city of Buffalo with a population of about 480,000 and the city of Niagara Falls with a population of 100,000. Less than half of the region's people live in these two cities. The remainder are spread throughout the region; however, settlement is relatively dense in the industrial belt along the Niagara River between Buffalo and Niagara Falls. A pronounced population movement from Buffalo to the outskirts has been in progress in recent years: between 1960 and 1966 the city of Buffalo itself lost more than 50,000 persons, declining from 533,000 in 1960 to 481,000 in 1966.

The Buffalo metropolitan area is one of the slowest growing urban areas in the nation, ranking fifty-second in rate of population growth between 1960 and 1966. Between 1900 and 1960, the rate of population growth for the whole Erie-Niagara area slowed to less than a third of the national rate. Outmigration is largely responsible for this decline. Since 1960, net outmigration from the region has been taking place at the rate of about 10,000 persons per year. Although year-by-year population figures for the late 1950s are not available, it is quite likely that the turning point in population growth occurred about the time of the completion of the St. Lawrence Seaway in 1957. (The seaway has had obvious negative effects upon Buffalo's economy. A drive along the waterfront reveals scores of vacant ship-handling facilities.) The area's overall population in 1950 to 1960 indicated sizable growth, so it is quite probable that the losses in the late 1950s were offset by some of the above-average gains made earlier in the decade.

Buffalo is primarily an industrial and transportation center, but most of the metropolitan region's territory consists of flat open land that is used for farming: over 60 percent of the area of Niagara County alone is devoted to agricultural production. Only 14 percent of the entire study's land area is currently devoted to urban purposes, the remainder being classified as "vacant," a classification that includes farms.

The Buffalo central business district, like most downtown areas, contains a large concentration of retail and office facilities and, to a lesser extent, wholesale and manufacturing. The office and government section of the downtown district is noticeably separate from the retail area. Recent trends show a continuing expansion of business offices in the center of the city and a decline in retail trade. Little residential development has occurred in the downtown section, particularly along the nearby waterfront. The Buffalo waterfront, one of the most seriously deteriorated portions of the region, consists of several miles of docks and piers, most of them now lying idle.

Urban growth in the Buffalo area shows a linear pattern of development, beginning at the Buffalo waterfront and the Niagara River and extending eastward. This basic pattern would normally be expected, and development over the past thirty years shows that the pattern has been maintained. However, there is a noticeable increase in urban development inland, southeast of the city of Buffalo toward Orchard Park. The Buffalo River, once thought to be a barrier to growth toward the southeast, has apparently become a minor factor.

Buffalo's strategic geographical location was a significant factor in its early rise to prominence as a major American city. Situated almost equidistant from New York City, Boston, Philadelphia, and Chicago, it was a natural junction point for rail, water, and highway transportation. During the railroad boom of the mid-1800s the city became a major focal point of eastern rail lines. Its role as the easternmost port on the Great Lakes shipping routes further added to its importance. During the mid-1950s the port of Buffalo handled approximately 19 million tons of cargo annually, thereby ranking first in value of commerce handled among the inland ports. In terms of volume, Buffalo was comparable to Boston, which handled about 20 million tons of cargo each year. Completion of the St. Lawrence Seaway in 1957 began a new era of transportation for the upstate New York or "Northern Frontier" area, but it eliminated Buffalo as the major transfer point of bulk goods between the Great Lakes region and the Middle Atlantic states. Between 1955 and 1965, total receipts declined by 3 million tons, or almost 30 percent, while shipments decreased by 1.4 million tons, or almost 60 percent.[1] As a result, many of the facilities are very much underused, such as the massive transshipment facilities along the Buffalo waterfront, including numerous slips for Great Lakes barges.

Buffalo remains a leading flour milling center, partly because of its accessibility to the Great Lakes grain carriers. Another area strength is low-cost electric power. The Niagara River, which drains Lake Erie into Lake Ontario

[1] U.S., Department of Commerce, Bureau of the Census, *Statistical Abstract of the United States* (Washington, D.C.: Government Printing Office, 1967), table no. 874, p. 575.

via Niagara Falls, has been exploited on a very large scale for electric power generation. As a result, considerable industry has been attracted to the area because of the availability of low-cost electricity. There are nearly 400 manufacturing establishments in the two-county region.

Economic conditions in Buffalo have been less than ideal in recent years, and the region has yet to recover from a series of economic blows: the 1958 recession, the opening of the St. Lawrence Seaway, and the accidental loss of an important power generating plant. A rock avalanche completely crushed the power station of the Schoellkopf powerhouse located about two miles downstream from Niagara Falls. In the five years following the Schoellkopf disaster, industrial employment in Niagara Falls dropped from 35,000 to 20,000, and the city's population declined 10 percent to 90,000.[2]

One element in the failure of the Buffalo area to recover from the 1958 recession has been the sluggish performance of the manufacturing sector. This has been related certainly to the construction of the seaway but even more to the region's failure to capture a proportionate share of the nation's growth industries, such as electronics and precision instrument manufacturing. While manufacturing jobs in the nation increased by over 20 percent between 1956 and 1965, the Buffalo area did not recover its 1958 level until 1965. In 1967, manufacturing employment was still more than 10 percent below 1956. In contrast, 1967 manufacturing employment in the country as a whole was 13 percent above 1956. As might be expected, the expansion of nonmanufacturing employment in the Buffalo area has fallen behind the national growth.

Total nonagricultural employment in the area in 1966 was 473,000, of which 180,000 was in manufacturing. The largest single category in manufacturing was primary metals, followed closely by transportation equipment. In the nonmanufacturing sector, which employed 292,000 persons, the largest grouping was in wholesale and retail trade, with 92,000, followed by government with 67,000 and by the service and miscellaneous categories with 64,000.

In one sense the 1956–1967 trend may overstate the area's losses. It is quite possible that the growth of the Buffalo area during the mid-1950s was bolstered by the construction activities connected with the St. Lawrence Seaway. This temporary boom in construction and related industries helped to provide the sharp contrast with the slackening employment after 1957.

Project Chronology

In 1960 the New York State Department of Public Works determined that the arterial plans prepared for the upstate urban areas in the early 1950s

[2] "Luring the Tourists to the American Side," *Business Week*, November 9, 1968, p. 134.

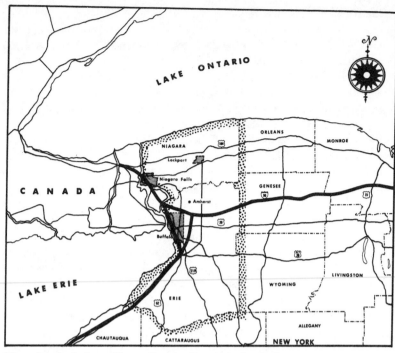

Figure 7.1. Study Area: Niagara Frontier Transportation Study

required updating. Partly because of the large number of areas—six large and five smaller ones—the department decided to create a separate planning organization to undertake this series of studies. The Buffalo area was chosen as the first to be analyzed by the newly created planning section. In effect the state decided to use the Niagara Frontier as a proving ground for new survey techniques and a new approach to study organization.

The technical organization established for the Buffalo study eventually became the core organization for all of the other Upstate New York Transportation Studies (UNYTS). The studies cover the six major urban areas of upstate New York: Buffalo (population, 1,300,000), Rochester (650,000), Albany (600,000), Syracuse (600,000), Utica-Rome (400,000), and Binghamton (225,000).[3] In addition the UNYTS group has undertaken studies in five smaller urban areas.

This operation probably represents the most centralized (and permanent) of

[3] New York, State Department of Public Works, *The Story of UNYTS* (September 1965), p. 1.

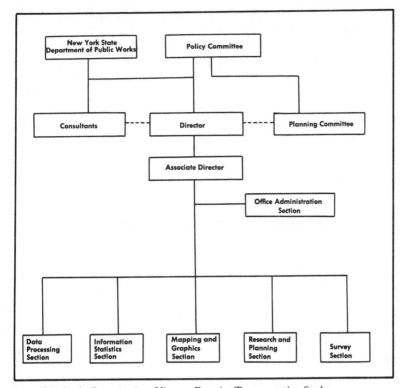

Figure 7.2. Study Organization: Niagara Frontier Transportation Study

the state organizations developed to conduct area transportation studies. In the larger urban areas most of the studies were conducted by staffs assembled specifically for a single project with the idea that they would be disbanded upon completion of the work or disintegration of the study. Such staffs have followed the available projects much as construction workers or migrant farm laborers do. Thus many of the technicians who participated in the Chicago Area Transportation Study (CATS), and later in the Pittsburgh study helped to initiate and conduct the Buffalo study and, subsequently, the other upstate New York studies. One objective of UNYTS was to develop standardized procedures during the Buffalo study and to train personnel to carry out the same type of study in the remaining upstate metropolitan areas.[4] The concept of conducting a transportation study for each upstate urban area was developed by the New York State Department of Public Works during the 1950s

[4] American Association of State Highway Officials, *Organizational Procedures of Seventeen Urban Transportation Studies* (Washington, D.C., 1963), pp. 45–48.

and was apparently successful enough to use once again.

The Niagara Frontier Transportation Study was to have been completed in two years; however, it still remained unfinished in 1969. Two factors were largely responsible for the delay. The first was a revision in computer technology, which during the early part of the study required a major change in data storage techniques. This was in response to the challenge of the large-capacity new computers that had become available. It is estimated that this factor alone accounted for nearly a two-year delay in the project. However, it should be noted that during this period the staff was able to develop procedures that have subsequently improved their ability to test alternative transportation mixes. Thus the two-year delay was not a total loss.

The second factor—which is still slowing the completion of a final report—is the issue of rapid transit. With a population of 1,300,000, the Buffalo area may be on the threshold of being able to justify some type of fixed-route rapid transit. Proponents have been successful in generating local citizen and political interest in rapid transit to the point where UNYTS has been reluctant to formulate a "final" transportation plan. In the meantime the NFTS Basic Corridor Plan, which indicates broad swaths of land through which future highways should be built, has not been adopted in its entirety by the state legislature, a prerequisite for state funding. Thus any final transportation plans have yet to be formulated or adopted.

The Buffalo study has been conducted from the New York Department of Transportation (NYDOT) headquarters in Albany, with little or no staff at the regional or local level. Local staff, or supervision of fieldwork, when required, has been provided through the central NYDOT organization. This centralization has been a source of criticism from local officials who feel that Buffalo, as the state's largest urban area outside of New York City, deserves a substantial resident area transportation planning staff. Local resentment of "absentee planning" has been compounded because Buffalo is the urban area most distant from the state capital in Albany.

In April 1961 a prospectus, based on work undertaken by a separate staff within the then Department of Public Works, was prepared for the Niagara Frontier Transportation Study. Technical work on the study was begun toward the end of 1961, a year and a half after the decision to study the area had been made and about six months after the prospectus had been prepared. At first the pace was brisk. Fieldwork was begun in the spring of 1962, and by the end of the year all of the basic inventories had been completed. These included a land-use survey, a vehicle-miles-of-travel survey, home interviews, roadside-interview origin-destination surveys, as well as supplementary air, rail, and bus studies and a railroad goods movement study. The latter may have been undertaken because of the availability of certain data on the movement of goods. Commodity data are usually complete, and, although historical trend data are obtainable, the information is rarely of significant value in an urban transportation study. Since little attention had been given to this aspect of area transportation, existing railroad commodity classifications were adopted. These included such extremely detailed categories as "swine," "hogs," and "pigs." The area transportation studies found little use for this information, so that goods movement was in most cases either ignored or treated as a brief postscript. When transportation planners have been tempted by such a feast of data, the most they have gotten is indigestion.

In 1962 the Niagara Frontier Transportation Study became incorporated as one of the Upstate New York Transportation Studies initiated by the state's highway agency. This move was coincidental with the passage of the Federal Highway Act of 1962, which required transportation plans for all urban areas of over 50,000 persons.

By late 1962, initial regional planning studies had been completed by both the Erie County and the Niagara County planning commissions. Although land-use data collection was a part of these county studies, the Niagara Frontier study undertook its own land-use analysis and, as indicated elsewhere, its own population projections. Although one document states that "a memorandum of understanding was executed between HHFA, BPR, and the New York State Department of Public Works concerning the use of '701' studies being conducted in Erie and Niagara counties,"[5] there is no indication that this countywide planning was coordinated with the NFTS either to provide data for the transportation study or to synchronize data collection procedures.

This experience of the NFTS, as well as of other area studies, should dispel a common bureaucratic illusion that agencies can be drawn together in a meaningful way simply by drawing a pen or pencil line to connect boxes on an organizational chart. A connecting line makes it appear that coordination is logical, desirable, and unavoidable, but in actual practice it is often most difficult to achieve. Given a deep mutual mistrust, casus belli can include incompatibility of data collected from different sources, personality conflicts, and simple disagreements over the project design and recommendations. Yet on paper, particularly in the Washington headquarters of federal agencies, interagency coordination on a regional project appears easy to achieve and to maintain.

The NFTS began to lose momentum when it reached the data-processing

[5] Ibid., pp. 45–46.

stage. From the completion of the fieldwork in late 1962 to the preparation of Volume 1 of the final report in mid-1964, the project was held up by various computer problems. This prolonged delay, it is estimated, eventually cost the study a vital two years. By the time its recommendations were presented, the climate of opinion had become decidedly stormy.

The technical difficulties with the computer were of two kinds: the first type was due to a changeover from relatively simple accounting machines to complex electronic data-processing equipment. Among other things, it entailed changes in the basic condition of the data collected in 1962. This was a physical problem and involved converting the data from one type of storage procedure and technology to another—from data-processing cards to electronic tape. It sounds uncomplicated but in fact proved to be frustrating and difficult.

The second type of technical problem involved establishing a system that would permit easy analysis of alternative transportation networks. The preparation of the output from the computers to permit evaluation by technicians and by committee members proved exceedingly burdensome. It was later claimed by the NYDOT staff that the system devised by UNYTS represented a "quick and inexpensive" method for testing different alternatives and the various combinations of new facilities. If this was indeed true, the delay in this initial upstate New York study was worth the effort, because the system would permit greater flexibility in making numerous alternative tests later in other study areas. Even in Buffalo the method devised facilitated the analysis of more alternative transportation systems than had originally been anticipated. One problem with the system, however, was that the alternatives, involving a mix of highways and rapid transit in the Buffalo area, were not easy to analyze because the NFTS highway and rail transit proposals were considered separately at different points in time. Buffalo aside, the determination of a modal split for the other upstate New York studies was not difficult to determine. As a rule of thumb, construction of new rapid transit facilities is difficult to justify in urban areas of under one million persons. Since the other urban areas had populations of a half million or less, rapid transit was not a serious factor in the preparation of a transportation plan. For these areas a highway plan was sufficient; highways can accommodate a system of bus routes, if required, without any additional expense.

Perhaps another reason for the slowdown between 1962 and 1964 was the desire of the study staff to use the Buffalo area as a testing ground for new research. The Chicago study was clearly identified as the model for the NFTS; the devising of advanced research methods was a prominent part of the technical process in the latter study. Since this was the pilot for ten subsequent studies, the innovative emphasis may have had more justification than an equivalent amount of research in a separate study. However, the NFTS may have suffered from its role as an experimental laboratory. The perception of earlier studies as ideal models can sometimes become a problem. No one can argue that CATS did not make significant strides in transportation planning techniques. Overlooked, however, has been the rather cool reception that its study recommendations received. The NFTS as well as other projects have often imitated the study techniques of CATS without recognizing the need to produce usable and acceptable plans—an objective that CATS failed to achieve. Certainly, the NFTS has had more success in securing agency approval for its plans than CATS did, but it still has a long way to go. This point has apparently been overlooked by those using the Buffalo area as a proving ground for studies elsewhere in the state. The innovations and procedures developed in the NFTS relate to the technical aspects of the study. In contrast, techniques of presentation and of ensuring acceptance of the final project have not received the attention they obviously need and deserve.

The NFTS began to encounter strong opposition once it began publishing its findings. The Basic Corridor Plan, prepared in 1965, identified wide strips of territory for proposed routes but carefully omitted detailed route locations. It provided grounds for the first major skirmish between the UNYTS staff and the local planners. Under New York practice, this plan was sufficient for approval (and subsequent funding) by the state legislature, which incorporated certain sections of the plan into the state highway system, thus making them eligible for state and federal aid. The procedure has been described as follows:

It is my understanding that the Basic Corridor Plan will be given to the Counsel of the Department of Public Works for the preparation of legislation to be submitted for consideration at the next session of the Legislature. If this legislation passes, we shall be free to start our advance planning and preliminary engineering, to employ our design squads, to let design contracts and to do those other needed things, including advanced purchase of right-of-way, which will make for an expeditious and efficient program of design and construction.[6]

Most of the sections of the expressway system proposed in the Corridor Plan were subsequently included in the New York State highway system.

One problem with the broad corridor approach is that it is apt to anger a much larger segment of the population than would a specific, relatively narrow route involving only a fraction of the corridor population and urban

[6] Norman W. Krapf, "Building the Basic Corridor Plan," in Niagara Frontier Transportation Study, *Remarks Made at the Presentation of the Basic Corridor Plan for Expressways, August 18, 1965,* Publication no. IR 44–251–01 (September 1965), p. 17.

development. On the other hand, the technical staff has a better chance of avoiding immediate and direct confrontation with soon-to-be-displaced families and businesses, particularly during the planning period when comprehensive plans are being formulated. Unfortunately, this approach leaves the hard-core location problems to either state highway agencies or city transit authorities, both of which normally lack the competence and sensitivity to handle them.

Because of the alleged need for haste in obtaining approval of the corridor system, NYDOT submitted proposals to the legislature for new routes in the NFTS area before making any study of the area's overall public transportation needs. This procedure had a negative political impact, and this was further exacerbated by the corridor recommendations themselves, which generated widespread opposition. By 1966, three factors, a growing public interest in rapid transit combined with UNYTS's apparent disregard for such a system, fears that a proposed highway corridor would demolish a number of high-income neighborhoods, and a U.S. special census revealing a significant error in the NFTS population projections, all converged to create strong resistance to the highway proposals. An equally important factor was the effort of the Buffalo Urban Renewal Department to block the proposed corridors. The department believed that at least two major projects were adversely affected by the NYDOT proposals.

Between early 1966 and mid-1968 little more progress was made on the project. Major regional land-use decisions, such as relocation of the state university and the location of a new sports stadium, have implications for the location and type of new transportation facilities that will be needed. The net result of the standoff between the study and local proponents of rail transit has been a temporary moratorium on approval of new transportation facilities. Meanwhile, it is apparent that there is continued interest in public transportation.[7]

HHFA's Influence and Involvement in the NFTS

The Niagara Frontier Transportation Study was totally financed from highway funds made available by the U.S. Bureau of Public Roads and the New York State Department of Public Works (absorbed by the New York Department of Transportation in 1967). HHFA (and its successor, the Department of Housing and Urban Development—HUD) was not a financial contributor in the transportation planning process; its only formal connection with the study was its ex officio membership on the ten-member Policy Committee

[7] State University of New York at Buffalo, Office of Urban Affairs, and Manufacturers and Traders Trust Company, *Niagara Frontier's Transportation Needs* (Buffalo, August 10, 1967).

(the regional administrator of HHFA's Region I was a member of this NFTS committee). Even though no HUD officials were on the Planning Committee, at least two or three members of this committee were executive directors of HUD-funded planning agencies. For example, key officials of the Erie County Department of Planning, the Niagara County Industrial Development and Planning Commission, and the city of Buffalo's Urban Renewal Department were all members. Furthermore, the New York State Office of Planning Coordination (OPC), created in 1966, had formal representation on both the Policy and the Planning Committee. Preparation of a comprehensive development plan was the primary mission of the OPC, although this office was also responsible for urban planning assistance and a variety of other planning tasks. Of significance is a study that began in 1968 to plan for the impact of the new campus for the State University at Buffalo (SUNYAB), a new expressway, a mental hospital, and a research institute in the Buffalo-Amherst area. The "Buffalo-Amherst Urban Impact Study" as outlined in the agency's annual report,[8] however, appeared to ignore local planning objectives as expressed by local planners.

HHFA or HHFA-related membership on the Policy and the Planning Committee of the Buffalo study increased considerably as the study moved on into the mid-1960s. In August 1964, only one of the ten members of the Policy Committee was a planner or a representative of a planning agency. Only four of the eleven members on the Planning Committee represented city or regional planning agencies or HUD-oriented agencies. By August 1966, however, with the addition of the director of the New York State Office of Planning Coordination, the Policy Committee had two members who were planning-agency oriented; and six of the thirteen members of the Planning Committee were concurrently members of city or regional planning organizations. This increase in HHFA-oriented participation occurred despite the fact that HHFA did not contribute any financial assistance to this area transportation study. Undoubtedly, the increase reflected attempts by the Bureau of Public Roads to develop more coordination at the federal level between the BPR and HHFA and to improve coordination at the metropolitan level between highway and regional planning agencies.

Based on a comparison with other projects, it seems unlikely that financial or technical participation by HHFA would have affected the design of the project or the scope of work. The agency would not have required the collection of significantly greater amounts of planning data, nor would the regional planning analysis have been expanded. Even during the course of the study,

[8] New York, State Office of Planning Coordination, *Annual Report, 1967–1968,* p. 26.

HHFA did not engage in any regional activities that were specifically geared to provide data for supplementary analysis as part of the NFTS. The principal reason was that the BPR's transportation planning techniques already required a substantial emphasis on regional planning, including population projections, land-use, employment, income, and labor force data, to name just a few. Thus the BPR was obliged to collect and analyze this type of data whether or not HHFA was a participant. The experience in Buffalo confirms the authors' earlier observation that HHFA-HUD involvement in the transportation studies did not necessarily add to the amount of planning work undertaken or to the quality of the finished product. For example, the NFTS project does not appear to be any more highway dominated than other studies in which HHFA-HUD has been a partner or contributor.

There is some local feeling that, if HHFA had been more deeply involved in the area transportation study and had financed certain work items, the recommendations of the NFTS would have been more broadly based or would at least have been more favorable to the urban renewal plans that were being developed by the city of Buffalo. Questions have been raised about the inability of the two federal agencies, both spending federal money, to coordinate plans and proposals. The planning financed by the Bureau of Public Roads and local highway funds has seemed to be incompatible with the project sponsored by HUD through Buffalo's Urban Renewal Department.

Reliability of Data: The Population Implosion

An error discovered in the NFTS population inventory of 1962 became a casus belli for opponents of subsequent NFTS recommendations. According to the 1960 census, the population of Niagara and Erie counties, the NFTS area, was 1,307,000. Volume 1 of the NFTS final report (August 1964) estimated that the July 1962 population of the area had risen to 1,350,000. (This figure was computed from the home-interview survey that covered 16,000 households in the study area, or 4 percent of the total.) The estimate was "verified" at the time by assuming a continuation of the 1950 to 1960 upward trend of population in the Buffalo area of 1.8 percent per year, which was slightly in excess of the national growth rate. However, the figures presented in the report apparently did not reflect the significant decline in the area growth rate that probably began in the late 1950s, as suggested by data on employment and migration. The NFTS data for 1962 were presumably derived from field interviews and were not based on any projection of population trends. The NFTS report stated:

By July, 1962, slightly two years later, the population of the area has risen to 1,350,000 persons. This figure is based on the home interview survey and can be presumed to be accurate; a comparison of 1962 home interview survey figures with those of the 1960 Census for Buffalo, whose population may be considered to be fairly stable over a two year period, reveals only a two percent variation. Since very fine adjustments are meaningless for planning purposes, the figure of 1,350,000 is used as the base 1962 population throughout this report.[9]

In 1966, however, a special U.S. census of the two-county area revealed that the population had increased to only 1,322,000. This figure represented a rise in six years of only half of what had been indicated by the NFTS for the two-year period between 1960 and 1962. The discovery of this apparent error was seized upon by opponents to cast doubt on the accuracy of the highway proposals and as proof of the failure of the NFTS—in their eyes—to give adequate attention to other important parts of the study.

The NFTS staff reacted defensively to the new population figures. Rather than admit that an error had been made and that the sampling technique was subject to substantial variations in interpretation, they issued a report presenting a spirited rebuttal of local criticisms.[10] In this report, the NFTS staff defended the population figures by suggesting that

Forecasting future events is a risky business at best. This is as true of population forecasting as it is of any other event. Perhaps it entails even more risk since the population is counted very exactly every ten years by the Bureau of the Census as required by law. Thus one's forecasts can be examined and compared with actual growth at a minimum of every ten years and sometimes at shorter intervals using shorter census and secondary data.[11]

In addition to its defensive tone, the quotation also appears somewhat plaintive in referring to the fact that population projections face the risks of subsequent exposure by the Bureau of the Census.[12]

This rebuttal further claimed that exact population forecasts are not really necessary in a transportation study and that examination of census data since 1930 reveals that the error in forecasts is a comparatively small factor in global, long-term trends. This is a weak argument at best, since a transportation plan normally includes a scheduling of program priorities together with recommendations for new and improved facilities. Obviously, if a road is not needed for several years in a particular location, premature investment in it may be imprudent.

[9] New York, Niagara Frontier Transportation Study, *Final Report,* vol. 1, *The Basis of Travel,* August 1964, p. 6.
[10] New York, Niagara Frontier Transportation Study, "Supplementary Remarks to the Report, 'An Evaluation of Alternative Public Transportation Facilities, Niagara Frontier Transportation Study' " (n.d.).
[11] Ibid., p. 8.
[12] See, for example, Melvin R. Levin, *Community and Regional Planning* (New York: Frederick A. Praeger, 1969), chap. 5, "Perils of Projection."

The problems of population forecasting that were encountered in Buffalo raise the broader issue of the accuracy of transportation planning techniques in general. Population is one of the key factors to be taken into account in transportation planning projections, since an increase in population is the largest single factor affecting any proposed expansion in future travel requirements. This was recognized in the first report of the NFTS. (It might be added that projections of land use and economic base upon which the origins and destinations of future trips are based are even less reliable than population forecasts.)

The problems surrounding the population estimates made by the NFTS point out one important lesson: study results should not be considered as scientific fact. If even the relatively simple inventory aspect of transportation planning processes is riddled with weak spots, any delusion that the process has the precision of a fine watch can lead only to serious problems.

Relations with Local Planning Agencies

Relations between the NFTS group and local planning agencies have varied widely from agency to agency. The Erie County Department of Planning, Niagara County Industrial Development and Planning Commission, Buffalo Planning Department, and Buffalo Urban Renewal Department were all involved in the study. The success and smoothness of interagency relations appear to be inversely related to the quality and capability of the local agency staffs. Perhaps the most effective coordination was achieved between the NFTS and Niagara County, the smaller of the two counties, which has a planning agency oriented toward economic development and a comparatively small staff. The county would benefit from the radial expressways proposed by the NFTS but opposed by the city of Buffalo. At the same time, Niagara County faces few problems over land acquisition or business and family relocation due to the construction of the proposed radial expressways. The Industrial Development and Planning Commission in Niagara County also viewed the elaborate highway proposals as a stimulus to economic growth. Thus the interests of the county were in fact enhanced by the highway proposals of the NFTS staff.

The situation was very different with the Erie County Department of Planning, which seemed to be a more conventional regional planning agency placing less emphasis on economic development and more on planning. Relations between the Erie County planning agency and the NFTS group were, and are, reserved, following the traditional pattern between highway engineers and planners. The planning director of the Erie County Department of Planning is one of the two local professional planners who have led the attack on the validity of the NFTS recommendations.

Perhaps some of the most difficult relationships were with the city of Buffalo agencies, including both the Planning and the Urban Renewal Department. These strains were to be expected. Other studies indicate that the greatest opposition to transportation planning recommendations comes from the central city, which stands to lose the most financially, physically, aesthetically, socially, and economically from the construction of major expressways through built-up areas.

In Buffalo, as in other large cities, the urban renewal agency has successfully attracted most of the planning talent. As a result, the Buffalo Planning Department is professionally understaffed. Furthermore, it is subject to political appointments, and many key jobs are held by persons apparently chosen for political loyalties rather than for professional credentials.

The question of public disclosure was one of the major issues that strained relations between the NFTS and the Buffalo Planning Department. The Buffalo planning agency effectively used the press as a weapon for gaining public support by publicizing criticisms of the NFTS recommendations. Moreover, the department received frequent and favorable treatment from the press, much to the chagrin of the NFTS staff, who in many cases felt betrayed and, at the least, maligned. The press may have been a factor in polarizing public opinion and in generally rallying public support against the NFTS recommendations. This experience was somewhat different from the usual conflict between city planning agency and transportation study staff, where the technical merits of the study are debated at length, the technicians lash out at each other, but the press does not become involved. Buffalo was the only area studied where the local press became involved with technical outputs. (Transportation planning is usually a dull subject for reporters.)

An interesting comparison can be made between Buffalo and Rochester; the studies in both areas were conducted by the same NYDOT staff. Rochester, which has a more qualified, professional central-city planning staff than Buffalo, has raised just as many doubts over the validity of certain study recommendations. However, relations between the transportation study and the planning agencies have not been adversely affected by leakages to a hostile press and by other affronts. Rochester's local planning agency evaluated the NYDOT proposals for over a year without expressing approval or disapproval of the study recommendations. One reason, of course, for the relative lack of rancor in Rochester is the absence of a public transportation issue. As noted, few areas with populations under a million have been seriously interested in fixed-route rapid transit, and bus service does not seem to arouse a similar intensity of feeling.

Perhaps the greatest single conflict in Buffalo has been between NYDOT and the city's Urban Renewal Department. This department has the distinction of possessing the most outspoken opponent of the NFTS in the region. As a result, there have been exchanges between the two agencies, including sharp and frequent rebuttal of opponents' objections and the proffering of alternative proposals. Such conflicts are a basic element in urban areas and reflect the typical stresses between downtown renewal objectives and highway objectives, as well as differences in long-range goals among various local, state, and federal agencies.

With one or two exceptions, the professional planners in Buffalo objected to the fact that the study was conducted out of Albany. In addition to sheer distance (Buffalo and Albany are 300 miles apart), the upstate New York weather, particularly during the wintertime, was an added deterrent to good communications. Although this communication gap may have been to some extent more psychological than real, it was a factor in worsening relations. Buffalo planners maintain that the economic base study was conducted in Albany without a single visit to Buffalo by the economist responsible. They also claim that the entire NFTS report reflects a lack of comprehension of area needs and local reactions to proposals made during the course of the study. While this charge may or may not have any basis in fact, the distance between the staff headquarters and the study area may well have reduced the opportunity for a fruitful dialogue. Transportation planning is difficult enough without courting unnecessary criticism. In most states, area transportation studies have been headquartered in the state highway agency's main office, but the use of consultants who establish local offices, if only for the collection of data, has tended to reduce ex post facto charges of colonialism.

The problem of interagency coordination for a study conducted out of Albany led to difficulties with Buffalo's city traffic engineer. Under normal conditions, a city traffic engineer could be expected to have a great deal of empathy with officials of state highway agencies because of the similarity of their backgrounds and interests.[13] Most transportation planning technicians and city engineers share a background in civil and highway engineering. Nevertheless, in Buffalo, there was a continuing lack of coordination between the city and the NFTS staff in Albany, and the influential traffic engineer became disenchanted with the project although he had initially considered his role an important one in the transportation study. The lack of coordination can probably be traced to the complicated techniques and avant-garde procedures used by the NFTS staff. A city engineer is usually more oriented toward signs, signals, and markings, a rather routine operat-

[13] See the comments in Alan A. Altshuler, *The City Planning Process* (Ithaca, N.Y.: Cornell University Press, 1965), chap. 1, pp. 17–83.

ing environment. During the course of the study, however, Buffalo's traffic engineer died; his replacement did not enjoy the same position of influence, and the dispute faded rapidly.

A development that is now complicating transportation planning in the Buffalo area was the establishment in 1967 of the Niagara Frontier Transportation Authority (NFTA). As part of New York State's efforts to improve transportation, the state legislature authorized the creation of local transportation authorities to develop regional transportation systems. These authorities have substantial funding potential, and there is every likelihood that they will operate as semi-independent empires similar in some ways to the Port of New York Authority. The transportation authorities may eventually preempt the whole transportation field because of their broad powers, including the power to construct highways. The relationships of these authorities with regional planning agencies, local planning and renewal agencies, and the NFTS have not been clearly identified. For example, although the bicounty planning organization for Erie and Niagara counties is responsible for "comprehensive" planning, particularly in relation to its Section 204 review power,[14] it is apparently barred legally from undertaking transportation planning. On the other hand, both the NFTS in its continuing phase and the Niagara Frontier Transportation Authority have broad legislative authority in this area.

Initially, the Niagara Frontier Transportation Authority seems to have been interested primarily in air transportation. Its emphasis apparently is to be focused on the development of a new and larger airport to serve both Buffalo and Niagara Falls. If this remains the only sphere of interest for the transportation authority, there may not be much overlapping and interagency conflict. However, if public transportation emerges as a high-priority issue for Buffalo, then the transportation authority may be the logical agency to undertake the planning and construction of a public transit system. In that event, difficult problems of coordination with NYDOT can be anticipated.

New York has one of the strongest state-oriented transportation planning programs in the nation, and certainly the direct impact of the state on planning and financing transportation facilities is greater in Buffalo than in any of the other areas discussed in this volume. With the continuing planning function being carried out in Albany, the imposition of a transportation authority that is also financed and controlled from Albany, and the requirement that any section of highway must be approved by the legislature in

[14] Section 204 of the Demonstration Cities and Metropolitan Development Act of 1965 calls for review by a regional planning agency of most types of federally aided construction to determine its consistency with respect to regional plans.

Albany, it is apparent that local planning or development efforts are completely dependent on transportation decisions reached in the state capital.

The Rapid Transit Controversy

One of the most fundamental of the current transportion planning questions in Buffalo is the role of public transportation in the future transportation system. At the present time the local bus company serves about 7 percent of all trips in the study area. Most of these trips are oriented toward the Buffalo central business district; surprisingly, the private transit company operates in the black.[15]

The basic controversy in Buffalo is not whether existing urban development justifies the construction of a rapid transit system but whether the region should continue to develop in the typical centrifugal pattern, as in the past, or whether it should attempt to grow more compactly, partly by concentrating more of its growth at the center of the region in Buffalo. Other cities, such as Atlanta, are confronting this same dilemma. The adolescent stage of public transportation development seems to occur, as we have noted, when urban areas reach a population of over one million. When large sums are to be invested in rapid transit facilities, a study is usually made of land-use alternatives, a procedure that HUD frequently encourages. In Buffalo two alternative land-use and development patterns are being proposed in an atmosphere of open conflict, and the choice of alternatives, and their collateral transportation systems, has perhaps been complicated by other factors. In most situations a single planning agency proposes and evaluates a variety of alternative land-use and development patterns, a process with a highly theoretical ring. In Buffalo, there are two genuinely opposed teams, and this may in fact be the only way to present alternative land-use and development patterns to the general public and measure realistically which option the majority favors. The opponents of dispersion are numerous and vociferous, but so far, it seems, development decisions have been based on an assumption that the sprawl will continue on the same basis as in the past. Many decision-makers, however, continue to place great reliance on automobiles and highways as the backbone of the transportation system.

The greatest impact of the rapid transit controversy has been to forestall the approval of the Kenmore Expressway to the north of Buffalo. Under New York State law, as noted, a highway must first be designated by the legislature as part of the state highway system before it can be funded and built. This designation has not been given to the expressway, and this theoretically keeps the door open for a rapid transit line.

[15]Robert E. Paaswell, "Transportation," Goals for Metropolitan Buffalo, Source Paper no. 1 [1967], p. 6.

In Buffalo the rapid transit concept has engendered a great deal of public support, to the point where local politicians, including state representatives, have publicly supported rapid transit proposals. As a result, some of the NYDOT staff feel that the political process is failing because representatives do not openly support highways, as opposed to rapid transit, although they must know in their hearts that rapid transit is not really feasible.

A significant factor in prolonging the issue has been the attitude of the NFTS staff. Because of earlier delays and a desire to produce some type of plan, the project staff made a blanket assumption that in the future (1985) 15 percent of all trips would be served by rapid transit, as opposed to 7 percent at the time of the field surveys. This percentage of trips was subtracted from the total future trips projected by the staff, and the Basic Corridor Plan for highways was prepared on the basis of the remainder. The NFTS staff had intended to prepare a separate rapid transit plan based on the 15 percent of the trips that had been excluded from the highway analysis. But the lack of urgency in preparing that second report provided highway foes with an excellent opportunity to show that rapid transit had been merely an afterthought in the Buffalo study. Furthermore, it provided ammunition for those who felt that the region should have been presented with realistic land-use alternatives involving mixes of highways and rapid transit. Although the NFTS was criticized for not properly considering rapid transit, it could have been applauded for allowing as much as 15 percent of future trips to be subject to public transportation usage. There is a problem with this type of statistic, however; if the percentage were applied to a single corridor it would more than justify a rapid transit line, but if it were spread throughout the region it might not justify any type of public transportation. In any case, it is clear that communications could have been improved between the protagonists.

Two major development decisions—the location of a major branch of the State University of New York in a Buffalo suburb, and the proposed construction of a sports stadium outside the downtown area—have dealt a further blow to proponents of rapid transit, who, under any conditions, were fighting an uphill battle. SUNYAB, with a 1968/69 enrollment of over 15,000 regular students and significant projected growth, would have been a major factor in enhancing the prospects for rapid transit if it had been located, as some suggested, on the Buffalo waterfront. However, its location in suburban Amherst has had the opposite effect: it has justified the proposed early construction of an expressway between Buffalo and Lockport to serve the new university site. On top of this, attempts to construct a sports stadium in Buffalo near the downtown area have not borne fruit: as of this writing, it appeared that the stadium would also be built outside the central area.

It should be noted that the proponents of public transportation were not merely planners working for HUD-oriented agencies. The Manufacturers and Traders。Trust Company, one of the city's largest banks, and the Office of Urban Affairs at SUNYAB jointly sponsored a public meeting, complete with distinguished speakers, to clarify the transportation needs of the Niagara Frontier. The report of the meeting described various types of rapid transit systems that have been considered or built in medium-density areas. UNYTS personnel were not participants at the meeting, even though they were involved in transportation planning in the region. Obviously, study personnel and rapid transit proponents were not on the best terms.

In late 1967 a group of people from Buffalo who were interested in rapid transit or otherwise connected with the NFTS visited Toronto to witness firsthand that city's new rapid transit system. However, the reactions of the persons who made the trip varied just as widely as the opinions about rapid transit in Buffalo. As in the classic Japanese story "Rashomon," the same event was described by different persons according to their own point of view. Persons favorable to rapid transit pointed to Toronto as a perfect example of how rapid transit could be successful, while anti-rapid-transit people pointed to the same trip, lectures, and interviews as providing evidence that rapid transit could not work in Buffalo.

Such activities indicate that the proponents of public transportation have been able to engender considerable popular support among the people of the region. The controversy seems to have produced an either-or situation, although, in reality, a reasonable transportation balance could be achieved. Proponents of public transportation are convinced that if a highway system is developed prior to commitments for the construction of rapid transit facilities, the latter may never be built, with the result that the region's development pattern will not change.

Proposals have been made for the construction of expressways that would provide rapid transit facilities in the median strips. The problem, however, as recognized by local officials, is that Buffalo's population and density may not be sufficiently great to warrant such facilities. In any case, Buffalo's citizens are now being faced with a choice in terms of transportation and land development patterns. If they support the NFTS findings and recommendations, then downtown Buffalo will continue to decline. If they support a dense urban core, rapid transit or improved public transportation will become more feasible. Obviously, if a rapid transit or improved public transportation system is initiated, it will have a significant effect on the density of Buffalo's central area.

Except for proposals for short sections of expressway in the downtown area that would conflict with urban renewal plans, much of the Buffalo controversy centers around one road, the Kenmore Expressway. This road would be one of the heaviest traveled highways, and it would also be the most expensive to construct in terms of financial and social-economic costs. The urban renewal staff contends that this highway would adversely affect the Downtown North project that is centered on Upper Main Street and could be the determining factor for the success of the renewal project as a whole. The staff believes that the Downtown North project is dependent to a large degree on rapid transit. The proponents of rapid transit see enough favorable signs, including the density and type of development in the Kenmore corridor, to spur them in their effort to obtain at least one rapid transit line for Buffalo in place of this highway. This would be a moral victory; moreover, a densely settled section of the city with numerous institutional uses might be spared the dislocations of a new expressway.

The State Transportation Agency as a Service Organization

Some state transportation or highway agencies see themselves as service organizations providing transportation planning services to a state's metropolitan areas. But the role of professional adviser, while perhaps desirable from the state's point of view, is an unrealistic one for a state transportation agency. There are two principal reasons for this. First, state transportation systems must be based upon a statewide capital improvement program that involves the problems of establishing priorities among areas, while transportation planning normally focuses on single metropolitan areas. Statewide programming is necessarily complex, since the importance of routes or public transportation facilities within any region must be judged in the final analysis by the state agency that also has to consider the competing needs of other areas.

There is a second and perhaps more important reason why a state transportation agency cannot function as a local service organization. In many cases, particularly where value judgments are a critical factor, the current state of the art in transportation planning does not permit easy, clear-cut evaluation of alternative proposals. Thus, before the state agency can function as an area transportation planning agency, the planning process must be capable of producing more convincing evidence of the need for specific transportation facilities. Local organizations must also have staffs fully capable of analyzing the data and evaluating alternative recommendations.

Local capability is a key issue. In New York State, the Department of Transportation has assembled a large and highly skilled transportation planning organization that would be difficult, if not impossible, to match in any one area. The local planning agencies are completely outclassed in terms of transportation planning. Furthermore, the complexity and cost of current data technology make it virtually impossible for a local organization to conduct its own analyses except through the state's transportation agency. This is one reason why local area personnel are often reduced to after-the-fact sniping rather than full participation in the design, research, and formulation of alternatives. In any case, the conflict between opposing professionals at the state and local levels would surely limit the possibility of harmonious relations. There are deep cleavages between state and area objectives, and between their frames of reference, and these can develop into technically sophisticated disputes or degenerate into simple name-calling.

The New York Department of Transportation has become unpopular in Buffalo: it has stressed the need for new expressways while the city's and the region's professional planners have been promoting an alternative transportation system with greater emphasis on public transportation. It is unlikely that a state transportation department can or would be willing to function merely as an adviser and provider of data to local planning agencies. NYDOT, by virtue of its staff size and quality, feels exceptionally well qualified to assume responsibility for transportation planning in the state's metropolitan areas. Yet in Buffalo, at least, reference to metropolitan goals has been virtually ignored in the state's transportation planning process. Goals for Metropolitan Buffalo, an informal group whose aim is to promote regional goals and to promote rail rapid transit, was formed in late 1967 to formulate and disseminate goals for the metropolitan area.[16] The lack of a clear and fully persuasive relationship between transportation proposals of the Department of Transportation and the goals of the metropolitan area has perhaps been most directly responsible for the growth of powerful local opposition to the NYDOT proposals.

Whether or not the state transportation agencies assume a more advisory role in metropolitan planning, there is the problem of handling data storage and processing so that the huge investment in data collection can be more fully utilized. Local planners have complained that the data developed by the Niagara Frontier Transportation Study are of no use to any local or regional planning organization because the material is "locked in computers." Another problem is that much of the data has been gathered and processed on the basis of traffic zones as the principal geographical units. These frequently do not coincide with the boundaries used by the local communities for planning districts and neighborhoods. Accordingly, local planners contend that,

[16] Goals for Metropolitan Buffalo, "1. Transportation," and "2. Downtown" (n.d.).

even if unfrozen, much of the data is of limited value.[17]

Relationship Between Area Size and Local Opposition

One hypothesis of this study is that large metropolitan areas usually employ higher-quality staff than smaller areas. Therefore, a state transportation or highway agency conducting a local transportation study is more vulnerable to effective local criticism and may as a consequence encounter significant obstacles in obtaining easy approval of transportation plans in the big city. Buffalo is a good example. Since the New York Department of Transportation does not concern itself with transportation planning for the New York metropolitan area, Buffalo is the largest urban area under its jurisdiction. (The Tri-State Transportation Study, a separate entity with its own staff, is responsible for the New York City area.) It has also been the most difficult for NYDOT in terms of securing approval for its proposed transportation plans. In Buffalo the understaffed city Planning Department has been augmented by the staff of the Urban Renewal Department, as well as by the county and bicounty planning agencies. The last two agencies have provided the local expertise for professional criticisms of the NYDOT proposals. In Rochester, where NYDOT is conducting one of the larger upstate New York studies, the city planning agency is raising most of the questions about the NYDOT proposals. In this case, however, the acrimony characteristic of relations in Buffalo has not developed, so far as can be determined. Although the upstate New York studies include a total of eleven areas, serious local opposition to highway plans seems to have developed only in the larger areas.

Another hypothesis that appears to hold true in Buffalo is that transportation planning becomes most controversial when rapid transit may be a realistic alternative. In smaller areas, transportation planning is, in effect, highway planning. Thus one of the most divisive issues in transportation planning —highway versus public transportation—has not been a significant issue. For example, upstate New York's Rochester area, with a metropolitan population of about 650,000, appears willing to accept the recommendations of NYDOT for an all-bus public transportation system.

Within the Niagara Frontier area, there are important differences between groups and communities in their response to the NYDOT recommendations. In the city of Buffalo and in Erie County, the possibility of rail rapid transit has produced sharp criticism of the highway plans prepared by NYDOT. In

---

[17] For example, in Manchester, New Hampshire, where the land-use data were collected before checking with the city planning department, it was later found that the planning districts used by the city planning department did not coincide with the zones and subzones that the transportation study had delineated for the city.

Niagara County, where the public transportation issue is not a factor, local planners seem satisfied with the NYDOT recommendations.

This is not surprising, since most outlying areas do not feel threatened by highway construction and, in general, believe that they have much to gain from new expressways. In contrast, built-up urban centers benefit less and suffer more. They can usually anticipate substantial social and economic dislocations as a result of new highway construction. The problem cannot be solved piecemeal by limiting construction to the suburbs, because it may be questionable practice to build radial outlying highways before connections to the urban center have been assured.

The Need for Transportation Goals and Objectives

A discussion of area transportation goals and objectives is touched on here only because the lack of suitable goals and objectives in Buffalo noticeably contributed to the confusion and conflict that resulted from the highway recommendations. There were a number of key objectives in the transportation plans. However, the question raised locally was whether these plans fulfilled city goals, since nontransportation goals may often be more important. Can transportation goals, in effect, be set independently of other needs? In the Niagara Frontier Transportation Study, early objectives included both transportation and nontransportation elements, as noted in a paper prepared in 1963:

As I see it, we have three main objectives. These are first, to minimize the sum of all transportation costs . . . secondly, we want to promote better land development . . . third, we want to promote economic growth. We are not sure how to measure gains to these last two objectives but they are important and we must acknowledge them.[18]

While a reduction in the overall costs of transportation is undeniably an important objective, it is questionable, in a given region, whether it should be the primary area objective. Furthermore, there is some question whether this goal was set by the NFTS staff or by the Policy Committee. The reduction of transportation costs may have been chosen as a goal because it presented an attractive objective that was comparatively easy to measure. For example, the NFTS statement of goals indicated that the greatest gains could be realized by reducing accidents and saving time. Costs for both factors are generally available; however, the costs of family dislocation, increased physical discomfort from fumes and noise, for example, which would affect central-city residents near new expressways, and measures to remove or reduce these hazards are usually excluded from consideration. Nevertheless, these costs are real

[18] Roger L. Creighton, "A Report on the Niagara Frontier Transportation Study," mimeographed (Albany: Upstate New York Transportation Studies and New York State Department of Public Works, July 1, 1963).

and show up elsewhere in the urban equation: often they turn out to be surprisingly high.

The difficulties of developing realistic comprehensive cost-benefit equations must be resolved before lowered costs alone can be used legitimately as a principal transportation objective. The greatest advantage of cost reduction as a goal in transportation planning is that costs and benefits are easy to identify when comparing a number of alternatives. In addition, the process is susceptible to computer applications. In these types of calculations large numbers of units are involved, each with a small incremental change. Unfortunately, the problem of allocating social costs or benefits where fewer units are involved but unit costs are high has yet to be resolved.

Perhaps the lack of any consensus on regional land-use objectives in Buffalo lay at the root of the basic highway versus rapid transit conflict. While highway proponents correctly preferred transportation solutions for what they predicted would be the character of the region at some future date, the proponents of rapid transit argued strongly that the continued outward development of the region must be curtailed and that increased downtown activity is vital to the region. The Buffalo Urban Renewal Department was (and presumably is) working on this latter premise, while NYDOT and others are obviously working in the other direction.

In the vacuum created by this standoff, the state agencies have had considerable influence in shaping the region. Legislative acceptance of most of the highway corridors and an executive decision to relocate SUNYAB in a Buffalo suburb instead of in a downtown location give evidence of this influence.

The majority of the area transportation studies conducted during the 1960s were initiated before the establishment of regional planning; therefore, regional goals were usually set by the study staff. Under these conditions, it is not surprising that a number of study recommendations do not meet with core-city or regional approval. This obvious lack of direction may have been the principal reason for the problems encountered in Buffalo. Presumably, by the next wave of urban transportation studies, metropolitan goals will have been defined by regional planning agencies, either broadly or specifically, so that the new studies will be provided with specific guidelines for the development of transportation plans. The production of generalized statements of goals and objectives is of course no guarantee of subsequent success in transportation planning.

Study Area Profile

Metropolitan Manchester was the only urban area in New Hampshire with a population of over 50,000, thus making it the only part of the state that met the comprehensive urban transportation planning requirements of the 1962 Federal-Aid Highway Act.

The Manchester Metropolitan Planning Study (MMPS) covered an area of 213 square miles with a resident population in 1964 of about 113,000 persons. Of this total, 92,000 lived in Manchester, and the remaining 21,000 were thinly spread throughout the five suburban communities constituting the MMPS region. One of the five suburbs, Goffstown, had a population of 8,000; the remaining four had populations under 5,000.

An examination of the distribution of employment and shopping in the area indicates the almost exclusive dormitory function of the suburbs. They rely on the city for jobs, for shopping facilities, and even for such public services as high schools, hospitals, and libraries. In its early history the city was a textile center with most of its population densely clustered around the Amoskeag Mills, a solid wall of brick and stone buildings stretching for over a mile along the banks of the Merrimack River. The persistence of the core orientation in the area is illustrated by the number of tuition students who live in outside communities and are enrolled in Manchester's high schools: they are the equivalent in school population to one of the city's three high schools. It is estimated that the tuition charged by the city and paid by the benefiting towns more than compensates the city for the operating cost of the schools, although tuition does not cover capital costs.

The surrounding communities continue diligently to preserve their independence of the central city, but the statistics gathered in the MMPS show that the city, through its sheer size and its provision of services, has perhaps more influence over local matters in the surrounding communities than might be observed superficially. This interdependence and, in fact, reliance on Manchester for many regional services were reflected to some extent in the suburban agreement to the creation of the Southern New Hampshire Planning Commission that was established during the course of the MMPS.

The pattern of development in the Manchester area is not complex. The urbanized core of the region is clustered close to the center of the city. Urban development has spread virtually symmetrically from the center. The availability of numerous bridges across the Merrimack River, the city's early development as a large mill town with close-in worker housing, and the completion of its major growth period prior to the advent of the automobile are all factors accounting for the distinctive development pattern. Apart from the Manchester urban area, which in two places spills over into adjacent communities, there are no other urban places of any significance in the region. Even strip development along arterial routes is not a critical planning factor. Driving out from the city along most arterials, one quickly passes through dense urban development and the suburban fringe and into a largely rural atmosphere long before reaching the outer boundaries of the study area. Suburban development has occurred either at the fringe of the urban area within the city of Manchester or in smaller, outlying "estate" areas, such as Bedford and Goffstown. There has been little small-lot tract development. In short, largely because of its relatively small population and its modest growth, the region consists of a small but densely settled core surrounded by low- and very low-density suburbs.

As in most urban areas, each individual community has developed certain stereotyped characteristics. The city itself is considered by outsiders as a working-class mill town, despite its size, its financial institutions, its opportunities for higher education, and its retail trade outlets. West of the Merrimack River, Goffstown and Bedford are considered high-income "Yankee" communities, although at their Manchester borders they contain some spillover of city growth. This polarization has created problems in Goffstown. Two town centers have developed, one with a higher-income, upper-class Yankee image, symbolized by the white (Protestant) church and a well-kept village green, and the other with a middle-class, French-Canadian (Catholic) label and a much less pristine appearance. These stereotypes have persisted despite efforts to bridge the gap between the two sectors. To the east of Manchester are the smaller communities of Hooksett, Auburn, and Londonderry. For the most part they do not enjoy the status of Goffstown and Bedford, although their population compositions are not dissimilar.

The median income statistics of the various communities in the 1960 census bear out the physical and social characteristics that seem obvious to the outsider. Bedford and Goffstown have the highest incomes, $6,800 and $6,200, respectively. Manchester is next, with a median income of $5,600. Ranking behind Manchester is Londonderry with $5,300, and Auburn and Hooksett bring up the rear with a median income of about $5,000 each. Median-income projections by the planning consultant did not change the rank order of the communities. The median income of the entire study area, $5,700, matches that of Manchester and clearly separates Bedford and Goffstown from the eastside suburbs.

Because of its location south of Manchester and close to the Massachusetts line, Londonderry has begun to feel the impact of new residents who work in Massachusetts but prefer to reside in rural Londonderry along its southern boundary. The projection made by the consultant did not consider this factor to be of major significance. However, it is possible that Londonderry has grown more rapidly than other communities in the study area as a result of the large-scale inmigration of workers employed in Massachusetts.

Politically, the city of Manchester presents a complex picture. The high residential densities in the city and the maneuvering for power and status among cohesive ethnic groups (the French Canadians, the Greeks, the Irish, and the Protestants) have created a highly charged political atmosphere. Ward politics in the city are rough and tumble; the representatives to the local legislative body are politically insecure and, at times, belligerent and uncompromising. Aldermen tend to reflect faithfully their constituents' biases, which include a measure of mistrust of other groups and their representatives. The composition of the Board of Aldermen changes frequently, and relations between the mayor and the Board of Aldermen are often strained. It is noteworthy, however, that the MMPS did not get caught up in the maelstrom of city politics, largely because its objectives and procedures seemed remote, technical, and unrelated to urgent city issues.

In any discussion of events in Manchester, one cannot ignore the *Manchester Union Leader*—the outspoken, highly opinionated, extreme right-wing newspaper serving Manchester and the entire state. The planning project was not among the topics on which the paper took a doctrinaire stand. Throughout the course of the study, events were reported with reasonableness and with accuracy. On the whole, the newspaper, which served as a reliable medium of information, can be discounted as having had any effect on the course or outcome of the study.

Project Chronology

For nearly a year before the beginning of the Manchester Metropolitan Planning Study, a committee composed of members of the New Hampshire Department of Public Works and Highways and the State Department of Resources and Economic Development (DRED), the official state planning agency, met regularly. The purpose of these meetings was to decide such basic questions as who should pay, what kinds of data should be collected, and who would perform the actual technical studies. Representatives of the U.S. Bureau of Public Roads (BPR) also participated, even though all decisions were theoretically made by the state agencies. A representative of the Housing and Home Finance Agency (HHFA) was on the committee, but HHFA's presence was not in evidence. Manchester's city planner was also a member of the committee, partly because the area was a city region and perhaps principally because the city contributed the bulk of the local funds to match the HHFA grant.

The Manchester Metropolitan Planning Study was authorized by the par-

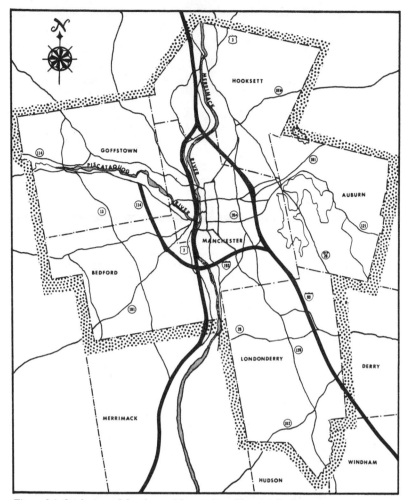

Figure 8.1. Study Area: Manchester Metropolitan Planning Study

ticipating agencies on June 9, 1964. A transportation consultant was hired, and during the summer of 1964 a number of field studies were undertaken, including home-interview surveys, origin and destination surveys using roadside-interviewing stations, and socioeconomic data on land use, income, employment, labor force, and retail sales. Preliminary interagency agreements called for a revolving fund, with approximately equal contributions from the Bureau of Public Roads ($110,000) and HHFA ($112,000) and

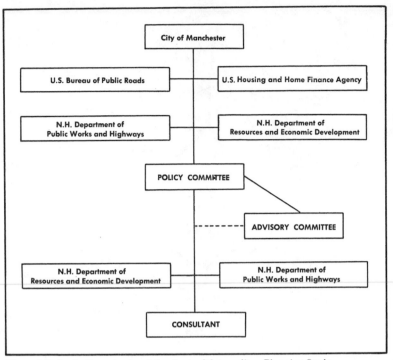

Figure 8.2. Study Organization: Manchester Metropolitan Planning Study

with each of the two participating state agencies contributing additional amounts as required. Because of administrative and funding problems, the first year of the study was financed completely by the Bureau of Public Roads and the state highway agency. The first year's work involved the collection of all travel data required in the study and the assembling of socioeconomic data, including land use, and the initial preparations of a regional land-use plan. It was not until June 1, 1965, that HHFA participated financially in the study, and by this time much of the planning effort had already been undertaken.

During the first year of the study, two contracts were signed between the state highway agency and the consultant to cover the initial phases of the study, amounting to $118,000 worth of work, the equivalent of the state highway agency's share of the project. The remainder of the study was to be financed through a single contract with the state planning agency (DRED). However, because of spasmodic federal funding, it took three separate con-

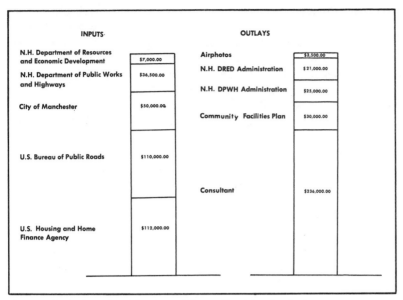

INPUTS			OUTLAYS		
N.H. Department of Resources and Economic Development	$7,000.00		Airphotos	$3,500.00	
N.H. Department of Public Works and Highways	$36,500.00		N.H. DRED Administration	$21,000.00	
			N.H. DPWH Administration	$25,000.00	
City of Manchester	$50,000.00		Community Facilities Plan	$30,000.00	
U.S. Bureau of Public Roads	$110,000.00		Consultant	$236,000.00	
U.S. Housing and Home Finance Agency	$112,000.00				

Figure 8.3. Funding of the Manchester Metropolitan Planning Study

tracts, following the initial state highway agency contract with the consultant, to complete the Manchester work.

The original study was scheduled over a fifteen-month period beginning in August 1964 and extending until November 1965; however, because of the uncertainty of HHFA funds during the summer of 1965 and the reluctance of the consultant to continue without a firm commitment, this schedule was disrupted. At the same time, the consultant reevaluated the time requirements necessary to finish the study and set a new completion date of April 1, 1966. Additional delays prolonged the technical work until October 1966. There were three reasons for the delay: the continued uncertainty of HHFA-HUD (the HHFA became the Department of Housing and Urban Development in September 1965) funds for financing the final stages, the consultant's staffing problems, and unanticipated adjustments to complaints. The Manchester City Planning Board and the Manchester Housing Authority (the city's urban renewal agency), as well as the state highway agency and DRED, raised a number of questions about the technical reports that had been issued. As a result, the consultant had to spend additional time responding to comments and making report adjustments.

The technical phase of the study was completed ten months after the originally scheduled completion date. Adding further to the study's duration was a lengthy review undertaken by the state and local agencies after presentation of a draft of the final report. This process, which involved numerous meetings between local technicians and the consultant's staff, lasted through the fall and winter of 1966/67. After an additional six-month period of official approvals, drafting, galley proofs, and printing, the final report was distributed to local officials in August 1967.

During the course of the study, in January and February 1966, DRED conducted an active campaign for the establishment of a regional planning commission. Representatives of DRED met with the town planning boards, the Manchester mayor and Board of Aldermen, the smaller-town boards of selectmen, and also resorted to newspaper and radio publicity. As a result of this campaign, Manchester and the surrounding communities approved the organization and financing of a regional planning commission, which was formally established in June 1966. However, because of the impending conclusion of the transportation study, and because a number of the members appointed to the new regional commission were also members of the Advisory Committee of the MMPS, it was decided that the regional planning commission would not function officially until the former study was completed. As the study was ending, there was an increase in attendance at the Advisory Committee meetings by future members of the regional planning commission who had not yet been assigned legal responsibilities but were interested in the Advisory Committee proceedings. This procedure permitted a smooth transition from the MMPS to the regional planning commission without any conflict between the two bodies. The new commission was thus able to begin its business with the transportation study no longer an issue and could devote itself more fully to other regional problems.

The MMPS had its share of administrative difficulties. The most severe interagency conflicts occurred during the summer of 1965 and coincided with the on-again, off-again financial support from HHFA. The initial contract with the consultant was signed in June 1964 for $110,000, a sum that committed most of the highway agency's contribution. In May 1965, with the money nearly spent and the consultant still working, the highway agency signed a supplemental contract for $8,000, presumably to tide the project over until HHFA funds were available. Finally, in June 1965, the first contract between DRED and the consultant was signed; however, some of this money was expended for work already undertaken under the presumption that a contract would be forthcoming. Within a month after signing the June contract, the consultant, unofficially supported by the state highway agency, created an issue over the lack of additional funds to continue the study. A final contract with the consultant firm was signed by the end of August 1965, but July and August were marked by increased questioning about HHFA's ability to finance the project and culminated in a major meeting to discuss the problem. Following this confrontation, in which neither side won any significant points, the project was marked by increased cooperation among the participating agencies. Apart from the problem of funding, the differences that arose concerned technical matters, specifically access to the central business district and the location of roads.

Despite its problems and conflicts, the MMPS can be considered a successful endeavor. A final report was prepared reasonably close to schedule. A regional transportation plan was developed that, for the most part, is acceptable to the technical and lay members of the community. The region now has completed a major component of its comprehensive regional plan for development. The project produced considerable data, both raw and processed, that should be useful in day-to-day operations as well as in supplemental and continuing long-range planning. The prime project sponsor seemed particularly well satisfied: the New Hampshire Department of Public Works and Highways secured a highway plan for metropolitan Manchester that provides the agency with programming guidance and meets federal criteria. Moreover, the plan has the special advantage of conforming with the agency's highway construction proposals made before the initiation of the transportation study. The comprehensive transportation plan also added a number of additional highway projects that officials of the state highway agency and local communities will undoubtedly recommend for inclusion in future federal-aid programs, although a source of funds for their construction has yet to be found.

This disparity between the cost of new proposals and financial reality, however, is not uncommon among highway-oriented studies. Few studies of the late 1940s or 1950s made any effort to relate the cost of building proposed highway facilities to the ability of the state or federal government to finance complete highway systems over a twenty-year, or longer, period. Such studies often produced plans that were unrelated to financial capabilities, and it is therefore understandable that after much disillusionment the trend is toward greater recognition of fiscal limitations in all types of studies.

The MMPS satisfactorily fulfilled its stated objectives by providing the region with a physical transportation plan showing where new highways should be built and where others should be improved. However, certain problems, which existed prior to the study, still remain, and others have been aggravated. For example, the problems of interagency coordination at the state level were still very much in evidence after the completion of the MMPS. Manchester was only one of several locations in the state where the state highway agency and the state planning agency found themselves in opposition—although the interagency conflicts in Manchester were much milder than in other places and were possibly exacerbated by events elsewhere.

Federal intervention helped to resolve disputes in other places, but participation in the MMPS project by the federal agencies was at times disruptive and counterproductive. This may have been due in part to lack of communication between Washington and the HHFA district office. In particular, there were early delays in HHFA financing and a continuing weakness in project supervision from its regional office.

The Role of the State Planning Agency

Although the Planning Division of the Department of Resources and Economic Development in New Hampshire was, to a large degree, responsible for the establishment of a regional planning commission in the Manchester area, this state agency did not fare well during the inception and early period of organization of the Southern New Hampshire Planning Commission, which occurred during the final stages of the MMPS. (The state planning agency in Maine also appeared to suffer a loss of local influence in the course of the Portland project. In the Boston area the state planning agency, which absorbed the Mass Transportation Commission, also suffered setbacks in authority, prestige, and influence as the transportation study progressed.)

It is useful at this point to review the status and functions of the state planning agencies. Although many of these organizations survived the lean period of the 1930s and 1940s, they were brought into prominence by the Housing Act of 1954, in particular its Section 701. This program was designed to assist small communities with populations of under 25,000 in preparing comprehensive plans (a later revision increased the maximum population level to 50,000). For nearly ten years the 701 program followed a set pattern. Federal 701 funds were available only to state planning agencies that contracted with the federal agency to perform these services, and in turn the state agency would contract with a private consultant to carry out the technical planning. This third-party contract arrangement was standardized, understood by all, and posed no serious problems. The state planning agency, at the hub of these contractual arrangements, was in complete control. It was in a position to guide the planning effort and to make sure that the work progressed to its own satisfaction and in line with federal requirements. As with most state planning agencies, the chief function of the New Hampshire organization was to ensure that the 701 program work in small towns was completed according to specifications and demonstrated an acceptable level of competence.

Many of the New Hampshire communities were small, and the state planning technician was the only planning professional that the town had anything to do with apart from the planning consultant or his field representative. In brief, there were no local planning staffs to second-guess state planning agency personnel, and the consultants, dependent on DRED approval, were naturally reluctant to criticize or to offer strong objections to the state planning agency procedures. Thus the state planning agency developed a secure and trusted position in administering a small, ongoing, and easily supervised program that had considerable local appeal. Relatively small amounts of money were involved, and there were no contentious local professionals to present technical alternatives and to challenge established planning policies. The program enjoyed wide public support, since comprehensive planning was considered a good thing and was so heavily financed by the federal government and the state that it caused little strain on the local tax base. As a result, DRED, like its counterpart in other states, developed a staff with strong capabilities in administering small-town planning studies. In addition, it developed some expertise in regional planning studies; it also sponsored and conducted regional studies in the fields of recreation, population, and natural resources.[1] These were small-scale affairs touching on little that was controversial and involving a close working relationship with local officials.

The urban transportation studies, which applied to urban areas with populations of over 50,000, used the same channels as the small-town 701 program and the same personnel and administrative techniques. However, this additional program proved to be a worrisome burden for DRED and similar state planning agencies. Numerous problems developed simply because procedures that had worked well at one level of magnitude were mistakenly expected to handle problems on a totally different scale. First, the amount of money involved was significantly greater in the new urban transportation planning program; hence accounting and monitoring became much more complicated. In the smaller studies, the state planning agency assisted small towns in financing their local shares by providing the services of state professionals, services that could be used to match federal funds. These services, as well as outright cash assistance from the state, were important to the towns and were often used as incentives for local support. The scale of the transportation study costs, however, made the state contribution in matching services much less significant. Project administrators and accountants were uncom-

[1] See, for example, New Hampshire, State Planning Project, *Forest Management for Better Living in New Hampshire*, Report no. 2 (June 1964), and idem, *The Water Resources of New Hampshire*, Report no. 10 (September 1965).

fortably aware that large amounts of cash were involved, that funds were being expended at an unusual rate, and that teams of federal auditors might one day call for an accounting of all the money spent.

Another, and perhaps more important, factor was the presence of a central-city planning staff, which introduced complications for the area transportation study. The Manchester City Planning Board was a good-sized agency of about ten people, four of whom were city planners by education and experience. With this type of local capability, there was little need to become involved with DRED, especially since the city itself was not eligible for any state or federal planning funds. Since the state planning agency had refrained from significant activities in the larger urban areas, there was frequently a genuine lack of communication, and occasionally animosity, between city planning professionals and the administrators in the state agencies, who were accustomed to dealing, as unchallenged experts, with acquiescent and grateful laymen in the small towns. (The differences are not so great between existing regional planning agencies and the state. In most cases, their planning is developed with the assistance or approval of the state planning agency, and their programs and staffs are frequently screened by the state agency. Thus a dialogue is established between the administering state agency and the regional planning body.) Having worked closely with many of the state's smaller communities, the state planning agency could call upon its local clients for support and assistance, especially in rural regions.

In Manchester, however, where the central city contains most of the regional population, the state agency's intimate links with the nearby smaller towns through the local 701 program did not give DRED a major advantage. DRED had administered or was involved in promoting 701 planning activities in all of the surrounding communities, but these communities accounted for only about one quarter of the total regional population. In Manchester, therefore, the state planning agency was working in a totally new environment when it tried to come to terms with the city's aggressive planning agency and related local agencies.

It appears that HUD's limited success in the urban transportation studies has been due, in no small part, to its reliance upon existing machinery and staff organization. Since these components were comparatively successful in administering a small-town planning program, HUD attempted to administer the same planning assistance program for transportation planning in large urban areas in the same manner. Perhaps the trouble was that HUD staff was simply not available to administer and operate the program. But it was not, and still is not, entirely clear what type of planning and administrative organizations can function effectively in metropolitan areas and what ends they should serve.

The Relationship Between Regional and Local Planning

The conflicting and frequently unclear relationship between local planning and the MMPS caused concern among small-town planning boards in the Manchester area. Their fears of being dictated to were allayed only after extensive discussions between the state planners and local planning boards. The Bureau of Public Roads and the state highway agency were not concerned with this problem because they had little if any interest in local planning activities. On the other hand, HUD was intimately involved because it was providing two-thirds of the financing for the local planning programs, and it was also the principal source of revenue for renewal activities in the city of Manchester. Thus potential conflicts between any one of the communities and the regional organization generally reflected on HUD but not on the BPR.

The problem of coordinating local and regional planning was complicated because, at the outset of the transportation study, the five communities surrounding Manchester represented five different phases of progress in local planning. Bedford, the most advanced, had already completed a comprehensive planning study under Section 701; Goffstown, next in order of progress, had engaged a planning firm and was in the process of preparing a local comprehensive plan; Auburn had decided to begin a 701 planning program, and not until midway during the course of the transportation study did it select a consultant who, by the end of the MMPS, was completing the initial studies. Londonderry also had decided to undertake 701 studies and, when the transportation project was concluded in late 1965, had reached the point of selecting a consultant. Hooksett, the last community in the region to become involved in comprehensive planning, by the very end of the transportation study had finally reached a decision to start on local comprehensive planning but had not gone beyond this point. A brief look at community attitudes toward regional planning efforts gives some indication of the problems of coordinating local and regional efforts.

In Bedford, the local planning board believed that its completed, published comprehensive plan would be adopted in toto by any future regional planning agency and incorporated into the regional plan. This, in fact, proved to be the case, although the local plan was prepared in greater detail than was required for regional planning purposes. This step had the advantage of freeing the regional planners of the responsibility for making arbitrary and often controversial decisions concerning local land uses. On the other hand, the adoption of an existing local plan can also lead to technical and policy problems. For example, local land-use categories are frequently incompatible with those used in regional planning, and assumptions about future economic and population growth and distribution may not be consistent with the assumptions of the regional plan. Moreover, local community objectives, in terms of land use and tax base, may not be wholly congruent with regional objectives. One obvious case is zoning for industry. (A study in Greater Boston, for example, revealed that the region contained over ten times as much industrially zoned land as could conceivably be utilized for industrial purposes.)[2]

In Goffstown, where work was in progress, the resolution of local and regional planning objectives created certain problems. The regional land-use plan incorporated the location of specific uses within Goffstown that were not compatible with the plan prepared by the local planners. These differences were only partially resolved. The presence of a local planner and a regional planner with differing responsibilities and allegiances generates problems that do not arise in communities not yet involved in local planning. In Goffstown, there was little if any conflict between local and regional objectives, although there was some apprehension about the local implications and legal status of regional land-use plans. Some felt that these plans were, in effect, regional zoning documents. Local planning boards often assume that the regional plan is controlling, that it delineates the framework of land uses within the town, and that any local planning must take place within that framework. In one small community, it was questioned whether a local planning program should be deferred until completion of the regional land-use plan. The natural instinct of the planner is to answer "no," since a "yes" would imply that local and regional planning cannot be carried on simultaneously. In fact, planning can proceed at two levels. However, in area transportation studies, there is always the danger that a regional decision derived from a transportation rather than a planning standpoint will be contrary to local planning and development concepts. In the transportation planning process, the regional land-use plan has primary significance. This traffic-oriented approach may have little or no relation to special local needs and goals and may have unanticipated and perhaps undesired consequences for the community.

The regional planning effort in the Manchester area had a significant impetus in stimulating local planning as a kind of self-protection program. Although the regional plan rarely has any binding authority, regional planning efforts often create a rush by planning boards to produce local plans that

[2] Melvin R. Levin and David A. Grossman, *Industrial Land Needs* (Boston: Greater Boston Economic Study Committee, 1961), p. 68.

can be plugged into the regional planning process. Interest in local planning may have been mild before the regional program began, but the latter became enough of a threat to trigger local planning action.

In a practical sense, it is desirable for participating local communities to have local comprehensive plans that can be fed into the regional hopper. The regional planner can then utilize existing data and does not have to speculate on community planning objectives. Even if the ultimate regional plan conflicts in some respects with the local plan, the local planning agency may not be overly concerned because it recognizes that, at least for the present, communities retain major control over land uses through zoning and subdivision regulations. The moment of truth may come, however, when vital but distasteful regional facilities are recommended for location in a specific community, as can happen with regional dumps, incinerators, or sewage treatment plants.

In the Manchester communities where local comprehensive planning had not begun or was just getting under way, there was, of course, some apprehension that the community would suffer because of its lack of preparedness. In such cases the regional planners had to assume an advocacy role, attempting to safeguard the interests of the community. Whatever their decisions, there was little danger of conflict from direct confrontation: the patient in the charity ward takes what he is given.

The greatest problems arose with the communities that were engaged in local comprehensive planning. These communities had their own technicians, usually a planning consultant whose stated or implicit assignment was to "defend" the community against the onslaughts of the regional planners. Direct conflicts of opinion over local land uses erupted. Their intensity depended on the size of the community, the depth of the differences of opinion, and the working relationships between professionals. For example, a highway proposal from the Goffstown planning board was considered unnecessary by the MMPS staff but essential by the town's planning consultant. After a period of mild and polite debate, the issue was shelved by the rather astute local planning board, which preferred to take the matter up at another time and another place.

No recommendations can be offered on how to avoid such a situation. It is hardly realistic to require that local planning be undertaken either prior to the initiation of regional planning or after the regional planning project is completed. Nevertheless, when both levels of planning are in simultaneous operation, the prospects for disagreement and delay are great.

The experience in Manchester indicates that regional agency coordination with individual communities has a greater chance of success if it makes contact directly with a "line" agency rather than through the frequently used "representative to the region."

The creation of a regional planning commission often results in the appointment of older persons in the community as local representatives. They are usually retired, with local reputations as advocates of good government, conservation, and self-help community projects, and they are rarely interested in political or controversial planning issues. Moreover, they frequently have little local influence or association with town government, although they may be part of the "establishment," serving as decorative embellishments to local government through membership on historic preservation committees, conservation commissions, or similar organizations. These representatives are rarely, if ever, asked to contribute suggestions or comments or to act as a liaison with other municipal agencies. State agencies would much rather deal with people who hold local office or are directly connected to the decision-making machinery.

Most representatives on regional commissions, particularly if the organization is advisory, show a rapidly declining interest in their role after the first meeting: in Boston, for example, as described earlier, the Advisory Committee meetings were hailed widely in the press at the outset and were attended by an impressive group of dignitaries. However, after the initial enthusiasm, subsequent subregional meetings covering virgin territory met with waning interest. In Manchester, some members from surrounding communities on the transportation study Advisory Committee were not much interested during the general proceedings because they could not comprehend the relevance of regional transportation to their own communities. On the other hand, when asked to establish meetings with local selectmen and planning boards, these same people were quite active, efficient, and even vocal. The role of listener and sounding board is apparently not a particularly satisfactory one for an elected or appointed local official. On the other hand, a position that permits him to contribute to decisions affecting overall policy is regarded as prestigious.

Local planning boards involved in the MMPS were noticeably enthusiastic about meetings between themselves and the technical staff from the Manchester study. The reason was twofold: first, local boards had a definite interest in the planning process, and this consultation gave them an opportunity to participate actively; second, and perhaps more important, the local planning board ordinarily had little access to transportation planners, and these meetings provided an opportunity to discuss the traffic and transportation problems of individual communities with experts who were already familiar with some of the local problems. In short, the towns used the meetings with transportation experts to secure free consultation on local traffic problems. (Free technical advice should not be overlooked as a device for eliciting local support. In Portland, for example, the regional planning agency was formed largely because of the potential savings and value to local communities of having an in-house advisory and consultant staff.)

As far as the general public is concerned, transportation planning as presently practiced is of little general interest, and any attempts to publicize the process are likely to remain ineffective unless accompanied by basic changes in approach and presentation. Exceptions occur in periods of conflict, when colorful accusations focus attention on disputing personalities. In the Manchester project, the local newspaper could have amplified the bickering. However, it did not choose to do so; in consequence, the project's image, for the public, was one of dull technicians working harmoniously on boring topics of interest only to themselves.

It might be observed that even in the larger cities, where interagency disagreements were more formidable, sharper, and more severe, the public was rarely exposed by the local press to these imbroglios. By and large the conflicts tended to be portrayed as personality clashes (which to a degree they were), but the basic policy differences rarely received notice. This is not to suggest that this lack of attention was necessarily an oversight. In a number of instances, what seemed to be significant issues to the participants were in fact tempests in teapots, of no concern to anyone but themselves. Perhaps the public and the press sense that the important decisions either have been made long since or would surely be reached by some other means.

HUD Objectives

HUD seemed to be overly optimistic about the potential contribution of small communities to the regional planning process. Despite the inclusion of representatives of the suburban towns on the MMPS Policy Committee, it was clear to all participants that the Manchester study was not subject to grassroots control by the small towns. The study was conducted by two state agencies, with a significant voice going to the central city, while the five suburban communities merely served as bystanders. Although HUD officials apparently felt that regional objectives and policies should have been agreed upon before development of the transportation and land-use plans, they also recognized that a study initiated and controlled by state agencies was not likely to develop goals that accurately reflected local opinion.

This raises another basic issue. The area transportation studies were not conducted in logical sequence. In theory a broad framework of regional goals should have been developed before the studies were initiated. Instead, the studies arrived at or, more accurately, reiterated and validated major decisions that were clearly going to have a major imprint on the region well before the community-controlled regional planning commissions could even be organized.

Most of the technical work prepared for the Manchester study was conducted by a transportation planning consultant firm, and it was principally initiated and controlled by the state highway agency. Under these conditions, HHFA was perhaps optimistic in its expectation that the smaller towns would be invested with a sound regional outlook as a result of exposure to and participation in a regional planning process.

The Manchester case also illustrates some of the problems that develop when a study is conducted for an area by outside agencies, and when the localities are only passive observers. It is difficult for a community to become involved in planning even if it has its own consultant working on local problems. Separation from the technical work, not always identifiable with local interests, by an additional layer of communities makes participation an almost impossible task. As one MMPS Advisory Committee member summed it up, "If this is regional planning, I'm all in favor as long as someone else pays the bill." It is interesting to note, however, that, although this individual's community subsequently participated readily in the formation of the regional planning commission and provided its proportionate share of funds for support, it subsequently refused to pay its assessment. Such a philosophy may also account for the notable lack of success of the advisory committees in the area transportation studies: the member communities had no significant financial or other interests in the proceedings, nor were they charter members of the organization.

Regional Planning versus Downtown Renewal

One of the principal conflicts in the Manchester study involved a dispute between the city's urban renewal agency, which was actively engaged in a number of projects, and the transportation planning project. The most important issue involved the priority of construction and improvement of bridges across the Merrimack River to serve the downtown area. There was an obvious difference of opinion between the planning consultant, retained jointly by HUD and the Bureau of Public Roads, and the city's urban renewal agency, which received its funds primarily from HUD. The transportation planning consultant used expansion factors in his traffic projections for the downtown area that did not take into consideration the impact of major proposals of the renewal agency. This meant that some major transportation improvements were not justified for the downtown area on the basis of projected traffic volumes that ignored the possible success of urban renewal plans. The urban renewal agency was understandably concerned; it felt that its plans to revitalize the downtown area should be considered fully, despite the fact that the trend had been toward a decrease in downtown activity and rapid growth in suburban and fringe retail and commercial traffic. It also believed that demonstrated traffic volumes should not be the only criteria for providing transportation facilities. (This raises the broader question of whether plans should be based upon developmental prospects or upon trend extrapolations. The latter method does not account for basic policy changes or shifts in local or national goals. On the other hand, planning for what might happen can be equally misleading. More than one city has been misled by attractive but unrealistic development plans.)

The argument was finally resolved by the transportation planning consultant. Anxious to avoid time-consuming delays and even more anxious to avoid technical warfare with a skilled and powerful renewal agency, the consultant determined, after due deliberation, that Manchester could have part of what it wanted: a new bridge to connect the Everett Turnpike on the west side of the Merrimack River to the central business district on the east side of the river. As a compromise solution, the consultant recommended one new bridge for the downtown area, but not for immediate construction. The urban renewal people, however, felt that this downtown bridge should be built right away to preserve and enhance downtown property values, and that a full interchange with an existing north-south expressway should also be built. Both the state highway agency and the Board of Aldermen felt that another bridge project outside the central business district was more important to the city. (The decision of the Board of Aldermen to side with the state highway agency can be explained only by a detailed study of politics in Manchester, long a favorite and productive area for political science researchers.) The compromise, while not particularly satisfying, was perhaps the only practical course of action under the circumstances. The MMPS was certainly in no position either politically or technically to dictate policy to settle a major dispute, and there was no regional executive authority that could force a resolution of this controversial issue.

Another aspect of the problem of downtown interests in gaining valid participation in regional planning efforts was the lack of participation by public transportation officials. Although trucking and other commercial highway transportation interests were well represented on the MMPS Advisory Committee, no members specifically represented public transportation. Furthermore, none of the important meetings to consider the public transportation system in the city were attended by any members of the private bus company's management. In at least one case, their absence was commented upon. When the consultant presented the findings of the mass transportation study to a meeting of the Advisory Committee, it was discovered that the owners of the local privately owned bus company were not present and had not even been informed of the study's recommendations. In retrospect, it was generally considered unfortunate that the management of the local bus company had not been invited to attend all the committee meetings.

The failure to provide a substantial role for public transportation in smaller study areas, in which virtually all travel takes place in private automobiles, illustrates a basic defect of the transportation studies—their tendency to accept and reinforce rather than revise existing transportation patterns. In both Portland and Manchester the percentage of trips made by public transportation was 4 to 5 percent. An urban population of about 75,000 appears to be the threshold at which some type of public transportation is required.[3] If genuine regional alternatives are to be considered (for example, a compact, high-density area served by efficient public transportation as opposed to low-density sprawl), it is not the most fruitful process to place basic control with the highway agencies. The latter do not see anything particularly wrong in continued urban sprawl as long as funds are provided to build the highways to serve expansive development. It quickly became apparent in Manchester, as in other areas, that minimal representation of public transportation by planners was not effective, particularly when the trends were running in the other direction. It requires courage, and a demonstration of feasible alternatives, to assert that a departure from these trends is not only necessary but feasible.

Financial Difficulties

Problems of cash flow plagued the early stages of a number of projects, and insecurity in this area clearly affected the progress of the Manchester study. This was less of a problem in Manchester than it might have been, however, because all the technical work was being conducted by one large consulting firm, which was presumably able to "carry" the project when payments were not forthcoming on schedule.

As noted earlier, although the BPR and state highway agency funds were committed and made available immediately at the outset of the Manchester

---

[3] Wilbur Smith and Associates, *Transportation and Parking for Tomorrow's Cities* (Detroit: Automobile Manufacturers Association, 1966), p. 90.

study, HUD funds were not available until after all of the BPR moneys had been expended. To complicate the problem further, the $118,000 that was to be supplied by HHFA and the state planning agency was not provided in a single lump sum but was spread out over three separate contracts. On each occasion, a separate contract with the consultant indicated the product and the sum of money to be paid. The consultant was assured verbally that he would be remunerated for his work, but he was reluctant to engage in any work not covered by a contract even though these activities were required in the normal conduct of the program. Whether this hesitation reflected a genuine concern that subsequent funding would not take place or whether it was an attempt by the consultant to assist his patron client, the state highway agency, in embarrassing HHFA-HUD is not known. However, there is little doubt that the uncertainty in funding did cause significant time loss in the conduct of the study. The consultant threatened to reduce his staff and curtail operations when funds were not immediately forthcoming, and on more than one occasion (for example, in June 1965 and again in August 1966) the firm virtually stopped operations.

It is possible that the charges of delays in funding were used to camouflage a gradual falling behind schedule on the part of the consultant. It is difficult to make this distinction, but the unfortunate funding arrangement undoubtedly had an adverse effect on study progress. It should be made clear, however, that HHFA-HUD, which was certainly responsible for some funding delays, was blamed by officials of the state highway agency for all of the time lost. Yet, in reality, there was not much to complain about on this score. Although the original time schedule for the MMPS was very optimistic, the study was completed rather faster than most of the other area transportation studies.

Part of HUD's problem arose from its organizational arrangement and budget limitations. State highway agencies, with large revolving funds that are usually allocated by state legislatures from motor fuel taxes, can control the flow of funds more uniformly. They can finance a planning program out of their current operating funds and hardly miss the money; it is an uncomplicated procedure and does not require federal approval. On the other hand, securing money from HUD for the Manchester project proved to be a time-consuming business involving more than normal amounts of patience.

The financial situation in the MMPS also partly explains a state planning agency's sense of inferiority to the highway agencies. State highway agencies normally assume full fiscal responsibility for funding transportation planning projects, knowing that the U.S. Bureau of Public Roads will eventually pay most of the cost. While BPR approval is pending, the highway agency can proceed with negotiations because it alone will be the contracting agency. What it means is that the relatively wealthy highway agencies can deal immediately and directly with contracts while their poor cousins, the planning agencies, have much less flexibility.

In most cases, the financially strapped state planning agency cannot make any commitments until it has contracted with HUD for project funds. The federal inputs from HUD do not follow channels comparable to those from the BPR. Two factors are involved. First, the state planning agency frequently acts as a collector of local and federal funds and then contracts with a consultant or agency to perform the specified task. Second, any major study usually represents a fairly high percentage of the state agency's total annual operating budget, because state planning agencies do not have the advantages and flexibility of revolving-fund financing. These cumbersome and time-consuming factors have placed the state planning agency at a distinct disadvantage in negotiating joint planning projects with their more affluent highway counterparts.

As time passed and HUD funds did become available for the Manchester study, this issue tended to fade in importance. Most of the local participants and the project Advisory Committee apparently decided that the argument over HUD funding involved nit-picking rather than real concern for the regional transportation study. Nevertheless, the issue forced the planning agency to be on the defensive during the critical design phase of the project. If the MMPS was almost exclusively directed toward highway agency objectives, the weak bargaining position of the planners was partly to blame.

It is noteworthy that neither the regional nor the headquarters staff of HHFA seemed to be aware of this problem. For example, after a disputative joint meeting of the project's Advisory Committee on August 11, 1965, attended by all the participating agencies and the consultant, the state planning agency received a letter from the HHFA regional office stating that the project appeared to be going well. The letter totally ignored the highway officials' allegations that the project might collapse because of problems in HHFA financing.[4] This letter can be interpreted in several ways. While it probably reflected a sheer lack of communication and understanding, it could conceivably have been a shrewd effort to shift blame from the shoulders of the responsible HHFA officials. In view of subsequent events, however, the first explanation seems more plausible. Private opinions were not always rosy, but

[4] Letter from HHFA Regional Director of Urban Renewal to Project Director, State Planning Project, August 13, 1965.

the HUD regional staff in charge of the project was officially pleased with both the conduct and the consequences of the MMPS.

One apparent effect of the sharp interagency bickering that erupted during August 1965 was a noticeable drop in attendance at Advisory Committee meetings, a drop that continued for several months until final recommendations began to come up for consideration. Interagency disputes were taken in earnest by the participants but were apparently quite boring to restive laymen. As a final point, it is worth noting the interesting financial arrangement between the Manchester City Planning Board, DRED, and HUD. In the MMPS, the city of Manchester contributed a large portion of the funds that were used to match the federal share. For every local dollar, HUD provided two dollars toward the MMPS study. The City Planning Board, partly as a reward and partly because it was capable of undertaking regional studies, was awarded a contract as part of the MMPS to prepare a regional public facilities plan. Inasmuch as the city made up a large portion of the region, this maneuver in effect helped the city accomplish its own planning objectives, since the surrounding towns relied heavily upon Manchester for a variety of services, including schools, libraries, and hospitals. Because the contract amount for this study exceeded the city's contribution to the MMPS, Manchester was able to amortize its contribution to the regional study by getting paid to do work it would have had to do eventually. Needless to say, this technique is growing in popularity.

Lack of Local Transportation Planning Expertise

On the face of it, one of the simpler tasks in area transportation studies is the designation of land-use categories. In practice, however, this is by no means the case. For example, initial errors in selecting suitable categories usually lead to significant problems. There is a pressing time problem, because the choices must be made early in the study before the actual work is undertaken. A certain risk is involved if categories are predetermined; categories peculiar to a particular area may be overlooked in the initial selection. In theory, the proper selection of land uses should be a task for which HUD and the planners are particularly well suited. However, neither HUD nor the state planning agency seems to be able to avoid substantial problems with land-use data.

For obvious reasons, HUD hopes to use its influence and funds to standardize land-use categories for transportation studies as well as for other types of regional planning efforts. It should be noted that the federal agency has been successful in stimulating the preparation of a standard land-use coding system; this is included and described in a manual prepared jointly by HHFA and the BPR, which has become widely used.[5] The land-use code follows the general concept of the Standard Industrial Classification system used by the U.S. Department of Labor. Virtually all land-use possibilities are covered in broad two-digit categories, while additional digits in coding system subcategories carry the classification into additional detail.

In Manchester, the land-use classification missed its mark on several counts. To begin with, the classification could make little use of existing data sources. The Manchester transportation study was begun at a time when the Department of Resources and Economic Development was nearing the completion of a statewide planning project, which, among its other tasks, had developed a set of preliminary land-use categories for use throughout the state. Initially, it was hoped that the transportation study categories could be coordinated with those used in the statewide study. However, the land-use categories used in the latter project were tailored to an effort that was oriented toward state resource and conservation planning rather than transportation. Thus the DRED categories were not applicable to a relatively urban planning region. For example, the State Planning Project separated agricultural land, forested land, and recreational land. In most cases, such land uses do not generate traffic, and for transportation analysis they can certainly be grouped together. On the other hand, residential density categories and industrial and commercial land uses were not detailed adequately for transportation planning purposes. In short, the land-use categories that had been found suitable for the resource-oriented statewide study could not be adapted for use in the traffic- and urban-oriented Manchester study.

In contrast, coordination of the land-use categories of the City Planning Board and the area transportation study was entirely feasible. In general the city land-use categories were adopted for use throughout the region, although it was subsequently discovered that they were not wholly satisfactory for the suburbs.

One serious defect in the land-use inventory did not become evident until it was too late to correct. About a year after the study had begun, it was discovered that the traffic zones adopted by the consultant at the outset of the transportation study did not have the same boundaries as the planning districts devised by the City Planning Board for its own inventory less than two years earlier. The two studies collected comparable information, but as a result of the boundary differences it will be extremely difficult for the city to make

---

[5] U.S., Housing and Home Finance Agency and Bureau of Public Roads, *Standard Land Use Coding Manual* (Washington, D.C.: Government Printing Office, January 1965).

detailed use of much of the expensive transportation study data in updating its own information. This error made the Planning Board mistrustful of the transportation consultants for the remainder of the project. The oversight could reasonably be laid at the door of the consulting firm on the grounds that it did not establish a working relationship with the City Planning Board staff before it started to collect its data. However, lack of state and federal supervision was also a contributing factor.

The City Planning Board, perhaps understandably, felt that Manchester's needs and potential contribution had been ignored in the design of the study. From one point of view, its displeasure eventually had beneficial results: in a painstaking attempt to utilize MMPS data for its own purposes, it uncovered a number of discrepancies, most of which were speedily rectified.

The city planning staff cannot be fully cleared of all responsibility for the failure to achieve maximum coordination with the regional transportation study. The inexperience of its staff in dealing with a regional effort, and particularly in comprehending the problems and procedures of an urban transportation planning study, was also a major factor. The city planning staff, on the other hand, felt that someone, either in the state planning agency or in HHFA, had been asleep at the switch in not alerting the city to the potential wasted effort and excessive work entailed by a lack of coordination. Since the state planning agency and HHFA were presumably financing the land-use data collection, there was perhaps some justification for the local staff's allegations.

This raises a basic question: Should a federal agency such as HUD finance large-scale planning efforts without exercising close supervision? On the basis of the Manchester study and other transportation projects, the answer is in the negative. Conversely, however, the extremely close supervision that the BPR normally exercises may not be necessary either. What HHFA-HUD perhaps needed most was a regional staff that understood the demands of regional analysis and, equally important, one that could devote the necessary time to a specific project. There does not seem to be any direct relationship between the size of an area and the amount of federal supervision required. Portland, for example, required little, while Manchester could probably have used more.

Although the state planning agency subsequently engaged staff to provide full-time supervision of the whole Manchester project, the important decisions relating to land-use categories were made at the very outset of the study before the full-time staff was on hand and before anyone locally seemed to know what was happening. Thus, while some inconsistencies and discrepancies were prevented during the remainder of the study, much of the advance work was completed before the adoption of final contractual arrangements. This suggests that HHFA should have exercised more supervision in the important decisions made at the start of the study program, which set its initial course.

Setting aside the special situation in the central city, the smaller towns around Manchester were totally oblivious to the need for coordination between the area study and local land-use planning. Yet, fortunately, this factor did not create any significant difficulties.

The Future Land-Use Plan

A "future land-use plan" is probably one of the most poorly defined terms in the planner's glossary. Perhaps the lack of definition of the techniques used in developing such a plan is even more significant.[6] To some, a future land-use plan is merely an extension of existing conditions modified by some recent trends. At the other extreme, it is an idealized model indicating a desirable state of affairs to which a city or region should aspire. According to some, a future land-use plan cannot be conceived until numerous alternative land-use configurations are reviewed and analyzed. To others, detailed, intensive consideration of alternatives is simply a waste of time.[7]

For a region, future land-use planning is, in essence, a guessing game; planners attempt to peer into the future to identify the scale and character of future development. Through the mid-1960s, there were virtually no statutory provisions for instituting regional land-use controls to ensure that regional development would occur in accordance with a preconceived plan. It remains to be seen if mandatory review and referral powers for regional planning commissions will alter this pattern.[8]

The land-use plan for the Manchester transportation study was based primarily on a consensus reached by individual planning boards and the consultant's staff. Although some effort was made to demonstrate potential land-use forms, such as satellite communities and radial development, the consultant's effort was largely put into meeting with local planning boards to assess their

[6] For a discussion of future land-use plans, models, and land-use configurations, see, for example, Edward C. Banfield, "The Uses and Limitations of Metropolitan Planning in Massachusetts," in *Taming Megalopolis,* ed. H. Wentworth Eldredge (Garden City, N.Y.: Anchor Books, 1967), pp. 698–709, and John Friedmann and William Alonso, eds., *Regional Development and Planning: A Reader* (Cambridge, Mass.: The M.I.T. Press, 1964), Introduction and chaps. 29 and 30, pp. 581–611.
[7] See Melvin R. Levin, "Planners and Metropolitan Planning," *Journal of the American Institute of Planners,* vol. 33, no. 3 (March 1967), pp. 78–89.
[8] Section 204 of the Housing Act of 1965 confers mandatory review of federally financed projects upon official regional planning agencies. The section has not been popular in Congress, which specifically denied HUD any money to administer the program in fiscal 1968 and again in fiscal 1969.

ideas about future growth and their opinions on the pattern they would like to see in the region. For the most part, the localities had little to suggest and were generally satisfied with an extrapolation of existing patterns. Thus the future land-use plan was a combination of a projection of current development together with some attention to "ideal" land-use arrangements injected by the regional planners. Both elements were modified to some extent by the consultant's analysis of realistic constraints on spatial development, such as holding capacity, soil conditions, and existing zoning.

Involvement of local planning officials in the preparation of the Manchester regional land-use plan had a twofold benefit: local planning boards had at least some voice in recommending future land uses affecting their individual communities, and cooperation with local planning boards (in many cases the selectmen of the smaller towns were participants) helped to secure subsequent approval of the resultant land-use plan. Thus the final plan developed for Manchester was a hybrid composed of consensus, ideals, projections, and analytical evaluation of existing conditions. How much impact on the real world it will have remains to be seen.

On the whole, the same procedure was applied to the preparation of estimates of future population. Population projections developed by the consultant were subject to review by local planning boards, and they were finally determined by the consultant after due consideration of local comments and reactions. As a result of this local involvement, population projections and the future land-use plan did not become areas of conflict as the transportation study moved along. In the city of Manchester itself, the relative decline in its proportion of regional population and economic activity created a few areas of sensitivity. Civic leaders resented the imputation that the recent adverse trends would continue. They seemed to believe that a projection is a form of magical incantation, that it has a genuine influence over future events—as indeed sometimes it has. There were also differences of opinion on the allocation of population within the city. By the time this dispute occurred, however, there was sufficient communication between the consultant and the City Planning Board so that serious arguments did not arise.

The Myth of Regional Land-Use Alternatives

Although the regional land-use plan prepared for the Manchester area evolved only after numerous meetings with local planning boards, HUD officials were still greatly concerned about whether the regional planners had fully discussed a number of land-use alternatives with local planning officials. HUD felt that the smaller communities might not have been aware of the growth options open to them because the consultant had not presented them with discrete alternatives. A first approximation of this plan was prepared by the regional planning consultant; this then provided the basis for the numerous conferences with local planners and planning boards; and, subsequently, a revised future land-use plan was prepared for the region. At this stage, it easily received the approval of the participating communities. (Each planning board formally reviewed the plan and approved its use for regional transportation planning purposes.)

This is not to suggest that the options were entirely neglected. Alternative transportation studies were prepared by the consultant to demonstrate alternative regional growth forms (satellite, concentric rings, radial, and so on). However, it was also the responsibility of the regional planning consultant to prepare a single, relatively realistic, and relevant future land-use plan for the region based on anticipated patterns of future growth.

The discussions of alternative land-use patterns may have been informative and interesting to local planning boards and other concerned people in the region, but the lack of any clear connection between the hazy, broad-brush treatment of land-use forms on the schematic maps and the current and anticipated growth patterns in the region made the discussion of alternatives a very theoretical exercise. As one Advisory Committee member put it, "All this land-use alternative stuff is very nice, but when are we going to get down to preparing a plan for the Manchester region?" As though to answer his question, an HHFA official had suggested earlier that, although regional growth alternatives are not necessarily possible, feasible, or valid, an investigation should nevertheless be undertaken as part of an authentic regional planning process. The effort seemed to be an unnecessary aspect of the planning study, which created bafflement and skepticism among the Advisory Committee members.

Project End—Advisory Committee Transition

The new regional planning commission that was established before completion of the MMPS assumed the role of the Advisory Committee, but in the process created a minor transition problem. The newly elected and appointed members of the commission were not interested in taking over a project that was so nearly finished. Fortunately, a number of members of the MMPS were ultimately appointed to the regional planning commission by their communities, so that a gradual transfer of responsibility was accomplished with a minimum of friction and hurt feelings. Nevertheless, some individuals on the MMPS Advisory Committee felt that the role of their committee should be expanded to retain some ex post facto responsibility in the regional planning process. It should be noted, however, that this was a minority reaction.

Another problem developed concerning responsibility for the continuing transportation planning function. The new commission, entitled the Southern New Hampshire Planning Commission (in effect, the Manchester region), hoped that it would be designated as the official transportation agency for the region and would thus be eligible for generous BPR funding for a wide variety of regional planning studies. The state highway agency, however, was not about to lose its birthright. Yet the disagreement was not a bitter one, since the regional representatives saw little chance of successfully challenging the BPR-backed highway agency, and they did not wish to become deeply and emotionally involved in a hopeless cause. In truth, they had more interest in obtaining federal planning funds for the region than in usurping the highway agency's traditional responsibilities.

Problems of a Joint Venture

The Manchester study is probably typical of the joint-venture types in which the BPR and HHFA-HUD participated. Some of the problems that developed between the federal agencies were inherent in their organization as well as in the standard operating procedures of the day. For one thing, the project schedule of only fifteen months as initially proposed was overly optimistic. Theoretical timing based on the minimum time path developed by a computer should not be confused with more realistic schedules that reflect agency delays, manpower turnover, and review procedures. The different techniques of financing transportation studies also proved to be a source of irritation among the agencies. The highway agency was able to deal directly with its own funds, which would be reimbursed at a later date by its federal counterpart, and was therefore in a much better position to commit itself to financing deadlines. On the other hand, HHFA-HUD financing in the Manchester study depended upon annual appropriations in Congress and was subject to congressional and administrative budget adjustments. For example, had the state's application to HHFA been submitted a few days earlier, it would not have been affected by a temporary halt imposed by the agency on 701 program funds. Such comparatively minor decisions at the federal level can have a significant impact on local operations.

The lack of adequate HHFA and DRED supervision at the outset of the study resulted in less than adequate treatment of certain areas of interest, thereby leaving the state planning agency dissatisfied with the results of the study, particularly with the data that were collected. The lack of firm federal policy was also a problem. The transportation project was half financed by HUD but found itself in conflict with HUD-sponsored urban renewal projects when decisions had to be made on transportation recommendations for the downtown area.

Because the technical work in Manchester was simple and uncomplicated, identification of the problems and some of their sources is not difficult. Some may have resulted from personality conflicts, but most of the rough spots were due to defects in the state organization created to administer the transportation study. The state planning agency's main problem throughout the project was apparently caused by its inexperience with area transportation studies compared with the expertise of the efficient and aggressive state highway agency. For example, during the first year of the study, when data were being collected and decisions on format were being made, DRED provided only token supervision. It did not have anyone available who was experienced with area transportation planning.

One overriding problem of the transportation study was a lack of expertise and even of general background on transportation planning. Although the Manchester Planning Board staff had a number of competent planners, none were familiar with the technical terms or the procedures used in comprehensive transportation planning. One result was a lack of communication between the City Planning Board and the MMPS consultant staff. This problem was partially overcome by appointing a state planning agency supervisor for the project. He was able to provide a link between the regional planning function and the City Planning Board, which proved useful to both the city and the surrounding towns in the study. However, this position was not filled early in the study, a factor that was partly responsible for the lack of communication concerning the designation of land-use categories.

One concluding note may have some bearing on HUD operations: because the state highway agency had financed the first half of the project, including most of the data collection, HUD and DRED funds financed the entire second half of the project, which covered the analysis and preparation of recommendations. Once the consultant's contract was solely with the state planning agency, the latter was in a position to ensure serious consideration of its objectives. This situation was not premeditated, but it gave the state planning agency a strong hand at the end of the project when recommendations were being formulated. The mechanics of the MMPS organization would still have given the planners a voice in the final critical stages of the study, but the contractual ties with the consultant were of particular value to DRED in the final stages of the study.

Study Area Profile

Portland, Maine, lies on the Atlantic coast approximately 100 miles north of Boston. It has strong highway connections to the Boston metropolitan area via Route U.S. 1 and, more recently, Interstate 95. The latter highway incorporates all of the New Hampshire Turnpike and the southern part of the Maine Turnpike. Current driving time between Boston and Portland is approximately two hours from city center to city center. Portland is the second largest seaport in New England. Its surprisingly heavy tonnage is directly attributable to the substantial oil storage and transmission facilities at the port. In 1962, while Boston's total port volume was slightly over 20 million tons, Portland handled nearly 16.5 million tons of cargo, 16 million of it in bulk oil shipments. The city is the terminus of major oil pipelines serving Montreal and eastern Canada and is also the terminal for oil deliveries to Maine, northern New Hampshire, and Vermont. However, the latter transshipments are normally made by tank trucks.

The Portland transportation study area of 335 square miles contains about one-sixth of the total state population and consists of the central city plus eight surrounding communities. All of these are within the jurisdiction of the Greater Portland Regional Planning Commission, which also covers a few other outlying communities as part of its territory. Established about two years before the initiation of the Portland Area Comprehensive Transportation Study (PACTS), the regional planning commission includes communities that were not made part of the transportation study because their outlying location and rural setting removed them from any significant role in regional transportation patterns. Portland is the only one of the five areas studied in this research that had a regional planning agency prior to the transportation study. (In the other areas, such agencies appear to have been a result of these studies.) Consequently, the size of the area was made smaller for transportation planning purposes, a move that reduced the data collection work load and overall technical requirements. Furthermore, it was a defensible move since transportation problems usually involve the inner parts of a region and only rarely appear at the outer edges of even a small region. This area limitation had another side effect: it reduced the membership on the PACTS citizen committees.

Although the population of Portland's metropolitan area at the beginning of the transportation study in 1963 was only about 5 percent of that of metropolitan Boston, the city at least in outward appearances is a small-scale version of Boston. The similarities include a compact downtown area, a close spatial relationship between the waterfront and the belt of old brick buildings between the waterfront and the business district, a small but distinct financial and insurance district, and a belt highway (consisting of the Maine Turnpike and its extensions to Falmouth in the north and to South Portland in the south). Most of Maine's important financial and insurance activities are located in Portland. A local branch of the University of Maine, with an enrollment of over 1,200 in 1968, is growing rapidly. It has the potential for eventually becoming larger than its parent institution at Orono. The city is also a major convention site for all of northern New England, particularly for Maine's civic and business organizations.

Portland's population of 72,000 represented slightly more than half of the regional population of 140,000 in 1963. Its sister city of South Portland, with 23,000 persons in 1963, shares harbor facilities and waterfront industrial sites with Portland and is the next largest community in the study area. South Portland lacks a central business district, however, and relies almost entirely on Portland for downtown services and shopping. Westbrook lies directly west of Portland and is a higher-income community, displaying a wide range of suburban characteristics—although it should be noted that this community is not a homogeneous suburb. It is the site of the region's largest employer, the S. D. Warren Paper Company, with an employment of over 2,000, which has the dubious distinction of being the region's most notorious air and water pollution nuisance.

Each of these three communities has a manager-council form of government with a full-time city manager. The municipalities in the Portland area have a reputation for progressive government. The city of Portland, for example, is considered a model for the Northeast. This reputation for good government extends to the state agencies, which have rarely been involved in scandals. The Maine State Highway Commission has a reputation for being highly efficient, nonpolitical, and competent in maintaining the state's far-flung rural and urban highways.

The remaining communities include Scarborough, Falmouth, Gorham, Cape Elizabeth, Yarmouth, and Cumberland, which range in population from 3,000 to 6,500 persons and are, for the most part, dormitory suburbs of Portland. Scarborough is an exception because of its close ties to the employment centers in nearby Biddeford and Saco to the south.

The Portland area has one unusual feature: approximately 1 percent of the region's population, about 1,400 persons, lives on offshore islands served by a regularly scheduled, privately owned ferry service and by licensed water taxis and miscellaneous unscheduled boat operations. During the summertime the population on the islands just about doubles its normal wintertime figure. The additional population is composed of out-of-state summer residents and mainlanders who maintain seasonal residences on the islands.

Portland's geographic location and its economic functions qualify it as a gateway to the entire state. Virtually all roads serving Maine converge on Portland. In poor weather, its airport is often the only one open in northern New England and it has modern instrument-landing equipment. In the past the airport has been used as an experimental location for new landing equipment. Despite Portland's urban orientation, only 65 to 70 square miles of the total study area of 335 square miles was in urban use in 1963. No additional surge of urban development is anticipated: by 1985 the amount of urban land is expected to increase by another 8 square miles.

The Portland area has traditionally been a strong mercantile, educational, medical, and financial region, with only a secondary role in manufacturing. In 1963 the area contained 40 percent of Maine's financial and business service employment. On the other hand, it had only one-sixth of the state's manufacturing employment.

One outstanding characteristic of the Portland area is its consistently low unemployment rate. In 1963 the jobless rate was 2 percent, or less than half the national average. This was due in part to the expansion of the local economy, but an even more important factor was the continuing and substantial outmigration of job seekers. The Portland area has succeeded in achieving a closer balance between available manpower and available jobs than many other areas in or out of New England. During the 1950–1960 period, net outmigration was roughly 10,000. As a result the population increased by only 5,000, or 0.6 percent, over the decade.

Projections of land use, population, employment, and labor force suggest that the Portland area will experience a gradual but modest growth in the next two decades. Employment is expected to increase by about 25 percent between 1960 and 1985. The city's role as the state's dominant administrative center will probably expand. It is estimated that between 1960 and 1980, 3,000 more persons, representing an increase of about one-third, will be employed in business and personal services.

Project Chronology

The Portland Area Comprehensive Transportation Study was in one sense a pioneer: it was one of the first transportation studies to meet the requirements of the 1962 Federal-Aid Highway Act, and it was the first study to be completed in Region I of the Housing and Home Finance Agency (HHFA).

A transportation study for the Portland area had been recommended by the State Highway Commission before enactment of the 1962 Highway Act and some four years before PACTS was initiated. The original proposal, calling for a straightforward highway study with only token consideration of land use, was very much in the pattern of other highway studies conducted during

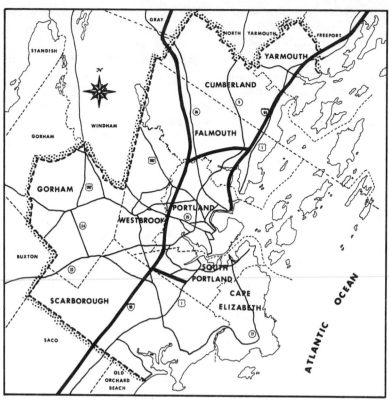

Figure 9.1. Study Area: Portland Area Comprehensive Transportation Study

the 1950s. However, the project lay dormant for a number of reasons, the main one being cost. The Portland study was initiated at about the time the cost of transportation studies underwent a quantum jump. During the 1950s a typical highway study conducted by a state agency was expected to cost about $1.00 per capita, and this is what the Maine highway agency expected; however, the consultant's estimate in 1959 for the proposed study in Portland was in the neighborhood of $4.00 per capita. Area transportation studies were apparently becoming much more elaborate at about this time. The use of massive data files, generated by extensive home interviews, other surveys, and gravity models, resulted in a substantial increase in total study costs. Another delay in the early study proposal was caused by the Maine State Highway Commission's attempt to secure the participation of the cities and towns in the technical work (perhaps by collecting local statistics) as well

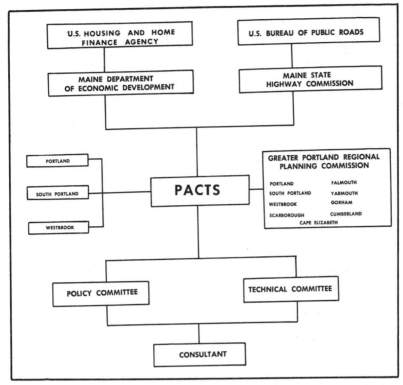

Figure 9.2. Study Organization: Portland Area Comprehensive Transportation Study

as in the financial obligations. Thus the Portland transportation study was on-again, off-again for more than four years.

The Portland study was initiated in June 1963 with a scheduled completion date of December 1964. The eighteen-month period was considered to be the minimum time necessary to conduct a study of this nature. Most remarkably, the final report was printed in April 1965, only five months after the scheduled completion date. PACTS was financed jointly, but not equally, by the U.S. Bureau of Public Roads (BPR) and the Housing and Home Finance Agency; however, unlike subsequent studies, such as those in the Boston and Manchester areas, there was no combined or "revolving" accounting arrangement. Each federal agency, through its state counterpart, financed and contracted with a transportation consultant for specified parts of the comprehensive study program. HHFA, together with its state and local partners, contributed about $70,000 and financed only those parts of the study

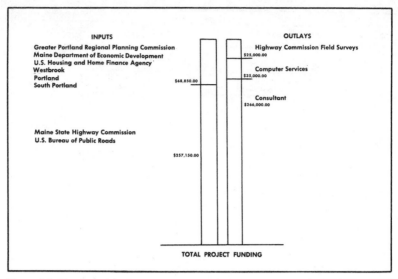

INPUTS

Greater Portland Regional Planning Commission
Maine Department of Economic Development
U.S. Housing and Home Finance Agency
Westbrook
Portland
South Portland

$68,850.00

Maine State Highway Commission
U.S. Bureau of Public Roads

$257,150.00

OUTLAYS

Highway Commission Field Surveys
$25,000.00

Computer Services
$35,000.00

Consultant
$266,000.00

TOTAL PROJECT FUNDING

Figure 9.3. Funding of the Portland Area Comprehensive Transportation Study

dealing with land use and socioeconomic considerations. The Bureau of Public Roads and its state partner, the Highway Commission, contributed about
$200,000, financing the remainder of the work, including the conversion of
land-use data to provide the necessary transportation parameters. The preparation of highway plans as well as other aspects of the study, except for the
regional planning item, was paid for from highway sources, which, all told,
provided nearly 80 percent of the total funds for PACTS.

The field studies conducted during the summer and fall of 1963 covered a
total of 3,700 home interviews and interviews with operators of 40 out of 80
registered taxis and 1,160 out of 7,000 trucks. Moreover, a cordon-line survey intercepted about 40 percent of the traffic and resulted in another 37,000
interviews. In addition, a land-use survey covering 300 square miles recorded
all identifiable land uses. (It may be of interest to note the survey costs
incurred in PACTS, which are perhaps typical of other studies conducted
during the early 1960s: home interviews cost $10.00 each; truck interviews
$9.00 each; taxi interviews $35.00 each; and individual roadside interviews
of car drivers $0.40 each.)

The winter of 1963/64 and the spring and summer of 1964 were devoted to
data analysis and collection. During the summer of 1964 an emergency arose:
a rush decision had to be made on the route location of an interstate highway
through Portland, which was to become the most important recommendation

of the study. In the fall of 1964, project recommendations were formulated, and the fieldwork for highway location recommendations was started. December 1964 saw the completion of the final draft of the report. Following a three-month review period, it was approved for printing in March 1965, and in June it was distributed to the appropriate agencies. The total consultant's fee for the project was $266,000. The State Highway Commission contributed an additional $30,000 worth of data-processing services through its arrangements with the Bureau of Public Roads. It also provided the personnel for all of the data collection, except for the land-use study, at an estimated cost of about $25,000. Thus the total cost of the Portland study is estimated at about $320,000.

The consultant's arrangements with the two participating state agencies involved separate contracts with each. The highway agency contracted to pay for the transportation inventory and all the necessary supplementary socioeconomic data, such as population and land use. The State Department of Economic Development (DED), the state's planning arm, contracted for work that it considered critical, such as the preparation of a future land-use plan showing what the region could attain—if regional land-use controls were adopted. DED also provided funds for a detailed analysis of the location of proposed routes to provide a basis by which to measure their impact upon the individual communities, an effort that was lacking in most area transportation studies.

In the PACTS organization, the relationships between the Policy Committee, the Technical Committee, and the transportation planning consultant were standard. The Policy Committee was established to act as the principal liaison body between the study organization and the various communities. It had little if any real policy-making power. The Technical Committee was to provide guidance on such matters as techniques and preliminary results of the intermediate steps in the study; it was also helpful in obtaining data from various public and private agencies.

The rather minor delays in the final stages of the study can be attributed to technical problems involving the correlation analysis and the gravity model. Each of these parts of the analysis utilized computer programs available through the Bureau of Public Roads. The principal delaying factors concerned use of the computer. Errors in machine operations, errors in programming, and misinterpretation of desired information proved costly and time-consuming. In other respects, however, the study's progress was very close to the original work schedule. The Portland study, although not unique in this regard, produced a complete and thorough set of technical memoranda describing the various aspects of the study for the Technical Committee and informed the federal agencies about the procedures and results of the study components. Such publication of background technical memoranda was also the practice in the Chicago and Penn-Jersey studies. Experience indicates that these technical publications provide the sponsoring agencies with a thorough description of what they are paying for and serve as a useful tool for establishing communication between the federal agencies and the transportation study.

Level of Detail of Highway Location

Some officials of the Department of Housing and Urban Development (HUD) maintain that the greatest lasting benefit from the department's funding of urban transportation studies comes through the subsequent creation of new regional planning agencies or the stimulus they provide for existing regional planning activities. From a long-range, high-level Washington point of view, this may be true. At the local level, however, HUD participation, in terms of money and supervisory staff, has a different meaning. The substantial allocation of HUD funds implied to local officials that urban transportation planning meant more than simply highway planning, and that, even if highway construction was to be proposed, location and relocation and other highway impacts would be given greater attention than in previous transportation planning studies. In short, it was anticipated that special attention would be given to land use, social and economic considerations, and housing. This was not necessarily the case, partly because most of the studies were dominated by highway agencies, despite HUD participation, and partly because public concern over highway dislocation and other local impacts seemed too parochial for most of the upper-echelon staff in the area studies. Many city planners and highway planners argue that regional transportation planning should not concern itself with the location of specific facilities (which is an urgent matter to the affected public) but should focus on the big picture, policies, concepts, overall system design, and corridor identification. The concerns of local politicians, local technicians, and the general public with the immediate problems of highway location in built-up areas and the impact on housing, land use, and the quality of urban life were not reflected in four of the five studies examined in this research.

Portland was an exception; a substantial effort went into a specific identification of the location of proposed highways. As a result, the Portland city planning department, as well as the Greater Portland Regional Planning Commission's technical staff, spent considerable time in evaluating alternative highway locations and assessing their probable impact on housing and land use. There were perhaps two reasons for this emphasis: the work items in the consultant's contract with the Maine Department of Economic Development called for special studies of highway location impact, and DED had a direct contract with the consultant and was able to control the study emphasis.

This type of detailed study of the highway proposal in an urban area often produces a confrontation between those in favor of a specific highway and its location and those opposed. This is one reason why prudent administrators attempt to avoid or at least postpone detailed analysis. If a consultant, or the project staff, does not have a contractual obligation to devote much time to such analysis, discretion is usually considered advisable. The Boston and Buffalo projects were typical in this respect; both studies carefully excluded consideration of specific highway locations. Transportation corridors were their finest level of detail. Although transportation planners generally agree that even in corridor analysis an awareness of potential highway location is necessary, most biagency studies have avoided the knotty issues involved in route location in favor of merely identifying transportation corridors. This decision not only relegates the hard-core problems of location to a state's highway engineers but also gives the latter responsibility for major decisions affecting social, economic, and land-use patterns within a broad swath of territory. Most of the studies either called for the construction of additional highways or served as implicit endorsements of past highway agency proposals calling for new roads. The Portland study was a departure from this practice, since planning funds were earmarked for detailed, on-the-ground location studies of major highway proposals. The contract with the transportation consultant on the Portland project specifically provided for such studies.

In the Portland project, HHFA (through its state counterpart) contributed only about 20 percent of the total cost. Its funds were allocated through contractual arrangements with the consultant, which were separate and distinct from those established between the consultant and the Bureau of Public Roads through the state highway agency. HHFA's influence resulted in a more comprehensive approach to transportation planning. Moreover, this separate arrangement was theoretically comparable to the letting of a single contract. In the Portland study, unlike the others, HHFA had the final word on the research it was financing. Thus the level of attention given to land use undoubtedly resulted from HHFA work specifications and financing through a separate consultant contract. This may suggest that an agency that for one reason or another tends to be the weaker sister in joint projects might do well to consider breaking off pieces of the work to ensure that its interests and objectives are not submerged. In contrast, the Manchester, Boston, and Penn-Jersey transportation studies were run on an integrated basis, and HHFA-

HUD did not press for (and probably was unable to assure) critical evaluation of the land-use impact of highway proposals.

HHFA policy for the area transportation studies in the early 1960s apparently centered on its concern for a long-range payoff in planning rather than on the problems of highway or facility location in urban areas, a role that Washington officials in the late 1960s regarded as critically important. Because of HUD's experience and statutory obligations for housing and urban planning, its participation in highway location studies is usually welcomed by local officials. Moreover, its involvement is eagerly sought by the Bureau of Public Roads on explosive "inner belt" and "cross-town expressway" issues in which family relocation, destruction of neighborhoods, and land use are critical problems. Specific highway location in urban areas entails much more effort, supervision, and potential conflict than studies confined to examining only broad policy and general location.

The question is whether HUD, in future broad-based, multiagency efforts, will concern itself primarily with policy, education, and the furtherance of regional thinking or whether it will show concern for more immediate, politically explosive location problems and other controversial issues facing the localities. The answer probably depends upon the role of the regional officials. It should be noted that the urban transportation studies required by the 1962 Federal-Aid Highway Act were not predicated on HHFA participation. Rather, the highway planning requirement reflected a growing nationwide demand for improved highway location techniques and for more attention to their impact on the urban landscape.

Intercity Travel Considerations

In studying the transportation problems of an urban area, there is some question of the need for and appropriateness of investigating intercity travel requirements, that is, air, bus, and rail transportation. Forms of transportation other than automobiles and local urban public transportation play a very minor part in the total urban transportation process. However, they frequently receive more attention than may be warranted because they are interesting both to transportation technicians and to lay committee members who are major participants in the planning studies. Such facilities are normally highly visible aspects of the community's transportation system, and it is therefore understandable that they command considerable attention. The tendency to devote more than necessary effort to regulated intercity transportation, such as that provided by scheduled airlines and buses, can also be attributed partly to the ready availability of voluminous statistics. The transportation planner, aware of the difficulties and costs involved in obtaining good urban transportation data and knowing also the rather fragile accuracy of much of the data, is frequently impressed by the reams of statistics collected by the state and federal regulatory agencies that supervise intercity transportation systems. Thus it is difficult for the planner, after spending considerable time in collecting numerous bits and pieces of automobile travel information, not to make more use of this vast body of statistics than is strictly necessary.

Nostalgia can also be a significant factor. Committee members are apt to be considerably older than the technicians and may well remember the important role that other modes of transportation used to play. For example, in the Portland area, many of the Policy Committee members retained happy memories of the old days, when frequent and relatively fast train service was available between Portland and Boston. Commuter rail service, however, had little current meaning for younger people in the community, who were accustomed to a convenient two-hour turnpike drive to Boston. It is also not unusual for appointees to transportation study committees to have some reputation as former transportation experts or, at least, as transportation hobbyists—collectors of memorabilia, testifiers at hearings, and frequent letter writers. More often than not, this interest extends mainly to railroads, but there are ferry buffs and technological enthusiasts for monorail and other more exotic forms of transportation.

In late 1964, while PACTS was in process, the Boston and Maine Railroad discontinued the last remnant of rail passenger service to Portland. With the passenger volume down to twelve persons per day, legal discontinuance was a mere formality. Nevertheless, PACTS did examine rail transportation as a viable possibility. The report suggests that, based on Boston and Maine figures, weekend operation was perhaps more feasible than normal commuter operations. This was justified by the recreational nature of Maine's economy and the volume of weekend travel on the railroad—when it did run—which was usually greater than on weekdays. Discontinuance of rail passenger service apparently represents the symbolic removal of a city from the major league of metropolitan areas. Passenger rail service is frequently considered to be a mark of visible success and importance. The rationale is as follows: the availability of interstate transportation is important to a region's economy and to its image as a growing and progressive area. While there is no doubt that commuter railroads may be important to an area, at least from the standpoint of morale, it is doubtful that much time should be spent on them in urban transportation studies in the smaller areas. Perhaps one solution might be to exclude railroads from area studies and examine them on a statewide, or even regional, basis.

At the opposite end of the transportation spectrum is aviation, a mode of transportation that is increasing in importance. In PACTS, the airport analysis was more detailed than would normally be the case. Although the city of Portland owned and operated the municipal airport and was making a profit from it, the City Council was interested in transferring it to state ownership because of alleged revenue losses. As PACTS progressed, the local Chamber of Commerce conducted a study which demonstrated that the airport was in fact a profitable operation. The City Council thereupon curtailed its efforts to transfer ownership of the facility and concentrated, instead, on developing a program of airport improvement. Because of this expression of interest, PACTS allocated more time and effort to the airport and its future.

PACTS' approach to the Portland airport was not unusual. In most transportation studies, airport facilities are treated primarily in terms of ground access and automobile traffic generation and only secondarily in terms of their growth potential and service to other areas. Airports constitute prime locations for industry and commerce, and are perhaps studied in more detail by transportation planners because of their potential internal surface traffic generation than because of their primary transportation function.

The Federal Aviation Administration (FAA) maintains liaison with the area transportation studies to ensure that airport access is given proper weight. Although that agency's interest is only minor in terms of the total picture, it is significant that such liaison was established in Portland and, moreover, that there was effective coordination between the federal agencies. HHFA kept the FAA well informed as the study progressed, so it could be assured that ground access was adequately considered. With both the Bureau of Public Roads and the Federal Aviation Administration now housed in the Department of Transportation (which also has been assigned responsibility for mass transportation), it is interesting to speculate on the trend in airport access proposals that will appear in future transportation studies. Certainly, the effort directed at alleviating access problems is likely to increase. A harbinger of things to come may be found in the Manchester study. As it entered its "continuing" phase, a member of the FAA held a technical-level position on the interagency coordinating committee.

The Portland study shows that there is a greater emphasis on intercity transportation in the smaller urban areas; there, economic relationships to major regional complexes are likely to be extremely important. In the larger urban areas, where there is less dependency upon other major regions, there appears to be less concern for the requirements of intercity travel, although the need is recognized for projections of airport passenger volumes and employment. The ground access problem has become critical in many larger areas. Airports are usually major generators of local traffic, and traffic projections must depend upon projections of air passenger services and of employment at the terminals and related industrial and business establishments.

Citizen Participation

The Portland area transportation study had two well-defined and active citizen participation groups. The Technical Committee (which included citizen members) met regularly to review and approve technical procedures and results. The Policy Committee, theoretically the highest study authority, was constituted to make policy decisions in connection with the transportation study, a task not easily defined in advance and an objective not easy to achieve. Several of the Technical Committee and most of the Policy Committee members were representatives from participating communities. Contingents from state and local agencies composed of officials serving in ex officio capacities rounded out the committees.

The Technical Committee became a useful tool for the consultant during the technical phases of the study. This committee, consisting of "working" officials of the Maine State Highway Commission, the Maine Department of Economic Development, the city of Portland, and the Greater Portland Regional Planning Commission, was reasonably well versed in regional planning concepts and could comprehend techniques and analyses at a fairly sophisticated level. The area's important transportation and planning agencies therefore had professional representation on the committee. In addition, South Portland and Westbrook, neither with an official local planning agency, were represented by their police chiefs, who turned out to be knowledgeable about local traffic problems. The remaining small communities were represented on the Technical Committee by one member, who was appointed by the Policy Committee as an ex officio member. In this case, the person elected had an engineering background, was able to give considerable attention to the study, and was well informed.

In small urban areas such as Portland, where the fringe communities are rural and have weak ties to the central city, transportation planning is usually restricted to small segments of the overall highway system, including bypasses, new access roads to recreation areas, or new proposed industrial parks—problems that can hardly be considered regional in nature.

Several members of the Technical Committee were engineers and planners, who contributed significantly to the development of the study and to its recommendations. Meetings were held on the average of once a month. Attendance was usually high and the sessions useful. Although the Technical

Committee included, ex officio, two representatives of HHFA, neither one attended a meeting. As a result, there was little contact or correspondence with HHFA in connection with Technical Committee activities, or for that matter in regard to the study as a whole.

In general, technical committees in the area transportation studies were either separate entities with memberships comparable to the policy committees or consisted of "working" members of policy committees. All the studies had representatives on their committees from each of the federal agencies involved. HHFA-HUD normally assigned personnel from the regional office, hundreds of miles away from the study area, while the BPR usually assigned men from the local district office, its district engineer serving on the policy committee and its planning and research engineer serving on the technical committee. This arrangement obviously put HHFA at a disadvantage because its committee members were in New York City, over 300 miles away. Moreover, HHFA-HUD staff were spread thin; they seemed to serve on many more committees than their BPR counterparts.

The Policy Committee in Portland consisted of representatives from each of the federal and state agencies as well as each of the participating communities. Federal and state members on the Policy Committee represented a higher level of authority than those on the Technical Committee. There were two HHFA members on the Policy Committee, and, as on the Technical Committee, neither one ever attended a committee meeting. HHFA apparently did not intend its officials to become an integral part of these committees. The inclusion of HHFA members at all was presumably to ensure participation in the decision-making process, since HHFA was footing a part of the bill.

The only HHFA official to visit the Portland project during its entire operation was a Region I official, an ex officio Technical Committee member, who attended a Policy Committee meeting. This token participation was occasioned by an HHFA request to change the name of the study from the Portland Area Comprehensive Transportation Study to the Portland Area Comprehensive Planning Study—to emphasize the role of HHFA in these studies. It is significant that neither committee responded favorably to this rather innocuous proposal, which would not have had any effect on the conduct of the study.

Unlike the Technical Committee, which was often involved in useful deliberations and discussions, the Policy Committee was unable to carve out a role for itself. Its meetings were less frequent, and its function was unclear to the membership. It was understood throughout most of the study that questions of procedure, review of technical results, and presentation of recommendations for improvements were the responsibility of the Technical Committee. As a result, the Policy Committee's activities were limited to providing educational information and liaison between PACTS and the communities. It was anticipated that its most important function would be to review proposals. The problem was that the proposals to be reviewed were not available until the very end of the technical study, thus leaving little to do in the interim. Further clouding the role of Policy Committee members was the procedure for submission of proposals. By the time that proposals and recommendations reached the committee, they had been thoroughly evaluated and discussed by the Technical Committee members. (Realistically, it would have been very difficult for Policy Committee members to alter any proposals or recommendations since they lacked technical expertise; this became especially difficult in the face of previous endorsements by the Technical Committee.) Drafts of the final report were sent to all Policy Committee members with the request that they evaluate the recommendations and be prepared to propose changes at a subsequent meeting. Although this request was taken seriously by some members, and their criticisms resulted in several minor changes in wording, most people on the committee felt they could do very little to the report at that late date.

The Portland organization, especially the Policy Committee, turned out to be less than ideal. It is perhaps significant that in subsequent studies, such as the one in Manchester, an advisory committee played a combined quasi-technical and quasi-policy committee role. The technical discussions in the Manchester study were confined to participating technicians and did not include laymen. Advisory Committee meetings discussed such matters as work schedules and the presentation of data to the public. Technical matters were discussed but, unless they dealt with public transportation or new highways, met with little interest.

Perhaps one of the few advantages of the Policy Committee was that it permitted limited participation by the smaller communities without enlarging the size of the Technical, or "working," Committee. In Portland, as in other urban areas, outlying parts of the region must be considered in area transportation studies even though most of the important problems do not concern them. In the Portland study, proposals relating to outlying communities did not involve large sums of money or entail the threat of community disruption. The inclusion of several core-city representatives on the Technical Committee reflected the obvious importance of the cities on both the Technical and the Policy Committee. The core cities assumed key roles while the smaller communities took a back seat.

One reason for establishing the Policy Committee in Portland was to ensure good public relations and increase the chances for community acceptance of proposals. This is a standard procedure in many civic endeavors; the cooperation of communities is elicited by placing local officials on committees even though they may play rather limited roles in the actual decision-making process. However, as this study points out, urban transportation studies did not hold much interest for most people. Thus the role of the Policy Committee as a public relations vehicle had little relevance to the study and carried little importance for its participants.

In general, the Policy Committee did not raise any significant or new issues. There was, however, one exception to this generalization. The Technical Committee and the consultant tended to downgrade the need for a detailed study of the ferry service to the offshore islands because they did not consider the islands important in regional transportation planning. Nevertheless, one community, Cumberland, felt that its offshore island, Great Chebeague, had great potential and was not adequately served by the ferry system. The Cumberland representative raised this issue at a Policy Committee meeting and persuaded the committee to get the consultant to conduct a detailed survey of ferry service to all of the islands. The Policy Committee thus exercised its greatest power by forcing the inclusion of another study item. This is not as marginal as it seems. While the vague functions of the Policy Committee, such as education and information, provided little satisfaction to its members, the ability of the participating communities to affect the conduct of the study even to a slight degree made a valuable contribution to morale. For the technicians it was important that this recommendation was fairly marginal; it did not interfere with the operations of the study or the activities of the Technical Committee. It might be pointed out that technicians, for the most part, did not participate in activities of the Policy Committee. This separation avoided any head-on confrontations; unfortunately, it also widened the distance between the Policy Committee and the key decisions.

It is not unusual for studies to be delayed by problems and conflicts within a committee that is not directly connected with the technical operation of the study. In the Boston project, for example, interagency conflicts at committee meetings and agency staff conflicts contributed to severe delays in the eventual completion of the project. In Portland, however, even though there was minor controversy at the Policy Committee level, it did not slow progress. When the Policy Committee wanted to affect a particular technical procedure, such as expanding the study to the ferry service, it voted on the issue rather than becoming embroiled in a dispute with the technicians. It is significant that this procedure of separation has been effective in other studies.

Coordination with Urban Renewal Projects

During the course of the Portland study, the cities of Portland and Westbrook both initiated urban renewal projects for their central business districts. In Portland the project began about six months after the area transportation study. This timing was fortunate because it gave the urban renewal planners an opportunity to make use of the data being collected for the transportation study and to discuss matters with the latter's staff. At the outset the local planning consultant's project director met with the transportation study project director to review the work of their individual projects and to determine which data would be transmitted to the urban renewal agency. The two directors also discussed the overall planning objectives of their respective studies.

Despite this preliminary contact and an auspicious beginning, the transportation and urban renewal planners soon parted company. Except for one or two additional contacts to find out when data would be delivered to the urban renewal agency, there was no direct contact between the two staffs. Using the same data, each reached somewhat different conclusions on the future layout of certain downtown streets. For example, the PACTS staff had been informed by the city of Portland that the renewal plans would call for creating a pedestrian mall that would eliminate the main downtown street and would require major improvements of circumferential streets. The transportation study plan incorporated, in effect, a street circulation plan for downtown Portland that was a component of the regional highway system. Although it did not call for banning traffic on the main business street, it did concede that a pedestrian mall could be developed without disrupting the proposed circulation plan. Despite the broad base of agreement on the overall approach to downtown circulation, the exact location of a bypass street generated friction between the two opposing bodies. This issue, which revolved around the question of how compact the central business district should be, was not resolved during the course of the transportation study.

The final plan, which included a circulation component for the downtown area, was not altered to reflect the criticisms of local urban renewal officials, but the project report did state, in effect, that alterations required by urban renewal plans could be accomplished with little difficulty.

The future possibility of a major urban renewal project in the downtown area may eventually warrant consideration of using Spring Street instead of Free Street as part of the central business district circumferential. If such a plan is adopted its only requirement should be that it conform to the basic traffic objectives of this report.[1]

The report contained another comment relating to urban renewal that underscored the divergence in objectives:

[1] Maine, State Highway Commission and Department of Economic Development, *Portland Area Comprehensive Transportation Study: Final Report* (April 1965), pp. 107–108.

Urban renewal plans now underway in the city of Portland anticipate the development of a pedestrian mall along Congress Street entirely eliminating traffic on this section of the street. This idea has merit and should be considered; however, the recommendations of this report are not based on the possibility of future developments but solely on the potential utilization of this street for traffic purposes. [2]

The latter statement may hold the key to the conflicts between highway agencies and urban planners that have developed in other areas. Transportation planners are often reluctant to include as "givens" the potential results of direct intervention by an urban renewal authority or any other agency to alter an existing, presently foreseeable land-use trend. When these developments affect a relatively small part of a large city, they may not conform to the expected or gradual growth trend used by the transportation planners. Thus the engineer may be hesitant to alter proposals on the basis of "possible" urban renewal plans that do not agree with the transportation planner's extrapolation of existing trends. In such cases the engineer feels that he has little alternative but to follow traditional practices unless directed to do otherwise.

City planners, however, convinced that the acceptance of their planning proposals and the subsequent economic benefits are imminent, feel that transportation planners should accept their proposals as future fact rather than as mere probability. In urban renewal projects, a Land-Use and Marketability Study (LUMS) is prepared, usually by a recognized expert in real estate values, showing the potential market and generally how a project can be designed to be economically successful. The renewal planners in Portland attempted unsuccessfully to inject these LUMS projections into the transportation plan.

The same situation arose in Manchester, where projections for downtown-area retail sales were not as optimistic in the transportation planner's report as those suggested by the urban renewal agency. The latter felt that a downtown renaissance was possible under certain conditions, one being improved access. In that case the urban renewal planners felt that any transportation recommendations that did not favor, or did not take into consideration, the changes brought about by renewal would be disadvantageous to the urban renewal process. What emerges is a chicken and egg situation. If new highways are recommended to serve the downtown area, it is possible that increased commercial activity will indeed occur. However, downtown retail trends in most central cities continue to decline or, at best, level off. It is a moot question whether improved access will increase downtown viability, and thus validate the urban renewal projections, or whether it will be only an

[2] Ibid., p. 107.

expensive development, unlikely to reverse the long-term trend.

On the whole, postproject events in Portland seem to confirm the state highway agency's view that roads should be constructed on the basis of existing trends. The agency believed that improved access (or the promise of it) to the downtown area would not necessarily result in increased commercial activity. An interstate expressway route is to be built adjacent to the downtown area, and major arterial connections from the interstate route to the downtown area have already been programmed and designed. But, despite this commitment, a major department store chain declined a downtown location late in 1968. Instead, it decided to develop a large new suburban shopping center on the belt highway. In addition, the downtown area's largest office employer (an insurance company with about 800 employees) announced plans to relocate and expand on a site farther from the center, although possibly within the city limits. Both decisions have no doubt seriously affected the renewal potential for downtown Portland.

While the Portland experience may not have direct application to other areas, it may serve to explain why transportation planners are reluctant to base decisions on proposals that run counter to past trends. The proponents of urban renewal, however, are legitimately concerned over any decisions that might prejudice the success of a major project.

On the whole the opposition raised by urban renewal agencies in many cities has been beneficial, because they have made the transportation planners aware of the impact of their highway location decisions. In both Portland and Manchester, because of their small size, successful resolution of these controversies was important in guaranteeing that the highway plans did not conflict at least with the urban renewal objectives.

In Westbrook, urban renewal planning was begun at the very end of the transportation study. Here the transportation planners recommended, as the first step toward a proposed major bypass route, the early construction of a short segment around the central business district rather than a total bypass of the built-up section of the city. The plan referred to the possibility of using urban renewal for land acquisition purposes and as a way of solving the comparatively small relocation problems created by the bypass. Arguments for the proposed route suggested the removal of substandard housing and the positive improvements in land use that would result from the highway.

One interesting development occurred in Westbrook. The transportation study staff and the urban renewal consultant who had been hired by Westbrook had reached agreement on a general location for the bypass, but the planning director of the regional planning commission strongly favored a bypass in a totally different location on the opposite side of the main street, although this alternative would have the same effect on traffic patterns. As a result, there was considerable discussion at technical meetings over the location of the bypass. It was subsequently discovered that the planning director was not representing the point of view of his regional planning commission but was merely expressing his personal opinion. When the lack of planning agency support became evident, the controversy evaporated.

This minor squabble points out a technical staff problem often recognized but rarely resolved: for all practical purposes the technical staff controls rather than serves its employer. In the case of Westbrook the regional planning commission members were not aware of the issues involved and probably did not know the extent of staff activities. While this is only one example, it has been repeated frequently, and usually in more important ways. Members of commissions and boards usually support staff recommendations because they are either indifferent to an issue or cannot offer technical alternatives. The staff point of view may or may not be the same as that of the majority of the planning commission members, but it carries great weight because it is presented with the full force of technical expertise. The reason for this state of affairs is quite simple: staff technicians operate on a full-time, paid basis while planning commission members, regardless of their background, are part-time and unpaid. This may be a serious problem as more planning commissions are established, secure their own financing, and obtain staffs that are technically qualified but not, as a rule, capable of giving genuine direction. Perhaps the membership of a regional planning commission should have a substantial technical background. The role of such a commission is discussed more fully in the last chapter.

The Highway Location Emergency

Halfway through the study, the need arose for a quick decision on the location of Interstate 95 through the city of Portland. Although it was known at the outset of PACTS that a decision on this route would have to be made, the study was not geared to provide a quick answer. Not until the technical work was under way and had progressed to the point of generating considerable data was it decided to ask the big question early in the game. The solution to this highway location problem was to become the most significant recommendation of PACTS. The consequences of this key decision would affect all other highway proposals for the region, yet it was made completely out of sequence, long before the scheduled completion date of the study.

The State Highway Commission gave assurances that a preliminary determination, based on hurriedly prepared statistics, could be changed if more thorough analysis subsequently dictated a different answer. In this as in other cases, however, an early decision based on scattered data confirmed assumptions based on no data at all. The decision was subsequently validated by the weight of later, serious analysis.

The location of Interstate 95 through the downtown Portland area and northward had been determined, but the best route south of the city to connect with the Maine Turnpike was not settled at the time PACTS began. Surprisingly, the problem was not over the desirability of a highway or its impact on adjoining neighborhoods, the source of most highway imbroglios. The chief issue in the Portland area involved a choice between a South Portland or a Westbrook location. Both communities wanted the road constructed for much the same reasons: to provide traffic relief to existing congested arterials and to reap the prestige of a location on the interstate system, thereby stimulating local economic development. (The situation was reminiscent of the early railroad location days and the struggles for county seat designation in the Midwest.) In both South Portland and Westbrook the route was likely to have minimum impact on existing land uses and very little effect on the relocation of homes and businesses. From a political point of view, the state highway agency was not happy with either location because the selection would result in sharp criticism from the rejected suitor. From a technical standpoint, the agency favored the route through South Portland, although this preference was based on earlier deductive reasoning rather than on any evaluation of a substantial body of travel data.

Pressure for an early decision was sharply increased when the state highway agency hired a consultant to prepare preliminary plans for the construction of Route 95 through the Portland area. This was a case of putting the cart before the horse—PACTS had barely completed collection of the field data that would be useful to the highway design consultant. It should be noted that the design consultant selected was not the project's transportation consultant but an engineer who had had experience in the design of structures over poor soil conditions, a factor of some importance for the choice of a route. Although the design consultant had instructions to evaluate all major proposals, only the South Portland alternatives received serious attention. To avoid charges of favoritism, the highway agency decided to ask PACTS for a preliminary judgment on the corridor location. There was some jockeying for the location among the communities of the area because, to many development-oriented officials, the new route represented a windfall opportunity to attract new industry and other tax base. The highway agency was equally concerned to avoid an embarrassing situation, such as preparing a location study for a highway in the wrong community. This possibility existed. The transportation study consultant had not yet reached the point in the study where a recommendation on the route could be made. It was perhaps more significant that the state highway agency had not dictated a particular route location to the consultant.

In such a situation the technical staff is on the spot. If the early returns clearly favor one route over another, they can proceed with little risk. On the other hand, if the data do not permit a clear-cut decision, they have to face the ever-present possibility of making the wrong choice on a key decision.

One should not overlook the psychological effect of such an early decision. An entire transportation plan may hinge upon one or two major decisions. An out-of-sequence procedure dilutes the impact of the final report, with the net result that other aspects of the transportation study do not receive the careful attention they might otherwise have had.

In retrospect it seems clear that the presence of a technical staff busily engaged in long-range planning tempts the administrator to ask for answers to urgent questions. This is a fact of life in most bureaucracies: long-range planning efforts are besieged with demands that divert time and staff to cope with crises. Planners, who by definition concentrate on tomorrow's problems, often find themselves facing today's decisions with little time for real planning. It is doubtful whether this endemic problem can ever be resolved, which suggests that planning activities should be organized so that only part of the staff is assigned to deal with day-to-day emergencies.

As noted in other chapters of this study, quick decisions also had to be made in Manchester and Boston. In Manchester it was a question of bridge priorities, and it was ultimately resolved independently between the state highway agency and the Manchester Board of Aldermen. The transportation study staff and the citizens' Advisory Committee were merely observers. In Boston, decisions relating to the extension of the MBTA to the South Shore had to be made years before the final transportation plans were completed.

The Transportation Consultant

The technical operations of the Portland study were conducted by an engineering consulting firm. The principal reason for this arrangement was to obtain manpower and experience not available within the state highway agency. At the time, there was no one in the state of Maine, either in the state highway or the state planning agency, who was familiar with the regional transportation studies. As in other states, the argument that the studies were intensive, short-term efforts militated against the permanent employment of an expensive in-house staff of transportation experts. Certain designated supporting services, for example, all of the manpower for the field-work, such as the home-interview survey, the roadside survey, traffic counts, and land-use surveys, were provided to the consultant by the state highway agency. The agency paid for them, but the responsibility for supervision and for the reliability of the data rested with the consultant. In addition, the highway agency also assumed the financial responsibility for all of the computer costs of the study. (The State Highway Commission, through its arrangements with the BPR, was able to provide computer time at a lower rate than the consultant was able to obtain on the open market.)

Surprisingly, none of the supporting activities of the state highway agency resulted in operational problems. The consultant was requested to determine the dollar cost of the computer programming and made a careful estimate based on computations by an experienced computer staff. His own skeptical project staff thereupon doubled the total. Their instincts proved sound: the final cost to the State Highway Commission for computer time was very close to this doubled estimate. Had the eventual cost exceeded the lower estimate by a factor of two, it would surely have strained the relations between the consultant and the state agencies.

A further probable reason why computer complications did not arise was that the computer made available through the state highway agency and the BPR was located in New York City close to the consultant's home office and computer staff. Had the computer been located in Maine, it is quite likely that problems would have arisen in machine time allocation, staff transportation, and supporting services. The computer portion of a transportation study, while not complicated, frequently causes delay and frustration. Problems in "getting on" the computer, language difficulties, lack of experience with programs, and carelessness are common.

Another possible explanation for the lack of administrative problems was that the state highway agency throughout the entire study made available well-qualified personnel to supervise the state employees hired for the survey and to coordinate efforts with the consultant. During and following the course of the data collection, state highway staff worked nearly full-time with the consultant's staff. As a result, few problems were encountered in the field, and the quality of the data collection was high. For example, when the consultant's staff detected improper data, the state highway personnel were ready to fire incompetent interviewers. In the land-use survey, field crews were closely supervised by the consultant's staff, since the highway agency did not have qualified personnel in this area.

It is worthwhile to look at the contractual obligations between the consultant and the two major state agencies, the Highway Commission and DED. Each agency had its own contract with the consultant to perform specific types of services. The highway agency's contract called for a series of highway planning studies. The state planning agency's contract specifically incorporated most of the planning inputs for the study, including an analysis of the land-use impact of highway location. This procedure enabled each client to assume primary responsibility in its area of interest. (While there was still a danger that interagency conflicts might develop, there was a greater opportunity for client satisfaction.) Moreover, under these circumstances, the consultant's staff became an effective intermediary between the agencies.

On the whole, consultants find it expedient to avoid entrapment by one dominant agency. Impartiality is advisable, because favorable relations with one client may threaten relations with the other. In summary, if agencies engaged in a joint endeavor hire a single consultant to conduct separate but simultaneous contracts, the result can be highly beneficial; insulation may help rather than hinder cooperative efforts. The hiring of a consultant represents a major joint effort at the outset of a project. It is perhaps the only time when participating agencies are in full agreement. As the study progresses, the chances for recrimination increase when technical problems arise, deadlines are missed, and, most important, when one agency's interest is given preference over another. The equal but separate status of the state agencies and the buffer role of the consultant's staff are important considerations in organizing a joint endeavor. Separate contracts may prevent the consultant and his staff from capitulating to the stronger agency on major issues.

At the state level, where open interagency warfare, bickering over minor points, and administrative ambushes are common, the consultant can often provide the needed buffer. For his own economic safety and mental tranquillity, he has an incentive to resolve interagency differences in a manner satisfactory to each of his clients.

A proliferation of technical staffs could become a problem under such separate contractual arrangements, although difficulties of this sort have occurred even when there has been a single client. Lack of staff coordination between two consultants doing different parts of the same study, and the hazards of harmonizing time deadlines and interlocking schedules, can make coordination difficult even with sophisticated computer programming and other management tools. When there is a single technical staff, however, coordination problems are obviously reduced. Individual parts of a single project may be contracted for with different agencies, but it generally does not alter study procedure if one consultant is responsible for all of the work. Thus another lesson of the Portland study is that it may be beneficial to concentrate rather than diffuse contractual responsibility for outside research.

The lack of rancor on highway location in the Portland study is particularly noteworthy, since a number of the proposals that emerged called for routes through densely settled parts of the city. PACTS was not marred by serious interagency disputes before, during, or after the technical stages of the project. The greatest opposition to highway proposals during the study came from the city of Portland's planning department and urban renewal agency, perhaps the most influential among the planning agencies responsible for shaping the final highway recommendations. Alan Altshuler, in his analysis of the problems involved in locating an expressway in St. Paul, Minnesota,[3] also found that the city's technical staff provided the only effective opposition to the state highway agency proposals.

The comparatively small size of the Portland study might suggest that smaller urban areas pose fewer problems in developing effective interagency coordination. This would be overstating the case, however, since interagency relations in other small urban studies were much less placid. It may well be that joint studies can best be approached by permitting each agency to fund its own areas of study interest and to bear sole responsibility for that part of the project. This seems to have been a major factor contributing to the ease with which the Portland study was conducted.

The Role of the Regional Planning Commission

Although the Greater Portland Regional Planning Commission was a financial contributor to the Portland study and provided the only technical representation for the smaller outlying communities, its importance, both in the technical conduct of the study and in the determination of recommendations, was extremely limited. The commission's planning director was a member of PACTS' Technical Committee and was active in its deliberations, but the regional planning commission itself declined in stature and regional importance during the course of the transportation study, although this decline was not attributable to PACTS. During the later stages of the Portland study, a prestigious group, the Portland Advisory Council, recommended to the City Council that either Portland withdraw from the regional planning commission or the regional planning commission reorganize and become a more effective body. Although some individual members of the City Council urged withdrawal, Portland continued to support the regional planning agency. One reason was the rather modest sum involved at the time—about $5,000. As in most urban areas the financial, as well as the technical, participation of the core city is essential to any successful planning effort.

[3] Alan A. Altshuler, *The City Planning Process* (Ithaca, N.Y.: Cornell University Press, 1965), chap. 2, "The Interagency Freeway," pp. 17–83.

In the Portland area the regional planning commission's greatest area of activity, before the transportation study was undertaken, had been to provide contract services to member communities for the preparation of various planning studies, including work financed with 701 planning funds. The preparation of regional analyses was only a secondary responsibility. This was perhaps a necessary arrangement in view of the limited financing available. Initial activities of the regional planning commission, however, did include a number of region-wide studies, some of which were published.[4] It is possible that this emphasis on providing assistance to smaller communities, and a lack of regional perspective, may have been important reasons for the central city's dissatisfaction. The latter had its own well-staffed planning agency to take care of its own problems.

But the city was also dissatisfied with the type of study being undertaken by the regional planning commission. For example, Portland had little interest in efforts to control cesspool and septic tank construction and in the establishment of model ordinances; yet these were under consideration during the Portland transportation study. The sequence of events in Portland suggests that a regional planning operation may logically provide useful contract services to member communities, but it cannot subordinate its regional responsibilities.

Throughout the study it was assumed that the regional planning commission would take over the continuing regional planning functions required to update the area transportation plan. (Theoretically, most area transportation studies were designed to be updated with a minimum of cost. Part of the standard planning procedure was to devise an administrative framework for this updating. In most cases, regional planning agencies were assigned the responsibility for collecting land-use data for inputs to future transportation studies, while the state highway agencies were generally left with the major responsibility for analysis and recommendations.) The regional planning commission was supposed to handle the collection of socioeconomic and land-use data necessary to transportation planning for the entire Portland region except for the city of Portland, where the planning department would be responsible for this function. The regional commission was also to maintain a library containing all reports, studies, and documentation relating to the social, economic, and planning aspects of the region. In addition to these

---

[4] See, for example, Greater Portland Regional Planning Commission, *Land Use and Highway Plan, 1975, for the Portland Region* (March 1958), and A. D. Little, Inc., *Greater Portland Planning Region: Economic Problems and Opportunities,* prepared for the Greater Portland Regional Planning Commission (Cambridge, Mass., March 1960).

broad responsibilities to be fulfilled at some later date, the regional planning commission in fact prepared an application for and eventually received funds under the Section 701 program for completion of a comprehensive regional plan. Clearly, the findings of the area transportation study would be accepted as "givens" in this plan.

The Greater Portland Regional Planning Commission still exists, has expanded its scope of activities since PACTS was completed, and has continued to obtain HUD funds for comprehensive planning. Nevertheless, it has played only a limited role within the region. Some of its problems do not necessarily stem from its own actions. It has been alleged, for example, that certain communities have used highly flexible tax policies as bribes to entice industries from their neighbors. This specific issue has added to traditional suspicions and jealousies among the area's communities and has tended to limit, as a result, the effectiveness of the regional commission.

It is doubtful whether the area transportation study in Portland affected the status of regional planning. Certainly, there is no evidence that the study enhanced the status of the regional planning commission or left it in a better position to serve the area. It is quite possible that the future value of the commission may be related to one of the alternatives suggested in the concluding chapter of this volume. Any strong role in metropolitan decision-making does not yet appear to be in the cards.

LEARNING FROM EXPERIENCE 3

Introduction

Historians are sometimes cynical about the validity of using lessons from the past as guides for present and future policies. Certainly, the constant reference to the same historical analogies for differing partisan purposes suggests that identical evidence can be variously interpreted according to the perceptions of the beholder. The area transportation studies are no exception to this rule. They have been labeled as successful operations, as useful experiments, or as outright money-wasting failures. It is apparent, however, that capsulized evaluations are both inaccurate and unfair. A balanced, objective appraisal of the studies results in complex conclusions that are wholly pleasing neither to the fervent supporter nor to the avid critic, nor, unfortunately, to the busy legislator.

The evaluator necessarily spends much of his time examining the temporal and spatial background against which the studies operated. For this reason, this research often raised questions that touched only tangentially on the ostensible subject matter.

The transportation studies themselves are only a corner of a seamless web of policies and programs affecting urban areas, and tugging away at one corner inevitably brings other problems to light. Part 2 has dealt with some of the problems—and accomplishments—of a sizable intergovernmental program. Most of the conclusions are far from startling. It is surely not surprising to discover once again that substantial program expenditures are not necessarily correlated with progress. Nor is it particularly revealing to suggest that each solution may drag in its train even more complicated problems than those it was designed to solve. (One by-product of many new programs is the revelation that so little is known about many basic issues.) Moreover, by this time, most will agree on the need for a scaling down in rhetoric. Surely, a reduction in volume of the preliminary trumpeting that usually heralds the birth of a new program would place subsequent modest accomplishments in better perspective.

Much of this research has focused on governmental weaknesses at all levels. In effect, the study has traced the unfortunate consequences of most of the administrative and intergovernmental problems outlined by Charles Schultze in his testimony for the Creative Federalism hearings in late 1966. These include

1. the problem of relating functional planning to overall area planning,
2. the serious shortage of qualified staff,
3. weaknesses in the federal field structure,
4. uncertainty regarding the availability and timing of federal funds,

CONCLUSIONS 10

5. federal actions and programs poorly related to state and local needs, capabilities, and structures,

6. a general need for more effective program evaluation, and

7. a matching of federal improvements in organization and management with vitally needed improvements in state and local capabilities.[1]

Our conclusions have fallen rather naturally into very similar categories.

The Absence of Goals and Priorities

Underlying all the primary problems is the fundamental one of the lack of national goals and priorities. There is a basic lack of agreement (or even hard, systematic thought) on goals, priorities, and objectives for the nation and its urban areas. While this chaotic state of affairs exists, decisions will continue to be made by a process of drift, piecemeal plans, and acquiescence to powerful single-interest agencies. The federal level is the logical place at which to begin to set the intergovernmental house in order. The concluding statement of the chairman of the Subcommittee on Intergovernmental Relations at the end of the Creative Federalism hearings can serve equally well as a finale to this study. Senator Muskie was concerned

over the confusion, conflict, and overlapping between too many of our Federal aid programs. Those programs have made a substantial contribution to the capacity of State and local governments to cope with the problems of an increasingly complex society. But the lack of policy coordination, different planning requirements, confusion of authority and lack of cooperation between different agencies at all three levels of government have reduced the potential value of these programs.[2]

An initial obstacle is the problem of sorting out the often conflicting goals of different public agencies, economic interests, and cultural entities that comprise the fabric of our complex urban society. Public policy is usually the resultant of many vectors, reflecting influences from various groups that differ widely in political power. Most of the groups seeking to influence public policy can make convincing claims to represent the public interest. In Robert B. Mitchell's terminology:

In the process of planning, ideals have to be translated into specific goals which specify ways in which the ideals can be attained. Then the goals—which really say, "Wouldn't it be nice if . . ."—must be tested for the probable costs and benefits, to various participants, of their attainment and for the feasibility of government action. When this has been done, government is in a position to commit itself to the actions necessary to attain a set of goals, which become committed policy objectives. Then they must be

[1] Charles L. Schultze, statement in U.S., Congress, Senate, Committee on Government Operations, Subcommittee on Intergovernmental Relations, *Creative Federalism: Hearings,* pt. 1, 89th Congress, 2nd session, 1966, pp. 388–393.

[2] Edmund S. Muskie, statement in ibid., p. 463.

translated into measurable criteria by which progress toward them can be evaluated.[3]

One of the principal difficulties in developing viable metropolitan policy lies in the absence of federal goals that can serve as meaningful guidelines. Federal policies on population size and distribution, on housing and economic development, as well as on transportation, tend to be contradictory or so generalized and hedged with verbiage that no consistent policy can be discerned, even by a trained observer. Perhaps a typical example of the problem is contained in the Intergovernmental Cooperation Act of 1968. This act calls for the president to establish rules and regulations governing "the formulation, evaluation and review of federal programs and projects having a *significant* impact on area and community development."

Such rules and regulations shall provide for full consideration of the concurrent achievement of the following specific objectives and, to the extent authorized by law, *reasoned choices* shall be made between such objectives when they conflict:
(1) *Appropriate* land uses for housing, commercial, industrial, governmental, institutional, and other purposes;
(2) *Wise* development and conservation of natural resources, including land, water, minerals, wildlife, and others;
(3) *Balanced* transportation systems, including highway, air, water, pedestrian, mass transit, and other modes for the movement of people and goods;
(4) *Adequate* outdoor recreation and open space;
(5) *Protection* of areas of unique natural beauty, historical and scientific interest;
(6) *Properly planned* community facilities, including utilities for the supply of power, water, and communications, for the safe disposal of wastes, and for other purposes; and
(7) *Concern* for high standards of design;
(8) *All viewpoints*—national, regional, State, and local—shall, to the extent possible, be *fully considered* and taken into account in planning Federal or federally assisted development programs and projects.[4]

Despite the declaration of purpose embodied in the act, the guidelines obviously obscure rather than clarify the basic problem: we have not as a nation reached hard choices on discernible goals and priorities, nor have we established a reliable mechanism for translating goals into meaningful public policy. Certainly, there is no indication of what constitutes "appropriate," "wise," "balanced," "adequate," "properly planned," or "concern." The act, in a real sense, reveals just how big a job of brush clearing is necessary

[3] Robert B. Mitchell, "Foreword," *Annals of the American Academy of Political and Social Science,* vol. 352 (March 1964), p. viii. This issue of the *Annals* is entitled "Urban Revival: Goals and Standards."
[4] U.S., Congress, P.L. 90–577, Intergovernmental Cooperation Act of 1968, 90th Congress, 2nd session, 1968, pp. 5–6. Emphasis added.

before federal programs can be sorted out. Moreover, there is no escape hatch in suggesting that the task of goal formulation can be shunted down to the area level. The lack of consensual agreement on policy goals is just as, if not more, apparent at the state and the metropolitan level, and the capability there for resolving conflicts is even less in evidence.

The absence of goals and priorities reflects the transitional nature of the nation's policies on urban areas. We have attained a high degree of proficiency in functional planning, but we have become increasingly aware of its limitations. It is clear that functional planning—including highway planning—is challenged to its very core once broader issues, involving interrelated problems of land use, human resources, and societal goals, are injected into the decision-making equation. It is easier to offer cogent criticism, however, than to develop plausible alternatives.

The area transportation studies represented a praiseworthy attempt to broaden the metropolitan perspective beyond the narrow functional limits of the past. However, it was discovered that little was known (or could quickly be discovered) about such issues as the impact of physical planning on human problems like poverty and race relations. This suggests that there is a need for more ventures into uncharted fields. Our experience also suggests that, in the future, more modesty and humility may be called for in setting out on the voyage of exploration.

The task of the area transportation studies would have been greatly simplified had there been a firm federal policy on such a basic issue as transportation in downtown areas. Because the federal government had not yet settled on a policy choice between urban renewal to revitalize core areas with the help of a good public transportation system and more highway construction to serve low-density suburbs, a major policy dispute was engendered in the Buffalo area, and less intense conflicts occurred in Portland and Manchester. In all the areas the lack of a countervailing federal policy permitted functional planning to take precedence.

The studies were based on the premise that it is possible to reach a meaningful regional consensus when local decision-makers and public agencies are confronted with technical alternatives. In practice the areas proved to be, as many students had indicated, pluralistic, polycentric congeries of interest groups with very different ideas of what constituted the public interest or how it could best be served. It seemed to those in charge that, if the studies were to function at all, they should avoid the sensitive, controversial issues—such as race—that came increasingly to the forefront in the mid-1960s. Even so, they had their share of clashes, which proved that technical "solutions" to problems that were formerly considered technical and noncontroversial can still generate considerable heat.

With no clear-cut national goals and priorities to guide them, the studies followed the traditional practice of regional planning agencies: they avoided controversial, divisive issues; they ignored questions concerning the wisdom of building more major highways in densely settled areas. The U.S. Bureau of Public Roads and the state highway agencies attempted to use the studies to secure an official metropolitan planning imprimatur on their previously developed highway plans. For the most part—the Niagara Frontier area was the exception—the area transportation studies did not get drawn into the great freeway controversy that had erupted in many urban areas by the mid-1960s. The antifreeway movement, which includes planners, people whose homes lie in the path of the freeways, conservationists, and others, is closely allied to the emergence of technical warfare between competing groups of professionals. After years of acquiescence and often support, planners, especially those charged with central-city urban renewal, are now in the forefront of the forces opposing the construction of more massive intown roads. That the controversy, and the subsequent paralysis of intown road-building proposals, occurred outside the parameters of the study organizations is one indication of their extremely tenuous connection with major issues. The studies were unable to realign their scope of work to consider emerging, relevant issues, such as the need to adjust transportation plans to help alleviate poverty and racial isolation. Many vital decisions were made during the time the studies were in operation, but there was no connection between the conduct and progress of these massive research operations and the actions taken at the state or metropolitan levels.

Despite the fact that both the Penn-Jersey and the Boston projects were paralyzed for years, changes did occur on a number of fronts, most of which had very little connection with the projects. Massachusetts reorganized the Metropolitan Transit Authority and the Department of Public Works, created the Massachusetts Department of Commerce and Development, the Boston Metropolitan Area Planning Council, a new Department of Community Affairs, and selected the location for a mammoth Boston branch of the University of Massachusetts—all with virtually no reference to the research and recommendations of a $5.4 million area transportation study.

The paralysis in the Boston project had no effect in either accelerating or delaying passage of a substantial amount of legislation that was directly relevant to the basic elements of regional planning, including transportation; the same observation can be made about the Buffalo project. The Niagara Frontier Transportation Authority was established in 1967 at a time when the conflicts between state and local planners over project recommendations remained unresolved. Furthermore, the new suburban site for the University of Buffalo, the largest single public investment in the region for a generation, was selected with no reference to the area transportation study.

No clear proof can be offered on this point, but, had there been a clear pattern of national priorities, the area transportation studies could very probably have been linked more closely to the critical issues facing the urban areas in the 1960s. The studies, lumbering along in deeply grooved tracks, reflected outdated priorities of the late 1950s and lacked the flexibility to redirect their attention to meet emerging issues. This obviously suggests that a certain amount of flexibility in urban organization is needed if only because priorities change over time. More cynically, it might also be suggested that the need for flexibility increases when completing an ostensibly short-term project takes the better part of a decade. The area studies spanned two major phases of urban planning: the nation's perception of its problems and priorities changed significantly, but the studies continued to proceed in their original direction.

Weaknesses in the State of the Art: The Planner Lacks Authority and Skill

A problem sharply underlined by the area studies is the lack of firm, standardized, regional planning techniques. Before the initiation of the area transportation studies, satisfactory methods had been devised to guide planning and construction of most of the physical components of the metropolitan area. Water and sewerage systems, highway and transit facilities, schools, and health centers were all designed to high standards and served as models for most of the world. It was recognized that improvements were needed in the highway planning process, but it was implicitly assumed by highway officials that these were more in the nature of refinements than correctives for basic deficiencies.

The situation with respect to area land use, social and economic development planning, and their relationships to physical planning was far different. A good deal was known about land-use planning at the community level, but area land-use planning and the social and economic aspects of area development were only slightly understood. The studies highlighted serious gaps in these vital components of comprehensive planning. Moreover, early expectations that the studies themselves would provide timely and definitive remedies to these glaring weaknesses in regional planning proved illusory. In part this was due to the disparity between the demonstrable, narrow, technical skills of community planning and the critical weaknesses in the state of the art for dealing with regional issues. Specifically, it quickly became apparent that while the highway engineers had perfected an efficient mechanism for coping with one type of metropolitan problem, there was no equally convincing expertise in comprehensive regional planning. As a result, the highway agencies were able to operate in a vacuum; the planners and other professionals could not offer plausible technical solutions to such problems as identifying and achieving desirable development patterns in metropolitan areas. In short, planners lack the hard-nosed certainty that gives the highway engineer the edge on credibility. As Alan Altshuler suggests, by using primitive origin-destination data sprinkled with simplistic desire-line maps, the highway technicians have been able to convey a sense of scientific certitude that planners until recently have been unable to challenge or copy.

It is extremely difficult to contend publicly with experts who display complex and supposedly conclusive technical justifications of their recommendations when one's own weapons are merely intuitive judgments of the public interest.[5]

Thus a key question raised by the studies is whether planners (and others) can, or wish to, develop technical arguments as convincing as those advanced by the highway engineers. However, many planners would regard hand-to-hand combat as a distasteful departure from the profession's traditional posture as a detached overseer of the public interest. In Altshuler's words, planners

could no doubt within a short while develop claims to expertness as evaluators of proposals rivaling those of highway engineers. They would no longer be generalists in their value orientation, however, and most planners would consider this a step backward for their profession.[6]

In short, planners conceivably can develop the necessary power base if they are genuinely interested in developing sound, defensible alternatives, but the state of the art and the supply of talent may not be up to the test. The talent shortage is probably the critical item: unless the planning profession can generate a number of rather remarkable men ready and willing to meet the challenges of the seventies, particularly the monumental challenge of spending tens of millions in planning funds, the experience in Boston and elsewhere suggests that its members will be elbowed aside by successful operators recruited from other professions.

The environment for large-scale metropolitan and state planning is far less tidy than many planners would like it to be. It is a world of action, of deeds not dossiers, of results not reports. The predilection of many planners for long overtures to action, in the form of work programs, has restricted their

[5]Alan A. Altshuler *The City Planning Process* (Ithaca, N.Y.: Cornell University Press, 1965), p. 341.
[6]Ibid.

usefulness in meeting legislative timetables at a time of constantly erupting, unpredictable crises that demand clarity and celerity. Yet the possibilities for bringing effective planning to bear on decisions have rarely, if ever, been more promising.

In recent years the bargaining power of the planning agencies at the state and local levels has been substantially enlarged by the federal government. This has come about in two ways: through increasing federal grants for planning studies, demonstration projects, and urban renewal and through increasing federal insistence that aid for actual construction be granted only when a project conforms to comprehensive city and regional plans. This requirement is frequently a pro forma, rubber-stamp affair, but proprietorship of keys to the federal treasury has worked a miraculous change on the status of many planning agencies.

At the regional level the availability of federal funds for research studies and demonstration projects has resulted in a remarkably increased interest in planning among political and consultant circles. Despite the availability of a conduit to the federal treasury, however, planners tend to play their hand poorly in the power game.

In Massachusetts, and in many other states, success in municipal and state politics has demanded a combination of the virtues of the biblical serpent, the shark, and the cooing dove—as William Allen White has written of Ohio at the turn of the century. The recent tendency to thrust the planner and the planning agency into a (theoretically) cooperative and (de facto) competitive relationship with other agencies has not been wholly successful. Early returns from this friendly confrontation, which pits the planning agency against powerful so-called cooperating agencies clad in ideological plate armor, indicate that the planning agency tends to be very much the junior, accommodating partner.

There are a number of reasons for this state of affairs. First, one must consider the nature of the planner and the planning agency. As a rule, a planner who considers himself a civilized believer in reason and compromise tends to be ill at ease, and perhaps awed, when confronted with blind certainty and violent opposition. He is often unskilled at infighting, except with professional colleagues. Moreover, since planning is a specialty that is fuzzily defined around the edges, it has been subject to constant encroachment by other professions claiming to have better answers to questions concerning transportation, resource development, and any number of other problems. Also, planning agencies are usually service operations rather than centers of political power; as a result they tend to bend easily under pressure. The planner, unless he becomes thoroughly embittered, is congenitally and sometimes almost pathetically optimistic about the future, his current project, and the possibility of educating the uneducable.

The nature of the staff in "cooperating" line agencies must also be considered. The staff are usually products of older professions and more encrusted with tradition. As has been suggested by students of state government, they are often rather inflexible, particularly at the lower echelons. Agency heads are fully aware of the need to protect the future of the line agency (and possibly improve its public relations) by devoting more attention to planning. This realization has prompted them to hire professional planning staffs and to engage in cooperative projects with planning agencies. But their willingness to hire a few planners does not imply that basic changes in convictions or operations have taken place. Nor does it often lead to any revision in their belief that planners are pretentious procrastinators and vague, useless moralizers.

Some planners have anticipated good results from the tendency of line agencies to develop their own planning staffs. For many years, planning societies and professional groups have urged the operating agencies to hire professional planners. Planners were convinced that this would provide the conduit for the introduction of vitally needed planning ideas into line agency policies and operations. This concept was put to the test in Penn-Jersey, where the BPR-financed study was directed by two bona fide city planners. The upshot in Penn-Jersey was that the planners, apparently attempting to emulate the highway researchers and to please their highway agency sponsors, quickly became entangled in a web of insoluble mathematical equations. Their efforts to enhance the image of the planning profession by creating complex land-use models were less than successful. On a smaller scale, the same attempt was made in the Boston project with a similar lack of substantive results.

Experience also suggests that planners are no less susceptible to co-optation than lawyers, economists, political scientists, or other professionals. One part of the planner's dilemma in reconciling his professional and agency loyalties arises from his subordinate position. An employee must evince loyalty to his employer, and since the planner's immediate future, including promotions and status, is derived from the employing agency, it is natural for him to adjust his outlook and actions accordingly even if this requires adjusting his professional conscience to fit his environment. There is no reason to expect that an intelligent planner cannot make as effective a presentation for his line agency as a lawyer can in preparing a convincing brief for a dubious client. Within the closely knit hierarchical structure and strong ideological framework of older line agencies, a newly hired planner tends to be regarded as an expedient instrument rather than as a senior contributor to policy. He is more likely to serve as a translator than an instructor, as a mouthpiece than a source of inspiration.

The planner may assume that an agency's interest in planning arises from an honest recognition of past deficiencies and future needs. He is likely to find, however, that his counterparts in other agencies regard the planner's contribution as a form of insulation against criticism. Planners often display a keen sensitivity to any suggestion of incompetence and are quite prepared to engage in a blanket defense of the entire record of their agency. Thus so-called joint, cooperative projects operated on equal terms may work smoothly only if planners and planning agencies remain close-mouthed pacifists. They are not, and perhaps cannot be, tough competitors unless they can draw on sustained strength from a powerful constituency or, failing that, receive effective backing from the governor.

Planners, as representatives of the broad public interest, tend to be very much at a disadvantage. Older operating agencies are supported by exceedingly well-oiled, strongly entrenched legislative machines and powerful special interests. There is frequently formidable resistance by both federal and state line agencies to new concepts, innovations, and, most of all, rival claimants in their fields of specialization. Since the planner has no unchallenged wisdom to call upon, nor any broad consensus on the future form or nature of urban regions, he finds it difficult to argue on equal terms with those whose concepts and techniques, although limited, have in fact worked. Furthermore, he is weakened because regional planning agencies lack any real control over vital elements in regional development (for example, land use, economic patterns, and urban design). Under these conditions, the planning agency, with no significant responsibilities for implementation or substantial contracts to award, may find it hazardous to offend powerful brothers.

In self-defense, planners have defined their mission as educational rather than operational, long term rather than short term. To some extent they have hoped that the force of public opinion can be brought to bear to implement the planning concepts that they cannot by themselves carry out. But there are definite limitations, in the short term, to missionary work among the adherents of strong rival faiths. Attempts at educating opposing bureaucratic dinosaurs have taught a simple but striking lesson: dinosaurs' brains may be small, but their teeth are sharp.

One obvious reason for the planner's relatively weak bargaining position within the line agencies is his lack of credible professional expertise as compared with, say, lawyers or economists. It had been thought that the area transportation studies would provide a vehicle for closing the credibility gap, but this was not to be. A number of planners involved in the studies seemed to feel, for example, that the answer could be found in the computer. With the help of the computer, they believed that planners would be able to attain technological parity with highway engineers. The studies proved, however, that a marriage between new technological devices and a formidable array of socioeconomic unknowns is difficult to consummate. It is not surprising that many of the transportation projects foundered on shoals of models and computers. As has been indicated, considerable money was wasted in the Penn-Jersey study in an attempt to produce a land-use model that would provide a basis for transportation planning for eventual use in other areas; similar problems of lesser magnitude were encountered in the Boston study. Some planners obviously embraced the computer with more enthusiasm than understanding. As one HHFA official stated:

For some in the [planning] profession, the computer is still a matter for religious and ideological battle. Others are accepting it, without much understanding or enthusiasm. The progress is substantial but it is still a devastating comment on the profession that so much of it has [been] rendered mute and defenseless in the face of a piece of hardware and mathematics of high school level.[7]

Later, in an issue of the *Journal of the American Institute of Planners*, the editor reflected:

While the planner accustomed to data processing aspects of computer utilization may be able to meet the computer and the programmer on his own terms, the computer as a device for simulating the real world seems to have a mysterious life of its own, and the complexities of its behavior consistently elude and frustrate its manipulators.[8]

Nevertheless, he continues:

I reject this inanimism and maintain that the computer can be the servant of the planner and the extension of his personality.[9]

Two years later, apparently somewhat chastened by his experience as a consultant to the Penn-Jersey study, the same author stated in another article:

Perhaps the best summary of the ideas and suggestions that I have outlined above is for the planning director who is interested in coming to terms with the computer to recognize that he has embarked on a process of adjustment, of education, and of seeking understanding.[10]

It is significant that Professor Harris, who apparently saw few limits to the use of the computer as a planning tool in 1965, was suggesting by 1967 that many planning activities are simply not susceptible to computerization.

[7] Frederick O'R. Hayes, "Urban Planning and the Transportation Study," in American Institute of Planners, *Proceedings of the 1963 Annual Conference, Milwaukee, Wisconsin*, p. 117.
[8] Britton Harris, "New Tools for Planning," *Journal of the American Institute of Planners*, vol. 31, no. 5 (May 1965), p. 90.
[9] Ibid.
[10] Britton Harris, "How to Succeed with Computers Without Really Trying," ibid., vol. 33, no. 1 (January 1967), p. 17.

Although a land-use model has been completed for the Penn-Jersey area, it has yet to be tested and used in the preparation of transportation plans. Moreover, the long search for the model was primarily responsible for a major schism within the study organization and for many of the disasters that dogged the project.

In recent years the use of computers in transportation planning has declined; the eagerly awaited modal split formulas, land-allocation models, and similar devices have so far proved less than satisfactory. Furthermore, early ideas of gathering immense volumes of data as a basis for decision-making have given way to more prudent evaluation of necessary data requirements. In view of past disappointments, agencies are now relying upon the computer as only one input in the decision-making process.

Talent Shortage

The planning profession must either do a better job of developing its own effective leadership or resign itself to a secondary or tertiary role in urban development. It must be made clear that simple, average competence is not enough when pioneering is to be done. Planning for small communities may call for modest abilities and traditional skills, but new programs involving penetration into uncharted fields through joint ventures with government demand unusual talents. What is needed is a high degree of technical ability combined with solid common sense. This rare combination is not often found.

Persons of this unusual caliber are prerequisites if the state of the art of planning is to reach the point where routinization and systematization will permit technicians of average competence to perform satisfactorily. This stage is remote in the case of area planning, and one of the principal reasons for the partial failures of the transportation studies was their inability to attract or retain star talent. This is not to suggest that the problem of staffing was ignored; on the contrary, a good deal of attention was focused on this issue, and working conditions, including salary levels, were made sufficiently attractive so that it was usually not difficult to find individuals to fill key jobs. The real problem lay in the inability to distinguish between persons of modest competence and the outstanding talent needed to lead large-scale, exploratory research.

Too much of the time, most of the line agency sponsors seemed to concentrate on manipulating organization charts, forgetting that some of the neat little boxes contained nothing but ectoplasm in the shape of bureaucrats occupying positions rather than making effective use of the potential opportunities. From its inception, such a staff tends to concentrate on process rather than product, to proliferate work rules, procedures, and protective mechanisms. By temperament, inclination, and training, such persons are unfit to operate consciously and effectively in a fragmented political environment. They are objects for manipulation in a world they do not really understand. Under these conditions, the hope that the area transportation studies would formulate bold new programs and secure broad support for innovative recommendations was simply unrealistic.

The planner in charge of an area planning operation, like any executive who seeks support for a sizable enterprise, must use the technique that Neustadt applies to presidents: he must persuade by bargaining, he must be persistent in following through on requests and orders, and "he must . . . induce them to believe that what he wants of them is what their own appraisal of their own responsibilities requires them to do in their own interest, not his."[11] This suggests that, among his other talents, the chief planner must have a good working grasp of the political process. This is understandably difficult in metropolitan affairs.

Robert Wood has noted the indigestible qualities in the intergovernmental mixture in metropolitan areas:

So in addition to the centrifugal local forces now scattering influence and power even further across the urban region, higher echelons of government erect separate bastions of authority for particularistic purposes. . . . We sketch a process chronically beset with such political tensions, conflicts, and diversity of participants as to be always in danger of flying apart.[12]

One of the present authors has enlarged on the implications of Wood's observation:

Assuming that this diagnosis is accurate, what is to be the prescription? Wood suggests that the planner should play a politically activist role, fashioning a strategy for the diverse interest groups, and building coalitions to implement them. It would seem, however, that the metropolitan planner is in an extremely weak position to undertake either task; he does not possess the leverage to succeed at the elaborate game of power politics needed in this highly-charged environment. Without the kind of power base which could be provided by metropolitan government, or perhaps by an aggressive governor, he has two alternatives: long term public and agency education for planning, which may pay off in five, ten, or twenty years and/or the kind of ritualistic charades which Adrian suggests is all that the metropolitan areas really want. Coalition-building in the metropolitan jungle is clearly no pathway to short-term or even longer-term injection of comprehensive planning in metropolitan areas.

Implementing metropolitan planning on an advisory basis calls for the qualities of a near-genius who is blessed with extraordinary luck. This combination seems to be in extremely short supply.[13]

[11] Richard E. Neustadt, *Presidential Power* (New York: Signet Books, 1960), pp. 51–53.

[12] Robert C. Wood, *Planning 1962* (Chicago: American Society of Planning Officials, 1962), p. 9.

[13] Melvin R. Levin, *Community and Regional Planning* (New York: Frederick A. Praeger, 1969), pp. 142–143.

Many planners tend to be objects rather than masters of the art of coalition-building. Persuasion is often limited to a technical presentation, shading off into sporadic discussions with friendly, already convinced audiences and terminating with disheartenment at the denseness, apathy, and obstinacy of an opposition that unaccountably assassinates their proposals. However, highway officials have a tough professional carapace. Conscious of their final power, they are not as susceptible to disheartenment as their planning colleagues. A long tradition of public controversy has tempered the highway-men, many of whom share a sincere sense of dedication toward highway construction and a contempt for its critics.

It soon became evident that a past history of success in small-town or city planning did not necessarily guarantee competence in regional planning. Planners were accustomed to opposition from small-town developers and others, but it would be fair to say that they tended to enjoy harmonious relations with the press and were in demand as speakers at meetings of local civic groups. In general, planners were accorded the status of honest, sincere professionals, engendering little of the suspicion, frustration, and rage engendered by highway agency staff. In consequence, they were quite unprepared for the hostile operating environment of the area transportation studies.

The planners' problems were compounded by their lack of sophistication toward transportation objectives, procedures, and personnel. And their initial ignorance was worsened by their frequent inability to master unfamiliar techniques and intricate administrative problems quickly enough to be able to present useful alternatives to plans submitted by the highway agencies.

The area studies helped to bring into focus the long-standing suspicion, current among planners, that highway engineers are narrow, callous technicians, heedless of the social impact of their efforts. Highway engineers were confirmed in their belief that planners are woolly-headed theoreticians lacking the practical sense to build a birdhouse, let alone to exert a useful influence on the routing of major expressways. The planning agencies were firmly committed to the concept of citizen participation, the highway agencies to the limited involvement of affected individuals and groups through statute-satisfying public hearings. The planning agencies, moreover, saw themselves as the guardians and protectors of the neglected public transportation sector. Yet the planner was not really given an overriding mandate to relegate highways to a secondary priority behind public transportation, or land use, or social considerations. Therefore, in the absence of clear national or area priorities and a highly developed state of the art to arrive at such priorities, the field was wide open. Either a planner of unusual talents will impose his vision, or powerful functional agencies will continue to win victories.

Another thorny problem uncovered by the studies involves the issue of government by expert. Area transportation planning, like other subjects that most people find both complex and boring, is relegated to professionals. Decisions are frequently made in back rooms on the basis of narrow technical criteria far removed from public discussion. Public hearings, until recently at any rate, have tended to be perfunctory pro forma affairs in which the participants are overwhelmed by masses of expensive maps and data. Accordingly, most significant development decisions are made by members of narrow professional guilds. Alan Altshuler has called this "creeping fait accompliism," in which agency professionals adopt a series of decisions under the guise of technical necessity until those decisions eventually, and sometimes unwittingly, accumulate into a major policy.[14] Contrary to some prophecies,[15] however, there has recently been a significant revolt against manipulation by the experts. This is evidenced in a number of areas, ranging from college campuses to poverty and renewal operations, as well as urban expressway construction.

The Buffalo and Philadelphia area studies reflected another facet of reaction against the experts. In both areas, local professionals and key political figures rejected a strong emphasis on the computer. In Philadelphia the issue involved alleged wastefulness in allocating time and money to an unworkable model, while in Buffalo there was considerable objection to a strong highway emphasis in the state-conducted study. The principle in both studies was the same—plans formulated by one group of officially designated experts were being challenged by other experts.

Planners were hopeful that the area transportation studies would provide a foothold for their profession in the metropolitan areas. They anticipated that a new brand of action-oriented research would emerge, in which a fruitful dialogue between the planner and the public would be maintained. This was one instance, among many, of the gap between initial expectations and subsequent reality. The federal and state planning agencies apparently expected that the planning techniques developed through the studies would be useful in the early stages of a continuing regional planning process. In addition the federal agencies hoped that new patterns of regional goals and priorities would emerge. The planners, for their part, were also sincerely (if naïvely) convinced that their conceptual approach, technical skills, and participation

[14] Altshuler, appropriately enough for our purposes, was referring to a tactic frequently employed by highway agencies. See Altshuler, *City Planning Process*, p. 59.
[15] Ibid., p. 339. In the early 1960s Altshuler foresaw a million persons being displaced with barely a murmur as a consequence of impersonal computerized decisions made by highway agencies.

were not only desperately needed but would be enthusiastically embraced by the highway engineers.

By and large, these hopes were not realized. The studies did not develop a corps of knowledge capable of generating plausible and defensible alternatives to the courses of action proposed by generally hostile and uncooperative highway officials. The research output has not come up to expectations; there seems to be no breakthrough on intown highway location decisions; and genuine citizen participation in major regional development is still a hope rather than a reality. Moreover, there is at best only a tenuous connection between current programs to extend public transportation and the highway-dominated area transportation studies.

The federal and state highway officials had more limited views about the benefits of the studies. By and large they shared an interest in developing a low-cost transportation model that would permit future highway studies to be conducted with considerably less data collection. In a sense, such a model was frosting on the cake. Despite the heavy wastage in model research in the Penn-Jersey project and the sizable sums spent elsewhere for this purpose, it would be fair to say that the highway engineers on the whole were perfectly satisfied with the outcome of the studies. Aside from the quest for universal models, they were not much interested in research or in exploring new forms of comprehensive regional planning. They were very much aware, however, of the need to secure sanction and validation for existing highway plans so as to neutralize a growing army of critics. Thus there was one major difference in approach: unlike the planners, the highway engineers were sure of their conclusions in advance. They had no interest in developing an elite corps of planners to challenge them on their home ground.

Because of this basic divergence in objectives, there was a division of labor that apparently suited the participants. Lacking outstanding talent, the planning agencies were assigned relatively innocuous and frequently unproductive research, such as the preparation of land-use maps and long deliberations over regional land-use and development "alternatives" (radial, concentric, core, and so on), while the traffic inventories and the major study conclusions were controlled by the highway agencies. Thus considerations dear to the planners, such as land use, aesthetics, economic base, public transportation, and other essential components of regional planning not directly related to highway proposals, were relegated to a secondary or tertiary priority or were frequently treated as research addenda having little influence on decisions.

One result of this working arrangement is clear: the area transportation studies totally funded by the U.S. Bureau of Public Roads were obviously highway oriented in their recommendations, but BPR officials and state highway officials are correct in maintaining that studies like the Penn-Jersey or Niagara Frontier were no more highway dominated than those in which HUD financing played a significant role. Without high-powered planners on the scene, HUD money had little impact on the design, conduct, or recommendations of the studies.

Modest as the planning input was in the decision-making process, the signs of progress were apparently pleasing to some planners. Our interviews suggested that spokesmen for the planning agencies were pleased that nonhighway factors in transportation planning, such as land use, employment, and economic development, were given substantial weight. They saw this as a significant step toward comprehensive transportation planning. In the absence of stronger leadership in the planning profession, this is perhaps all they could expect.

Introduction

Governmental coordination in metropolitan areas was the principal theme of this research, and it is therefore fitting that most of the attention of the concluding chapters should be devoted to the serious problems in this area. The absence of clear national priorities and the underdeveloped state of the art of planning were major stumbling blocks for the area transportation studies, but the problems encountered in coordinating interagency efforts constituted an insurmountable obstacle to the formulation and implementation of viable regional plans.

The fragmentation of powers among a variety of agencies and levels of government reflects to a degree a similar fragmentation in the larger society. It would be an oversimplification, however, to suggest that the participating agencies were permitted to mire the studies in endless argument and esoteric research because the public fundamentally opposes genuine metropolitan planning. As Mowitz and Wright stress in their Detroit area study, on most issues the metropolitan public is highly pragmatic, much more interested in high-quality services than in ideology.[1] There is much less concern over which agency performs the function, such as highway construction and maintenance, than that the function be performed satisfactorily. Because there was no discernible connection between the area transportation studies and the performance of any tangible public function, the bureaucracies were free to maneuver as they saw fit. The complex machinery governing the projects did not provide for a clear expression of the public will.

Perhaps the key problem in translating the desires of the public into effective policy is that the public interest cannot always be identified easily in a fragmented region. Inevitably, as time went on, unforeseen interrelationships between transportation and such matters as poverty, open space, and economic development emerged into clearer view, and interagency policy committees began to grow in Washington and in the metropolitan areas.

The federal agencies increasingly found themselves overlapping into each other's jurisdictions. As we have indicated, their response was not a thorough rethinking and reordering of policy to achieve consistency at the federal level but a shifting of the burden of goal formulation and coordination to the local level. The area transportation projects and their successors, the metropolitan planning agencies, were to work with other government agencies and government levels, to enlist the participation of elected officials and the citizenry in the planning process, and thereby to arrive at a meaningful and acceptable plan. The plan would then be implemented because it represented the fruits

[1] Robert J. Mowitz and Deil S. Wright, *Profile of a Metropolis* (Detroit: Wayne State University Press, 1962), pp. 629–634.

of the agencies that possessed the necessary implementing powers.

The difficulties in arriving at this type of metropolitan consensus are too well known to bear extensive repetition. Metropolitan areas are polycentric, and class differences, clashing agency interests, and other factors tend to reduce, if not entirely eliminate, the possibility that any metropolitan agency can fashion and carry out comprehensive plans in the absence of strong central executive power.[2]

The federal government is in a position to influence the planning process in metropolitan areas, but fragmented federal authority has often created rather than solved problems. The disparity in funding procedures between the Department of Housing and Urban Development (HUD) and the Bureau of Public Roads (BPR), which engendered trouble in the Manchester project, is a minor example. The tendency to attack such potential policy inconsistencies between federal agencies through the medium of a gentlemen's agreement at the Washington level may satisfy higher-level bureaucrats, but these ecumenical treaties ignore the formidable barriers posed by what has been called the "pyramidal mass"[3] or the "permanent government"[4] lower down in the agencies.

To cite the example most relevant to this study, by the late 1950s, cooperation was in full swing in Washington between the Bureau of Public Roads and HUD. In practice, however, it was not always possible to transmit this spirit to local offices or even to the third or fourth Washington echelons. Interagency harmony as established in the stratospheric supergrades in Washington was often out of step with the realities of life in the provinces. The need for coordinated planning and the development of transportation facilities, an objective avowed by the uppermost layer of the Bureau of Public Roads in Washington, was difficult to relay to the final, and perhaps most important, link in the transportation planning chain—perhaps best stereotyped as a recalcitrant highway engineer who had been building rural roads for the past fifty years. Officials of the Bureau of Public Roads wielded considerable authority at the national and regional levels, but it is clear in hind-

[2] See Edward C. Banfield, "The Uses and Limitations of Metropolitan Planning in Massachusetts," in *Taming Megalopolis,* ed. H. Wentworth Eldredge (New York: Anchor Books, 1967), vol. 2, pp. 710–718.

[3] The phrase is from Smith Simpson, *Anatomy of the State Department* (Boston: Houghton Mifflin Company, 1967), p. 24.

[4] The phrase is from Arthur M. Schlesinger, Jr., *A Thousand Days: John F. Kennedy in the White House* (Boston: Houghton Mifflin Company, 1965), pp. 681–684. Both Simpson and Schlesinger were referring to the problem of injecting new life and ideas into the State Department, but, unhappily, their observations apply to other agencies as well.

sight that the bureau's personnel in the state offices were often cowed by the state highway agencies.

The situation was no better in HUD. HUD's basic operating procedure was to arrange for state planning agencies to function as its designated organization at the state level, but this system failed to produce a better administrative organization than that used by the Bureau of Public Roads. State planning agencies lacked adequate staff and sufficient funds to carry out their assignments, and HUD was unable to provide the necessary expertise. In this regard, the BPR held one advantage over HUD. The BPR, with its formally organized district offices in each state, was able to do a much better job of supervising its projects than HUD, with its understaffed and less experienced (in transportation planning) regional office personnel. There was also an interesting difference in temperament: HUD and state planning officials for the most part were gentle persuaders; state highway officials were rough-riders, politically strong, and single-minded. It is not surprising, therefore, that the highway engineers seemed to win all the battles.

The area transportation studies did shed some light on the advantages and disadvantages of adopting a cooperative or an integrated organizational arrangement for interagency efforts. Under a cooperative arrangement, the individual agencies arrange for and finance their own portion of a broader unified study. Under an integrated procedure, both agencies agree on the scope of the work to be done and place their funds in a joint account, so that neither agency theoretically has direct control over the outcome of any portion of the study. The research for this volume indicated that the cooperative effort, as applied in Portland and in the later stages of the Penn-Jersey project, was a more satisfactory arrangement both for the sponsoring agency and for the technical staff and the local committees. Not everyone agrees with this view, however.

On the basis of experience to date we regard the coordinated project as probably less effective than the integrated project as a device for reconciling the views and satisfying the desires of the participants in this study. The limitations of the coordinated approach have perhaps been most evident in areas where the comprehensive community planning program has up to the time of the study been weak or nonexistent or where the director of the planning agency has been lacking in either professional competence or aggressiveness.[5]

At the time of this statement (1963), coordinated efforts had been abandoned for the most part by HUD in favor of the joint "revolving account" proce-

[5] Frederick O'R. Hayes, "Urban Planning and the Transportation Study," in American Institute of Planners, *Proceedings of the 1963 Annual Conference, Milwaukee, Wisconsin*, p. 112.

dure. In Portland the HUD portions of the studies did seem to be neglected. Experience has shown that, given the same deficiencies in competence or aggressiveness, the coordinated effort is apt to provide more satisfying results for the sponsoring agency. Perhaps this explains why HUD by 1966 had decided to finance portions of the work of the Delaware Valley Regional Planning Commission (heir to the Penn-Jersey study) on a coordinated basis.

Whatever else the projects prove, they suggest that the combination of transportation and comprehensive planning requires complicated chemistry. Transportation studies seem to preserve a smooth, unruffled surface only if they are unilateral—that is, if they are dominated by highway concepts. A one-agency transportation planning operation can perform its task efficiently, but there is no guarantee that it is any more effective in producing widely acceptable transportation plans. Under the single-agency administrative alternative, conflict is externalized; it tends to be delayed until the recommendations have been delivered and opponents have finally had a chance to make their voices heard. In contrast, studies conducted on an interagency basis may bog down before they produce significant results. Even in a cooperative study, the competitors can submerge their conflicts; they can avoid painful choices among alternatives by denying that they have provided alternatives. In the Boston area, for example, the highway and transit agencies each presented plans for expansion that were based on the assumption that neither agency would openly attack the other's maximum plan. On the other hand, in Buffalo the proponents of public transportation claimed that adoption of their proposals offered a viable alternative to new intown highway construction. There is an obvious similarity in the traditional posture of the three branches of the U.S. military establishment. (Despite frequent outbreaks of open rivalry for prestigious missions and limited funds, the Secretary of Defense is presented with a "balanced" system incorporating the maximum of each participant's branch, designed to purchase harmony at enormous public expense.)

The gap that sometimes exists between the headquarters and field commanders of federal agencies creates serious problems at the operating level. The cooperative relationship is formulated by top-level personnel who not only enjoy the broad perspective but are also spared the difficult problems of translating general agreements into specific working arrangements. Moreover, a certain amount of selectivity is to blame; headquarters staff generally tend to be brighter than the field hands in local offices. To an even greater extent than their superiors, middle-echelon field personnel tend to be regulators, reviewers, and concurrers rather than innovators of the type required in complicated intergovernmental projects. Only rarely is a local official a pioneer who dares to move rapidly and to depart boldly from established, bureaucratic routine.

This problem is by no means unique to transportation planning, or for that matter to the United States. Delineating the proper boundary between maintaining stability and providing receptivity for innovation is a problem that afflicts private as well as public bureaucracies in most parts of the world. In Anthony Down's phraseology, long-established bureaucracies tend to be dominated by "conservers" rather than "innovators," people who adhere religiously to the rules to stay out of trouble. Downs suggests that the middle ranks of a bureaucratic hierarchy normally contain relatively high proportions of conservers. He sees the conservers as risk avoiders who constitute a special threat to innovation, since they have devised an ingenious way of simultaneously making decisions and avoiding the responsibility for doing so.

This consists of rigidly applying the rules of procedure promulgated by higher authorities. Instead of "playing it by ear" and adapting the rules to fit particular situations, many conservers eschew even the slightest deviation from written procedures unless they obtain approval from higher authority. Thus, rigid rule-following acts as a shield protecting them from being blamed for mistakes by their superiors, and even from having to obey any orders that conflict with "the book."[6]

Clearly, one special hazard to the success of an innovative enterprise is the danger that prime responsibility for the pioneering will be placed in the hands of enervated, fearful executives.

One hypothesis advanced to explain the failure of federal agencies in coping with regional projects suggests that the agencies lacked both the ability to distinguish between failure and achievement and the humility to admit error. In this view, bureaucracy is unwieldy, dogmatic, and self-perpetuating, capable only of unenlightened, routinized survival. If this extremist view is accepted, the miasma of the area transportation studies was as inescapable as the early crudities of urban renewal programs.[7] If this is the case, errors in both programs would be assessed not as unfortunate, isolated mistakes but as an accurate reflection of the shortcomings of some key HUD officials.

However, this kind of root-and-branch attack cannot be given full credence. While the BPR and HUD did not, at times, perform either intelligently or

[6] Anthony Downs, *Inside Bureaucracy* (Boston: Little, Brown and Company, 1967), p. 100.

[7] Considerable stresses between regional HUD offices and local officials are characteristic of the urban renewal program. Greer blames part of the regional office rigidity, slowness, and other administrative ills on a "simple shortage of trained personnel." See Scott Greer, *Urban Renewal in American Cities* (Indianapolis: Bobbs-Merrill Company, 1965), pp. 106–113.

admirably, the problems confronting the agencies were often, as in Boston, local in origin. HUD often inherits rather than generates administrative problems. For example, it may be recalled that the interagency bickering between the Department of Public Works and the Mass Transportation Commission in Massachusetts was none of HUD's doing, and neither was it HUD's fault that the project director had created a host of local enemies. Similarly, the frictions between the central-city urban renewal agencies and the highway agencies in the Buffalo, Manchester, and Portland areas were not of HUD's making. Nonetheless, when every allowance is made and every excuse is entered, the HUD record is still faulty. The decision to evade the responsibility for continuing close supervision and to concentrate on a paper world of committees, memoranda, community conferences, and work programs rather than on meaningful accomplishment were matters of choice rather than necessity.

Federal, State, and Local Relations

Lateral sparring among line agencies is a long-established tradition, and it is most likely that interagency conflict will flourish rather than diminish in coming years. More and more agencies will be locked up together in the metropolitan box, directing their attention to urban problems through programs that impinge on, encroach on, overlap, and, on occasion, duplicate each other. With two-thirds of the nation's population already living in 231 metropolitan areas,[8] and virtually all of its economic and population growth gravitating to large urban aggregations, agency survival and power must be linked to urbanism. Bureaucratic empires can no longer be founded on trees, corn, village highways, county airports, or village schools. The agencies that tie themselves closely to the urban aspects of national development are the most likely to be rewarded with status, power, and legislative bounty. Considering the number of agencies operating in urban regions and the importance of victory, the potential for violent infighting is virtually unlimited.

But the battle for a share of urban programs is not limited to the federal agencies; the arena of intergovernmental conflict also involves strains and abrasions between the federal agencies and their state and local counterparts. In part this struggle is a continuation of the ancient struggle for state sovereignty, the most recent manifestation of which is the eruption over civil rights.

The federal-local conflict presents an interesting dilemma. As a rule, planners and administrators in or out of the federal establishment have been very

[8] This was the number of Standard Metropolitan Statistical Areas in the continental United States, defined by the U.S. Bureau of the Budget, as of July 1, 1967. There are an additional 3 SMSAs in Puerto Rico. (The 1960 census listed 212 SMSAs.)

much on the federal side of the fence in the belief that the federal government epitomizes progress and liberalism while, relatively speaking, the states have stood for retrogression and mediocrity. (Obviously not all officials in state and local government agree with this unflattering evaluation.)

To a degree the conflict is historic, but smoldering embers burst into flame in the 1960s with the growing self-confidence of the federal bureaucrats of the New Frontier and its successor, the Great Society. During the past decade the enormous expansion of complex federal programs had resulted in serious strains, particularly in initiating and supervising a multitude of grant-in-aid operations.

It would be fair to say that federal agencies in the relatively passive Eisenhower decade appeared eager to treat state and local agencies as equal partners. This was a period of uncertainty, reductions in force, and insulting political speeches and newspaper editorials by conservatives still reacting to the growth of a big federal establishment during the New Deal of the 1930s, denigrating allegedly parasitic or disloyal "payrollers." Beset by enemies, federal executives earnestly solicited the support of their fellow professionals in the states and localities to intercede with the Congress and their grass-roots constituencies. When a federal agency dragged its feet or otherwise proved uncooperative, local agencies could resort to arm-twisting with the aid of cooperative legislators. It was relatively easy to change frowns to smiles, hesitation to celerity, and grave doubts to quick approval of applications.

A radical change occurred in this pattern in the space of only a few years. President Kennedy's new enthusiasm markedly improved agency morale, bringing in new, vigorous staff and apparently confirming federal officials in the conviction that they were morally superior to and far more intelligent than their local clients. The local administrators have a different story to tell. Local jurisdictions welcome federal money but resent what they interpret as dictatorial behavior, inconsistent supervision, and arbitrary changes in ground rules. They are quick to charge that federal criticisms are often self-fulfilling prophecies, for example, when strict federal limitations on administrative funds prevent local agencies from hiring the administrative staff necessary to run new programs effectively.

There are, of course, two sides to this story. Sometimes what appears to the local officials as arbitrary or inconsistent behavior is due to the fast-moving milieu in Washington. A number of programs have been changing with bewildering speed, and administrators are hard put to keep abreast of new developments. The constant shifts in rules are explained by federal officials as an inseparable concomitant of the administration of pioneering programs, since the amount of funds available for a given activity can change almost overnight, and instructions must be adjusted accordingly. But at the state or local level, this looks suspiciously like an arbitrary reneging on commitments.

To a degree the federal officials must share some of the blame for local failures. Some key officials are afflicted by a tendency to confuse organization charts with organization, personnel changes with progress, and progress reports with products. What enrages local and state officials, however, is the fact that the rule book in the administrative game is not only subject to constant, unilateral changes by the guardians and composers of the sacred text but is modified by verbal understandings that get local agencies into trouble and are later disavowed by the federal officials. The aggrieved, frustrated local official may wish to protest, but his complaint is hopelessly snarled in contradictory discussions and convenient lapses of memory. Fortunately, this uniquely American tradition—name-calling and private ferocity—does not end in bloodshed. No one has been physically liquidated for failure to play crack-the-whip with federal directives, nor have Washington officials been exiled for insulting the intelligence or the person of a state official.

Another federal characteristic that seems to arouse adverse local reactions is the humorless moralizing prevalent in some government agencies. Federal officials often seem to view the day-to-day operations of their client agencies as a kind of moral gymnasium in which the local agency's ethical musculature, competence, and intelligence are continually tested and frequently found flabby. To the irritated state and local official, it appears that his Washington colleagues endow temporary administrative expedients with the status of moral principles. A shortage of program funds may be transformed into admonitions on the virtues of thrift; indecision may be passed off as prudence; and failure to act on applications, memoranda, and letters may solemnly be explained as time spent in grave reflection and ponderous weighing of alternatives. The federal officials, on the other hand, regard many state and local agency officials, often with cause, as simple-minded, wayward duffers. They feel that, honest or not, competent or not, many of their state and local counterparts operate in a slough of corrupt local politics. In view of these manifold deficiencies, colleagues at the state and local level are totally unable to grasp either the higher morality or the reality of the Washington scene, and those in Washington can cite chapter and verse of cases in which nasty messes were either prevented or quickly mopped up only by dint of timely federal intervention.[9] Moreover, many top federal

[9] For a concise summary of the low opinions of many federal officials concerning their state and local operations, see U.S., Advisory Commission on Intergovernmental Relations, *The Federal System as Seen by Federal Aid Officials* (Washington, D.C.: Government Printing Office, 1965). See also Melvin R. Levin, *Community and Regional Planning* (New York: Frederick A. Praeger, 1969), pp. 17–38.

executives seem to be imbued with a strong missionary spirit; there is a streak of paternal concern, an eagerness to rescue clients from their baser instincts and the limitations and consequences of their environment. Some of the intervention in the Boston project was clearly of this nature.

Perhaps the singular ineptness that often characterizes federal intervention is partly attributable to a Washington double standard. Extremely careful in their own hiring practices and always on the lookout for outstanding talent, federal officials are sometimes inclined to tolerate dullards in their field offices (often recruited from state and local government) and to expect and to accommodate sheer incompetence at the state and local levels. To a degree this is inescapable, since there is little enough talent to go around and no certain way of forcing it on reluctant local agencies. Nevertheless, there is room for suspicion that certain federal executives prefer weak, dependent clients rather than self-reliant potential rivals.

In recent years the primary expression of federal initiative has been the grant-in-aid for specific programs, which has served to convert state and local government into semivoluntary instruments of federal policy. Senator Muskie has termed the grant-in-aid programs a "hidden dimension of government." In fiscal 1968, over $17 billion in federal grant-in-aid funds were allocated either to or through state agencies or were sent directly to municipalities, bypassing the state governments. All told, grants-in-aid amounted to almost one-seventh of total state and local government expenditures in 1965, and present trends indicate that the proportion may rise to perhaps a third of the total in 1970.

The grant-in-aid technique clearly has its virtues. Through a variety of matching arrangements, poorer states and poor people benefit from federal program supervision as well as federal funds. The former role can range from a fairly loose rein—in states and localities deemed to be sober and reliable—to thoroughly restrictive controls in the case of the bigoted or irresponsible. The grant-in-aid system is a major method of persuading relatively backward and passive state and local governments to participate in new programs.

The unfortunate fact is that, with a few notable exceptions in the past three decades, the states and localities have not been playing much of a role as innovative laboratories. In Alan Campbell's words:

There have been no major policy breakthroughs by the State-local parts of the governmental system. In fact, only the Federal Government, with a few notable exceptions, has provided any new major policy thrusts. On the whole, it seems fair to say that as the system now stands the policy initiatives come from the national part of the system while the administration of the new programs are left in the hands of State and local officials, with considerable supervision by the national bureaucracy.

But fundamentally, I don't think we can ever get away from what is essentially the paperwork requirements of Federal aid, as long as the Federal aid remains specific. I am not, however, ready to take the next step and say we ought to move away from that and give more general grants to State and local governments until I am more confident that the State and local governments are ready to receive them and use them well.[10]

Despite the weaknesses of state and local government, several nonideological technical problems militate against a greater reliance on the grant-in-aid system. Regulation can easily shade off into strangulation, and federal agencies are not a suitable replacement for state and local government. There is also a tendency for federal standards, controls, and impulses to be applied uniformly and mechanically, stifling independence and initiative.

Although few federal agencies match the low standards found in the worst state and local governments, some regional offices shine only by comparison with their country cousins. For one thing, the federal selection process sweeps too high a proportion of the best people in the agencies up to Washington headquarters. The regional offices, which are responsible for most of the day-to-day supervision, are less attractive to ambitious civil servants. Consequently, the caliber of staff available to work closely with the states and localities on such matters as the area transportation studies is less than adequate. The correlation is not necessarily close between the intelligence necessary to secure a top-echelon job in Washington headquarters and subsequent performance. Despite earlier promise in lower echelons, a Potomac assignment often seems to lead to disorientation. The successful local functionary all too frequently goes to Washington and turns into a skillful paper shuffler and prolific memorandum writer. Critics assert that some upper-echelon executives seem to have left their common sense at the borders of the federal district. They are often tempted to provide procrustean straitjackets for their local clients for the sake of ease in record keeping and avoiding the danger of disastrous congressional investigations and recrimination. Under this system a bungled operation in New Orleans or Kalamazoo may be translated into a blanket national directive that smothers initiative in New York and Seattle. Since the mind of man is capable of conceiving of an infinite variety of error, regulatory manuals tend to reach infinite lengths, and the honest and competent are harassed with procedures designed for the delinquent and the cloddish. The deadly fear is that some wayward local official will steal some

[10] Alan K. Campbell, testimony in U.S., Congress, Senate, Committee on Government Operations, Subcommittee on Intergovernmental Operations, *Creative Federalism: Hearings,* pt. 2–B, 90th Congress, 1st session, 1967, pp. 848, 860.

money and that at the trial the theft will be laid at the door of a hapless federal bureaucrat who slipped up on one of the procedural safeguards.

Is there a need for worry over sticky fingers in state and local government? While it is entirely true that scandals in welfare, poverty, and highway programs, among others, have provided fuel for political bonfires, most programs and, in fact, most government operations do not lend themselves to theft. Despite the losses often attributed to graft and administrative incompetence in the states, losses through corrupt practices are actually rather nominal. As one experienced Massachusetts observer (long since run out of town) suggested, banner headlines are misleading: "more money goes down the drain through stupidity than cupidity." Honest but worse than useless chairwarmers are a thousand times more wasteful than the handful of crooks. Close examination discloses that most state budgets are stretched too thin to provide minimum support levels for education and other basic functions, let alone to permit significant amounts of thievery. It is probable that most of the elaborate, costly, and time-consuming procedures in grant-in-aid programs could be substantially abbreviated without increasing the risk—provided there is a credible threat of an ex post facto audit of finances and program output. This approach would relieve the administrator of most impediments, reduce the burden of record keeping, and speed up operations significantly. Certainly, the area transportation projects could have proceeded more smoothly with less regulatory paperwork.

State-Metropolitan Relations

The research shed additional light on a much discussed problem of fractionated decision-making in metropolitan areas. Some maintain that the present fragmented system works reasonably well, while others consider it critical and call for sweeping governmental reorganization.[11] This study suggests that the solution to most metropolitan problems of whatever severity cannot be found within the metropolitan areas. Instead, metropolitan planning and development can best be approached as a branch of state government.[12] With all its glaring weaknesses, state government offers the most realistic level for responsive metropolitan decisions.

Having offered this observation, the authors must hasten to add that the research offers no simple recommendations to expedite this task through the

[11] For good presentations of both sets of view, see Michael N. Danielson, ed., *Metropolitan Politics: A Reader* (Boston: Little, Brown and Company, 1966).

[12] For example, writing about the Boston area, Meyerson and Banfield comment that "it is hard to see how the Commonwealth can fail to become the equivalent for all practical purposes of eight or more metropolitan governments." See Martin Meyerson and Edward C. Banfield, *Boston: The Job Ahead* (Cambridge, Mass.: Harvard University Press, 1966), p. 24.

governor's office or other state decision-making avenues. We are simply stating a fact: if experience with the area transportation studies is any clue, the knottier metropolitan problems tend to gravitate toward the state house for resolution as well as for program funding and implementation. Except for an occasional tour de force effected by a leader with unusual charisma, it seems unrealistic to expect metropolitan planning agencies to function as effective political mechanisms. Aside from securing their own survival and attracting a steady stream of local and state money to attract federal matching funds for research, metropolitan planning agencies seem fated to function as only one of a number of competing lobbies within the state.

If a metropolitan program is to be meaningful, the authors contend, it is far more likely to develop under the jurisdiction of state government. First, in practical terms, the state governments are not likely to consent to the creation of 250 or so strong metropolitan governments because this would imply a transfer of power that would emasculate them. Second, many metropolitan problems are extraregional and require state or even interstate action for their solution. Yet the experience of the area transportation studies suggests that metropolitan planning cannot be successfully conducted by federal agencies. For the most part, the direct intervention of federal officials in the area transportation studies proved to be clumsy and defective. All of the studies support the conclusion that direct federal participation cannot be looked upon as a desirable administrative arrangement. On the other hand, there was strong participation from an unexpected source—state executives—which proved necessary because of unresolved differences between state and federal participants. In the Boston study, for example, HHFA looked to and encouraged the governor to resolve impasses that had developed between state and federal agencies. In the Niagara Frontier study, the governor was called upon for help. And in the Penn-Jersey study, the governor of Pennsylvania eventually entered the picture in an attempt to settle a conflict between the two major factions. In the two small studies, gubernatorial intervention was unnecessary; because the state highway departments were willing to adjust their own plans to accommodate those proposed by the local urban renewal agencies, there was no serious controversy. Major decisions in both of these studies were made by the state agencies with no countervailing dissent from regional or local planning organizations.

Based on this experience, it is reasonable to suggest that metropolitan area planning and development should be, in fact, a branch of state government and, accordingly, should be administered through the state rather than through regional agencies that must look to the federal agencies for financing and to the state agencies for decisions.

State agency executives, unlike local elected officials, can profess no loyalties to one metropolitan area over another. Even in sparsely populated states such as Maine and New Hampshire, state agencies cannot be exclusively concerned with one or two principal urban areas lest they alienate the remainder of their constituency. Nevertheless, most of a metropolitan area's development programs are the responsibility of state agencies and are financed under programs that must allocate and distribute available funds throughout a state. For example, the Department of Public Works in Massachusetts is responsible for highways in metropolitan areas, including their planning, design, programming, and actual construction. Public transportation facilities are still for the most part financed and operated by regional public transportation agencies, but even here the picture is changing. The establishment of state transportation departments in both New York and New Jersey, and the consideration being given to a similar agency in other states, will lead to more state control over the planning and programming of public transportation facilities as well as highways. For this reason alone, more of the major decisions affecting a metropolitan area are being made at the state level. Naturally, this implies that, with the exception of the larger central cities, local communities will continue to play only a minor role in major metropolitan decisions.

Federal highway grants are made directly and only to the state agencies. Grant distribution and priority determinations within a state, while subject to BPR supervision, are state responsibilities. The Inner Belt in Cambridge, Massachusetts, is a good example. The state highway agency posed an early threat to the city by suggesting that the money, if not allocated to Cambridge because of local opposition to routes preferred by the highway agency, would be spent elsewhere in the state. While many city officials and neighborhood residents regard highway construction as a threat to residential areas, the highway agencies remain convinced that all of their construction projects are highly sought after prizes and that withholding such favors constitutes severe chastisement for a recalcitrant community. In California, state highway officials made good on their threat to deprive the San Francisco area of a large sum of highway funds because of the city's refusal to permit construction of an expressway. Regardless of the merits of either of these cases, they indicate that metropolitan decisions have been advanced by a state agency and not by the Bureau of Public Roads, and certainly not by a metropolitan agency.

A few areas like Dade County (Florida) and metropolitan Nashville have established a form of metropolitan government, but no metropolitan areas in the United States have strong, central decision-making machinery equivalent to a city or state government because they do not have an elected chief executive. The functional metropolitan agencies, created to provide specific services, are usually dependent on state financing, although they may develop into powerful empires and tend to be self-serving organisms that then become obstacles to publicly responsive decision-making. For conflicts involving any of the autonomous "metropolitan giants," to use Robert Wood's term for regional authorities, solutions must be sought in state government.[13]

City, state, and federal governments have one feature in common: they all have chief executives who possess the statutory authority to overcome paralysis and, on occasion, to inject into decisions considerations that transcend the political muscle of the participants. In short, where there is a central decision-making process and elected leaders who presumably reflect the will of the people, there are provisions for settling interagency disputes, and the pressure is considerably greater for resolving them. Metropolitan-level conflicts often result in protracted wrangling; each side expends considerable effort on complex maneuvers to bring gubernatorial and other pressures to bear on its opponents. While awaiting gubernatorial action, the situation can become paralytic, as evidenced in the Boston and Penn-Jersey projects.

The control of regional development by the state is not a new concept. In 1962 the Council of State Governments produced a report that noted:

State government possesses singular qualifications to make profound and constructive contributions to urban regional development practice. The state is in fact an established regional form of government. It has ample powers and financial resources to move broadly on several fronts. Far ranging state highway, recreation and water resource development programs to name a few have had and will continue to have great impact on the development of urban and regional areas. Moreover, the state occupies a unique vantage point broad enough to allow it to view details of the development within its boundaries as part of an interrelated system yet close enough to enable it to treat urban regional programs individually and at first hand.[14]

This view has become increasingly popular after a decade of experimentation by HUD in dealing directly with metropolitan areas. In New England the establishment of the New England Regional Commission, and more particularly the strengthening of the state planning agencies in the component states, points to a stronger federal-state relationship. It is more than likely that a stronger state role will inevitably limit any transfer of decision-making power to metropolitan agencies. In a real sense, strong metropolitan governments would represent the creation of miniature "statelets" that would compete with state government to the extent that they were given independent funding and power. Yet it is difficult to imagine states abdicating authority over the

---

[13] See Robert C. Wood, *1400 Governments* (Cambridge, Mass.: Harvard University Press, 1961), chap. 4, "The World of the Metropolitan Giants," pp. 114–172.
[14] Council of State Governments, *State Responsibility in Urban Regional Development* (Chicago, 1962), p. 17.

most populous and vital portions of their territory, the metropolitan areas. Genuine metropolitan government, therefore, including the election of metropolitan officials and the establishment of agencies fully capable of dealing with metropolitan problems, does not seem to be a realistic possibility.

The practical alternative to a metropolitan political structure is the strengthening of state government. But HUD, like its HHFA predecessor, has had an ambivalent attitude toward state governments. It has provided funds to state planning agencies for statewide planning, and it has used them as conduits for federal funds to support small-town planning. In a few cases, state agencies have performed planning services for small towns. In this approach, Tennessee is the most notable. Yet HUD at the same time deals directly with larger communities in housing, model cities, urban renewal, and other programs involving substantial expenditures. HUD money for planning is also available for the metropolitan agencies sandwiched between state and local governments, which have been assigned administrative and coordinating functions.

As a result of these extensive dealings with agencies at the local, regional, and state levels, HUD is often in the position of financing both sides in a guerrilla war as, for example, when local renewal plans clash with regional transportation plans. Certainly, in the area transportation studies, HUD has given technical and financial support to both parties. In Manchester, for instance, much of the dispute centered around urban renewal plans for the downtown area, which conflicted with the highway plans of the HUD-BPR-sponsored transportation study. Similar urban renewal–highway agency struggles were evident in the Portland and Buffalo areas.

The issue of metropolitanism versus state power has a number of implications. For example, one can ask whether it is more desirable to maintain a resident planning staff in metropolitan areas or to obtain the benefits of having a larger and perhaps more proficient state organization perform metropolitan planning from a central office. Two basic objectives may be in conflict. Officials in the New York State Department of Transportation stress the advantages of centralization: a variety of staff can be hired and retained; procedures can be standardized to cut costs, improve results, and avoid errors; and a high level of service to outlying areas can be maintained in an age of swift communications. Others suggest that a strong resident area staff is necessary to reflect local needs accurately, ensure broad community participation, and serve as area advocates in Washington and in the state capital. This was the view of several local officials in the largest metropolitan region, the Niagara Frontier, served by New York's Department of Transportation.

Insofar as the area transportation studies are concerned, HUD's efforts to deal with the large metropolitan areas directly, while simultaneously working closely with state and local planning agencies, created a number of administrative and jurisdictional problems. On the basis of this experience, a closer look should be given to the possibility of utilizing state government more extensively as a way of obtaining improved metropolitan organizational and development patterns.

The Need for Reorganization and Centralization

The experience of the transportation studies suggests that it may be far too early to expect regional planning organizations to make significant contributions to regional development decisions. There is neither an adequate underpinning of useful research on regional goals, plans, alternative strategies, and consequences nor a recognized, coherent set of findings and conclusions to guide such decisions. The regional planning organizations are generally controlled by technicians with varying political expertise, operating under the loose direction of laymen. They are not suitable political and administrative structures for arriving at consensual regional goals—if such there be—nor are they capable of requiring community and agency adherence to such goals. When the regional agencies attempt to exercise a serious impact on area decisions, they are caught in a complicated game involving an intricate mix of local, state, federal, quasi-public, and private agency participants. There is a basic internal contradiction in the assumption that a weak political and administrative entity can develop and impose broad goals on the operations of other well-entrenched, influential agencies.

Extraordinary difficulties occur in developing and translating broad general goals into realistic objectives in a polycentric society. One highly skeptical observer maintains that no one can "point to an example of successful comprehensive planning in the United States." This critic suggests that

in the American political system the making of comprehensive plans, as distinguished from the manufacture of documents to satisfy federal requirements, has never been a real possibility. . . .
The metropolitan area . . . is a political no-man's land into which a planning body ventures at its peril. [15]

The federal agencies accurately reflect the state of mind of a nation that has not yet made a judgment on metropolitan problems and priorities. The appointment of a presidential adviser on urban affairs probably guarantees that the right questions will be asked, but this is no assurance of interagency harmony or of a federal consensus on metropolitan policy. Presidential intervention can help to resolve overt interagency conflict, but the disparate interests operating in metropolitan areas will revert to their original directions. Metropolitan planning agencies, on their own, are even less likely to be able

[15] Banfield, "Uses and Limitations of Metropolitan Planning," p. 715.

to resolve the issues that remain unresolved in the nation and its Congress.

Alan Campbell suggests that the present system of government militates against rational choice on an area basis:

the housekeeping orientation of the present local system makes it impossible for any kind of areawide planning to be undertaken. As a result, basic decisions concerning the fundamental nature of American metropolitanism are simply not made because there is no institutional system to make them. Under the present system there is no overall planning of metropolitan areas. There are, indeed, metropolitanwide planning agencies but they are only advisory and seldom possess those tools necessary for effective planning. Without such metropolitanwide planning controls the present dispersal of metropolitan population will continue. It is possible that this distribution of residences and jobs is what we want, but the present system does not provide any method for decisionmaking.[16]

At the very least, both the federal and metropolitan levels will continue to be characterized by conflicting interest groups maneuvering for agency and personal advantage. "Intragovernmental gamesmanship," to use Totton Anderson's apt phrase,[17] is likely to remain a way of life within the federal system, doubtlessly growing more complicated each year as interagency and intergovernmental programs proliferate.

The pattern of federal-metropolitan relations is a mosaic of lobbying pressures, each always under the threat of being outmaneuvered by one of the dissatisfied claimants. Michael Danielson's description is valid for the larger area transportation studies considered in this research. He sees

a system in which the many pathways to the national capital attract numerous metropolitan actors, each motivated by a different perspective of the urban landscape and none representing the metropolis as a whole. From a constellation of federal agencies, commissions, committees, and individuals, most seek particular remedies for the maladies of their particular fragments of the metropolis. Few of the federal participants can satisfy urban demands independently, but most can block action unilaterally. In this scramble, capabilities and influence are unequally distributed; perceptions, attitudes, interest, constituency concerns, and goals vary widely. From the interplay of these many variables comes the characteristic pattern of federal-metropolitan politics.[18]

It is only fair to indicate that some modest optimism remains over the possibility of effective metropolitan planning albeit on a less-than-comprehensive scale. Robert Wood, for example, has observed a growing discontent among metropolitan leadership cadres, which he feels can be harnessed to secure backing for federal incentives to stimulate metropolitan programs in such key

[16] Campbell, in U.S., Congress, Senate, *Creative Federalism,* p. 852.

[17] Totton Anderson, "Pressure Groups and Intergovernmental Relations," *Annals of the American Academy of Political and Social Science,* vol. 359 (May 1965), pp. 121–122.

[18] Michael N. Danielson, "The Pattern of Federal-Metropolitan Politics," in idem, *Metropolitan Politics,* p. 342.

fields as housing and land use.[19] Regardless of the nature and scope of federal incentives, however, great disparities will undoubtedly remain among metropolitan areas, depending on the quality of area leadership. The enormous variations existing from city to city in the scale of urban renewal programming suggest that there are definite limitations to federal assistance to local areas. Grant-in-aid programs offer opportunities to state and local governments, but there is no guarantee that the latter possess the capability for exploiting such opportunities.

By this time the reader may share the authors' conclusion that the obstacles to creating and implementing coordinated plans for metropolitan development are formidable, if not entirely insurmountable. It would clearly be immensely helpful if federal activities bearing on urban development could be rendered moderately consistent, but the present treaty-making approach does not seem to offer much hope in this regard. Certainly, the history of the larger area transportation studies indicates the weak holding power of paper agreements when agency interests and personal ambitions clash. Since the problem of federal coordination has a direct relevance to the future of metropolitan areas, it may be useful to offer a tentative suggestion of how such a realignment may come about. Metropolitan problems are so inextricably linked that, like the magician's string of handkerchiefs, tugging away at one problem inevitably drags along all the others. Given this difficulty, what is clearly required is not a readjustment of one, two, or three federal departments but a broad reorganization of the functions of agencies directly related to urban areas.

Not much dismantling of existing agencies or programs is a likely possibility. The situation in late 1966 was concisely stated by Charles L. Schultze, director of the Bureau of the Budget:

We have tried to do a great deal in a short time, and the federal system has been hard put to digest so much so quickly. The inevitable gap between the creation of new programs and the retooling of the administrative process has resulted in the array of unfinished business that constitutes the agenda for these hearings. But, paradoxically, the problems in administration and intergovernmental relations which these programs have created are themselves a tribute to their realism and their vigor.

We could have sat on our hands and played it safe. There would certainly be fewer complaints. There would also, however, be an even worse gap—that between mounting social costs and responsible policy initiatives. In closing one gap, we opened another, but it is the one we prefer. I dislike to see evidence of faulty coordination, spinning wheels, frustrating delays, failures of communication, and all the other dross that comprises the symptoms of uneven administration and program execution. At the same time, it would be surprising if everything clicked smoothly in the wake of an immensely productive period of legislation which in the last Congress produced 21 new

[19] Robert C. Wood, "A Federal Policy for Metropolitan Areas," in ibid., p. 334.

health programs, 17 new educational programs, . . . to meet the problems of our cities, 4 new programs for manpower training, and 17 new resource development programs.[20]

Schultze suggested a partial solution (at the federal level) to the dilemmas he poses. For the most part these involve structural changes:

As I see it, there are three roads we can travel to solve our crisis in coordination and management:
(1) We can combine Federal programs to reduce the proliferation which confuses State and local administrators;
(2) We can reorganize the executive branch to concentrate programs under fewer agencies; and
(3) We can develop an effective and flexible method of policy coordination in Washington and in the field.
I suspect we shall have to travel all three roads at once. No one proposal and no one technique will be adequate.
My mind is still open on the most effective approach to the problem. But, on the basis of these hearings, it is evident that the interagency committees and the convener authorities fall far short of the standards we must achieve. Single agencies or departments, acting under delegated authority or in concert, are not adequate to the task. The final answer, or answers, must rest in the Executive Office of the President. The coordination must have a broader base than budget considerations, a deeper significance than effective operations, and a bigger goal than day-to-day management.[21]

It is not inconceivable that disenchantment with the present pattern of polycentric power in metropolitan areas will lead to a centralization of federal urban authority under a presidentially backed czar. Such a development might do more for coordinated development in metropolitan areas than is being accomplished under the present system. Perhaps the most outstanding example of a successful reorganization of power centers was the effective control over the armed services instituted by President Kennedy through Secretary of Defense McNamara. It may be noted that the key feature in the reform was not merely a shuffling of boxes on organization charts but the achievement of vigorous leadership over a management team.

The situation that Secretary of Defense McNamara took over has a direct parallel to the present situation with respect to urban areas. There were similar gentlemen's agreements among the services, which barely concealed rivalries for limited annual appropriations, key missions, and intricate arrangements with congressional and private constituencies. As one author describes the Pentagon prior to McNamara's arrival:

in the previous thirteen years, and despite the ministrations of some of the most highly regarded professional managers in the U.S., the Defense Department had never developed a systematic procedure for translating strategic requirements into budgetary requests. What happened each year, according

[20] Charles L. Schultze, statement in U.S., Congress, Senate, *Creative Federalism*, pt. 1, 89th Congress, 2nd session, 1966, p. 389.
[21] Ibid., p. 464.

to Comptroller Charles J. Hitch, who introduced the new system into the Pentagon, was a "process of bargaining among officials and groups having diverse strengths, aims, convictions, and responsibilities."[22]

The fundamental change within the Defense Department was the subordination of the three services to a single overall defense mission. This by no means eliminated interservice struggles, but it did introduce a pattern of coherent and consistent management:

McNamara's critics are probably right in identifying the scientific attitudes he has brought to the Pentagon as the major ingredient of his management revolution; they are wrong, however, in suggesting that computers are at the bottom of it all. What is at the bottom is an absolute insistence on being rational and systematic. In practice, this means that the assumptions underlying positions must be made explicit, that issues must be defined rigorously, that possible courses of action must be examined in light of their consequences, that data must be precise (e.g., quantified) whenever possible— and that nothing at all will be accepted on faith.[23]

Our study modestly concludes that centralized management is desirable to produce a coherent federal approach to the metropolitan areas. At the very least this would eliminate some of the grosser examples of unnecessary overlapping, interagency friction, and general frustration that bedevil federal-metropolitan relations. We must hasten to add, however, that while centralization provides some guarantees of efficiency, it does not promise wisdom. As with the Pentagon, there is always the possibility of large-scale error, partly because effective management is still exposed to political pressure and partly because some major and crucial factors defy quantification.

This approach would have two other important consequences: for example, it would bring into sharp focus the lack of any national pattern of goals and priorities. The need for such priorities will become critical as the nation begins to harness rather than dissipate its resources that are aimed at improving the situation in urban areas. In turn, this would probably create pressures for the establishment of a single federal agency with overall responsibility for urban policy. At a minimum, this could involve a merger of half a dozen major federal departments, including HUD, HEW, DOT, and Labor.

A clarification of federal policy and a rationalization of the machinery relating to urban areas would have a profound effect on intergovernmental relations. There would be less demand by state and metropolitan emissaries to journey to Washington to promote pet solutions, and state-metropolitan relations would improve. For example, the classic conflict between state highway

---

[22] David Seligman, "McNamara's Management Revolution," *Fortune Magazine,* July 1965, p. 117.

[23] Ibid., p. 120. See also Aaron Wildavsky, "The Political Economy of Efficiency: Cost-Benefit Analysis, Systems Analysis and Program Budgeting, *Public Administration Review,* vol. 26, no. 4 (December 1966), pp. 292–310.

departments and rapid transit systems would be reduced to minimal proportions, and new-town efforts could be combined more meaningfully with new investments in transportation. This managerial approach would permit a more orderly investment of the national resources; as we have indicated, however, better arrangements such as these would provide a tool rather than a substitute for basic decisions on goals and priorities.

A Role for Metropolitan Agencies

Major improvements in federal policy and programs are a prerequisite for any significant upgrading in the quality of decisions affecting metropolitan areas, but much can be accomplished before such sweeping structural changes are realized. It must be made clear that although the functions proposed in this section do not necessarily require federal action, it is vital that they gain approval by state government. Metropolitan agencies represent a potential threat to state government, and any meaningful activities on their part must rest on state acquiescence.

Within this framework, there appear to be three principal roles that metropolitan agencies can play:

1. Education: The Regional University. Analysis of the regional decision-making process reveals that a long educational campaign in the press and other media leading to a near consensus among civic, political, and other public opinion leaders is usually necessary for action. The time that elapses between the real beginning of such a campaign and the completion of a major development project may range from as few as five to as many as thirty years. In metropolitan Boston the first major educational campaign for mass transit extensions began in 1926 and was picked up again in 1945. Two decades later the necessary enabling legislation was passed, and the extensions proposed in 1925 may be completed in the 1970s. This is only one illustration from a number of cases, ranging from regional water and sewerage systems to incinerators, parks, and airports, of proposals requiring two or three decades of promotion before they become a reality. It suggests that public education should be one of the principal functions of regional planning agencies. This educational function obviously includes research on goals, environmental needs and problems, and other major regional concerns, including transportation. Over and above the task of informing the general public, the regional planning organization should be expected to engage in a long-range educational program directed toward other government agencies. The area transportation studies indicate that such a job is badly needed, particularly for the highway agencies. The metropolitan planning agency does not have to do this single-handed. There is every reason to develop close working relationships with local colleges and universities to draw on their research resources and to develop a solid, broadly based interest and capability in planning. If the agency is to play this role effectively, it can also make extensive use of existing and newly established credit and noncredit courses, of university faculty and fellows, and of scholarship and internship programs.[24]

The regional planning organization would serve, in effect, as the core faculty of a regional university without a campus or formal curriculum. With the assistance of local educational institutions and other available resources, the regional planning agency would conduct a continuing instructional program for laymen, and intermediate and advanced seminars for administrators and technicians. Certainly, there is much to be done. Emerging issues such as new towns, dispersion of the city ghettos, urban design, aesthetics, new approaches to waste disposal, and easing of congestion in the urban core will require years of preparatory research and education before effective decisions can be reached.

It is apparent that the staff of the regional agency must possess a reasonable working acquaintance with modern communication skills and techniques. The citizenry cannot be forced to attend classes nor to listen to lectures, and it risks no explicit personal disadvantage by flunking examinations. In the face of legitimate competing claims for attention, the regional planning agency cannot expect to have much public impact unless it succeeds in making its work at least moderately interesting. There is an entire world of graphics that government agencies are only beginning to explore. The cinematic dramatization of the gravity model for metropolitan Hartford prepared by the Federal Bureau of Public Roads offers proof that even a difficult, technically complex subject can be made understandable to a lay audience. Making effective use of these techniques is all the more important because it is in this critical area—education and communication—that the regional transportation studies experienced a serious failure. The permanent agencies can surely do better if they recognize the importance of this function at the outset.

2. The Judicial Function: A Regional Supreme Court for Area Planning and Development. A second function closely related to education is a judicial one, which devolves on the regional planning agencies through the statutory referral and review powers conferred by Section 204 of the 1967 Housing Act.

The goal should be to create a prestigious regional agency, whose decisions would have the status of a supreme court ruling on significant regional plan-

[24] Title VIII of the 1964 Housing Act and Title IX of the Demonstration Cities and Metropolitan Development Act of 1965, along with Title I of the Higher Education Act of 1965, provide sizable funds for this function. Since the allocation of money under these programs is controlled by state agencies, the metropolitan agencies are in this, as in other instances, required to establish a modus vivendi as clients of state government.

ning and development issues. This, obviously, is not feasible with an unwieldy, loose administrative structure consisting of a relatively large number of locally elected officials, variously appointed laymen, part-time members of community planning boards, and representatives of public agencies who can be easily manipulated by a full-time technical staff. Effective performance of this review function requires a small, distinguished, and knowledgeable policy-making board that can exercise continuing and full control over an experienced, qualified staff.

The board should have direct access to the major centers of recognized statutory authority that possess substantial influence and control over public agencies operating in the region. In effect, this means another close working relationship with state government. In this case the link is to the governor's office, and the regional agency must be careful to avoid partisan coloration and thus retain its freedom from manipulation as a political instrument in the governor's orchestra. Achieving close cooperation with the governor's office while retaining its own autonomy may be difficult but should be feasible on the basis of mutually compatible interests. Both parties are interested in improving the quality of regional decisions and of agency performance. Both play a significant and not dissimilar educational and communication role. Both wish to prevent messy public wrangles between affected agencies and the regional board. Moreover, governors usually welcome a fresh source of informed and objective advice on major policies and issues. It is more than likely, in fact, that an effective regional planning agency could develop into an invaluable advisory and research resource for the governor, serving, it may be hoped, as an auxiliary rather than as a rival to the state planning agency.

The regional planning board might consist of a limited number of well-known persons of outstanding background who would serve on a part-time, remunerated basis. Some members might be appointed to represent major interests, including such constituencies as public transportation, conservation, and the disadvantaged. Valid participation by persons representing conflicting viewpoints usually strengthens rather than weakens citizen commissions. Depending on the size of the area and other circumstances, however, experimentation could be undertaken with alternative membership patterns. It may well be that no one general arrangement is suitable for all areas. The area transportation studies indicated that citizen boards lacking interest-group representation and motivation tend to consist of relatively weak, apathetic participants. The staff would, among its other functions, perform the necessary background research on issues coming before the board.

Under such conditions, the regional planning agency's mandatory referral and review power can be elevated to a quasi-judicial plane, vested with an aura of objective sanctity as well as technical expertise. Moreover, as the agency gains solidity and prestige, it can and should be expected to advise on program proposals of federal, private, and other interests affecting the region, over and above its special role with the governor. If it is a storehouse of knowledge, a clearinghouse for research, and a respected source of informed counsel, the influence of the regional agency will inevitably spread well beyond its statutory perimeters.

3. Technical Planning Assistance. Experience with the area transportation studies, and, indeed, with similar regional planning ventures, indicates that one of the potentially most rewarding functions of the regional planning agency is not really a regional responsibility at all. This is the provision of technical assistance to local communities and public agencies. Few regional agency activities evoke such tangible appreciation and support; it is noteworthy that the 1968 amendments to federal housing and urban development legislation specifically added metropolitan agencies to the list of agencies eligible for federal aid to undertake local planning assistance. An increasing number of states are providing technical assistance for communities through departments of community affairs (as in Connecticut, New Jersey, and Massachusetts) or similar mechanisms. To the extent that there is political mileage in the function, the regional agency may find itself in competition with a state agency for the privilege of providing local technical services.

One problem in undertaking this type of service is that it may drain away scarce staff time from basic regional planning tasks; alternatively, it may lead to the creation of a staff empire dependent for its main support on a variety of research and planning contracts with other agencies. Perhaps the most effective way of handling this function, therefore, is to draw on the help of a list of selected, approved consultants. The agency could act as a clearinghouse-referral service or as a prime contractor issuing and overseeing subcontracts. In either approach, the regional agency would be improving the quality of technical decisions affecting the region and simultaneously securing broader support for itself by performing useful, visible activities. Under either arrangement, the regional planning agency would assume part of the role now performed by state planning agencies. Clearly in this, as in most of its functions, the metropolitan agency must develop a modus vivendi with state government.

The Role and Importance of Program Evaluation

The experience gained in this research underscored the difficulty as well as the critical importance of evaluating ongoing programs. Thanks to natural human inertia, most government programs are difficult to start and equally difficult to change and to stop. It is no easier for a troubled bureaucratic organization than for an individual to undertake self-criticism and act on its findings. Some people and agencies are capable of this kind of self-surgery, but they are rarities. As a result the impetus for change often comes from the sources of funding; the hot breath of legislative committees is often a prime stimulus.

For ob.ious reasons, agencies seem to be relying increasingly on outside critics to assume the onerous burden of program evaluation. This is not an easy task, as a seasoned evaluator has noted:

Commenting on the performance of on-going programs is at best a hazardous occupation. Program content, if not direction, is usually in a state of flux. Data valid at the time an evaluation is written may be obsolete by the time the report sees the light of day.

Nevertheless, those who assess current government programs need not feel guilty about their occupation. As long as Congress must make decisions involving billions of dollars with only a modicum of information about the impacts of the activities it funds, there is a need for objective evaluations which present to Congress and the public whatever data are available on existing programs with the hope that the information and judgment will pass the test of time. Since those administering the program cannot be expected to approach the task objectively, the need for outside evaluation is clear.

If evaluations are to be useful to decision-making, then the evaluator cannot afford to wait until all returns are in and all precincts are heard from. Every time Congress renews an appropriation it declares a program a winner. Since Congress annually invests billions of dollars for the continuation of on-going programs, the program evaluator should not hesitate to analyze whatever data the program operators will provide to help those who shape policy to arrive at their decisions on the basis of the best available information.[25]

One special problem for our particular research deserves mention. It was unusually difficult to make an objective analysis of organizations that were characterized by rapid turnover in the top echelon and by major administrative reorganizations. This kind of turmoil was found in both the Boston and the Penn-Jersey projects. Moreover, all of the participants in the projects considered in this research were subjected to some administrative surgery before the studies were closed out. HHFA became HUD, the BPR became part of DOT, the Massachusetts DPW was overhauled, and so on.

A new broom is an implicit admission of past failures. As a rule, a new managerial team is only too willing to discuss (with informed outsiders) the mess it inherited. Under these circumstances it is almost churlish to undertake an open review of past errors while newly appointed chiefs are manfully struggling to correct them. It is tempting to reserve judgment until the new men have had a chance to assemble staff, revise operating procedures, and bring long-missing vitality back to an administration. Unfortunately, there is

[25] See Sar A. Levitan, "Vista: The Great Society's Domestic Volunteers," pt. 1, *Poverty and Human Resources Abstracts,* vol. 3, no. 5 (September–October 1968), p. 19.

a strong likelihood that members of the new team will quit in frustration or will be replaced. In turn, their newly appointed successors will again be eager to discuss their troubled legacy, and again any appraisal would be premature until the dust has had a chance to settle. Since the air continues to be obscured by clouds of freshly inked organizational charts, meaningful criticism may be deflected until, at long last, there is a period of relative calm. This may not occur until the money runs out. Deferred until this terminal coma, an analysis takes on the air of an autopsy.

As events moved, this research proved to be more of an ex post facto assessment than a biopsy of living organisms. Each of the larger studies was, in its lifetime, afflicted by maladies that caused much pain and expense, suggesting that timely criticisms may have some value as preventive medicine—provided the patient is willing to listen. This obviously involves a mutual spirit of accommodation on the part of analyst and subject. It is particularly necessary that the critique be constructive and be viewed by the subject as at least potentially helpful.

Quite probably the critics should be outsiders, not tied to any previous commitment or faction. This, of course, raises some interesting questions about their attitudes and roles.

What is constructive criticism from outside? If one is not a government bureaucrat or a politican or a professional social worker working in an agency, what kind of role does one have as an outside critic looking at these programs? To what extent do you make criticisms which are only within the perspective of those operating the program? . . .

We are groping, I think, towards a new kind of social role of criticism which lies between the large-scale sweeping indictment of society along the lines of the New Left and talks about really large-scale value changes in society and the kind of very small-scale pragmatic concerns of those who are administering programs or benefiting from certain programs and are only concerned with bolstering, rather than re-examining, these programs. I think that the role of many independent social scientists is in between the two positions of large-sweeping social change and very incremental kinds of social improvements.[26]

The role Miller proposes for the outside critic clearly makes demands equally on the abilities of the evaluator and on the receptivity of the client agency. It is not easy to be optimistic on either count. Peter Rossi has observed that

The will to believe that their programs are effective is understandably strong among administrators. As long as the results are positive (or at least not negative), relations between practitioners and researchers are cordial and even effusive. But what if the results are negative?

. . . I do not know of any action program that has been put out of business by evaluation research, unless evaluation itself was meant to be the hatchet. Why? Mainly because practitioners (and sometimes researchers) never seri-

[26] S. M. Miller, "Criteria for Antipoverty Policies: A Paradigm for Choice," ibid., p. 10.

ously consider the possibility that results *might* come out negative or insignificant. When a research finding shows that a program is ineffective, and the research director has failed to plan for this eventuality, then the impact can be so devastating that it becomes more comforting to deny the worth of the negative evaluation than to reorganize one's planning.[27]

Rossi points to a relatively neglected aspect of the area studies and, indeed, of metropolitanism in general: the tendency to concentrate on organization charts and flow diagrams, on tables of staff requirements, and on technical prerequisites for personnel to the detriment of certain important nontechnical considerations. For example, a problem that plagued each of the three major transportation studies revolved around jarring clashes between sensitive personalities. There was a marked tendency for the participants, whatever their level of skill, to cling tenaciously to counterproductive courses of action. The old saw about the lack of correlation between intelligence, wisdom, and tolerance was very much in evidence. One participant pointed to the special danger of throwing good money after bad by giving, in his words, "the new money to the old men." The tendency to equate blocks of expenditures with progress and production must be avoided. Unfortunately, program evaluation is not one of the highly developed arts, and there are all too many instances in which governmental machinery, once set in motion, continues to grind out appropriations for unproductive endeavors. Sometimes even congressional pressures for rigorous agency evaluation may not prove effective. But there is little doubt that more searching critiques are on their way.

Program Evaluation and Agency Reform

This analysis of area transportation studies has underscored the need for an upgrading of agency performance, including substantial improvements in program conceptualization and the capability of an agency to adjust its programs to meet realities. Program evaluation is at best a thankless task. Those who undertake it may be accused of a morbid propensity for exhuming half-forgotten mistakes. Nevertheless, this book strikes a modestly hopeful note with its finding that a faulty system of organization and inflated expectations were more to blame for later paralysis and confusion than were failings of the individual participants.

The research also made it extremely clear that the defects of the area studies were only surface manifestations of deeply rooted problems. This society has not decided on its urban goals and priorities, has not developed accurate information on the nature of its problems and on how best to solve them, and has not produced a sufficient number of highly talented practitioners to lead pioneering efforts. It is not surprising that interagency and intergovernmental

[27] Peter Rossi, "Evaluating Social Action Programs," *Trans-Action,* vol. 4, no. 7 (June 1967), pp. 51–52.

relations, as manifested in the area transportation studies, faithfully reflected these underlying deficiencies.

Finally, the research indicated that the real choices in many situations lie between almost equally unpalatable alternatives. The Department of Housing and Urban Development seems to view programs as offering choices between the good and the bad: well-planned administrative operations and effective citizen participation are sharply contrasted to their opposites. More optimistically, the Bureau of Public Roads seems to operate on the implicit assumption that most of its choices range between the good and the even better: highways are always helpful, but some route locations generate greater benefits than others.

Yet in reality, in the larger area transportation studies, the choice seemed to lie between the barely tolerable and the much worse. The Boston project required a choice between the retention of an unpopular but forceful administrator and the imposition of a leadership and organizational structure that looked good but worked badly, permitting the project to run down. In Penn-Jersey the choice lay between a decision to write off years of effort and millions of dollars or to make a fresh start under new management. In Buffalo the choice lies between clinging to a costly, technically impressive highway corridor that local interests find unacceptable, or starting over with new assumptions, some of which may challenge the fundamental bases of highway construction in urban areas. Perhaps all this can be summarized under the heading of maturity. It requires wisdom and calm reason to decide that opponents are not necessarily wicked, stupid, shortsighted, or untrustworthy, and even more inner security to create viable working relationships with people and agencies holding very dissimilar views.

In this respect, the area transportation studies may be a way station toward reasoning together, a transition from old-style, ad hoc approaches and exhortation toward new dimensions in interagency and intergovernmental coordination.

Books

Abrams, Richard M. *Conservatism in a Progressive Era: Massachusetts Politics, 1900–1912.* Cambridge, Mass.: Harvard University Press, 1964.

Altshuler, Alan A. *The City Planning Process: A Political Analysis.* Ithaca, N.Y.: Cornell University Press, 1965.

American Municipal Association. *The Collapse of Commuter Service: A Survey of Mass Transportation in Five Selected Cities.* Washington, D.C., 1959.

American Transit Association. *Transit Facts and Figures: Annual Report, 1968.* Washington, D.C., 1968.

Banfield, Edward C. "The Uses and Limitations of Metropolitan Planning in Massachusetts." In *Taming Megalopolis.* Edited by H. Wentworth Eldredge. Vol. 2. New York: Anchor Books, 1967.

Council of State Governments. *State Responsibility in Urban Regional Development.* Chicago, 1962.

Courtney, Joseph F. "State and Municipal Government Law." In *Annual Survey of Massachusetts Laws.* Boston: Little, Brown and Company, 1964.

Danielson, Michael N. *Federal-Metropolitan Politics and the Commuter Crisis.* New York: Columbia University Press, 1965.

——, ed. *Metropolitan Politics: A Reader.* Boston: Little, Brown and Company, 1966.

Downs, Anthony. *Inside Bureaucracy.* Boston: Little, Brown and Company, 1967.

Fitch, Lyle, and Associates. *Urban Transportation and Public Policy.* San Francisco: Chandler Publishing Co., 1964.

Friedman, Robert S. "State Politics and Highways." In *Politics in the American States.* Edited by Herbert Jacob and Kenneth N. Vines. Boston: Little, Brown and Company, 1965.

Friedmann, John, and Alonso, William, eds. *Regional Development and Planning: A Reader.* Cambridge, Mass.: The M.I.T. Press, 1964.

Gilbert, Charles E. *Governing the Suburbs.* Bloomington: Indiana University Press, 1967.

Gottfield, Gunther M. *Rapid Transit Systems in Six Metropolitan Areas.* Staff report prepared for U.S., Congress, Joint Committee on Washington Metropolitan Problems, 86th Congress, 1st session, November 1959.

Greer, Scott. *Urban Renewal in American Cities.* Indianapolis: Bobbs-Merill Company, 1965.

Levin, Melvin R. *Community and Regional Planning: Issues in Public Policy.* New York: Frederick A. Praeger, 1969.

Mansfield, Harvey C. "Political Parties, Patronage and the Federal Service." In The American Assembly, *The Federal Government Service.* Edited by Wallace S. Sayre. Englewood Cliffs, N.J.: Prentice-Hall, 1965.

Meyerson, Martin, and Banfield, Edward C. *Boston: The Job Ahead.* Cambridge, Mass.: Harvard University Press, 1966.

Milgrim, Grace. *The City Expands.* Philadelphia: University of Pennsylvania, Institute for Environmental Studies, 1967.

Mowitz, Robert J., and Wright, Deil S. *Profile of a Metropolis: A Case Book.* Detroit: Wayne State University Press, 1962.

National Committee on Urban Transportation. *Better Transportation for Your City.* Chicago: Public Administration Service, 1958.

Neustadt, Richard E. *Presidential Power.* New York: Signet Books, 1960.

Owen, Wilfred. "What Do We Want the Highway System to Do?" In Tax Institute, Inc., *Financing Highways.* Princeton, N.J., 1957.

Schlesinger, Arthur M., Jr. *A Thousand Days: John F. Kennedy in the White House.* Boston: Houghton Mifflin Company, 1965.

Simpson, Smith. *Anatomy of the State Department.* Boston: Houghton Mifflin Company, 1967.

Smerk, George M. *Urban Transportation: The Federal Role.* Bloomington: Indiana University Press, 1965.

Smith, Wilbur, and Associates. *Transportation and Parking for Tomorrow's Cities.* Detroit: Automobile Manufacturers Association, 1966.

Whalen, Richard J. *The Founding Father.* New York: New American Library, 1964.

Wood, Robert C. *1400 Governments.* Cambridge, Mass.: Harvard University Press, 1961.

——. *Planning 1962.* Chicago: American Society of Planning Officials, 1962.

Zettel, Richard M., and Carll, Richard R. *Summary Review of Metropolitan Area Transportation Studies in the United States.* Berkeley: University of California, Institute of Traffic and Transportation Engineering, 1962.

Reports

American Association of State Highway Officials. Committee on Urban Transportation Planning. *Organizational Procedures of Seventeen Urban Transportation Studies.* Washington, D.C., 1963.

Automobile Manufacturers Association. *Automobile Facts and Figures.* Detroit, 1967.

Boston. Park Department. *Future Parks and Playgrounds.* Prepared by Shurcliff and Merrill. 1926.

Creighton, Roger L. "A Report on the Niagara Frontier Transportation Study." Mimeographed. Albany: Upstate New York Transportation Studies and New York State Department of Public Works, July 1, 1963.

Delaware Valley Regional Planning Commission. *Delaware Valley Planning News,* vol. 2, no. 4 (June 1968).

——. *Important Facts about the Delaware Valley Regional Planning Commission.* Philadelphia, 1967.

——. *1985 Regional Projection for the Delaware Valley.* Plan Report no. 1. Philadelphia, 1967.

Greater Portland Regional Planning Commission. *Land Use and Highway Plan, 1975, for the Portland Region.* March 1958.

Highway Research Board. *Transportation System Evaluation.* Highway Research Record no. 238. Washington, D.C., 1968.

——. *Urban Development Models.* Special Report no. 97. Washington, D.C., 1968.

Krapf, Norman W. "Building the Basic Corridor Plan." In Niagara Frontier Transportation Study, *Remarks Made at the Presentation of the Basic Corridor Plan for Expressways, August 18, 1965.* Publication no. IR 44–251–01. September 1965.

Levin, Melvin R., and Grossman, David A. *Industrial Land Needs.* Boston: Greater Boston Economic Study Committee, 1961.

Little, Arthur D., Inc. *Greater Portland Planning Region: Economic Problems and Opportunities.* Prepared for the Greater Portland Regional Planning Commission. Cambridge, Mass., March 1960.

Lowry, Ira S. "Seven Models of Urban Development: A Structural Comparison." In Highway Research Board, *Urban Development Models.* Special Report no. 97. Washington, D.C., 1968.

Maine. State Highway Commission and Department of Economic Development. *Portland Area Comprehensive Transportation Study: Final Report.* April 1965.

Massachusetts Bay Transportation Authority. *A Comprehensive Development Program for Public Transportation in the Massachusetts Bay Area.* 1966.

Massachusetts. Boston Regional Planning Project. *Policy Objectives and the Scope of Planning for the Boston Regional Planning Project.* Special Report no. 4. May 1, 1964.

Massachusetts. Mass Transportation Commission. "Approved Work Program." Boston, May 1962.

———. "Demonstration Project Progress Report No. 5." Boston, November 1963.

———. *Mass Transportation in Massachusetts: Final Report.* Boston, July 1964.

———. "Memorandum on Management of the Boston Regional Planning Project." Boston, January 24, 1964.

New York. Niagara Frontier Transportation Study. *Final Report.* Vol. 1. *The Basis of Travel.* August 1964.

———. 'Supplementary Remarks to the Report, 'An Evaluation of Alternative Public Transportation Facilities, Niagara Frontier Transportation Study.' " n.d.

New York. State Office of Planning Coordination. *Annual Report, 1967–1968.*

Paaswell, Robert E. "Transportation." Goals for Metropolitan Buffalo. Source Paper no. 1. [1967].

Penn-Jersey Transportation Study. Vol. 3. *1975 Transportation Plans.* Philadephia, May 1965.

———. *Prospectus.* Philadelphia, December 11, 1959.

———. *Prospectus Supplement, 1963–64.* Philadelphia, November 1963.

———. Vol. 1. *The State of the Region.* Philadelphia, 1964.

Seidman, David R. "Report on the Activities Allocation Model." Penn-Jersey Paper no. 22. Philadelphia, November 17, 1964.

Simmons, W. R., and Associates Research, Inc. *Philadelphia Market News-*

paper Profile: Sunday Newspaper. 1967 edition. Philadelphia: Philadelphia Bulletin Co., 1967.

State University of New York at Buffalo, Office of Urban Affairs, and Manufacturers and Traders Trust Company. *Niagara Frontier's Transportation Needs.* Buffalo, August 10, 1967.

U.S. Advisory Commission on Intergovernmental Relations. *The Federal System as Seen by Federal Aid Officials.* Washington, D.C.: Government Printing Office, 1965.

——. *Intergovernmental Responsibilities for Mass Transportation Facilities and Service in Metropolitan Areas.* Washington, D.C.: Government Printing Office, 1961.

——. *Metropolitan Councils of Government: An Information Report.* Washington, D.C.: Government Printing Office, August 1966.

U.S. Army. Corps of Engineers. *Waterborne Commerce of the United States.* Washington, D.C.: Government Printing Office, 1967.

U.S. Congress. Senate. Committee on Government Operations. Subcommittee on Intergovernmental Relations. *Creative Federalism: Hearings.* Pt. 1. 89th Congress, 2nd session, 1966; Pt. 2–A and Pt. 2–B, 90th Congress, 1st session, 1967.

Articles in Periodicals

"Federal Road Aid Extended Despite D.C. Project Dispute." *Congressional Quarterly Weekly Report,* vol. 26, no. 35 (August 30, 1968), p. 2321.

Harris, Britton. "How to Succeed with Computers Without Really Trying." *Journal of the American Institute of Planners,* vol. 33, no. 1 (January 1967).

——. "New Tools for Planning." *Journal of the American Institute of Planners,* vol. 31, no. 5 (May 1965).

Hayes, Frederick O'R. "Urban Planning and the Transportation Study." In American Institute of Planners, *Proceedings of the 1963 Annual Conference, Milwaukee, Wisconsin.*

Huxtable, Ada L. "Politics of Expressways." *New York Times,* July 17, 1969, p. 51.

Levin, Melvin R. "The Big Regions." *Journal of the American Institute of Planners,* vol. 34, no. 3 (March 1968).

——. "Planners and Metropolitan Planning." *Journal of the American Institute of Planners,* vol. 33, no. 3 (March 1967).

Levitan, Sar A. "Vista: The Great Society's Domestic Volunteers." *Poverty and Human Resources Abstracts,* vol. 3, no. 5 (September–October 1968).

"Mayor Abandons Plans for Expressways." *New York Times,* July 17, 1969, p. 1.

Meier, Richard L., and Duke, Richard D. "Gaming Simulation for Urban Planning." *Journal of the American Institute of Planners,* vol. 32, no. 1 (January 1966).

Miller, S. M. "Criteria for Antipoverty Policies: A Paradigm for Choice." *Poverty and Human Resources Abstracts,* vol. 3, no. 5 (September–October 1968), p. 10.

Mitchell, Robert B. "Foreword." *Annals of the American Academy of Political and Social Science,* vol. 352 (March 1964).

Plotkin, A. S. "The Crisis in Greater Boston's Public Transportation." *Boston Globe,* January 12–19, 1964.

Richardson, Elliot L. "Poisoned Politics: The Real Tragedy of Massachusetts." *The Atlantic,* October 1961.

Rossi, Peter. "Evaluating Social Action Programs." *Trans-Action,* vol. 4, no. 7 (June 1967).

Seligman, David. "McNamara's Management Revolution." *Fortune Magazine,* July 1965.

Shepard, Lyn. "The Highway Revolt." *Christian Science Monitor,* June 4–July 9, 1968.

Urban Development Models: New Tools for Planning. Special issue, *Journal of the American Institute of Planners,* vol. 31, no. 4 (May 1965).

Wildavsky, Aaron. "The Political Economy of Efficiency: Cost-Benefit Analysis, Systems Analysis and Program Budgeting." *Public Administration Review,* vol. 26, no. 4 (December 1966).

Index

Abrams, Richard M., 65n

"Absentee planning," 146, 152, 162, 163, 262

Acceptability of results, 5, 145, 155, 179, 217, 251

ACIR, *see* Advisory Commission on Intergovernmental Relations

Activities Allocation Model (AAM), 138–140; *see also* Models, land-use

Advisory Commission on Intergovernmental Relations (ACIR), 37, 38

Air transportation, 163, 210, 211–212

Albany, N.Y., 150

Alonso, William, 196n

Altshuler, Alan A., 15n, 162n, 225, 237, 245, 245n

American Municipal Association, 40, 54

American Transit Association, 31

Amherst, N.Y., 157, 165

Anderson, Totton, 264n

Atlantic, The, 65

Auburn, N.H., 173, 183

Automobile
versus public transportation, 29–30, 34, 35, 36, 42, 164
registrations, 29–30
traffic congestion, 27, 31, 37, 38, 54–55

Banfield, Edward C., 196n, 249n, 258n, 263n

"Baystatology," 65

Bedford, N.H., 173, 183

Biddeford, Me., 202

Binghamton, N.Y., 150

Blatnik Committee, 76

Bistate planning efforts, 23, 131, 134, 136–137, 145; *see also* Delaware Valley Regional Planning Commission; Penn-Jersey Transportation Study

Boston, Mass., study region
area, 49, 56 (map)
automobile traffic volume, 54–55
central city, 51, 87
economy and employment, 50–51, 120
family relocation and highway plans, 55
highway agencies, 54, 56–57, 251; *see also* Massachusetts, Department of Public Works
highway facilities, 53, 54–55, 155, 266
highway plan of 1948, 69, 71
income, per capita, 51

land-use patterns, 50

mass transit ridership, 61, 73, 107–108, 110

politics, 65–66

population, 49–50, 73

public transportation, 52–54, 71, 105, 116, 251

railroads, commuter, 53–54, 60–61, 68, 73, 106, 109, 110

regional planning agency, 64, 115, 116, 180

zoning patterns, 50

Boston Planning Board, 74

Boston Redevelopment Authority (BRA), 68, 74

Boston Regional Planning Project (BRPP)
administrative structure, 62–63, 77–78, 85–86, 92
committees, 57, 63, 70, 80, 82, 89–90, 91, 102, 114, 116, 186, 222
consultants, 62, 64, 71, 75–76, 79, 82–84, 86, 90, 92, 96, 98, 99, 104–105, 112
continuation of, 60, 82; *see also* EMRPP
control of, 56, 61, 62, 63, 69–70, 72, 74, 75, 76, 77–78, 79, 81, 89, 90, 92, 95–97, 98–101, 104, 275
cost-benefit analysis, 72, 171
costs, 60, 71, 88
and DCD, *see* Massachusetts, Department of Commerce and Development
delays, *see* schedule
demonstration program, 60–61, 63, 67, 68, 79, 80, 83–84, 86, 93, 106–108, 110; *see also* planning project studies
director of MTC, *see* Mass Transportation Commission, director
DPW and, *see* Massachusetts, Department of Public Works
effects of, 55–56, 67, 117–118, 235
federal role in, 62–63, 64, 85, 88, 90–92, 97, 100, 110, 115; *see also* BPR; HHFA-HUD
funding, 23, 56, 59, 60, 66, 88
and governor, 63–64, 66–67, 78, 81, 85, 87, 90–91, 93–95, 96–97, 98, 99–104, 105, 110, 111–112, 259
and highway location, 55
highway orientation of, 56–57, 89, 210
interagency agreements, 61, 62, 63,

Boston Regional Planning Project (BRPP) (continued)
  77–80, 82, 84, 86, 98, 111, 115–116
  interagency conflicts, 62–63, 77, 98–99, 216; see also control of
  land-use inventory, 60, 62, 104–105, 112–113, 239
  local participation in, 91
  mass transit, extension of, 53, 61, 68, 71, 72, 73, 95, 108, 109, 222, 268
  name of, 87
  objectives, 4, 70, 72–73, 114
  offices, 97–98, 113
  organization, 57, 60, 61; see also administrative structure
  overhead support, 88, 89, 92, 113
  patronage and, 68–69, 70, 74, 75, 78, 81, 85, 90, 108, 109
  planner (planning project director), 62, 64, 69, 74–75, 76, 77, 78, 84, 105
  planning project studies, 60, 67, 70–72, 83, 85–86, 90, 97, 109–110, 114; see also demonstration program
  and political change, 64, 78, 113
  and press, 102, 112
  and public transportation, 56, 60, 116; see also demonstration program
  and railroads, see demonstration program
  reorganization of, 58, 63–64, 100–104, 115–118; see also EMRPP
  report, final, 64, 117
  schedule, 60, 64, 73–74, 82, 96, 98–99, 113, 115, 118, 216
  staff, 69, 70, 88, 95, 105, 108–109, 113, 217
  supervision of, 56–57; see also BPR, and Boston study; HHFA-HUD, and Boston study
  traffic inventory, 62, 83–84
  see also Boston, Mass., study region; Massachusetts; Mass Transportation Commission; Transportation planning, urban comprehensive
BPR (Federal Bureau of Public Roads)
  and Boston study, 57, 60, 61–62, 65, 74, 85, 89, 91–92, 97, 98, 99–100, 113, 115
  and city planners, 36–37
  committee participation, 136, 214
  and DVRPC, 136, 144
  funding, 6, 21, 23, 38–39, 191–192, 200, 249; see also 1.5% planning funds

  and HHFA-HUD cooperation, 39, 45–46, 60, 69, 157, 210, 249
  and land-use categories, 195
  and land-use model, 138, 144; see also Penn-Jersey Transportation Study, model entries
  and local participation, 80–81, 135
  and local planning, 184
  and Manchester study, 174–176, 181, 188, 190–191
  and model research, 14, 139, 143–144
  and Niagara Frontier study, 23, 156–157
  objectives, 14, 127–128, 139
  and Penn-Jersey study, 126–128, 131, 133, 135–136, 143–144, 145
  and Portland study, 205–206, 207, 209, 214, 223
  and regional planning, 157, 158
  rural highway bias, 23, 35, 38, 44
  and state highway agencies, 31, 33, 39, 43, 44, 46, 235, 250, 260
  supervision, 4, 13, 45–46, 195, 250
  transportation responsibilities, 32, 45, 143, 159
  and urban transportation, 38–39, 45
  see also specific studies, federal role in
BRA, see Boston Redevelopment Authority
Brooke, Edward W., 102n
BRPP, see Boston Regional Planning Project
Buffalo, N.Y., 148
  development pattern, 164–166, 171
  downtown area, 147–148, 165, 166, 167, 171
  geographical location, 148
  planning agencies, 156, 157, 158, 160, 161, 162, 167, 169
  Planning Department, 160, 161, 169
  port, 148
  public transportation trips (%), 123
  and rapid transit issue, 165
  sports stadium location, 156, 165–166
  traffic engineer, 162–163
  Urban Renewal Department, 156, 157, 158, 160, 161, 162, 167, 169, 171
  see also Niagara Frontier study region; Niagara Frontier Transportation Study
Buffalo River, 148
Bureau of Public Roads, see BPR
Burlington County, N.J., 122

Buses, *see* Public transportation, buses

Camden, N.J., 120, 124, 125, 137
Campbell, Alan K., 256–257, 264
Cape Elizabeth, Me., 202
Carll, Richard R., 38n
CATS, *see* Chicago Area Transportation Study
Charlestown, Mass., 68
Chicago Area Transportation Study (CATS), 9, 14, 87, 127, 132, 151, 154–155, 208
Chicago Transit Authority, 15, 52
Christian Science Monitor, 7
Citizen participation, *see* local participation entry under BPR; HHFA-HUD; specific studies
"Collapse of Commuter Service," 40–41
Committees, 136, 188, 215; *see also* committee entries under Transportation planning, urban comprehensive; specific studies
Commuter railroads, *see* Railroads, commuter
Computer
  problems, 131, 141–142, 143, 154, 207, 223
  software, 138, 143
  technology, 141, 152, 154, 168
  in transportation planning, 4, 8, 137–138, 142–143, 241–242, 245
  see also Data; Models
Consultants
  and interagency conflicts, 224
  role of, 12, 18, 162, 224
  and 701 program, 180, 183
  single, 224; *see also* Portland Area Comprehensive Transportation Study
  or staff, 7, 105, 131–132, 223–224
  see also entry under specific studies
Council of State Governments, 261
Councils of local government (COGs), 134
Courtney, Joseph F., 111n
Creative Federalism hearings, 231–232, 265–266
Creighton, Roger L., 170n
Cumberland, Me., 202, 216

Dade County, Fla., 260
Danielson, Michael N., 87, 258n, 264
Data
  incompatibility of, 153, 168–169,

194–195
  processing problems, 131, 137, 140, 168
  quantity, 131, 141, 142, 153
  reliability of, 160, 211, 223
  storage and collection, 141, 152, 154, 168
  see also Computer; Models
DED, *see* Maine, Department of Economic Development
Delaware River, 119, 122
Delaware Valley Regional Planning Commission (DVRPC), 134
  federal role in, *see* DVRPC entry under BRP; HHFA-HUD
  funding, 133–134, 144
  land-use model, 139–140
  organization, 128, 132, 137, 250–251
  responsibilities of, 132–133, 134–135
  and state planning agencies, 136
  see also Penn-Jersey Transportation Study
Demonstration Cities and Metropolitan Development Act of 1965 (Section 204), 163n, 269n
Demonstration programs, 43; *see also* Boston Regional Planning Project, demonstration program
Detroit transportation study, 130
Dilworth, Ray, report, 40–41
Downs, Anthony, 252
DRED, *see* New Hampshire, Department of Resources and Economic Development
Duke, Richard D., 87
DVRPC, *see* Delaware Valley Regional Planning Commission

Eastern Massachusetts Regional Planning Project, *see* EMRPP
Electronic Accounting Machine (EAM), 131, 141, 142
Emergency Relief and Construction Act of 1932, 32
EMRPP (Eastern Massachusetts Regional Planning Project), 22, 49, 58, 87, 116–117
Engineering News-Record, 9
Erie County, 163, 169
  Department of Planning, 153, 157, 160
Evaluation techniques, 7, 11, 22–26, 271–274
Executive authority, 17–18, 87, 189, 249, 259, 261, 263, 266, 270, 271; *see also*

Executive authority (*continued*)
specific studies, governor entry
Expressways, *see* Highways

Falmouth, Me., 201
Federal-Aid Highway Act
of 1944, 34
of 1956, 30n, 36
of 1962, 12, 27, 45, 46, 153, 172, 203,
210
of 1968 (S. 3418), 28–29, 28n
Federal-Aid Road Act of 1916, 31–32, 33
Federal Aviation Administration (FAA),
212
Fischer, Victor, 81n
Fitch, Lyle, and Associates, 38n
Freeway revolt, 7, 235; *see also* Highways, impact of
Friedman, Robert S., 35n
Friedmann, John, 195n
Funding of studies, 6, 21
federal, *see* BPR, funding; HHFA-HUD, funding; Section 204 program;
701 program
revolving account, 23, 44, 175–176,
191, 192, 205
see also specific studies, funding entry
Furculo, Foster, 59

Gasoline taxes, 30n
Gilbert, Charles E., 121n
Goals for Metropolitan Buffalo, 168
Goals and priorities, 159, 162, 167, 168,
170–171, 187–188, 232–235, 236, 244,
245, 248, 263, 268, 269, 274
Goffstown, N.H., 172, 173, 183, 184,
185
Gorham, Me., 202
Gottfield, Gunther M., 52n
Gravity model, 143, 207, 269
Great Chebeague Island, Me., 216
Greater Portland Regional Planning
Commission, 188, 201, 208, 213,
225–227
Grossman, David A., 185n

Harris, Britton, 8, 241–242
Harrisburg, Pa., 141, 146
Hartford, Conn., 269
Hayden-Cartwright Act (1934), 33, 35;
see also 1.5 percent planning funds
Hayes, Frederick O'R., 241n, 250n
HHFA-HUD (Housing and Home

Finance Agency–Department of Housing and Urban Development)
administration of programs, 182
and Boston study, 56–57, 60, 61–62, 74,
85, 91–92, 97, 99–100, 115, 259
and BPR cooperation, 39, 45–46, 60,
69, 157, 210, 249
committee participation, 136, 214
Community Facilities Administration,
3n
and Congress, 196n, 199
and DVRPC, 133, 136, 251
funding, 6–7, 21, 23, 39, 144, 176–178,
179, 180, 184, 191–192, 199, 200,
201, 249, 250–251; *see also* 701 program
HHFA becomes HUD, 3, 3n
and land use, 39, 164, 193–194, 206,
208, 209–210
and local participation, 80–81, 135,
187, 197, 275
and local planning programs, 182–183
and Manchester study, 174, 175–179,
180, 187, 191–193, 195–196, 197,
199–200
and mass transportation, 43–44
and Niagara Frontier study, 156–158
participation, effects of, 5, 12, 143–144,
158, 183, 208, 210, 246–247
and Penn-Jersey study, 143–144
and Portland study, 203, 205–206,
209–210, 214, 251
and regional planning, 11, 208
regions, 24
and research, 139, 144, 146
and state and local government, 214,
261–263
supervision, 4, 13, 45–46, 182, 195–
196, 250
Urban Renewal Administration, 3n, 37
urban renewal and transportation function, 28n, 39, 188, 199, 262
Higher Education Act of 1965, 269n
Highway agencies
versus city planners, 34, 44, 217–218
and development patterns, 190
goals in transportation studies, 4, 14,
246
functions of, 15–16, 32–33, 44, 199,
226
versus planning agencies, 44, 157, 160,
191–192, 199
state, 30, 42, 167–169, 191–192

see also BPR; specific state agencies
Highway Research Board, 132, 137n, 144
Highways
and cities, 31–32
corridor approach, 155–156, 208, 209
costs versus financing, 179
federal expenditures for, 30–31
funding, *see* BPR, funding
impact of, 7, 9–10, 32, 39, 55, 155–156, 167, 170–171, 207, 208–210, 219, 224
route location of, 3, 19, 155–156, 207, 209–210, 219, 222, 246
socioeconomic aspects of, *see* impact of
versus urban renewal, 156, 158, 162, 167, 190, 218–219, 234, 253
versus urban streets, 27, 30, 32, 35, 44
Highway Trust Fund, 30n
Hooksett, N.H., 173, 183
Housing Act, U.S.
of 1954, 37, 38, 41, 180; *see also* 701 program
of 1961, 42–45
of 1965, 163, 196n, 203
Huxtable, Ada L., 7n

Interagency and intergovernmental projects
agreements, 36, 39, 60, 63, 69, 78–80, 82, 111, 115–116, 175
conflicts, resolution of, 17–18, 140, 180, 189, 224, 261, 263; *see also* Executive authority
coordination of, 11, 39, 42, 45, 69, 134, 153, 157–158, 160, 162, 180, 224–225, 250, 251, 266
federal, 265–267
federal-local, 253, 256
federal-state, 253–256, 261
and innovation, 256–257
integrated, 250–251
metropolitan, 17, 233, 248
and political change, 18–19
problems, 117–118, 231–234, 236, 242
versus single agency, 15, 164, 251
and size of area, 12–13, 225
and staff level, 20, 39, 45–46, 153, 162, 249, 251, 255–257
verbal agreements, 98, 255
Intercity transportation, 31, 210–213
Intergovernmental Cooperation Act of 1968, 233
Intergovernmental relations, *see* Inter-

agency and intergovernmental projects
Interstate system, *see* National System of Interstate and Defense Highways

Johnson, Lyndon B., 3n, 29
Journal of the American Institute of Planners, 7, 241

Kenmore Expressway, 164, 167
Kennedy, Edward M., 109
Kennedy, John F., 44, 266
Kluczywski, John C., 29
Krapf, Norman W., 155n

Land Economics, 7
Land use
alternatives, 14, 70, 164, 165, 196–198
categories, 169n, 184, 193–194, 195, 200
and highways, 3, 4, 32
models for, 8, 137–140, 144, 240, 242; *see also* Penn-Jersey Transportation Study, model entries
plans for, 3, 38, 156, 164, 171, 176, 184, 196–198, 209
and regional planning, 185, 186, 236–237
surveys, 14, 62, 104–105, 112–113
see also HHFA-HUD, and land use; specific studies, land-use entries
Land-Use and Marketability Study (LUMS), 218
Legislation, federal, 3n, 31–46; *see also* specific acts and programs
Legislatures, state, rural control of, 35, 44
Levin, Melvin R., 106n, 184n, 196n, 243n, 255n
Levitan, Sar A., 272n
Levittown, Pa., 122, 123
Little, A. D., 226n
Lockport, N.Y., 165
Londonderry, N.H., 173–174, 183
Lowry, Ira S., 140n

Maine
Department of Economic Development (DED), 180, 207, 208, 222, 223–224
State Highway Commission, 202, 203–204, 206, 207, 209, 220–224
University of, 201
see also Portland Area Comprehensive Transportation Study

Manchester Metropolitan Planning Study (MMPS), 22
  Advisory Committee, 178, 186, 189, 192, 193, 198, 215
  and central city, 187, 188, 189, 193–195, 200
  chronology, 174, 176–178, 179, 191, 199
  commercial transport participation, 189
  and computer, 141
  conflicts, resolution of, 189
  consultant, 175, 176–177, 178–179, 181, 188, 189, 190, 191, 196–197, 198, 200
  continuation of, 178, 180, 198–199
  data, 175, 176, 179, 195
  delays, 177–178, 191
  effects of, 179, 180, 197
  and FAA, 212
  federal intervention, 180
  federal role in, see Manchester study entry under BPR; HHFA-HUD
  funding, 23, 174, 175–177, 178–179, 190–192, 193, 199, 200
  highway orientation of, 192
  impact of, 179, 180, 197
  interagency relations, 175, 178, 179–180, 193, 200
  land-use categories, 169n, 194–195, 200
  land-use plan, 176, 184, 196–198
  local participation in, 186–187, 188, 196–198
  and local planning, 183–185, 186–187, 196–198, 200
  organization, 176
  Policy Committee, 188
  population projections, 197
  and press, 174, 187
  public transportation, nonparticipation of, 189–190
  reports, 177–178, 179
  and regional planning commission, 180, 198–199
  and state highway department, see New Hampshire, Department of Public Works and Highways
  and state planning department, see New Hampshire, Department of Resources and Economic Development (DRED)
  supervision, 195–196, 199, 200
  and urban renewal, 188–189, 218, 262
  see also Manchester, N.H.; Manchester, N.H., study region; New Hampshire
Manchester, N.H.
  Board of Aldermen and Mayor, 175, 179, 190, 222
  central role of, 172, 174, 193
  City Planning Board, 169n, 177, 193, 194–195, 200
  downtown area, 188–189, 199, 218
  and funding of MMPS, 174
  Housing Authority, 177, 188–189
  politics in, 174, 189
  population decline, 197
  renewal and HUD, 183, 262
  urban renewal agency, see Housing Authority
  see also Manchester Metropolitan Planning Study
Manchester, N.H., study region
  area, 172, 175 (map)
  bus service, 190
  core-city orientation, 172, 182, 193
  development pattern, 172–173, 196–197
  economy, 172
  highways, 189
  income levels, 173
  inmigration, 173–174
  local planning, 183–185
  public transportation trips (%), 123, 190
  regional planning, 172, 178, 180, 183, 198–199
Manchester Union Leader, 174, 187
Mansfield, Harvey C., 69n
Manufacturers and Traders Trust Company, Buffalo, N.Y., 156n, 167
MAPC, see Metropolitan Area Planning Council
Massachusetts
  attorney general, 102–103
  Department of Commerce and Development (DCD), 63–64, 112, 113, 116, 117, 181
  Department of Public Works (DPW), 54, 60, 61, 65, 74, 76–77, 87, 88–89, 116, 260
  Executive Commission for Administration and Finance, 63, 64
  federal agency investigations, 62, 65, 93
  patronage in, 68–69; see also Patronage, and Boston study
  politics, 65–66
  see also Boston, Mass., study region; Boston Regional Planning Project; Mass Transportation Commission
Massachusetts Bay Transportation Au-

thority, *see* MBTA
Massachusetts Port Authority, 54
Massachusetts Public Transportation Authority (MPTA), 109, 110–111
Massachusetts Turnpike Authority, 54, 65
Mass transit, fixed-route, 29–30, 154
city and state interest in, 44
federal government and, 28–29, 37–38, 44
versus highways, 27–29, 35, 37; *see also* Niagara Frontier Transportation Study, and rapid transit
ownership of, 27, 28, 35, 36
ridership, 29, 35, 36, 42, 61, 73, 107–108, 110
and size of area, 152, 154, 161, 164, 169
see also Boston Regional Planning Project, mass transit, extension of; Public transportation; Railroads
Mass Transportation Commission (MTC)
abolished, 63, 112, 113
composition of, 67
contract (1962), 61, 62, 79
director, 57, 59, 62, 63, 66–67
and federal agencies, 61–62
statutory powers, 58–59
and transit authority, 63, 68, 70–71, 72
see also Boston Regional Planning Project, control of, demonstration program; Massachusetts, Department of Commerce and Development, Department of Public Works
MBTA (Massachusetts Bay Transportation Authority), 15, 52–53, 61, 63, 64, 68, 70–71, 72, 73, 107–108, 111, 116–117
McNamara, Robert S., 266–267
MDC, *see* Metropolitan District Commission
Meier, Richard L., 87
Merrimack River, 172, 188, 189
Metropolitan Area Planning Council (MAPC), 64, 115, 116, 180
Metropolitan District Commission, 54, 62, 65
Metropolitanism, 264, 274
Metropolitan planning agency
educational role for, 268–269
federal government and, 259, 271

judicial role for, 269–271
versus regional agencies, 259
and state, 258–263, 268, 269n, 270
and technical assistance, 271
see also Interagency and intergovernmental agencies; Planning and planning agencies; Regional and metropolitan planning
Meyerson, Martin, 258n
Milgrim, Grace, 121n
Miller, S. M., 273
Mitchell, Robert B., 232–233
MMPS, *see* Manchester Metropolitan Planning Study
Modal split formulas, 137–138, 154, 242
Model Cities Program, 11, 163
Models, 8, 14
alternatives, 1, 70n, 139
development of, 8, 14, 70n, 137–138, 140, 142, 143, 245, 246
land-use, 8, 137–140, 144, 242
and size of area, 140
see also BPR, and model research; Computer; Penn-Jersey Transportation Study, model entries
Mowitz, Robert J., 99, 248
MTA (Metropolitan Transit Authority), *see* MBTA
MTC, *see* Mass Transportation Commission
Muskie, Edmund S., 232, 256

Nashville, Tenn., 260, 262
National Committee on Urban Transportation, 40
National Industrial Recovery Act of 1933 (NIRA), 33
National System of Interstate and Defense Highways, 15, 28n, 30, 30n, 34, 36, 37
National Transportation Policy, 37–38
Neustadt, Richard E., 95, 243
New England Regional Commission, 261
New Hampshire
Department of Public Works and Highways, 174, 176–177, 179, 180, 183, 188, 191, 199
Department of Resources and Economic Development (DRED), 174, 176, 178, 181–182, 191, 199
State Planning Project, 194
see also Manchester Metropolitan Planning Study

New Jersey
  Community Affairs commissioner, 136
  Highway Department, 126, 128, 131, 136
  role in Penn-Jersey study, 128, 136–137
  state planning agency, 136
  as transportation center, 136–137
New York State
  Department of Public Works, 149–150, 151–152, 156
  Department of Transportation (NY-DOT), 151, 156, 158–160, 161–162, 163, 167–168, 169–170, 262
  legislature, 152, 155, 163, 164, 171
  Office of Planning Coordination (OPC), 157
  regional transportation authorities, 163
  see also Niagara Frontier Transportation Study; UNYTS
New York Times, 7
NFTS, see Niagara Frontier Transportation Study
Niagara County, 147, 153, 163, 169–170
  Industrial Development and Planning Commission, 157, 160
Niagara Falls (city), 147, 149
Niagara Frontier study region
  air transportation, 163
  area, 147, 150 (map)
  bus service, 164
  development pattern, 164–166, 171
  economy and employment, 120, 147–149
  land use, 164
  outmigration, 147
  population, 147, 149, 150, 152, 156, 158–160
  urban growth, 148
Niagara Frontier Transportation Authority (NFTA), 163, 235–236
Niagara Frontier Transportation Study (NFTS), 22
  "absentee planning," 152, 162, 163, 262
  alternative transportation systems, 154
  Basic Corridor Plan, 152, 155–156, 164, 165, 167, 171, 275
  and central city, 161, 162
  computer problems, 141, 152, 154
  data storage techniques, 152, 154
  delays, 152, 154–155
  effects of, 235–236
  federal role in, see Niagara Frontier

  study entry under BPR; HHFA-HUD funding, 23, 156
  and governor, 259
  highway emphasis, 158, 245, 251
  highway route location, 210
  land use, 156, 164, 165, 171
  name of, 87
  objectives, 170–171
  organization, 151
  and planning agencies, 153, 155, 156, 157, 160–164
  Planning Committee, 157
  Policy Committee, 156–157, 170
  population projections, 156, 158–160
  and the press, 161
  prospectus, 152
  and public transportation, 154, 156, 164, 165, 166, 169
  and rapid transit, 152, 154, 156, 163, 164–167, 169, 171, 251
  reports, 154, 155
  research, 154–155
  schedule, 152; see also delays
  staff, 23, 152
  surveys, 152–153, 158, 162
  see also Buffalo, N.Y.; New York State; Niagara Frontier study region; UNYTS
Niagara River, 147, 148
NYDOT, see New York State, Department of Transportation

1.5 percent planning funds, 33, 35, 38–39, 45, 77, 129
OPC, see New York State, Office of Planning Coordination
Orchard Park, N.Y., 148
Owen, Wilfred, 36

Paaswell, Robert E., 164n
PACTS, see Portland Area Comprehensive Transportation Study
Patronage, 65, 69, 161
  and Boston study, 68–69, 70, 74, 75, 78, 81, 85, 90, 108, 109
Peabody, Endicott M., 67, 91n, 93–95, 105, 114–115; see also Boston Regional Planning Project, and governor
"Penn-Jersey Papers," 132
Penn-Jersey study region
  area, 119, 126 (map)
  development pattern, 122–123

economy and employment, 120, 121
highways, 124–125
inmigration, 120
land use, 121–123
population, 120–121
public transportation, 123–124, 125
traffic volumes, 124–125
travel patterns, 123
urbanization, 121–122
see also Philadelphia, Pa.
Penn-Jersey Transportation Study, 22
administrative organization, 127, 128,
 134–136, 137, 145–146
bistate effort, 134–135, 136–137, 145
chronology, 125–126, 133, 144–145
computer problems, 131, 141–142
consultants, 131
continuation of, 126–127, 129, 132–133,
 136, 144, 145–146; *see also* Delaware
 Valley Regional Planning Commission
cost, 130
data, 130, 131, 141–142, 144
delays, 130, 141
director, 132–133, 145, 239
Executive Committee, 135
federal role in, *see* Penn-Jersey study
 under BPR; HHFA-HUD
funding, 129, 133
and governor, 132, 133, 259
home-interview survey, 131
impact of, 8
land-use model, *see* model, land-use
local participation in, 126, 129, 137,
 144, 145
model, land-use (AAM), 137, 138–140,
 144–145, 146, 239, 241, 242, 245
model research, 130–131, 132, 133,
 139–140, 142, 144
objectives, 129–130
organization, 127, 128, 134–136, 137,
 145
Organizing Committee, 125
Policy Committee, 135–136, 138, 145
Program Planning Committee, 125–126
prospectuses, 125–126, 130
public transportation, 116, 123
and RCEO, 133–134
regional growth model, *see* model
 research
reports, 132, 133
research orientation of, 127–128,
 129–130, 132, 133, 144
schedule, 130–131, 133

staff, 131, 132, 142, 145, 146
Technical Planning Committee, 135,
 145
see also Delaware Valley Regional
 Planning Commission; Penn-Jersey
 study region
Pennsylvania
Department of Highways, 125, 128,
 131, 141, 142, 146
State Planning Board, 136
Pennsylvania, University of, 128
PERT, *see* Project Evaluation and
 Review Technique
Philadelphia, Pa.
employment, 121
location, 119
nonwhite population, 121, 123
and Penn-Jersey study, 127, 135
population growth, 119, 120–121
public transportation, 52, 123–124
railroads, 54, 119
Philadelphia Transit Company, 134
Pittsburgh, Pa., 140, 151
Planners
versus administrators, 18
versus highway engineers, 3, 9–10, 32,
 34, 146, 160, 237, 241, 244, 245–246
and politicians, 16–17
regional, shortage of, 4, 18, 66; *see also*
 Talent shortage
see also Planning and planning agencies; Regional and metropolitan planning
Planning and planning agencies
basis (trend or development prospects?),
 164, 188–189, 190, 196–197, 218–219
federal aid, 238, 271; *see also* Section
 204 program; 701 program
and functional agencies, 11, 15–17, 234,
 238–240, 242, 243
and highway agencies, 44, 157, 160,
 191–192, 199
local, 21, 167–168, 182
metropolitan roles for, 268–271
regional versus local, 155, 183–184,
 185–186, 244
and size of area, 5, 181, 213, 215
state, 180–182, 192, 250, 261–262
state versus city, 182
state versus local, 157, 163, 168–169,
 187–188, 236
urban versus small-town, 181–182, 183,
 194

Planning and planning agencies (*continued*)
weak position of, 17, 191–192, 224, 240
see also Metropolitan planning agencies; Regional and metropolitan planning
Plotkin, A. S., 110n
Portland Advisory Council, 225
Portland Area Comprehwnsive Transportation Study (PACTS), 22
and airport, 212–213
and central cities, 215
citizen participation, *see* local participation
committee membership, 213–214; *see also* Policy Committee, Technical Committee
computer costs, 207, 223
computer problems, 141, 207, 223
consultant, 205, 207, 209, 213, 221–224
continuation of, 226–227; *see also* Greater Portland Regional Planning Commission
costs, 204, 206–207
data collection, 206, 223, 226
delays, 204–205, 207
federal role in, *see* Portland study entry under BPR; HHFA-HUD
ferry service survey, 216
funding, 23, 205–207, 209, 223
highway location, 206–207, 208–209, 220–222, 224, 225
impact of, 227
interagency conflicts, lack of, 224, 225
land-use data, 206, 226
land-use plan, future, 196–198, 207, 209
local participation in, 201, 213–216
name, 214
organization, 205, 215, 250–251
Policy Committee, 207, 211, 213–216
public relations, 216
and regional planning commission, 205, 225–227
reports, 205, 207–208, 215, 217–218
schedule, 205, 207, 208
staff, 222, 223
Technical Committee, 207, 213–215, 216, 225
and urban renewal, 216–220, 225
see also Portland, Me.; Portland study region
Portland, Me.

airport, 203, 212
Chamber of Commerce, 212
City Council, 212, 225
committee representation, 215–216
description, 201–202
downtown area, 201, 217–218, 219
planning department, 208, 225, 226
population, 202
port, 201
public transportation trips (%), 123, 190
rail service, 211
and regional planning commission, 225–226
suburbs, 202
urban renewal, 216–219, 225
see also Portland Area Comprehensive Transportation Study
Portland study region
area, 201, 204 (map)
economy and employment, 203
highways, 202, 221–222
islands, offshore, 202, 216
outmigration, 203
population, 201, 202
regional planning agency, *see* Greater Portland Regional Planning Commission
surveys, 206, 222
urban development, 203
Press, 67, 102, 112, 161, 174, 178, 187
Project Evaluation and Review Technique (PERT), 14, 96, 105
Public transportation
air, 164
versus automobile, 29–30, 34, 35, 36, 42, 164
buses, 31, 35, 63, 73, 107–108, 154, 161, 164, 169, 190, 210
facilities, 30–31, 42
federal government and, 27–46, 234, 267–268
or highways, 21, 28–29, 138, 154, 169, 170–171, 190, 234, 268
intercity, 31, 210–213
investment in, 31
ridership, 29, 31, 35, 36, 42, 123–124, 190
and size of area, 12–13, 23, 107, 161, 164, 190, 211
see also Mass transit; Railroads

Railroads
Boston and Albany, 53, 61, 68, 107

Boston and Maine, 53, 61, 68, 73, 83, 106, 109, 211
commuter, 36, 40–41, 43, 53–54, 61, 73, 125, 211
New York Central, 53, 61, 68, 107
New York, New Haven and Hartford, 53, 61, 73, 106, 109
Pennsylvania, 125
Reading, 125
and size of area, 211
subsidies for, 40, 43, 108n; see also Boston Regional Planning Project, demonstration program
see also Public transportation
Rapid transit, rail, see Mass transit, fixed-route
RCEO, see Regional Conference of Elected Officials
Reading, Mass., 68
Regional Conference of Elected Officials (RCEO), 133–134
Regional and metropolitan planning, 5, 183, 226
and central cities, 4, 188–190, 225, 226
and federal government, 238, 249, 259, 264–267, 268
versus local, 155, 183–186, 244
and local issues, 22
review powers, 196, 196n
and state government, 17, 182, 258–263, 268
talent shortage for, 4, 18; see also Talent shortage
techniques, 236–237
and transportation planning, 5, 171, 187–188
see also Interagency and intergovernmental programs; Metropolitan planning agency; Planners; Planning and planning agencies
Revolving-fund financing, 23, 44, 175–176, 191, 192, 205
Richardson, Elliot L., 66n
Rochester, N.Y., 150, 161, 162, 170
Rome, N.Y., 150
Rossi, Peter, 273–274

Saco, Me., 202
St. Lawrence Seaway, 147, 148, 149
San Francisco, Calif., and state highway agency, 260
Scarborough, Me., 202
Schlesinger, Arthur M., Jr., 249n

Schocken, Thomas B., 6n
Schofer, Joseph, 6n
Schultze, Charles L., 231–232, 265–266
Schuylkill River, 119
Scranton, William P., 132, 133
Section 701 (of 1954 Housing Act) program, see 701 program
Section 204 (of 1965 Housing Act), 163, 163n, 196n, 269
Seidman, David, 267n
Seligman, David, 267n
SEPTA, see Southeastern Pennsylvania Transportation Authority
701 program (1954 Housing Act), 3n, 8, 37, 38, 39, 41, 44, 144, 153, 180–183, 199, 227
Shepard, Lyn, 7n
Simpson, Smith, 249n
Size (population) of planning area, 5, 6, 7, 11, 12–13, 23, 107, 140, 152, 154, 161, 164, 166, 169–170, 182, 190, 211, 212–213, 219, 225
Smerk, George M., 33n
Smith, Wilbur, and Associates, 190n
SMSA (Standard Metropolitan Statistical Area), 49, 51, 253n
Southeastern Pennsylvania Transportation Authority (SEPTA), 134
Southern New Hampshire Planning Commission, 172, 180, 187, 198–199
South Portland, Me., 202, 213, 221
Staff, 58, 74–75, 142, 151, 252
commitment of, 20, 79
versus consultants, 7, 23, 83, 105, 116, 131–132, 223–224
effectiveness of, 58
level, 20–21, 58, 169, 251–252
technical, role of, 220, 222
see also Talent shortage
Standard Industrial Classification, 194
SUNYAB (State University of New York at Buffalo)
location, 156, 157, 165, 171, 236
Office of Urban Affairs, 156n, 166
Syracuse, N.Y., 150

Talent shortage, 4, 18, 57–59, 131, 237, 242–246
Toronto, Canada, 166
Traffic congestion, 27, 31, 37, 54–55
Traffic Quarterly, 6, 7
Transit, mass, see Mass transit, fixedroute

Transportation, public, *see* Public transportation

Transportation planning, urban comprehensive
acceptability of results, 5, 145, 155, 179, 217, 251
and airports, 212–213
avoidance of issues, 8–9, 234–235
and central cities, 161, 162, 165–166, 170, 171, 172, 182, 220, 225, 234
chronology, 9
citizen participation, *see* local participation in
committees, 20, 136, 145, 189, 214, 216, 270
communication problems, 15, 19–20, 98, 99, 142–143, 155, 188, 198, 269
computer and, *see* techniques
conflicts, resolution of, *see* Executive authority; specific studies, governor entry
continuation of, 208, 226, 245; *see also* entry under specific studies
costs of, 204
crises, response to, 17, 222
educational aspects of, 14–15, 72
expectations of, 186, 231, 274
and experts, 245
federal requirements for, 12, 60, 67, 72, 127, 153, 172, 210, 238; *see also* Federal-Aid Highway Act, of 1962
flexibility, lack of, 17, 20, 22, 235–236
funding, *see* funding entry under BPR; HHFA-HUD
highway orientation of, 4–5, 158, 192, 208, 209, 246–247, 251
highways, rural, or urban streets, 31–37
impact of, 5, 7–8, 9–10, 13, 14, 21, 55–56, 118, 208, 222, 235–236, 246, 248
local capabilities for, 168–169, 200
local participation in, 3, 126–127, 129, 168, 188, 244, 246, 270
and local planning agencies, 183–185, 195
local support for, 22, 187
methodology of research on, 23–26
models, use in, *see* techniques
nonhighway factors in, 4, 10, 55, 144, 157, 162, 167, 170–171, 208, 236, 247, 248
objectives, 4, 9, 14, 21, 127–128, 139, 245, 246
organization, 7, 19, 250–251
and political change, 18–19, 78
public interest in, 19–20, 187, 216
public transportation, 8, 116, 190, 244, 246
and regional planning, 5, 171, 184, 187–188, 226
reorganization of, 272
reports, 10, 222
research orientation of, 8, 14, 127, 141, 246
scope of, 3
sequence of, 187–188, 220, 222
and size of area, 5, 23, 164, 169–170, 213, 219
socioeconomic factors in, *see* nonhighway factors in
staffing, 18, 142, 151, 242; *see also* Talent shortage
and state, 167–169, 180–182
supervision of, 195–196, 200; *see also* supervision entry under BPR; HHFA-HUD
techniques, 4, 8, 137–138, 141–143, 158, 160, 242; *see also* Penn-Jersey Transportation Study, model entries
and urban renewal, 2, 158, 199, 218–219, 262
as validating instruments, 4, 22, 117, 188, 190, 235, 246

Trenton, N.J., 120, 122, 123, 124, 137
Tri-State Transportation Study, 169

United States
Bureau of Public Roads, *see* BPR
Census Bureau, 158–159
Department of Housing and Urban Development (HUD), *see* HHFA-HUD
Department of Transportation (DOT), 27, 28n, 212
grant-in-aid program, 41, 254, 256–257, 258, 265
highway expenditures, 130–131
Housing and Home Finance Agency (HHFA), *see* HHFA-HUD
legislation, *see* Legislation, federal; specific acts and programs
and public transportation, *see* and urban and public transportation
Special Study Group on Transportation Policies, 37n, 38
urban goals and priorities, lack of, *see*

Goals and priorities
and urban and public transportation,
27–46, 234, 267–268
Urban Renewal Administration, *see*
entry under HHFA-HUD
United States Steel Company, 122
UNYTS (Upstate New York Transportation Study)
and local planners, 155
model, 140
objectives, 151, 170–171
and rapid transit in Buffalo area, 165,
166
urban areas studied, 150
see also New York State, Department of
Transportation;   Niagara   Frontier
Transportation Study
Upstate   New   York   Transportation
Study, *see* UNYTS
Urban Affairs Quarterly, 7
Urban transportation, *see* Highways;
Mass transit; Public transportation;
Transportation planning, urban comprehensive; United States, and urban
and public transportation
Urban renewal, *see* Highways, versus
urban renewal; Transportation plan-
ning, urban comprehensive, and urban
renewal; entry under specific transpor-
tation studies
Utica, N.Y., 150

Volpe, John A., 60, 66–67, 81

Wachs, Martin, 6n
Washington, D.C., 29
Weaver, Robert C., 80–81
Westbrook,   Me.,   202,   213,   216,
219–220, 221
Whalen, Richard J., 65
Wildavsky, Aaron, 267n
Williams, Harrison A., Jr., 41
March 1960 bill, 41
January 1961 bill, 42–43, 44
Wood, Donald F., 6n
Wood, Robert C., 243, 261, 264–265
Wright, Deil S., 99, 248

Yarmouth, Me., 202

Zettel, Richard M., 38n
Zoning, 50, 184